Investigating the Truth

In the *World Library of Psychologists* series, international experts present career-long collections of what they judge to be their finest pieces – extracts from books, key articles, salient research findings, and their major practical theoretical contributions.

The selected works of Professor Ray Bull include some of the most influential insights into the psychology of investigative interviewing. Whether it has been determining whether a suspect is lying or telling the truth, enabling children to provide reliable testimony, or understanding how the dynamics of the interview process itself can affect what is achieved, Professor Bull has been at the forefront in researching this fascinating area of applied psychology for over 40 years, his work informing practice internationally. An elected Honorary Fellow of the British Psychological Society and the first Honorary Life Member of the International Investigative Interviewing Research Group, Professor Bull also drafted parts of the government's Memorandum of Good Practice and of Achieving Best Evidence on Video Recorded Interviews with Child Witnesses for Criminal Proceedings.

Including a specially written introduction in which Professor Bull reflects on a wide-ranging career and contextualises how the field has evolved, this collection will be a valuable resource for students and researchers of forensic psychology.

Ray Bull is Professor of Criminal Investigation at the University of Derby, UK. He has previously held the position of President of the European Association of Psychology and Law. In 2008 he received from the European Association of Psychology and Law the Award for Life-time Contribution to Psychology and Law. He regularly acts as an expert witness and conducts workshops/training on investigative interviewing.

World Library of Psychologists

The *World Library of Psychologists* series celebrates the important contributions to psychology made by leading experts in their individual fields of study. Each scholar has compiled a career-long collection of what they consider to be their finest pieces: extracts from books, journals, articles, major theoretical and practical contributions, and salient research findings.

For the first time ever the work of each contributor is presented in a single volume so readers can follow the themes and progress of their work and identify the contributions made to, and the development of, the fields themselves.

Each book in the series features a specially written introduction by the contributor giving an overview of their career, contextualizing their selection within the development of the field, and showing how their thinking developed over time.

Attention, Perception and Action
Selected Works of Glyn Humphreys
By Glyn W. Humphreys

Facial Expression Recognition
Selected Works of Andy Young
By Andy Young

From Obscurity to Clarity in Psychometric Testing
Selected Works of Professor Peter Saville
By Professor Peter Saville
With Tom Hopton

Discovering the Social Mind
Selected Works of Christopher D. Frith
By Christopher D. Frith

Towards a Deeper Understanding of Consciousness
Selected Works of Max Velmans
By Max Velmans

Thinking Developmentally from Constructivism to Neuroconstructivism
Selected Works of Annette Karmiloff-Smith
By Annette Karmiloff-Smith

Acquired Language Disorders in Adulthood and Childhood
Selected Works of Elaine Funnell
Edited by Nicola Pitchford, Andrew W. Ellis

Exploring Working Memory
Selected Works of Alan Baddeley
By Alan Baddeley

Investigating the Truth

Selected Works of Ray Bull

Ray Bull

Routledge
Taylor & Francis Group
LONDON AND NEW YORK

First published 2019 by Routledge

2 Park Square, Milton Park, Abingdon, Oxfordshire OX14 4RN
52 Vanderbilt Avenue, New York, NY 10017

Routledge is an imprint of the Taylor & Francis Group, an informa business

First issued in paperback 2019

British Library Cataloguing-in-Publication Data
A catalogue record for this book is available from the British Library

Library of Congress Cataloging-in-Publication Data
A catalog record for this book has been requested

ISBN: 978-1-138-04886-7 (hbk)
ISBN: 978-0-367-34509-9 (pbk)

Typeset in Times New Roman
by Sunrise Setting Ltd, Brixham, UK

Contents

Contributors

Lucy Akehurst, Department of Psychology, University of Portsmouth, Portsmouth, UK.

Pedro B. Albuquerque, School of Law and Criminology, University of Derby, Derby, UK.

Jehanne Almerigogna, Department of Psychology, University of Portsmouth, Portsmouth, UK.

Julian Boon, Leicester University, UK.

Ray Bull, School of Law and Criminology, University of Derby, Derby, UK.

Julie Cherryman, Department of Psychology, University of Portsmouth, Portsmouth, UK.

Coral J. Dando, Department of Psychology, University of Wolverhampton, UK.

Rhona Flin, Robert Gordon University, Aberdeen, UK.

Peter Horncastle, PA Consulting Group, London, UK.

Anne Knox, Glasgow Caledonian University, UK.

Guenter Koehnken, Institut für Psychologie, University of Kiel, Germany.

Samantha Leahy-Harland, Bournemouth University, Poole, UK.

Samantha Mann, Psychology Department, University of Portsmouth, Portsmouth, UK.

Amina Memon, School of Human Development, University of Texas at Dallas, USA.

Rebecca Milne, Institute of Criminal Justice Studies, University of Portsmouth, UK.

Thomas C. Ormerod, Department of Psychology, Lancaster University, UK.

James Ost, Department of Psychology, University of Portsmouth, Portsmouth, UK.

Rui M. Paulo, School of Psychology, University of Minho, Braga, Portugal.

R. L. Reid, Department of Psychology, University of Exeter, Exeter, UK.

Alexandra L. Sandham, Department of Psychology, Lancaster University, UK.

S. Soukara, Athens Metropolitan College, Athens, Greece; School of Psychology, University of Leicester, UK.

Mark Turner, Department of Psychology, University of Portsmouth, Portsmouth, UK.

Aldert Vrij, Psychology Department, University of Portsmouth, Portsmouth, UK.

Dave Walsh, School of Law and Criminology, University of Derby, Derby, UK.

Linsey Wark, Department of Psychology, University of Southampton, UK.

Introduction

This introduction contains an overview outlining the evolution of my research career from (i) first working with/researching the police in the 1970s and 1980s to investigate the truth in relation to their expectations of increased effectiveness regarding recruit training and the memorability of briefings (Part 1); to (ii) developing and assessing the effectiveness of the 'cognitive interview' that had been designed to assist witnesses to recall what truly happened (Part 2); to (iii) conducting research on how best to interview/question children in order to get to the truth (Part 3); to (iv) researching people's (false) assumptions about liars' behaviour and effective ways to detect truth/lies (Part 4); to (v) developing ways to get suspects to tell the truth (Part 5).

Part 1: Police

Several months after graduating with a BSc in psychology (with mathematical statistics) I was invited by Professor Leslie Reid (my head of department) to (temporarily we thought) move away from my research towards gaining a PhD in psychophysiology (see Bull & Gale, 1971, 1973, 1974, 1975) to work for 12 months on a research project funded by the Police Scientific Development Branch of the Home Office. This project involved assessing the truth in relation to the police organisation's expectation that television broadcasts would make the contents of daily operational briefings that contained a variety of information more memorable to patrol officers (e.g. who or what to look out for). (In 1971 this was a novel idea.) Traditionally, in England such briefings had been delivered face-to-face by a duty sergeant who typically read out to a group of officers a rather long list of items selected from an even greater number of available items. In contrast, not only did the televised briefings present more visual information, they also contained fewer items. We first of all found that more televised briefing information was later recalled than the face-to-face briefing information. However, we were aware of seminal research in the domain of cognitive psychology that people might better be able to recall around seven items than a larger number of items (e.g. Miller, 1956).

This was one of the reasons why the police and the Home Office agreed to fund our research project for a further 12 months and to our conducting of an experiment in which the number of items (and indeed the briefing items themselves) was controlled and similar for both the television and face-to-face presentations to officers. Indeed, the script used for both conditions was identical. For one presentation the number of items was seven, for another it was six, and for another eight. We found (Bull & Reid, 1975 – included in the present volume) no recall difference between the two types of presentation that supported our view that our earlier finding of better recall of the televised briefings could well be due to their containing fewer items. We also found that eight items resulted in significantly less (absolute) recall than did seven or six (that did not differ). Furthermore, by systematically varying the order in which items appeared within the scripts we innovatively found support for the 'serial position effect' (i.e. items in the middle of lists are less well recalled) that heretofore had been studied with lists containing simple items such as digits or nonsense syllables.

Our findings a few years later (after my appointment to a lectureship in cognitive psychology in London) led on to another study (Bull & Peace, 1978) conducted in a different, large police organisation in England where we found the traditional style of briefing at a busy police station to contain an average of 15 items. When we assessed the recall of such briefings we found that only 4% of officers recalled more than seven items and that the average number of pieces of information (an item would contain a number of pieces) recalled was 22.1. At a different, less busy station the average number of items per traditional briefing was nine, yet the mean recall was 22.6. The chief of this police organisation then instructed the officers who presented the face-to-face briefings in these two stations to restrict the briefings to seven items, which led to increased average recall of 29.0 and 27.3 (respectively). In light of our findings (i.e. investigating the truth of 'less means more'), restricting such briefings to seven items immediately became force-wide policy, and later added to national policy.

Also, eventually resulting in national policy was my later work in the 1980s with the London Metropolitan Police Service (the 'Met') (see Bull & Horncastle, 1994 – available in the present book). For a variety of reasons the Met decided in 1981 to enhance the training it provided to its recruits and 'probationers' (i.e. in their first 24 months of service). The initial, full-time recruit training was substantially extended to incorporate sessions on (a) interpersonal skills, (b) self-awareness, and (c) community relations that now constituted a quarter of the 20 week course (these components being referred to as 'Human Awareness' and later as 'Policing Skills'). The initial version of the new course began in April 1982, it having been developed by police officers, some of whom had knowledge drawn from the behavioural sciences. The Met also decided to commission (via the independent Police Foundation) an external evaluation of the three new components of the course, which I was asked to conduct in order to investigate the truth in relation to the Met's expectation that the new training would be effective. Initially, this external evaluation was funded to last just 12 months but in the light of its findings it was annually extended/funded for over five years.

For the first phase (i.e. year one) of our evaluation we used some available psychometric instruments to provide reliable and valid assessments of the impact of the training, comparing cohorts of recruits in (i) week 1, (ii) week 20, (iii) week 26, and (iv) week 50 – on the last two occasions the recruits had been assigned to work (under supervision) in a variety of police stations. Although some existing, standardised psychometric questionnaires did address some of the training's stated aims, we had to design our own for some aspects. For the existing questionnaires we found that the recruits' social-evaluative anxiety did decrease substantially, but there were no clear trends regarding either the self-esteem or the interpersonal relations questionnaires. The questionnaire that we devised detected a number of changes across this period of a year, but several of them were in the opposite direction from what the Met had anticipated. During this first year we also designed a questionnaire that directly sought the views of the trainees, and these were incorporated into our progress reports to the Met.

In the light of our findings the Met decided to amend several aspects of the course and invited me to continue evaluating it (see Bull & Horncastle, 1994 – available in the present volume, and Bull & Horncastle, 1989, 1988). Here, I can briefly mention that in the later years of our evaluation we also (i) compared the number of complaints made by the public about probationer officers who had received either the new training or the training that preceded it, (ii) conducted an extensive patrol observation study, (iii) developed and then employed a supervisors' questionnaire, and (iv) interviewed members of the public about their interactions with probationers. The information we thus gained again fed back into amending the training, the resulting version of which was subsequently adopted nationally – our having investigated the truth that psychology can improve policing.

Part 2: The 'cognitive interview'

Above I mentioned my research on improving the memorability of police daily operational briefings. My liaison person within the relevant government ministry (i.e. the Home Office) subsequently asked me in around 1974 to write an overview of psychological research on the topic of person/face recognition. I have no knowledge of whether my overview was passed to members of the government-appointed 'Devlin Committee' who in 1976 produced their report on 'Evidence of Identification in Criminal Cases' (Devlin, 1976). Even so, this seminal and very extensive report gave explicit mention to the then available, relevant psychological research. However, the report added that 'a gap exists between academic research . . . and the practical requirements of courts of law . . . we recommend . . . the possibility . . . of undertaking research . . . in which the insights of psychology could be brought to bear on . . . all matters relating to evidence of identification' (p. 73).

During my lectureship in London I shared an office with another of the department's cognitive psychologists who, after this Devlin Report had been published, suggested to me (or I suggested to him – my memory is not perfect) that we together write a book on the topic of person identification, which we did (Clifford & Bull, 1978 – reprinted in 2017). Here I should add in passing that I first sent our proposal to a major international publisher of academic psychological books which replied saying that, although their reviewers had informed them that our proposal had high academic/intellectual merit, it had been decided that the topic would not attract sufficient sales. Fortunately, the second publisher accepted our proposal. The next year two other books on the topic were published in North America (Loftus, 1979; Yarmey, 1979). Together, these three books encouraged many people around the world to conduct research relevant to the recommendation in the Devlin Report, not only in terms of identification but also regarding 'What happened?'

The fruits of this fast expanding body of research (largely on memory) had relevance, of course, to how to interview people (e.g. witnesses, victims) in ways that best assist them to access their memory. One outstanding example of this is the 'cognitive interview' originally developed in the 1980s in the USA by Fisher and Geiselman (Geiselman, Fisher, MacKinnon, & Holland, 1985). (For an overview see Milne & Bull, 1999.) In my first academic post in cognitive psychology I had been impressed by the research of the famous British cognitive psychologist Donald Broadbent who said in an interview that those of us who wished their research to have impact in the real world should start by examining a 'problem' (here I can suggest poor witness memory) and work back from that towards theory. This is what Fisher and Geiselman had done.

In 2000 in England and Wales the government commissioned (in the light of a growing body of research) the writing of a document that would not only be an updated version of the 1992 Memorandum of Good Practice 'MOGP' guidance (see below) but would also provide guidance on the interviewing of particularly vulnerable witnesses/victims, whether adult or child. This very extensive document [known as 'Achieving best evidence in criminal proceedings: Guidance on interviewing victims and witnesses' ('ABE'), published in 2002 and updated since then] was written by a team of people (led by Professor Graham Davies) that involved psychologists (including myself – I wrote most of the new section/chapter on interviewing vulnerable people).

Whereas up to 1992 there were insufficient peer-reviewed research publications on the possible contribution of a new technique called the 'cognitive interview' (CI) for the interviewing of children, when drafting ABE it was decided that by then there were more than enough published research studies to justify its inclusion (for the first meta-analysis of studies of the CI see Koehnken, Milne, Memon, & Bull, 1999). In 1991 we published an overview of the original cognitive interview procedure (Memon & Bull, 1991) which contained four mnemonic techniques that Fisher and Geiselman had derived from research in cognitive psychology. In doing this I had realised that their original version of the CI did not focus on the importance of interviewers establishing and maintaining rapport with interviewees that I had emphasised in the 1992 MOGP. (Indeed, in their seminal 1992 book Fisher and Geiselman also recognised this.)

Therefore, in the early 1990s we conducted a series of studies in which some participants were interviewed in line with the guidance in the MOGP (this we called a 'structured interview') and others were similarly interviewed but also using the four original mnemonics of the early version of the CI. For example, in Memon, Wark, Bull, & Koehnken (1997) we found that children (aged 8 to

9 years) who saw a magic show when interviewed two days later recalled more correct information when the CI techniques were used. They also reported more incorrect information but this was numerically much smaller than the increase in correct recall (at 3 and 20 units of information, respectively). This superiority for correct recall found using the original CI mnemonics (compared with a well-conducted interview without them) we replicated in other studies (e.g. Memon, Holley, Wark, Bull, & Koehnken, 1996; Memon, Wark, Holley, Bull, & Koehnken, 1997; Milne & Bull, 1996; Milne, Clare, & Bull, 1999). However, in our study (described above) we found no superiority of the CI mnemonics for interviews conducted 12 days after the event, this perhaps being due to the fading in memory of contextual cues.

In one of our 1996 studies (i.e. Memon *et al.*) we also examined if use of the CI would reduce the negative effect of (subsequently asked) mis-leading questions (which at that time were apparently common in possible abuse cases in other countries such as the USA). We found that it did. Therefore, we decided that it was important to see if we could replicate this finding (Milne & Bull, 2003 – contained within the present 'selected works'). We were also interested (as we had been in some of our other studies) to see whether use of the CI techniques would increase the correct recall about persons, this being an area of human frailty noted in prior work on witness memory. Furthermore, because a theoretical base of one of the original four CI mnemonics (i.e. recall now in a different order, for example, reverse order) related to people's use when attempting recall of 'scripts' (i.e. what usually happens), we wanted the event to be recalled to contain both script-consistent and script-inconsistent aspects. This is why in our studies with child participants we used a magic show and a magician who was willing to include in his show not only typical aspects but also atypical aspects that would be unfamiliar to children. In our 2003 study we did replicate the finding of our 1996 study in which the CI reduced the effects of subsequently asked mis-leading questions, especially those that were script-consistent. We also found that use of the CI increased the correct recall of person information.

Such studies as these, which investigated the truth of the CI being effective, led us to include CI in the 2002 official government guidance document ('Achieving Best Evidence' – see Part 3). Since then research has continued on the CI and additions to the original CI techniques (see Fisher, Milne, & Bull, 2011), including in countries new to such research such as Brazil (Milnitsky Stein & Memon, 2006) and recently in Portugal. At the University of Minho in Portugal an aspiring PhD student (Rui Paulo) contacted me to ask if I would be willing to co-supervise his PhD there (on the CI) if he successfully applied for a prestigious doctoral scholarship that required him to study for some periods outside Portugal (i.e. with me in England). I agreed and he was successful.

In our opening study (Paulo, Albuquerque, Saraiva, & Bull, 2015) adults watched a recording of a mock bank robbery and were interviewed with either a (newly translated) Portuguese version of the CI (as described/updated by Fisher and Geiselman, 1992) or our 'structured interview'. Those interviewed with the CI provided more information without compromising accuracy. A novel finding was that those participants who more highly rated the appropriateness of the interview procedure provided more correct recall. We sought such ratings because I had always been concerned when first learning about Geiselman and Fisher's pioneering CI studies in the 1980s that the interviewing with which they compared their original version of the CI was uncontrolled. Such interviews sometimes merely involved interviewers doing what came naturally (i.e. they received no training), which might not be an appropriate comparison because the motivation of witnesses (and other important factors) could differ between these interviews and the CI interviews.

Similarly, I had been concerned that in Fisher and Geiselman's ground-breaking studies only one group of interviewers had received training; this might have increased their motivation which could have been noted by their interviewees and thus affected their recall performance. Indeed, many psychologists who conduct experiments often ignore this motivation issue when comparing performance across different conditions/parts of their studies. For example, I was recently asked by a leading international research journal to review a manuscript that was good except that one of the experimental conditions was far less interesting/more boring than the others, so no wonder performance was poorer in that condition.

In our second Portuguese CI study (Paulo, Albuquerque, & Bull, 2016a – included within the present volume) we again found a CI superiority effect but we also found that participants' self-ratings of motivation were significantly associated with recall accuracy, in that the more motivated interviewees provided more accurate information. In this study we also found witnesses' spontaneous verbal expressions of uncertainty while recalling (e.g. saying 'I think', 'maybe', 'I believe') to be associated with lower accuracy of the directly associated information being recalled. In our other Portuguese studies we found that replacing one of the original four CI mnemonics with 'category clustering recall' (i.e. asking participants to now recall in the categories of 'actions' or 'objects' etc.) enhanced the recall of correct information (see Paulo, Albuquerque, & Bull, 2016b; Paulo, Albuquerque, Vitorino, & Bull, 2017).

Part 3: Investigative interviewing of children

I mentioned above the growing contribution of psychology to investigating the truth/obtaining valid information from suspects in an ethical way. This has a parallel development regarding the interviewing of witnesses/victims, especially children. In 1992 in England and Wales the government innovatively encouraged those who interview children in connection with their possibly witnessing crimes to video record such interviews – this soon became national practice and can be part of a child's evidence at court. When doing this the government realised that those who undertake this difficult task would benefit from guidance on how best to do this, particularly as prior investigations in the UK and the USA had involved unskilled or inept interviewing/questioning. Together with a law professor I was commissioned to develop this extensive guidance, known as the Memorandum of Good Practice on Video Recorded Interviews with Child Witnesses for

Criminal Proceedings (MOGP), which was firmly based in the findings of psychological research, including our work on the questioning of children in criminal trials.

However, while it could be considered an achievement to have government guidance extensively informed by the findings of psychological research, a crucial question is the extent to which such guidance can be put into practice. In the 1970s and 1980s a growing body of research by psychologists (especially in the USA, for example see Ceci & Bruck, 1993, 1995; Ceci, Crossman, Scullin, Gilstrap, & Huffman, 2002) found that not only parents but also relevant professionals had questioned children about possible abuse in ways that may have unduly influenced what children said about what had happened. Here in the UK we studied professionals' questioning of child witnesses in judicial proceedings (Flin, Bull, Boon, & Knox, 1993 – available within the present book). As part of a research project funded by the Scottish Home and Health Department, we conducted the first British study of lawyers' questioning of child witnesses during criminal trials conducted in the major city of Glasgow. Among our surprising findings was that during a 15-month period in the late 1980s no fewer than 1,800 child witnesses were cited for criminal trials (i.e. formally notified that they may be called to give evidence). The relevant cases mostly related to their (possibly) witnessing as 'bystanders' assaults, thefts, breaches of the peace and road traffic accidents. Some cases related to child abuse, but at that time (unlike now) there was little media activity that encouraged victims to come forward.

At the time of our study there was, however, growing media focus in the UK that some child witnesses to/victims of sexual abuse were not coping in a system designed for adults, though no study had yet been conducted on this.

We observed 89 children actually giving evidence (ten 5 to 8 year olds, twenty-five 9 to 13 year olds and fifty-four 14 to 15 year olds). The proportions of these children who appeared 'unhappy' when being questioned by the lawyers (many of whom at that time had little or no training on how to talk to children) were high at 55% for their evidence-in-chief and 50% for their cross-examination. (Similar data were found for 'tense' at 57% and 48%, respectively.) Nevertheless, the majority of the children were 'fluent' when giving their evidence, but few provided 'a lot of detail' with most providing only 'a little' or 'some' detail. The main difference between their examination-in-chief and their cross-examination was regarding the age appropriateness of the lawyers' vocabulary (at 88% and 59%, respectively). One clear implication of our innovative study's findings was that lawyers would benefit from relevant guidance and training (which subsequently took place in the UK) and perhaps be 'selected' to work on child cases (as indeed they now are, as are judges). For an impressive body of subsequent work on the questioning of children in courts in New Zealand see Zajac (2009).

In our Glasgow study we also found that lawyers during their examination-in-chief were significantly more 'supportive' to the children than were the lawyers during cross-examination. A few years later, having co-drafted the government guidance on good practice when interviewing children (i.e. the MOGP mentioned above), I began to receive requests from lawyers, social workers and the police to examine video-recorded investigative interviews with children in order to offer an opinion on the extent to which the interviewing was in line with the guidance (this continues to happen nowadays). Among the many things I noticed in those 'early days' in the mid-1990s was that interviews conducted by social workers were typically more supportive (in appropriate ways) than those conducted by police officers (who had hitherto interviewed children less often than had social workers and who often were more experienced at interviewing suspects). So I decided that the effects in interviews of the degree of supportiveness was deserving of research attention.

Some years later we conducted an experiment that did examine the effects of 'supportiveness' that involved children (aged 8 to 11 years) being interviewed about what they had witnessed/seen (i.e. part of a movie). Given that by now it had become even clearer to me that conducting a perfect child interview that gathers lots of information is rarely achievable (see Bull, 2010 and below), I also wanted to investigate the extent to which the official guidance's emphasis on establishing rapport with interviewees (and maintaining it – see Walsh & Bull, 2012 and below) might reduce the effects of the inevitable suggestive/leading questions that even well-trained interviewers find difficult to avoid. Therefore, our interviews contained some mis-leading questions (Almerigogna, Ost, Bull, & Akehurst, 2007). Among our findings were that children interviewed with a supportive style were less likely to go along with mis-leading questions than were those with a rather less supportive style (also found by Bull & Corran, 2003). Additionally, (i) the less supportive style was associated with an increase in child witnesses' state anxiety (i.e. pre- versus post-interview) whereas the supportive style was associated with a decrease; and (ii) those children whose anxiety decreased provided fewer incorrect answers to the mis-leading questions. We concluded that since supportive style is under the control of interviewers and is thus amenable to manipulation (whereas some other important factors, for example age of child, are not), it should be emphasised in training.

However, training seems never to have been fully effective. For a special issue of the highly regarded research journal *Legal and Criminological Psychology* I was invited by its editors to provide an overview of psychological research and professional practice regarding the investigative interviewing of children and other vulnerable witnesses (Bull, 2010). In that article (contained in the present volume) I made it clear that psychological research has found that people (including professionals who have to interview/question children) are typically very poor at this task and I mentioned the rather obvious, but largely ignored, point that training requires them not only to do new things but also to stop doing 'what comes naturally'. At the request of the editors I also mentioned two topics much in need of further research. One of these was the effects of interviewer style, such as their supportiveness (mentioned above) and the other was the effects of long delays (e.g. between an event occurring and later being interviewed about it).

Contrary to what 'common sense' might suggest (and to what some psychologists have claimed in criminal court cases in which I have testified), the limited number of ecologically valid studies of children's ability to recall 'negative' events after long delays (if interviewed appropriately) tell us that such recall can be accurate. Understandably, ethical approval committees will not permit researchers to cause 'negative' events to children, and I have never been clever enough to design a study that includes a naturally occurring 'negative' event. However, we did conduct a study involving a long delay in which we found (Bull, Paterson, & Vrij, 2003) that a week after watching a magic show children could, on average, correctly recall 24 'pieces of information' from it (with 97% accuracy). The same children one year later could only recall seven 'pieces of information' (with 41% accuracy). These children were then shown a small number of items used in the magic show and they then recalled (discounting these shown items) a further 31 'pieces of information' (with 83% accuracy).

Of course, investigating the truth can be hampered not only by unskilled interviewing (e.g. involving suggestive questioning) but also by people lying/being untruthful (see Part 4).

Part 4: Detecting truth/lies

In the early 1980s (courtesy of some generous referees, I suspect) my application to the Scientific Committee of the North Atlantic Treaty Organization (NATO) to fund a three week lecture tour of universities in North America was successful, during which I spoke on witness memory topics. One of the professors in Canada who invited me was John Yuille, with whom we later obtained substantial funding from NATO to hold a week-long conference in 1985 on 'The role of psychology in police selection and training' (in Skiathos, Greece) for over 70 international delegates. This 'Advanced Study Institute' was deemed to have been a great success, which led John Yuille to apply successfully to NATO to hold another on 'Credibility assessment' in 1988 (in Italy) at which he invited me to present on the topic of 'Can training enhance the detection of deception?'. During my presentation I mentioned the importance of skilled interviewing.

A few years later I attended another NATO-funded conference, this time on child witnesses where (in the hotel bar) I first met Aldert Vrij. A short time after that, while working in Amsterdam, Aldert contacted me suggesting that he would like to use his sabbatical leave to come to the University of Portsmouth where I was Head of the Psychology Department. During his months in Portsmouth Aldert and I chatted on the topic of detecting deception/truth. In 1994 Aldert took up a permanent position (then as a Senior Lecturer) in my department and we soon started publishing together research on lying (e.g. Akehurst, Koehnken, Vrij, & Bull, 1996; Vrij, Semin, & Bull, 1996), with Aldert usually taking the lead (e.g. Akehurst, Bull, Vrij, & Koehnken, 2004; Vrij, Edward, Roberts, & Bull, 2000; Vrij, Akehurst, Soukara, & Bull, 2002). Here there is space to mention just one publication, Mann, Vrij, & Bull (2004).

In this highly cited 2004 article we were able not only to study police officers' ability to detect suspects' lies, but also to use actual police video-recorded interviews – a very unusual thing at the time (and since). In part, our being given access to such interviews came about via my work on interviewing and because the chairperson of the national police committee on interviewing was open-minded about the possible benefits of quality research. When I approached the chairperson about the possibility of some real world research on the detection of truth/lies in interviews with suspects, this chief police officer (of a relatively large organisation) was supportive, with a number of caveats. For example, while access was granted to a large number of interviews with suspects in serious cases, use of these was restricted to our research team, and they were shown only to officers in this large police organisation of several thousand personnel.

As part of her PhD studies Samantha Mann had to spend many days at this police organisation going through case files (i) to find those that involved video recorded interviews with suspects, (ii) of these, those that involved the suspect both lying and telling the truth, (iii) of these, those in which the lying was of investigative relevance, (iv) of these, those in which truth telling was not cognitively easy. Eventually, we had an appropriate sample of interviews, parts of which were shown to 99 police officers most of whom were detectives. Almost all prior studies of police detection of truth/lies had found performance levels very close to chance (e.g. 50%) but these had rarely if ever used real-life police interviews with suspects. We found an average performance level of 65% (66% for lies and 64% for truths) that was significantly above chance level. Furthermore, participants' amount of experience in investigative interviewing correlated significantly and positively with performance. Also, when asked prior to viewing the recordings to report which cues each participant usually used, those who reported mostly using content (i.e. what suspects said) performed better than did those who said they typically focused on behavioural cues – a finding that supports the training given to police in England and Wales to interview suspects in order that they provide information (see Part 5 below for details).

In the late 1990s there was a knock on my office door in the Department of Psychology at the University of Portsmouth and in came a person that I did not know, but I had a feeling that I had seen her once before. She explained that during her studies at the university (in another department) for an MSc in Criminal Justice Studies I had presented a lecture on research on investigative interviewing (including my own earlier work commissioned by the Home Office on whether the new philosophy and training in investigative interviewing introduced in 1992 (see Part 5 below) was translating into practice) (see Cherryman & Bull, 1996, 2000). She (Stavroula Soukara) went on to say that having come from outside the UK she was enjoying her time in England and she now was thinking about conducting a PhD on the interviewing of suspects and wanted me to be her doctoral supervisor. I asked her to send me a copy of her CV and we met again some days later. I then told her that although I was willing to supervise her undertaking a PhD on investigative interviewing, no one in the UK at that time other than government-commissioned researchers or police officers doing a higher degree had ever been granted permission to access real-life recorded police interviews with suspects. Therefore, I suggested that she should consider doing her PhD on the interviewing of (mock) witnesses. Stavroula and I readily agreed that police interviewing of suspects (with all its complexities and pressures) could never be replicated in a 'mock' or laboratory setting, whereas this might be possible to a fair extent for the interviewing of uninvolved, bystander witnesses. Stavroula seemed adamant that she wanted to study the real-life interviewing of suspects, and when I asked her why she said that she wanted to go back to her country and change the way this was done (which she subsequently has contributed to). We eventually agreed that we would try to gain access to real-life interviews of suspects, but that if we failed to do so within six months she would do her PhD on the interviewing of witnesses.

We then contacted and met with a number of highly experienced interviewers whom I knew, seeking their views (see Soukara, Bull, & Vrij, 2002), and eventually permission was granted. A number of other publications arose from this successful PhD (Bull & Soukara, 2010; Soukara, Bull, Vrij, Turner, & Cherryman, 2009 – also see Part 5 below), the final study in which was a close examination of the rather rare interviews in the 1990s (Baldwin, 1993; Pearse & Gudjonsson, 1997) in which suspects 'shift' from denying/not admitting (for a considerable period of time) to then giving an incriminating, comprehensive account. In that study we found that two of the many police skills/tactics that we focused on were very substantially associated with the timing of such shifts, these being the asking of 'open questions' and the interviewer 'disclosing information'. I then realised (in 2003) that the latter finding meant that in these interviews the officers had not given away to the suspects all the information/evidence they already had near the beginning of the interviews (this not being required by law in England), which earlier research had found to be typical (Moston, Stephenson, & Williamson, 1992) and which is still done in other countries (Tsan-Chang Lin & Chih-Hung Shih, 2013). Instead, they had been doing so gradually as the interviews progressed. I then set about securing funding to investigate this further (not being aware of a few publications in Dutch that had mentioned this – see van der Sleen, 2009). Eventually, as part of a new government fund for research on counter-terrorism I obtained support for a 33-month project.

This project was designed to compare the 'early' disclosure of information with 'gradual' disclosure, and with 'late' disclosure innovatively studied in Sweden (Hartwig, Granhag, Stromwall, & Vrij, 2005). It was not possible to analyse real-life interviews with terrorism suspects in which information disclosure was either 'early, 'late' or 'gradual' (for an excellent study of interviews with terrorists see Alison, Alison, Noone, Elntib, & Christiansen, 2013). Therefore, we had to devise a scenario as similar as we could make it. We needed to think of one in which (i) covert observation would be made of participants who might be conducting a terrorism plot or who might be conducting somewhat similar behaviour but not wrong-doing, (ii) that such observation would produce lists of items of possibly incriminating information but none that by itself or in small combinations would confirm terrorism, (iii) that such lists should contain several items, five of which would be available to the police officer interviewing the suspects, (iv) that the suspects should be clever people, and (v) that the scenario be topical, interesting and take a fair while to complete. One evening in a hotel bar near to where I worked at the University of Leicester we were able (with the help of creativity inspired by white wine) to devise such a scenario which we called 'Dodgy Builders' in which all participants built a new sports stadium but some planted bombs within it (Dando & Bull, 2011).

Using this scenario we conducted two large studies. In the first study 150 university students participated (as terrorists or builders) and were then individually interviewed by a person who had ten years' police investigative interviewing experience. This interviewer followed a schedule in which one-third of the participants were interviewed employing 'early' disclosure, another third using 'late' disclosure and the remaining third with 'gradual' disclosure. All of these interviews were video recorded. Each of 30 laypersons watched ten interviews from each of the three disclosure conditions (five terrorists who lied about some of their activities and five builders who told the truth) but they were not made aware of our hypotheses. For each interview they had to decide whether the interviewee had lied or told the truth. For the 'early' and the 'late' disclosure interviews performance was at chance level (i.e. 49% and 50%, respectively) but for the 'gradual' interviews it was 68%. For more on this study see Dando, Bull, Ormerod, & Sandham (2015) (contained within the present volume), including that participant motivation was similar across conditions.

This finding that gradual disclosure occasioned superior performance (while keeping the same interviewer constant throughout) justified our asking five experienced police interviewers to devote several days to taking part in our second study (Dando & Bull, 2011 – contained within the present volume). Another 150 university students participated in the same way as in our first study but were interviewed by one of the five interviewers whom we had trained to disclose information gradually or late or early using 11 pieces of information. At the end of each interview the interviewers had to decide whether that interviewee had lied or told the truth. For the early disclosure interviews their average performance was 50%, for the late it was 48%, and for the gradual it was 71%, thus replicating our prior finding.

Of course, it would be useful to know if the gradual disclosure that we had found in these two scenario studies, and had noticed in 2003 in those real-life interviews, would be of benefit to investigations. Though merely an anecdote, having shared our findings with a number of the most experienced police officers in a number of organisations in England (who are called 'interview advisors' or 'tier five qualified'), I subsequently received a message from one of these, the gist of which was 'Ray – gradual disclosure worked really well in a crucially important interview'. More importantly, with my colleague Dr Dave Walsh, we later found that in real-life interviews with people suspected of fraud, when the evidence/information was disclosed gradually interviews were both more skilled and involved the gaining of comprehensive accounts. Whereas when evidence was disclosed either early or late, interviews were found to be both less skilled and less likely to involve this outcome (Walsh & Bull, 2015).

Part 5: Investigative interviewing of suspects

In the previous paragraph I mentioned the gaining of comprehensive accounts. 'Investigative interviewing', in contrast to 'interrogating', seeks to gather relevant and truthful information from suspects (whether innocent or guilty) rather than confessions. This enormous change in police/investigators' mind-set was initially brought about by the promulgation in 1992 in England and Wales of the newly developed 'PEACE' method. In 1990 the Association of Chiefs of Police (ACPO) set up a working party of highly experienced investigators/detectives to develop new training. At around the same time the senior London police officer Tom Williamson convened a different small working party of detectives and psychologists (including Eric Shepherd, Stephen Moston and myself) who met on Sundays and who produced (in 1991) an unpublished overview of aspects of psychology that might be useful to the improvement of such interviewing/interrogating. This large document was passed to the detectives' working party. Once that team of detectives had drafted their guidance documents they sent such drafts to me asking if they had 'got the psychology correct?' – they indeed had. Thus, this innovative model/approach involved substantial guidance documents and training courses (that all police interviewers in England and Wales must attend) which contained much research-based cognitive and social psychology (see Milne & Bull, 1999).

As stated in Part 1, my first experience of sharing psychology with the police in England commenced in 1971, when few were doing this, and ten years later I began a commissioned project (lasting over five years) with the Metropolitan Police in London that involved evaluating and improving the new style of recruit training that innovatively involved considerable amounts of psychology. Both of these projects resulted in considerable changes/improvements nationally. Given this (and possibly our 1983 book entitled *Psychology for Police Officers*), it is perhaps not that surprising that in 1992 the findings of psychological research were incorporated by the working party of experienced detectives into the PEACE method (also see Bull, 1984).

Many years later the United Nations (UN) appointed a law professor (Juan Mendez) to the post of Special Rapporteur on 'Torture and other cruel, inhuman or degrading treatment or punishment'. In 2016 the UN published an extensive report by Professor Mendez which in its summary stated that:

> The Special Rapporteur . . . advocates the development of a universal protocol identifying a set of standards for non-coercive interviewing methods and procedural safeguards that ought, as a matter of law and policy, to be applied at a minimum to all interviews by law enforcement officials, military and intelligence personnel and other bodies with investigative mandates.

When mentioning this 'universal protocol' the UN Special Rapporteur noted that:

> Encouragingly, some States have moved away from accusatorial, manipulative and confession-driven interviewing models with a view to increasing accurate and reliable information and minimizing the risks of unreliable information and miscarriages of justice . . . The essence of an alternative information-gathering model was first captured by the PEACE model

> of interviewing adopted in 1992 in England and Wales . . . investigative interviewing can provide positive guidance for the protocol.

In producing his 2016 report the UN Special Rapporteur (and his team) read as many relevant documents as possible, including those that I had co-authored/authored. These included not only the four articles (mentioned below) that are available within the present book, but also others (such as Bull, 2014; Bull & Soukara, 2010; Walsh & Bull, 2010, 2012). In our 2009 article (available within the present book) we analysed police interviews with suspects (in a variety of cases) at a time when (as now) it is understandably a complex and time-consuming procedure to try to obtain permission to access such interviews (that nationally have since 1986 been audio recorded). A major aim of our 2009 study was to see to what extent the interviewing was in line with the training the interviewers had received regarding the PEACE method (as we had done around a decade earlier; Cherryman & Bull, 1996).

In other countries then, and nowadays, police often used coercive interrogation strategies in the hope that these would cause suspects to confess. For example, in the USA, Kassin, Kukucka, Lawson, & DeCarlo (2017) found frequent use of tactics such as 'maximisation' (e.g. 'threatening with consequences', 'exaggerating seriousness'), 'minimisation' (e.g. 'leniency') and 'false evidence' (e.g. 'lying about existing evidence'). Also see Kassin, Kukucka, Lawson, and DeCarlo (2017). One of the major assumptions underlying justification for the use of coercive interrogation techniques is the widespread 'common-sense' belief (aptly summarised by Leo (2008) that 'suspects almost never confess spontaneously but virtually always in response to police pressure' (p. 162) and that 'Confessions, especially to serious crimes, are rarely made spontaneously. Rather they are actively elicited . . . typically after sustained psychological pressure' (p. 119).

However, even way back in the early 1990s the PEACE method avoided use of minimisation, maximisation and false evidence. In our 2009 study of real-life police interviews with suspects we found that such tactics were never or almost never employed. Instead, the most frequent tactics (I prefer to use the word 'skills') were 'disclosure of evidence', 'open questions', 'emphasising contradictions' and 'challenging suspect's account'. These are all in line with the basic principles of PEACE such as 'The role is to obtain accurate and reliable information from suspects, witnesses or victims in order to discover the truth about matters under investigation' and 'Interviews should be approached with an open mind. Information obtained from the person who is being interviewed should always be tested against what the interviewing officer already knows or what can reasonably be established' (see Milne & Bull, 1999).

Of course, although the PEACE method was (and is) partly based on the findings of available psychological research, a crucial question is to what extent the PEACE method is effective. Probably the first research designed to directly address this question was our 2010 publication (Walsh & Bull, 2010) in which we reported finding in real-life investigative interviews with suspects that interviewing in line with the PEACE method was associated with securing a greater number of comprehensive accounts, including exculpatory ones as well as admissions/confessions. For the 'account' phase, several significant positive associations between interview skills and interview outcomes were found, including for 'encourages suspect to give an account', 'develops topics', 'uses appropriate questions', 'explores received information', 'open-mindedness', 'active listening' and 'cognitive interviewing'. Overall, 63% of those interviews that were rated as satisfactory or above for the account phase obtained a comprehensive account or a full confession whereas only 12% of those rated as 'needs further training' did so.

Also, in the early/mid-2000s, we wanted to particularly study the effects of establishing and maintaining rapport with suspects (as emphasised in the training of the PEACE method, also in ABE and the MOGP mentioned in Part 3). To a considerable extent rapport is the opposite of coercion, and even nowadays some investigators/interviewers find it difficult to understand why it might be effective. We found (Walsh & Bull, 2012 – available within the present volume) that when examining the relationship between rapport building/rapport maintenance and subsequent interview outcomes, those interviewers who were rated as at or above PEACE standard of performance in their rapport building skills in the 'Account' phase were three times as likely to achieve a comprehensive account from the interviewees than those who were assessed as below minimum acceptable standards. Also, interviewers rated as at or above PEACE standard in both their rapport building and maintenance skills were over five times more likely to obtain satisfactory outcomes. Subsequent to our study, other researchers around the world have found rapport to be considered an essential skill (for reviews see Abbe & Brandon, 2013; Alison, Giles, & McGuire, 2015; Bull, 2013; Bull & Baker, in press).

We also were able to examine real-life interviews with suspects in another study (Leahy-Harland & Bull, 2017) that focused exclusively on real-life taped interviews with serious crime suspects. We found that interviewers employed a range of strategies with 'presentation of evidence' and 'challenge' being the most frequently used. Closed questions were by far the type of question most frequently used, and open questions, although less frequent, were found to occur more during the opening phases of the interviews. The frequency of ineffective question types (e.g. negative, repetitive, multiple) was low. We also found a number of significant associations between interviewer strategies and suspect responses. For example, rapport/empathy and open-type questions were associated with an increased likelihood of suspects admitting the offence, while 'describing trauma' and 'negative questions' were associated with a decreased likelihood. We further found that the interviewers of these suspected murderers and rapists did not demonstrate a 'dominating approach' in these long duration interviews. We examined which strategies were associated with a continuing relevant response by interviewees and found positive associations for 'rapport/empathy', 'presentation of evidence', 'requests attention', but negative associations for 'explicitly asks for account/tell truth', 'emphasises seriousness of offence' and 'situational futility'.

The last three tactics mentioned in the previous paragraph are part of an interrogation procedure that is widely taught in the USA and many other countries. During the time that Barack Obama was president, in the USA an initiative commenced designed to develop research-based methods for obtaining information/intelligence from those suspected of being involved in or planning serious wrong-doing such as terrorism (for an overview see Meissner, Surmon-Böhr, Oleszkiewicz, & Alison, 2017). In the very early days of this 'High-value detainees interrogation group' research programme (known as HIG) I was on two occasions invited to the USA largely to explain the reasons why in England and Wales the PEACE method was developed, its psychological underpinnings and its effectiveness. Following this I was commissioned by the HIG to write an overview of work on what is 'believed' or actually 'known' about characteristics that may contribute to being a good/effective interviewer (Bull, 2013 – available within the present volume).

This 2013 article overviewed what is known regarding beliefs about important attributes of good interviewers, the actual relationships between skills/abilities and information gain in interviews, and actual differences between 'good' and 'not so good' investigators/interviewers. I concluded that there seemed to be an international consensus that the following may well be very important: preparation, planning, knowledge of topic, being well-organised, flexibility, open-mindedness, communication, rapport, listening, questioning, emphasising contradictions, compassion/empathy, courtesy, respect, patience, being calm and appealing to cooperation; and that a humanitarian interviewing style is more likely to lead to comprehensive, truthful accounts.

I would like to finish this introduction to my selected works by saying how very important it is to have several teams of quality researchers around the world working/researching on the same topic. Without my many wonderful collaborators and co-authors this book of selected works would not have been possible. I have been fortunate to be involved in networks of amazing people – **n**etwork **i**mplies **n**ot **a**lone – I dedicate this book to the memory of **Nina**, who devoted her far too short police then academic life to investigating the truth (see Westera, Kebbell, & Milne, 2011, 2013; Westera, Kebbell, Milne, & Green, 2016; Westera, McKimmie, Kebbell, Milne, & Masser, 2015; Westera & Powell, 2017).

References

Abbe, A. & Brandon, S. (2013). The role of rapport in investigative interviewing: a review. *Journal of Investigative Psychology and Offender Profiling*, *10*, 237–249.

Akehurst, L., Bull, R., Vrij, A. & Koehnken, G. (2004). The effects of training professional groups and lay persons to use Criteria Based Content Analysis. *Applied Cognitive Psychology*, *18*, 877–891.

Akehurst, L., Koehnken, G., Vrij, A. & Bull, R. (1996). Lay persons' and police officers' beliefs regarding deceptive behaviour. *Applied Cognitive Psychology*, *10*, 461–473.

Alison, L., Giles, S. & McGuire, G. (2015). Blood from a stone: why rapport works and torture doesn't in 'enhanced' interrogations. *Investigative Interviewing: Research and Practice*, *6*, 5–23.

Alison, L., Alison, E., Noone, G., Elntib, S. & Christiansen, P. (2013). Why tough tactics fail and rapport gets results: Observing Rapport-Based Interpersonal Techniques

(ORBIT) to generate useful information from terrorists. *Psychology, Public Policy, and Law, 19*, 411–431.

Baldwin, J. (1993). Police interview techniques: establishing truth or proof? *British Journal of Criminology, 33*, 325–352.

Bull, R. (1984). Psychology's contribution to policing. In D. Muller, D. Blackman & A. Chapman (eds.), *Psychology and Law*. Chichester: Wiley.

Bull, R. (2014). When in interviews to disclose information to suspects and to challenge them? In R. Bull (ed.), *Investigative Interviewing*. New York: Springer.

Bull, R. & Gale, A. (1971). The relationship between some measures of the galvanic skin response. *Psychonomic Science, 25*, 293–294.

Bull, R. & Gale, A. (1973). The reliability of and interrelationships between various measures of electrodermal activity. *Journal of Experimental Research in Personality, 6*, 200–206.

Bull, R. & Gale, A. (1974). Does the law of initial value apply to the galvanic skin response? *Biological Psychology, 1*, 213–227.

Bull, R. & Gale, A. (1975). Electrodermal activity recorded concomitantly from the subjects' two hands. *Psychophysiology, 12*, 94–97.

Bull, R. & Peace, D. (1978). Improving the effectiveness of daily briefings. *Police Research Bulletin, 31*, 4–7.

Bull, R. & Horncastle, P. (1988). Evaluating training: the London Metropolitan Police's recruit training in human awareness/policing skills. In P. Southgate (ed.), *New Directions in Police Training*. London: HMSO.

Bull, R. & Horncastle, P. (1989). An evaluation of human awareness training. In R. Morgan & D. Smith (eds.), *Coming to Terms with Policing*. London: Tavistock.

Bull, R. & Corran, E. (2003). Interviewing child witnesses: past and future. *International Journal of Police Science and Management, 4*, 315–322.

Bull, R. & Soukara, S. (2010). A set of studies of what really happens in police interviews with suspects. In G. D. Lassiter & C. Meissner (eds.), *Interrogations and Confessions*. Washington, DC: American Psychological Association.

Bull, R. & Baker, B. (in press). Obtaining from suspects valid discourse 'PEACE'-fully: what role for rapport and empathy? In M. Mason & F. Rock (eds.), *The Discourse of Police Interviews*. Chicago: University of Chicago Press.

Bull, R., Paterson, B. & Vrij, A. (2003). *Child witness recall after a one year delay*. Paper presented at Sixteenth European Conference on Developmental Psychology, Milan.

Ceci, S. J. & Bruck, M. (1993). Suggestibility of the child witness: a historical review and synthesis. *Psychological Bulletin, 113*, 403–439.

Ceci, S. J. & Bruck, M. (1995). *Jeopardy in the Courtroom: A Scientific Analysis of Children's Testimony*. Washington, DC: American Psychological Association.

Ceci, S., Crossman, A., Scullin, M., Gilstrap, L. & Huffman, M. (2002). Children's suggestibility research: Implications for the courtroom and the forensic interview. In H. Westcott, G. Davies & R. Bull (eds.), *Children's Testimony: Psychological Research and Forensic Practice*. Chichester: Wiley.

Cherryman, J. & Bull, R. (1996). Investigative interviewing. In F. Leishman, B. Loveday & S. Savage (eds.), *Core Issues in Policing*. London: Heinemann.

Cherryman, J. & Bull, R. (2000). Investigative interviewing. In F. Leishman, S. Savage & B. Loveday (eds.), *Core Issues in Policing* (2nd edn). London: Longman.

Clifford, B. & Bull, R. (1978). *The Psychology of Person Identification*. London: Routledge & Kegan Paul.

Devlin, P. (1976). *Report to the Secretary of State for the Home Department of the Departmental Committee on Evidence of Identification in Criminal Cases*. London: HMSO.
Fisher, R. & Geiselman, R. E. (1992). *Memory-Enhancing Techniques for Investigative Interviewing: The Cognitive Interview*. Springfield, IL: C. Thomas.
Fisher, R., Milne, R. & Bull, R. (2011). Interviewing cooperative witnesses. *Current Directions in Psychological Science*, *20*, 16–19.
Geiselman, R. E., Fisher, R., MacKinnon, D. & Holland, H. (1985). Eyewitness memory enhancement in the police interview: cognitive retrieval mnemonics versus hypnosis. *Journal of Applied Psychology*, *70*, 401–412.
Hartwig, M., Granhag, P. A., Stromwall, L. & Vrij, A. (2005). Detecting deception via strategic disclosure of evidence. *Law and Human Behavior*, *29*, 469–484.
Kassin, S., Kukucka, J., Lawson, V. & DeCarlo, J. (2017). Police reports of mock suspect interrogations: a test of accuracy and perception. *Law and Human Behavior*, *41*, 230–243.
Koehnken, G., Milne, R., Memon, A. & Bull, R. (1999). The cognitive interview: a meta-analysis. *Psychology, Crime and Law*, *5*, 3–28.
Leo, R. (2008). *Police Interrogation and American Justice*. Boston: Harvard University Press.
Loftus, E. (1979). *Eyewitness Testimony*. Cambridge, MA: Harvard University Press.
Mann, S., Vrij, A. & Bull, R. (2004). Detecting true lies: police officers' ability to detect suspects' lies. *Journal of Applied Psychology*, *89*, 137–149.
Meissner, C., Surmon-Böhr, F., Oleszkiewicz, S. & Alison, L. (2017). Developing an evidence-based perspective on interrogation: a review of the US government's high-value detainee interrogation group research program. *Psychology, Public Policy, and Law*, *23*, 438–457.
Memon, A. & Bull, R. (1991). The cognitive interview: its origins, empirical support, evaluation and practical implications. *Journal of Community and Applied Social Psychology*, *1*, 291–307.
Memon, A., Holley, A., Wark, L., Bull, R. & Koehnken, G. (1996). Reducing suggestibility in child witness interviews. *Applied Cognitive Psychology*, *10*, 503–518.
Memon, A., Wark, L., Holley, A., Bull, R. & Koehnken, G. (1997). Eyewitness performance in cognitive and structured interviews. *Memory*, *5*, 639–656.
Miller, G. (1956). The magic number seven plus or minus two: some limits on our capacity for processing information. *Psychological Review*, *63*, 91–97.
Milne, R. & Bull, R. (1996). Interviewing children with mild learning disability with the cognitive interview. In N. Clark & G. Stephenson (eds.), *Investigative and Forensic Decision Making*. Leicester: British Psychological Society.
Milne, R. & Bull, R. (1999). *Investigative Interviewing: Psychology and Practice*. Chichester: Wiley.
Milne, R., Clare, I. & Bull, R. (1999). The use of the cognitive interview for adults with mild learning disabilities. *Psychology, Crime and Law*, *5*, 81–100.
Milnitsky Stein, L. & Memon, A. (2006). Testing the efficacy of the cognitive interview in a developing country. *Applied Cognitive Psychology*, *20*, 597–605.
Moston, S., Stephenson, G. & Williamson, T. (1992). The effects of case characteristics on suspect behaviour during police questioning. *British Journal of Criminology*, *32*, 23–40.
Paulo, R., Albuquerque, P., Saraiva, M. & Bull, R. (2015). The enhanced cognitive interview: testing appropriateness perception, memory capacity, and estimate relation with rapport quality. *Applied Cognitive Psychology*, *29*, 536–543.

Paulo, R., Albuquerque, P. B. & Bull, R. (2016a). The enhanced cognitive interview: expressions of uncertainty, motivation and its relation with report accuracy. *Psychology, Crime and Law, 22*, 366–381.

Paulo, R., Albuquerque, P. B. & Bull, R. (2016b). Improving the enhanced cognitive interview with a new interview strategy: category clustering recall. *Applied Cognitive Psychology, 30*, 775–784.

Paulo, R., Albuquerque, P., Vitorino, F. & Bull, R. (2017). Enhancing the cognitive interview with an alternative procedure to witness-compatible questioning: category clustering recall. *Psychology, Crime and Law, 10*, 967–982.

Pearse, J. & Gudjonsson, G. (1997). Police interviewing techniques at two south London police stations. *Psychology Crime and Law, 3*, 63–74.

Soukara, S., Bull, R. & Vrij, A. (2002). Police detectives' aims regarding their interviews with suspects. *International Journal of Police Science and Management, 4*, 101–114.

Soukara, S., Bull, R., Vrij, A., Turner, M. & Cherryman, C. (2009). A study of what really happens in police interviews with suspects. *Psychology, Crime and Law, 15*, 493–506.

Tsan-Chang, L. & Chih-Hung, S. (2013). *A study of police interrogation practice in Taiwan*. Paper presented at the Asian Conference of Criminal and Police Psychology, Singapore.

van der Sleen, J. (2009). A structured model for investigative interviewing of suspects. In R. Bull, T. Valentine & T. Williamson (eds.), *Handbook of Psychology of Investigative Interviewing*. Chichester: Wiley-Blackwell.

Vrij, A., Semin, G. & Bull, R. (1996). Insight into behaviour displayed during deception. *Human Communication Research, 22*, 544–562.

Vrij, A., Edward, K., Roberts, K. & Bull, R. (2000). Detecting deceit via analysis of verbal and nonverbal behaviour. *Journal of Nonverbal Behavior, 24*, 239–263.

Vrij, A., Akehurst, L., Soukara, S. & Bull, R. (2002). Will the truth come out? The effect of deception, age, status, coaching, and social skills on CBCA scores. *Law and Human Behavior, 26*, 261–283.

Walsh, D. & Bull, R. (2010). What really is effective in interviews with suspects? A study comparing interview skills against interview outcomes. *Legal and Criminological Psychology, 15*, 305–321.

Walsh, D. & Bull, R. (2012). How do interviewers attempt to overcome suspects' denials? *Psychiatry, Psychology and Law, 19*, 151–168.

Walsh, D. & Bull, R. (2015). The association between interview skills, questioning and evidence disclosure strategies, and interview outcomes. *Psychology, Crime and Law, 21*, 661– 680.

Westera, N. & Powell, M. (2017). Prosecutors' perceptions of how to improve the quality of evidence in domestic violence cases. *Policing and Society, 27*, 157–172.

Westera, N., Kebbell, M. & Milne, R. (2011). Interviewing rape complainants: police officers' perceptions of interview format and quality of evidence. *Applied Cognitive Psychology, 25*, 917–926.

Westera, N., Kebbell, M. & Milne, R. (2013). It is better, but does it look better? Prosecutor perceptions of using rape complainant investigative interviews as evidence. *Psychology, Crime & Law, 19*, 595–610.

Westera, N., Kebbell, M., Milne, R. & Green, T. (2016). Towards a more effective detective. *Policing and Society, 26*, 1–17.

Westera, N., McKimmie, B., Kebbell, M., Milne, R. & Masser, B. (2015). Does the narrative style of video evidence influence judgements about rape complainant testimony? *Applied Cognitive Psychology, 29*, 637–646.

Yarmey, A. D. (1979). *The Psychology of Eyewitness Testimony*. New York: Free Press.

Zajac, R. (2009). Investigative interviewing in the courtroom: child witnesses under cross-examination. In R. Bull, T. Valentine & T. Williamson (eds.), *Handbook of Psychology of Investigative Interviewing*. Chichester: Wiley-Blackwell.

With thanks to APA, John Wiley & Sons, Springer, Taylor & Francis and SAGE for use of the following:

Part 1: Police

Bull, R. & Reid, R. L. (1975). Police officers' recall of information. *Journal of Occupational Psychology*, *48*, 73–78.
Bull, R. & Horncastle, P. (1994). Evaluation of police recruit training involving psychology. *Psychology, Crime and Law*, *1*, 143–149.

Part 2: The 'cognitive interview'

Memon, A., Wark, L., Bull, R. & Koehnken, G. (1997). Isolating the effects of the cognitive interview techniques. *British Journal of Psychology*, *88*, 187–198.
Milne, R. & Bull, R. (2003). Does the cognitive interview help children to resist the effects of suggestive questioning? *Legal and Criminological Psychology*, *8*, 21–38.
Paulo, R., Albuquerque, P. B. & Bull, R. (2016). The enhanced cognitive interview: expressions of uncertainty, motivation and its relation with report accuracy. *Psychology, Crime and Law*, 22, 366–381.

Part 3: Investigative interviewing of children

Almerigogna, J., Ost, J., Bull, R. & Akehurst, L. (2007). A state of high anxiety: how unsupportive interviewers can increase the suggestibility of child witnesses. *Applied Cognitive Psychology*, *21*, 963–974.
Bull, R. (2010). The investigative interviewing of children and other vulnerable witnesses: psychological research and working/professional practice. *Legal and Criminological Psychology*, *15*, 5–23.
Flin, R., Bull, R., Boon, J. & Knox, A. (1993). Child witnesses in Scottish criminal trials. *International Review of Victimology*, *2*, 309–329.

Part 4: Detecting truth/lies

Dando, C. & Bull, R. (2011). Maximising opportunities to detect verbal deception: training police officers to interview tactically. *Journal of Investigative Psychology and Offender Profiling*, *8*, 189–202.
Dando, C., Bull, R., Ormerod, T. & Sandham, A. (2015). Helping to sort the liars from the truth-tellers: the gradual revelation of information during investigative interviews. *Legal and Criminological Psychology*, *20*, 114–128.
Mann, S., Vrij, A. & Bull, R. (2004). Detecting true lies: police officers' ability to detect suspects' lies. *Journal of Applied Psychology*, *89*, 137–149.

Part 5: Investigative interviewing of suspects

Bull, R. (2013). What is 'believed' or actually 'known' about characteristics that may contribute to being a good/effective interviewer? *Investigative Interviewing: Research and Practice*, *5*, 128–143.

Leahy-Harland, S. & Bull, R. (2017). Police strategies and suspect responses in real-life serious crime interviews. *Journal of Police and Criminal Psychology*, *32*, 138–151.

Soukara, S., Bull, R., Vrij, A., Turner, M. & Cherryman, C. (2009). A study of what really happens in police interviews with suspects. *Psychology, Crime and Law*, *15*, 493–506.

Walsh, D. & Bull, R. (2012). Examining rapport in investigative interviews with suspects: does its building and maintenance work? *Journal of Police and Criminal Psychology*, *27*, 73–84.

1 Evaluation of police recruit training involving psychology

Ray Bull and Peter Horncastle

Introduction

In March 1981, before the disturbances in Brixton and other parts of London, a working party was formed in the London Metropolitan Police with a mandate to examine and to report on all current methods of formal and informal behavioural training for recruits and probationers (i.e. those in their first two years of service) and to make recommendations for improvements in these. From the findings of the working party came recommendations to develop what became Human Awareness Training (HAT). The first version of this training was implemented by the Metropolitan Police in April 1982. In June of the same year the independent evaluation described in this paper began under the auspices of the Police Foundation and at the request of the police. Our evaluation began not only after the training had been designed, but some months after it had been implemented. Thus, a before and after study was not possible. However, such evaluations are rarely organized and conducted under ideal circumstances. Nevertheless, our yearly reports to the London Police were to lead them to amend aspects of the training each year.

"Human Awareness Training" comprises three related areas of training: interpersonal skills (said to embody conversational skills and the ability to manage encounters with others); self-awareness (self-knowledge and insight into one's effect on social situations); and community relations (embracing awareness of and knowledge about different cultures and subcultures). The training programme, designed by police officers with a background in the behavioural sciences, accounts for approximately a quarter of the initial 20-week training course for those recruited to the Metropolitan Police. Much of the training is practical in its approach, and considerable use is made of such teaching techniques as role-play exercises and video feedback of students' performance.

The aims of the training (as stated by the Metropolitan Police, in 1985–6) were that the recruit should:

1. reflect credit upon the police force in appearance and behaviour on and off duty;
2. be capable of dealing impartially with people irrespective of background or circumstances;

3 identify how his/her personality affects others;
4 display knowledge of how people are likely to respond in given circumstances;
5 display professionalism in handling and concluding a wide variety of incidents;
6 show skill in recalling events and in helping others to do so;
7 identify the effect of group behaviour upon members of both the police and public;
8 apply a wide variety of interpersonal skills when dealing with members of the public;
9 understand the customs, viewpoints and traditions of minorities;
10 demonstrate flexibility and judgement in dealing with varied situations.

An outline of (phase one) of the evaluation

The behavioural science literature on attitude and social skills training evaluation was reviewed with that on police training to identify appropriate standardized, valid and reliable questionnaires which had been used in similar kinds of situations.

Two groups of recruits (31 per group) completed these questionnaires in Week 1 and in Week 20 (i.e. at the end) of initial training, then again six months and twelve months into their probationary period. The questionnaires used were as follows:

- a social-evaluative anxiety questionnaire (measures social avoidance and distress);
- a self-esteem questionnaire (measures perceived interpersonal threat; self esteem; faith in people; and sensitivity to criticism);
- an interpersonal relations questionnaire (measures need to establish satisfactory relationships; need to control them; and need for affection).

Groups of around 30 officers each answered the questionnaires.

These questionnaires were supplemented by one specifically designed to assess the attitudes, beliefs and behavioural set which the training aimed to inculcate. This instrument, subsequently called the recruit training questionnaire (RTQ), was administered to two groups of officers ($n = 30$) on the four testing occasions. In addition, data concerning complaints made about the police by members of the public were gathered, as were supervisors' comments.

Summary of findings (phase one)

Social-evaluative anxiety questionnaire

Police constables have to enter social situations which are often characterized by conflict between the participants or overt aggression. Constables may have to initiate interactions with members of the public in order to control or manipulate their behaviour, often against the other's will. To manage such social interaction constables need to be able to control the anxiety which such situations engender and be able to put up with the negative evaluations made of them by those with whom they must interact. For obvious reasons police constables must not avoid entering social situations, however unpleasant these situations may appear. The social-evaluative anxiety questionnaire can be used to generate two measures:

(i) the tendency to be distressed and to avoid social situations;
(ii) the tendency to be afraid of being negatively evaluated by others.

With respect to the task of the constable, social distress, avoidance and fear of negative evaluation are prima facie undesirable characteristics, and one of HAT's aims should be to minimize recruits' tendencies in these directions.

Officers' scores decreased progressively and significantly over the testing period (from 13.27 to 7.39). Not only did the above tendencies decline significantly during HAT but they continued to decline during probation. However, the changes during initial training were larger than after it. While it is not possible to identify precisely the cause of this effect from the evaluation design, the utility of the questionnaire is established in this context, and the effect in line with HAT objectives is powerful suggestive evidence.

Recruit training questionnaire

With regard to our own especially constructed recruit training questionnaire, this questionnaire was sensitive enough as a research instrument to generate some significantly different scores between the beginning and end of the study period. However, these changes were often in the *opposite* direction to that predicted from the training objectives. More recruits, for example, disagreed with the idea that social science concepts would be useful to them at the *end* of the course than at the beginning. Fewer trainees thought they would try to understand minority viewpoints by the end of training than at the beginning. Likewise, the importance attached to community relations decreased over training. The welfare/service aspect of police work remained important to trainees but declined in importance for probationers once they began operational duties.

One or two beliefs and attitudes changed in *appropriate* ways. Notably fairness and trustworthiness grew in importance as characteristics of "the good police officer". But overall, basic attitudes and beliefs remained much the same, and given that the effect of training is being pitted against a lifetime of family and school experience, this is scarcely surprising. On balance it must be said, however, that such changes as we observed were more in line with the expected peer group effect and institutional effect than they were in line with avowed intentions of the human awareness component of the course. The other two questionnaires used (i.e. self-esteem and interpersonal relations) revealed few significant differences over time.

Complaints

How supervisors respond to probationers and how the public respond to them are two crude but vital indicators of the success of initial training. Space prevents mention of our work on supervisors' assessment, but mention can be made of complaints data. With the assistance of the Complaints Investigation Bureau at Scotland Yard a comparison was made of complaints made against police officers trained under the new system with those trained a year earlier under the old system.

Data on police complaints often reveal a relationship between frequency of complaints and length of service. Consequently, the two samples needed to be matched in terms of length of service. It was found that the HAT-trained officers received 17% fewer complaints per officer, per month of service, compared to the officers trained under the older system. This difference was found not to be due to those officers having, on average, 12 months longer police service. When the complaints data were statistically analysed with regard to the number of complaints per officer, per month of service, the difference in these two sets of data would have occurred by chance in only eight out of 100 occasions. Thus, the 17% reduction in the rate of complaints was probably not a chance finding but seems likely to have been a result of the training, as this was the major factor consistently differentiating the two groups of subjects. While tying this reduction to HAT specifically is problematic, HAT, which emphasizes the *discretionary* role of the police officer, at least cannot be said to increase the probability of officers so trained incurring complaints.

Phase one conclusion

It was our recommendation that the Metropolitan Police's recruit training programme in human awareness was a worthwhile achievement of considerable substance and promise. However, we were concerned by whether the achievements of the initial training were to some extent dissipated by post-initial training experiences. Now that the force's initial recruit training in HAT appeared to be operating with considerable efficiency it seemed appropriate to determine the extent to which the effects of this training were manifested in constables' policing behaviour.

Partly in the light of the information presented so far, the Metropolitan Police agreed to fund a second phase of the evaluation. This second phase examined the extent to which officers were putting HAT skills into practice on the street. By this time the title of the training has been changed from Human Awareness Training to Policing Skills Training (PST).

Phase two of the evaluation

Three components for the phase two evaluation were agreed upon:

1. Psychometric evaluation

Four valid and reliable questionnaires were completed by officers at the end (week 20) of initial training and then again 20, 40 and 66 weeks later. These week 40, 60 and 86 testing dates coincided with the completion of the Street Duties Course (Part 1), the Street Duties Course (Part 2) and Continuation Training Classes (Part 2) under the then-current probationer training programme. The questionnaires used were as follows (with the first three having been used in phase one):

- a social-evaluative anxiety questionnaire;
- a self-esteem questionnaire;
- an interpersonal relations questionnaire;
- a self-monitoring questionnaire (measures amount of self-observation and self-control).

These four questionnaires were completed by three cohorts of 40 officers. Additionally, one other questionnaire was used which we specifically designed to assess the attitudes, beliefs and behavioural set which PST aimed to inculcate, especially those attitudes concerned with the use of discretion in police work. This instrument, subsequently called the district training questionnaire (DTQ), was administered to two groups of officers (61 in total) on the four testing occasions. (The DTQ was based, in part, on the recruit training questionnaire employed in phase one.)

As with the first phase of the evaluation, it was not possible to use police recruits as controls. As scores were obtained over time. subjects acted as their own control and, provided the training had a systematic effect, then scores over time should have exhibited some significant and coherent pattern of change.

2. Patrol observation study

In order to examine the utility of PST in the field a sample of 64 police officers with between 18 and 43 months service (i.e. those who received PST after most of the authors' phase one recommendations had been implemented) were accompanied on patrol on one or more days by one or two trained observers. This observational evaluation took place in each of eight police stations which together formed a representative sample of policing opportunities in London. Observations were made according to our specially designed schedule containing some 89 data scales. Observers recorded data on 550 police officer–citizen encounters. On some occasions two observers accompanied an officer on patrol. This was for two reasons. One was to gather data on the inter-judge reliability of the behavioural observations and the other was to conduct the third component of the evaluation: interviewing the participants of encounters.

3. Interviewing the participants of encounters

On fifty occasions observers conducted interviews with a constable and with an encountered member of the public (separately) once an encounter had finished. The questionnaires used for these interviews were concerned not only with the respondents' view of the behaviour objectively recorded (but not disclosed) by the observers, but also with matters which may be important in police–citizen encounters which were not easy to observe objectively (e.g. inner feelings).

Summary of findings (phase two)

1. Psychometric evaluation

Officers' scores indicative of distress, avoidance and fear of negative evaluation by others in social situations decreased progressively and significantly during the period over which we tested them (from 14.81 to 9.74). (A similar result was reported in phase one.) These findings are in line with the aims of PST. However, at the end of the initial twenty-week training, phase two officers' scores on these dimensions were higher (and hence less in line with the aims of PST) than phase one officers' scores had been at the same point in their training (14.81 vs. 10.33). Such a finding might indicate a deterioration in training standards.

As we found in phase one, the other extant psychometric questionnaire revealed very few significant changes.

On the district training questionnaire, like the phase one officers, the phase two officers had some favourable attitudes towards the training at the end of initial training. (Their views were, if anything, more positive than phase one officers' had been.) However, they tended to become rather more undecided about the usefulness of their training as they gained operational experience. This was particularly true for the race awareness aspects of training. For example, as their probationary period progressed, officers placed less emphasis on the importance of trying to understand the customs, viewpoints and traditions of minority groups.

2. Patrol observation study

The six-month observation period allowed the researchers to gather quantitative and qualitative data on 550 encounters between PST officers and members of the public. The effects of observers on officers' behaviour was judged to be minimal, and there was a high degree of reliability between the observers' perceptions of encounters. The incidents observed involved a large number of occasions where police officers had the potential to use their discretion in dealing with the public.

In a majority of encounters the police officers observed showed themselves to be competent managers of people. Many of the specific "people handling" skills which instructors attempt to impart to recruits during their initial training were effectively translated into desirable, professional behaviour on the streets (e.g. conducting stops on the street, opening encounters, handling disputes between people, control of self and others' aggression). However, there were several areas of police performance which were less effective and which did not fully meet the stated intentions of initial training (e.g. the interviewing of a number of victims of crime was less effective than it could have been, as was the use of a multi-agency approach to the treatment of victims). Other areas of performance were more variable: these included self-monitoring ability, closing encounters and interviewing skills.

3. Interviewing the participants of encounters

The fifty interviews with police officers and members of the public after an encounter involved a wide variety of different encounters (some 44% involved traffic-related matters in which the member of the public had committed an offence).

The public's evaluation of officers' performance was usually favourable. This trend was evident regardless (in most cases) of the status of the individual concerned (i.e. whether they were an offender, witness, informant, etc.). Officers who were interviewed tended to underestimate the views held by the member of the public concerning the quality of the various policing skills they had demonstrated. They also tended to evaluate members of the public less favourably on certain dimensions (e.g. compliance, satisfaction, disposition to the police service) than those members of the public viewed themselves. Such findings have important implications for the aspects of initial Policing Skills Training which deal with issues such as stereotyping and self-evaluation.

Recommendations (phase two)

Our phase two evaluation provided little evidence to suggest that the concepts and skills which Policing Skills Training sought to impart to recruits were significantly undermined by those recruits' subsequent operational experience. While the training had many strengths, there none the less remained areas in which it could be improved. Our evidence suggested that further thought should be given to the following:

(i) At the end of initial training, recruits' ability to monitor their own behaviour and their sensitivity to the expression and self-presentation of others was not as good as it might be. This ability did not improve with subsequent operational experience. While patrolling officers were observed to be competent managers of the people they encountered, they sometimes found difficulty in closing encounters. The self-evaluation and self-awareness components of PST should be enhanced and assessment of them examined.

(ii) As their probation proceeds, probationers became less positive about the Policing Skills Training they received. In the police force as a whole misunderstandings about the nature and objectives of PST were fairly common. The force should consider ways in which it can continue to reinforce the values which recruit training seeks to impart. The programme of force-wide Policing Skills Training (which sought to inform all officers recruited before the introduction of PST about what PST is) needed to be given full support by all ranks.

(iii) One of the goals of PST is that officers understand and are sympathetic towards victims. Officers did not always appear to show sympathy for victims, nor were they always aware of local arrangements for referring victims to other agencies. In some cases local policy on dealing with victims was at variance with what officers had been taught was desirable: in other words officers lacked the opportunity to put into practice what they had learned. The force needed to re-examine its policy towards victim support so that local policy and what is taught as desirable practice are brought more into line with one another.

Conclusion

Our recommendations were based on the belief that it is important that trainees find the objectives of their training to be compatible with those of the force as a whole. We felt that such compatibility did not exist in all parts of the force. We concluded that Policing Skills Training marked an important turning point in police training. We judged it to be a most worthwhile development which merits the considerable funding and other support it still receives from the force. Since receiving our final report the London Metropolitan Police has acted on all its recommendations.

2 Recall after briefing: television versus face-to-face presentation

Ray Bull and R. L. Reid

Introduction

The investigation was concerned with the effectiveness of television as a means of presenting daily informative briefings to police constables. Before television was introduced, briefings were normally carried out by a duty sergeant reading aloud to a group of constables items of information selected from those which had recently arrived at his station. With television in operation, items were selected by the studio staff and presented in the form of a recorded programme relayed to the stations.

The style of programme adopted by the police was similar to that of a public television news bulletin, save that it was rarely possible for them to present action pictures. Each programme contained three or four items concerning wanted persons, two concerning vehicles and one or two other items. A typical script might, for example, include details of an indecent assault, a burglary, a series of thefts, a missing child, a stolen vehicle and a 'hit and run' vehicle. For the television briefings a police officer acted as presenter, occupying the screen for a substantial part of the programme. Captions were frequently shown together with photographs of persons or vehicles, and descriptions were often displayed and simultaneously read out by the presenter.

At an early stage in the research it was found that in an operational setting television briefings led to significantly greater immediate recall than face-to-face briefings. However, a survey of the contents of briefings disclosed that the introduction of television had led to a substantial change in the amount of information contained in briefings and in the frequency with which various types of items were appearing. A typical face-to-face briefing would contain eight items, whereas a television briefing would contain only six or seven but these would be longer. The net result was that television briefings contained much more information (up to 50 per cent more) than did the traditional face-to-face briefings, although the time taken up by each type of briefing was the same (about 8 min.).

A controlled comparison of recall was undertaken in a training context presenting exactly the same information by the two briefing methods. In the earlier operational tests free recall was measured immediately after briefing and after intervals of 24 and 48 hr. Results indicated that the immediate test would provide the best return for police time taken up by the experiment. Because it had been suggested that cued recall rather than free recall might be more closely related to effectiveness 'on the beat', a cued recall test was added, although it proved to be impossible to simulate the kind of cueing that seemed most likely to occur in the life situation.

The primary aim was to compare the two methods of presentation. At the same time it was possible to examine the effect on recall of varying the number of items presented in each programme. This was of particular interest because there was some feeling among the police that an optimal size of briefing had been reached. The experiment was planned also to obtain some information about two other variables. The subjects who were available for testing comprised a group of probationary constables, half of them in their first and half in their second year of duty. Before the investigation several senior officers had suggested that assimilating the kind of information given in a briefing is a skill acquired by years of practice. Here was an opportunity to find out by keeping the two groups separate and comparing results.

Finally, it had been decided that some variation of the order within scripts should be made to ensure that the comparisons of script length would not be affected by any adventitious effect of a particular order within a particular script, e.g. through having the most memorable items at the end or beginning. Accepting that random variation could not be used because each script could be presented to four groups only, and also because there would have been problems of editing the videotapes, it seemed that the best variation would be to shuffle the items so as to try to eliminate any serial position effect (Kintsch, 1970). For administrative reasons the different orders of items within the same script had to be presented to groups of probationers with different lengths of experience, but it was thought unlikely that there would be any interaction between the two variables. Thus a situation arose in which it was possible to check, although under less than ideal conditions, whether a serial position effect would occur. Many studies with nonsense syllables or words have found that items are better recalled when placed at the beginning or end of a list rather than near the middle, and that items placed in the first half are better recalled than those in the second half, but there is no clear evidence that these effects occur in the recall of larger units of meaningful information.

Method

Subjects

Two groups of probationary constables acted as subjects, each group being available for 1 hr. on each of three alternate Thursdays. One group (A) comprised officers in the first year as police constables, the other (B) officers in their second year.

Procedure

Upon each attendance the subjects were divided into two equal subgroups, one to be briefed by television and the other by a training sergeant using the same script.

Table 2.1 Sequence and content of trials

Week	*Group*	*No. in group*	*Medium*	*Script*	*Item order*
1	B1	16	Tele }	6	123456
	B2	16	F-to-f		
2	A1	9	Tele }	6	456123
	A2	9	F-to-f		
3	A2	12	Tele }	8	12345678
	A1	11	F-to-f		
4	B2	13	Tele }	8	67845123
	B1	13	F-to-f		
5	A1	12	Tele }	7	1234567
	A2	13	F-to-f		
6	B1	14	Tele }	7	5674123
	B2	13	F-to-f		

Thus on each occasion it was possible to compare the effect of the face-to-face and the television methods.

In alternate weeks groups received the same items presented in different orders (see Table 2.1). Three different scripts were used. The first script (6) contained six items and a total of 99 units of information, the second (8) contained eight items and 162 units of information and the third (7) seven items and 138 units of information. For each script the items were similar in type but, as will be apparent from the figures given above, the items in the smallest script turned out to be somewhat smaller than the items contained in the other two scripts.

Both item orders were presented by the same person, either a training sergeant for face-to-face, or a member of the studio staff for television presentation. In the case of television the presenters were used to appearing on the recorded versions of briefings. For the face-to-face briefings the presenters were three training sergeants who received previews of the scripts, and who, through their role as teachers, were experienced at presenting information of this kind. Thus, although different presenters were used, all were fully experienced.

Immediately after the officers had been briefed they were handed a questionnaire, the first section asking them to write down everything they could remember of the items of information given at the briefings and telling them not to turn to the second section until they had recalled all that they could. The second section supplied a few key words from each of the briefing items to act as cues and asked subjects to write down any extra information about the item which they had not already written down in the first section. Thus scores were available for free recall and for the extra recall occasioned by the added cues.

There is no universally accepted way of assessing the recall of information presented in the form of ordinary sentences. In the present study recall was scored using a method which was found to work well during the programme of research.

One point was awarded for every correctly recalled unit of information within an item, analysing items as indicated below:

1 2 3
Arthur Smith/escaped from Dartmoor/6' 4" tall/

4 5 6
black hair/blue eyes/walks with a limp/. (Total: six units)

1 2 3 4 5
Stolen car/blue/Ford Anglia/ABC/123D. (Total: five units)

Results

Results were analysed in terms of the number of units of information correctly recalled, taking no account of incorrect recall since this occurred only very infrequently.

Television versus face-to-face presentation

Table 2.2 compares recall after the two methods of presentation. There was no overall difference (Mann–Whitney *U* test; Siegel, 1956) between the methods with regard to either free recall (37 units versus 36) or recall with cues (6 versus 5).

Number of items per briefing

Table 2.2 provides some experimental support for the practice of restricting briefings to six or seven items. For both methods of presentation the absolute

Table 2.2 Units of information recalled after television and after face-to-face briefings

	Free recall		*Cued recall*	
	Television	*Face-to-face*	*Television*	*Face-to-face*
Script 6 (6 items, 99 units)				
Order 1, Group B	42.8	44.4	7.1	3.1
Order 2, Group A	34.7	34.9	3.9	6.7
Mean	39.1		5.2	
Script 7 (7 items, 138 units)				
Order 1,Group A	39.8	37.7	6.2	5.6
Order 2, Group B	42.6	40.9	5.6	3.5
Mean	40.3		5.2	
Script 8 (8 items, 162 units)				
Order 1, Group A	30.5	24.6	8.8	5.7
Order 2, Group B	34.1	32.8	5.1	6.6
Mean	30.5		6.6	

amount of recall from briefings containing eight items was significantly less than from those containing six or seven (Mann–Whitney *U* test). The finding of less recall after the longest script would be difficult to explain in terms of the order in which the three scripts occurred, because this script happened to be the middle one and the subjects did not know that the third script was to be the last.

Experience of subjects

As shown in Table 2.2 the probationers in their second year of duty (group B) recalled significantly more information (Mann–Whitney *U* test) than did those in their first year (group A). The 'experience' variable is confounded with order of presentation, but orders were arbitrarily assigned and in any case would not be expected to affect overall performance.

Item order

As shown in Table 2.1, the tests for an item–order effect were made by comparing group A with group B. Since these groups differed in amount of free recall the data analysed in this section were converted to percentages of an individual's total free recall arising from each item remembered. Preliminary analysis gave no evidence of any systematic difference between the two briefing methods with regard to the relative recall of an item in each of its two positions within a list, and so the data for the two briefing methods were pooled. Considering, within each list, the six items which were presented in each of two different positions, a prediction can be made (first half better than second half and ends better than middle) concerning the position which will be more favourable to recall. The results confirmed 13 out of 18 possible predictions (binomial test, $P = 0.048$), indicating the occurrence of a serial position effect in the recall of large units of meaningful information.

Discussion

The failure to find a difference between television and face-to-face presentation, when the same information was presented by each method, suggests that the virtue of the television system as disclosed by operational testing lay in the preparation of television scripts. Face-to-face briefings based on these scripts contained better organized, more memorable material than their operational counterparts. This raises the question whether some of the advantages of television might be obtained more cheaply by centralized preparation of good scripts for traditional briefing, but if this system were to be adopted problems of control might arise and the puppet-like role of the presenter of a prepared script might prove to be unacceptable in the long term.

The police seem to have been right to suspect that adding to the load of information to be remembered could result in less being recalled. The overload effect may well be important in other practical learning tasks, but recognition of the possibility of overloading has tended to remain within the realms of common sense rather than psychological theory.

There may be some practical implications of the suggestion that serial position has an effect upon recall of large meaningful units of information as well as nonsense syllables: if better recall is required of one item than of others it should be put first in a list, but if all items are equally important those which are more difficult should not be placed in the middle.

Acknowledgement

This research was supported by a grant from the Police Scientific Development Branch of the Home Office to Professor Reid. The authors would like to acknowledge the cooperation which they received from the police.

References

Kintsch, W. (1970). *Learning, memory and conceptual processes*. New York, NY: Wiley.
Siegel, S. (1956). *Nonparametric statistics*. New York, NY: McGraw-Hill.

3 Isolating the effects of the cognitive interview techniques

Amina Memon, Linsey Wark, Ray Bull and Guenter Koehnken

Introduction

The ability to obtain full and accurate information is critical in an investigation, yet according to the eyewitness literature, accurate and complete recall is difficult to achieve (e.g. Goodman, Aman, & Hirschman, 1987). The cognitive interview (CI) was developed by Fisher and Geiselman in response to the many requests received from police officers for a method of improving recall in witnesses. It draws upon experimental research on memory and is presented as a package of techniques that can be used to facilitate memory search and retrieval (Fisher & Geiselman, 1992). The present study attempts to identify the most effective components of the CI and compare it with current practices for interviewing children (see Bull, 1995a, 1995b). The extent to which variables such as interviewer training, motivation and effective communication/rapport with the witness may contribute to gains in information are also explored. The research therefore addresses both theoretical and practical questions.

The CI procedure

The CI procedure essentially comprises four techniques and some strategies for improving communication in an interview (Fisher & Geiselman, 1992). One of the principal CI techniques is the mental reinstatement of the physical and personal contexts that existed at the time (see Memon & Bruce, 1985, for a review). Context reinstatement involves (a) emotional elements ('How were you feeling at the time?'), which may work via state-dependent effects (Eich, 1980), (b) perceptual features ('Put yourself back at the scene of the crime and picture the room; how did it smell, what could you hear?'), and (c) sequencing elements ('What were you doing at the time?'). The rationale for context reinstatement comes from the encoding specificity principle (e.g. Tulving & Thomson, 1973). The other CI strategies include instructions to search for details extensively (which can lead to the recall of additional relevant information; Geiselman & Fisher, 1988), to recount events in a variety of orders (Loftus & Fathi, 1985) and from a variety of perspectives (e.g. the perspective of the victim, suspect, another witness). These techniques are based on the assumption that memory trace inaccessibility is a result of a limited search.

The four techniques described above formed the basis of the original version of the CI. Further refinements of the CI (Fisher & Geiselman, 1992) include 'cognitive techniques' for activating and probing a witness' mental image of the various parts of an event, such as a suspect's face, clothing, objects etc. A distinction is drawn between conceptual image codes (an image stored as a concept or dictionary definition) and pictorial codes (the mental representation of an image; Paivio, 1971). In addition to the 'cognitive' components, the CI in its current form places considerable emphasis on social communication techniques, similar to those recommended to interviewers not employing the CI 'cognitive techniques' (Bull, 1992; Memorandum of good practice, 1992). These techniques include 'transfer of control' of the interview from the interviewer to the witness. The latter is put into place during the rapport building phase in several ways. For instance it allows witnesses to dictate the pace of the interview and structure their own recall. This is achieved through use of open questions, by not interrupting witnesses, by timing questions carefully so that they are related to witnesses' retrieval patterns and not to a protocol that an interviewer may be using. For example, if a witness is describing a suspect's face, an appropriate question would be to ask about eye colour rather than to ask about the suspect's shoes. These social communication strategies are said by Fisher & Geiselman (1992) to facilitate the effective implementation of the cognitive CI techniques described earlier. For example, by not interrupting witnesses while they are attempting to recreate context, and by pausing between questions, the interviewer allows the witness time to form an image and to engage in a more exhaustive search, and this may induce more elaborate responses.

In early tests of the CI, the interviewers (students or police officers) received some instruction in use of the 'cognitive' components of the CI and collected memory reports of simulated events that students had witnessed two days earlier. In the first study, instructions were given to interviewees in a written form so interviewer–witness interaction was minimal. With relatively brief training, interviewers obtained up to 35 per cent more correct information without an increase in errors, as compared to a no-training control group (e.g. Geiselman, Fisher, MacKinnon, & Holland, 1985, 1986). When the revised version of the CI was tested it was found to generate even more information than the original CI (Fisher, Geiselman, Raymond, Jurkevich, & Warhaftig, 1987). These results were taken as strong evidence of the effectiveness of the CI. However, upon closer examination of the studies it was apparent that there was one major drawback, namely, the lack of a suitable control group.

Control group

From a practical perspective, it is important to show that the CI is more effective than the techniques currently recommended for use by police officers and others who conduct investigative interviews. However, an effective control group is needed to demonstrate that the CI cognitive techniques themselves are causing the positive effects and not other factors such as social communication, quality of questioning, rapport building skills or interviewer (or interviewee) motivation.

The use of the term 'Standard' in earlier studies itself implies inferiority. In the present research we sought to construct a control interview (the structured interview: Koehnken, Thürer, & Zorberbier, 1994) in which the quality of training in communication and questioning techniques was comparable to the CI and which followed that recommended to professionals who interview children (e.g. Memorandum of good practice, 1992). The essence of the Memorandum's guidelines on interview structure is to treat the interview as a procedure in which a variety of interviewing techniques are deployed in relatively discrete phases proceeding from free recall to open and then specific, closed-form questions. Rapport building, active listening and not interrupting (transfer of control) are also emphasized as important components. The CI techniques fit nicely into this basic framework.

The CI and children

Given current concerns about the vulnerability of children in criminal proceedings (e.g. Goodman & Bottoms, 1993) and the skills of those who interview child witnesses (Bull, 1992; Clyde, 1992), it is timely to focus on the utility of the CI with this group. In earlier tests, six–seven-year-old children did not show any advantage when interviewed with a CI as compared with a structured interview (Memon, Cronin, Eaves, & Bull, 1993; Memon, Cronin, Eaves, & Bull, 1996). A subsequent study suggested that young children had difficulty using some of the CI strategies (e.g. the 'reverse order' recall instruction). This could be due to developmental limitations (Flavell & Wellman, 1977) or task demands (Cronin, Memon, Eaves, Küpper & Bull, 1992). More recently, the CI procedure has been further modified for use with child witnesses. Saywitz, Geiselman & Bornstein (1992) evaluated the CI using seven–eight-year-olds and 10–11-year-olds as witnesses to a live event. A 'practice session' was included (Expt 2) to familiarize the children with the interview techniques. The interviewers were college students (practice interview) or experienced police officers (interview about main event) who received written instructions and a two-hour training session which included information about child-appropriate language, rapport building, interview preparation and procedure, and information on the use of the four original cognitive components of the CI. In the control (standard) condition police officers were instructed to use the techniques they would normally use. The CI led to the recall of more correct details as compared with the standard interview without increasing errors. The CI benefited the older children more than the younger children.

The CI has been investigated in Germany in several studies designed to examine separately any effects of the CI on (a) the incidence of errors and (b) confabulation (Koehnken, Finger, Nitschke, Höfer, & Aschermann, 1992; Koehnken, Schimmossek, Aschermann, & Höfer, 1995; Koehnken *et al.*, 1994; Mantwill, Koehnken, & Aschermann, 1995). With adults, there was an increase in correct details and errors with the CI in two studies (Koehnken *et al.*, 1995; Mantwill *et al.*, 1995). With children (aged 9–10 years), it was found the CI did substantially increase the amount of correct information recalled. However, confabulations (the report of details not present in the event) also increased significantly (Koehnken *et al.*, 1992). Several more recent studies where the children have ranged in age from seven–nine years have also reported increases not only in correct information but also in errors with the CI (McCauley & Fisher, 1995; Milne, Bull, Koehnken, & Memon, 1995). From a theoretical and practical perspective it is clearly important to identify why the errors occur and whether they can be minimized.

Repeated testing with the CI

So far, research has primarily examined the effects of CI under optimal encoding conditions (a single interview after a relatively brief delay). In the real world a witness may be interviewed many days after the event. Studies of children's delayed recall show that inaccuracies increase over time (Flin, Boon, Knox, & Bull, 1992; Poole & White, 1993). Also, a witness may be interviewed more than once. While there has been concern addressed about the possible effects of repeated poor interviews with children (Clyde, 1992), laboratory studies of memory and memory development have documented two main positive effects of repeated testing using a variety of stimulus materials. The first is 'reminiscence', or the recall of material that did not appear in an earlier test. When this new information exceeds the amount of information that is forgotten, the 'hypermnesia' effect has occurred (Payne, 1987). Both these phenomena have been demonstrated in eyewitness contexts using videotaped (Scrivner & Safer, 1988) and staged criminal scenarios (Turtle & Yuille, 1994). We know that memory improves for a short period of time after exposure (Brainerd, Reyna, Howe, & Kingma, 1990). Another advantage of repeated testing shortly after an event is that it inoculates against forgetting (Brainerd & Ornstein, 1991; Warren & Lane, 1995).

It is predicted that an initial CI interview will produce hypermnesia effects at second interview on the basis that its techniques such as context reinstatement increase overlap between encoding and retrieval conditions and enrich connections between episodic traces and semantic features (Brainerd *et al.*, 1990). These factors will improve children's performance on a second test relative to those who had no first test or an inferior first test. An alternative explanation of increased reporting with CI following repeated testing would be that the CI merely shifts a witness' criterion for how much to report. (Note that one of the CI instructions to witnesses is to report everything, even that which they are unsure of.) Multiple retrieval attempts with the CI may act as conversational training (Hudson, 1990). Poole & White (1995) made the useful point that a forensic interview is both a memory test and a conversation, and so it is difficult to predict which of these two aspects will most influence recall.

The conclusions of previous CI studies are contradictory. Some have found an increase in correct information, some find an increase in errors and others get no effects (see Koehnken, Milne, Memon, & Bull, 1994, for a review). Moreover, it may be possible for an interviewer armed with a range of 'good' interviewing techniques and effective communication skills to achieve the same results as a CI interviewer. The present study aimed to determine, through careful matching of experimental and control group, whether any CI effects reflect improved retrieval searches or whether they are a result of improved interviewer–witness communication. The primary aim of the present study is to test this hypothesis and to assess the nature of inaccuracies that may occur when the CI technique is used with children. In order to directly compare the results of this study with previous research, children aged eight–nine years are used. Previous research has shown this age group show a smaller advantage of testing with CI as compared to older children (Saywitz *et al.*, 1992) and make more errors in their reports (Koehnken *et al.*, 1992; McCauley & Fisher, 1995; Milne *et al.*, 1995).

Method

Participants

One hundred and nine children aged between eight and nine years of age participated in the study. There were 53 males and 56 females.[1] There were 29 cognitive interviews and 32 structured interviews performed at time 1. The number of children in each of the four repeat testing groups was as follows: CI/CI = 10; CI/SI = 16; SI/CI = 15; and SI/SI = 13. In addition, the following numbers of children were interviewed at time 2 only: NCI (none, CI) = 16 and NSI (none, SI) = 17.

The event

Children took part in a magic show, an event chosen because of its interest to children. A local magician was contacted and agreed to take part in the study. The magic show lasted for approximately nine minutes and there were 12 performances to small groups of children. The magic show was videorecorded.

The magic show was performed to groups of between 8 and 12 children (mean = 9) over a period of two mornings in a room (not their classroom) which the children, although familiar with, did not use often. After a delay of between one or two days (equally distributed across the conditions) some of the children were interviewed in school using a cognitive or structured interview. The remainder were not interviewed at that time. After a further delay of between 10 and 13 days (equally distributed between the conditions) all of the children were interviewed (some now for a second time) by either a cognitive or structured interviewer. The children interviewed twice had different interviewers at each time.

Design

A 3 (cognitive, structured or no first interview) by 2 (cognitive and structured) design was used to examine the effects of interview technique and repeated testing.

Interviewer training

Four interviewers were trained solely in the cognitive interview and four in the structured interview. The cognitive interviewers were two male and two female students. The structured interviewers were three female and one male student. The cognitive interviewers and structured interviewers were trained separately by a highly qualified researcher (GK) with many years of interview training experience. The structure and content of the training for each group will be described fully as this is something earlier researchers have failed to do. Similarities and differences between the SI and CI should be noted.

Each group of interviewers was trained in two four-hour sessions that began with an introductory lecture on the importance of the interview in psychological assessment and information gathering in various situations. Both groups were given some guidelines about non-verbal behaviour in the interview (e.g. seating position, eye contact, pauses and speech rate). For each step in the training there was a demonstration role play excerpt (a CI/SI child witness interview conducted by a trained interviewer) which was followed by several live practice role plays (interviewers were asked to choose an event, playing the part of a child and interviewer) and these were video recorded. Individual feedback was given. There were plenary discussion and question sessions at the end. In addition to active role plays, the interviewers were encouraged to rehearse mentally the various stages of the interview. For each group the interview was divided into the following phases.

Rapport. Boggs & Eyberg (1990) pointed out that the essential first phase of the interview is to establish rapport between child and interviewer. She is asked to describe a familiar event, for example, a favourite game. Follow-up comments such as 'that sounds fun, tell me how you play it?' increase rapport and prime the child to give elaborate responses. Both the CI and SI group practised rapport building in this way (see Saywitz *et al.*, 1992). An important part of the rapport building was the transfer of control from interviewer to interviewee (which included active listening, not interrupting and effective use of pauses). As part of this transfer of control the interviewer makes it clear that he or she does not have the information about the event but rather it is the child who holds the information. This procedure typically forms part of the CI but it has also been advocated in other interviewing guidelines (e.g. the Memorandum of good practice, 1992) and therefore this component formed part of the training for the SI as well as the CI group.

Free recall phase. The SI interviewers were asked to request a free narrative account from the witness and this was used as a strategy for obtaining information in the subsequent questioning phase. The CI group received identical instructions for the free recall phase, but in addition they were given training in encouraging witnesses to reinstate the context mentally (as described in the introduction) before they began. The CI interviewers also employed the 'report everything' instruction at this stage.

Prompt phase. At the end of the free recall phase, CI and SI interviewers paused briefly and used one prompt, 'Please tell me more', before commencing the questioning phase.

Questioning phase. In the next phase both the CI and SI interviewers were asked to use the information reported by the witness in their free recall phase as a guide for follow-up questions. Both the CI and SI interviewers were instructed in the use of appropriate types of questions. They were asked to begin with open questions and then follow these with closed questions. In general interviewers were asked to use the free recall to find out who was present at the event and what they did. Where a person was mentioned, interviewers were asked to elicit details about clothing. They were specifically instructed to avoid leading, misleading and forced-choice questions. The CI interviewers received additional training in the activation and probing of images relating to various parts of the event. (For example, the children were told to 'picture the magician's face, and then describe it'.)

Second retrieval phase. The purpose of this phase was to examine the effects of additional instructions on the recall of new information. The second retrieval phase of the interview was different for the two groups. The CI interviewers employed the CI 'reverse order' recall instruction at this point. This took the following form: 'Tell me about the very last thing you remember in the magic show and then what happened before that, and before that, so you're working your way back to the first thing you remember.' It was placed towards the end of the interview so that any extra information it elicited could be identified. The SI group also attempted to elicit additional information at this stage by asking children to go through the event again, recalling additional details if possible.

Both groups received a summary of the theoretical background material relevant to their training and a detailed handout containing all the training material to study. Each group was led to believe they were the 'experimental group'.

Coding and scoring of the interview transcripts

Using the videos of the 12 magic shows, two research assistants identified the details that could be recalled. This produced some 650 details. The information contained in the verbatim transcript of each interview was checked with the corresponding video and classified as correct, as an error (that is, wrongly describing something that was present or did happen) or as a confabulation (e.g. saying a 'pig' was present when it was not).

Information was classified into four detail types describing persons, actions, objects or surroundings. Although any classification of detail type is dependent on the sort of event used, there were several concerns that we wanted to address. Firstly, we wanted to test the hypothesis that the CI, by encouraging reinstatement of context, merely increases the reporting of details about surroundings (Memon *et al.*, 1996). The present coding classification therefore includes a separate count of such details. Secondly, we wanted to examine whether the CI might increase the reporting of all types of erroneous information, or whether errors (if they occurred) may reflect the difficulty children have in giving descriptions about persons as compared to actions (Davies, Tarrant, & Flin, 1989).

The stage at which information was reported in the interview was noted with a distinction being made between free recall (FR), prompt (PR), questioning (QU), and second retrieval (SR) phases. After the information contained in the child's free report was scored for accuracy, recall appearing in the other subsequent sections of the interview (QU, PR and SR phases) was only scored if it was new. This is illustrated in Appendix 1.

Two research assistants coded and scored the interview transcripts and any uncertainties were resolved by discussion. In addition to this, 10 transcripts were coded by both of the research assistants and inter-coder reliabilities were calculated: inter-coder agreement for total accurate was 96 per cent ($r = .93$, $p < .0001$) and for total errors 89 per cent ($r = .86$, $p < .001$).

Results

Two types of measures are reported throughout. Firstly, the absolute number of errors and confabulations are reported. Secondly, instead of simply reporting the absolute number of correct details, these are expressed as a proportion of that available to be recalled because each of the 12 magic shows contained slightly different information (i.e. descriptions of the children who helped, what they were wearing etc.). This will be referred to as 'percentage correct' in the results described below.

As is now the convention in research on the CI, the number of correct, incorrect, and confabulated details are also each expressed as a proportion of the total number recalled. The proportion is calculated by dividing the number of each type of detail (i.e. correct, or incorrect and confabulations) by the total number of details reported (i.e. correct plus incorrect plus confabulations). This measure is usually referred to as accuracy (and sometimes as reliability).

First interviews

Amount recalled at time 1. A series of one-way ANOVAs was performed to test the prediction that the CI would increase the amount of correct and of incorrect information (errors and confabulations).[2] For percentage correct recall there was a significant effect ($F(1, 59) = 6.17$, $p < .05$) with the CI producing more correct recall. Similarly, the absolute numbers of errors was significantly higher in the CI condition ($F(1, 59) = 4.17$, $p < .05$). There was no significant effect of type of interview on confabulated details ($F < 1$). The increase in percentage correct information with the CI was a difference of 20 units of information. This was accompanied by an increase of 3.31 units of erroneous details. So with a control group matched in every respect to the CI save the 'cognitive' components of CI, there is a positive effect on the percentage of correct recall. There is also an increase in the absolute number of errors (although not in the proportion of recall that was inaccurate) and this is considered at length in the discussion.

Accuracy at time 1. It was found that, on average, 88 per cent of the children's recall was correct with 8 per cent errors and 4 per cent confabulated details. This is consistent with earlier research (Saywitz *et al.*, 1992). A one-way ANOVA (interview type) was performed on the accuracy of recall (amount correct expressed as a function of total amount reported). From this no significant differences in accuracy emerged across interview type ($F < 1$).

Recall at each phase of the interview at time 1. The 'percentage correct', total number of correct details and absolute amount of inaccurate information reported

Table 3.1 Percentage correct recall, total correct and errors by interview phase (time 1)

	Cognitive interview			*Structured interview*		
	% correct	*Total correct*	*Errors*	*% correct*	*Total correct*	*Errors*
Free recall						
M	7.5	48.1	2.1	7.3	46.4	2.2
SD	4.4	28.2	2.3	3.8	24.0	2.0
Prompt						
M	0.7	4.5	0.1	0.2	1.2	0.0
SD	1.8	11.38	0.6	0.6	3.5	0.2
Questioning						
M	6.6**	42.7	6.8**	4.0	25.7	4.0
SD	2.8	18.0	4.7	2.3	14.8	3.2
Second retrieval						
M	1.0	6.5	0.9	1.3	8.1	0.9
SD	1.3	8.4	1.5	1.3	8.5	1.3
Total						
M	15.8*	101.9	10.0*	12.7	81.5	7.1
SD	4.9	31.9	6.6	4.9	31.4	4.6

* $p < .05$; ** $p < 01$.

Note: The 'percentage correct' measure shows the percentage of *possible* accurate recall for event.

at each phase of the interview can be seen in Table 3.1. Most of the accurate information the children recalled was in the FR and QU phases of the interview, as would be expected given information was only scored later if it was new.

Previous research with child witnesses has not established where in the interview the effects of CI appear. In the present study the CI instructions were given prior to both the FR and QU phases. As indicated earlier, information from the FR phase was used to probe for further detail in the QU phase. On this basis it would be expected that the CI would show an increase in new information at each of these phases. A series of one-way ANOVAs were performed to look at the 'percentage correct' information, errors and confabulations at each phase of the interview.[3]

The only phase to yield significant effects of interview type was the question phase. The percentage correct information was significantly higher in the CI as compared to the SI group ($F(1,59) = 16.22, p < .001$). This was accompanied by a significant increase in errors ($F(1, 59) = 8.43, p < .01$). There was no effect of interview type on confabulations in the QU phase ($F(1,59 = 1.32, p > .05$; means = 3.62 for the CI and 2.59 for the SI).

One question that was of particular interest in this study was the effects of multiple retrieval attempts within a single interview session on recall. We were interested in whether the reverse order recall (CI) instruction could generate any more information than a simple request to try again. There was no beneficial effect of using the CI reverse order recall instruction over a simple instruction to go through the event one more time. In other words, there were no significant CI–SI differences in the SR phase ($F < 1$). Averaging across these two conditions, there were approximately six additional units of information generated within the additional retrieval attempt.

Recall by type of detail at time 1. So far the analyses show that the significant CI–SI difference in percentage correct and errors only occurred in the questioning phase. It was important to examine the question phase in more depth to ascertain the types of details (person, action, object and surrounding) being recalled. The next series of analyses breaks down the 'percentage correct' recall and errors at the QU phase into types of information recalled (see Table 3.2) and a series of one-way ANOVAs was conducted to compare performance across CI and SI for each dependent variable (confabulations are not reported in this section as there were no significant main effects).

The person category was of most interest in the present study as it is known that both adults (MacLeod, Frowley, & Shepherd, 1994) and children (see Davies *et al.*, 1989) have difficulty in describing people accurately (Clifford & Bull, 1978). An ANOVA revealed a significant effect of interview type on person errors in the QU phase ($F(1, 59) = 6.38, p = .01$) with the CI having significantly more person errors in this phase. Contrary to prediction, there were no effects of interview type for person correct ($F(1, 59) = 2.65, p > .05$).

Taking action details next, the CI was found to increase percentage correct information ($F(1,59) = 11.77, p < .001$) but not action errors ($F(1,59) = 1.89$).

Finally, for objects there was an effect of interview type on percentage correct in the QU phase ($F(1,59) = 5.40, p < .01$) with more correct information in the CI. There was no significant effect for object errors ($F(1,59) = 3.37, p = .07$) or details about surroundings ($F < 1$) across conditions.

Table 3.2 Percentage correct information, total correct and errors in the QU phase by detail type (time 1)

	Cognitive interview			*Structured interview*		
	% correct	*Total correct*	*Errors*	*% correct*	*Total correct*	*Errors*
Person						
M	7.5	8.7	3.4*	5.7	6.6	1.9
SD	4.7	5.5	3.0	3.7	4.4	1.5
Action						
M	6.2**	22.7	1.7	3.1	11.5	1.1
SD	4.0	14.9	1.8	2.8	10.2	1.9
Object						
M	8.6**	10.8	1.8	5.3	6.7	1.0
SD	4.3	5.4	1.9	3.8	4.8	1.4
Surrounding						
M	1.6	0.55	0.0	2.8	1.0	0.0
SD	2.8	0.95	0.0	4.5	1.5	0.0

* $p < .05$; ** $p < .01$.

Note: The 'percentage correct' measure shows the percentage of *possible* accurate recall for event.

Number of interviews and event knowledge. The eight interviewers (four cognitive and four structured) conducted between 5 and 10 interviews at time 1 and 9 and 12 interviews each at time 2. As the interviewers were unfamiliar with the event when they started interviewing at time 1, it was important to check that they were not eliciting more information at the end of their series of interviews than at the beginning, due to their increased knowledge of the event. For each interviewer, interview position (first interview, second interview etc.) was correlated with amount of accurate information obtained. There were no significant correlations (interviewer A, Fisher's $r(5) = -.09$; interviewer B, $r(8) = -.16$; interviewer C, $r(6) = .24$; interviewer D, $r(9) = .16$; interviewer E, $r(10) = .10$; interviewer F, $r(8) = .34$; interviewer G, $r(6) = .24$; interviewer H, $r(7) = -.09$).

To summarize the results of the first interview, those children having a CI interview at time 1 recalled more correct information than did those having an SI. They also made more errors. However, accuracy rates did not differ. The significant effects occurred in the QU phase and examination of performance in this phase revealed that in the CI group there was more correct recall about actions and objects and more person errors.

Second interviews

When analysing the data yielded at time 2 a series of 2 × 3 ANOVAs were performed to examine CI–SI differences at time 2 taking into account type of interview at time 1 (CI/SI/none).

Amount recalled at time 2. Examination of percentage correct, amount of errors and amount of confabulations revealed a significant effect of interview type on percentage correct information only ($F(2,81) = 5.38$, $p < .01$). *Post hoc* analyses revealed that those children who had either a CI (Fisher's PLSD = 3.10, $p < .05$) or an SI (Fisher's PLSD = 4.43, $p < .01$) at time 1 recalled significantly higher percentage correct at time 2 than those children who were not interviewed at time 1 (see Table 3.3 for means). There were no significant differences in accuracy of recall. The mean accuracy rate (across all conditions) was 84 per cent.

Having identified an increase in percentage correct information in the groups who experienced two interviews, analyses were performed to look at differences at each stage of their second interview (as with the time 1 data).

Recall at each phase of the interview (time 2). When a series of 3 × 2 ANOVAs was performed on the data, with percentage correct, errors and confabulations at each phase of the interview as the dependent measures, the following results were obtained. Taking the FR phase first, ANOVA revealed a significant effect of first interview on percentage correct free recall ($F(2,81) = 7.06$, $p < .01$). *Post hoc* analyses showed that the children who had no interview at time 1 recalled a lower percentage of correct information during the free report phase of their interview at time 2 than those who had either a CI (Fisher's PLSD = 3.73, $p < .01$) or an SI (Fisher's PLSD = .25, $p < .01$) at time 1. No other significant effects were noted in the FR phase.

Table 3.3 Percentage correct information, errors and confabulations means at time 2

Time 2	*Time 1*					
	CI		*SI*		*None*	
	% correct	*Total correct*	*% correct*	*Total correct*	*% correct*	*Total correct*
CI						
M	16.4	105.4	18.1	115.7	13.5	86.5
SD	4.0	26.5	6.9	44.5	6.7	42.8
SI						
M	15.6	100.5	16.3	104.5	12.2	78.2
SD	5.5	35.3	4.3	28.2	3.2	20.1
Errors	*CI*		*SI*		*None*	
CI						
M	16.2		12.2		11.2	
SD	7.9		7.6		6.9	
SI						
M	15.0		16.3		11.3	
SD	8.5		12.4		11.0	
Confabulations	*CI*		*SI*		*None*	
CI						
M	6.8		7.4		4.1	
SD	10.3		6.8		4.6	
SI						
M	5.7		8.4		9.3	
SD	7.1		19.4		13.0	

Note: The 'percentage correct' measure shows the percentage of *possible* accurate recall for event. Due to dropouts at time 2, the N for CI and SI at time 1 were 26 and 28.

In the QU phase, there was an effect of first interview on percentage correct ($F(2,81) = 4.11, p < .05$). Contrary to prediction, those children having an SI interview at time 1 reported more correct information in the QU phase at time 2 compared to those having a CI interview at time 1 (Fisher's PLSD = 1.82, $p = .01$) and compared to those having no interview at time 1 (Fisher's PLSD = 1.44, $p < .05$). There were no other significant effects in the QU phase and no significant effects in the SR phase.

Proportion of new and repeated information at time 2. The coding scheme developed for the second interviews enabled the information to be categorized as either new (not mentioned at time 1) or repeated information (mentioned at time 1 and repeated at time 2). For those children having two interviews ($N = 54$), the amount of repeated and new information and the proportion of their recall that was either new or repeated were noted. The amount of new and repeated information did not vary as a function of interview method. Interestingly at time 2, 59 per cent of accurate information was repeated and 41 per cent was new; 23 per cent of errors were repeated and 77 per cent were new; 12 per cent of confabulations were repeated and 88 per cent were new. There are many possible reasons for the new information at time 2 (including the children having talked amongst themselves and to others between interviews). It is worthy of note that a number of script-relevant intrusions occurred at the second interview and this may reflect the influence of schema on gaps in memory (see Milne *et al.*, 1995; Wark, Memon, Koehnken, & Bull, 1995, for specific examples).

Number of questions asked and recall performance. Both groups of interviewers (CI and SI) were instructed to ask questions concerning only what the children had told them during the free report phase of the interview. As stated above, no differences in the amount recalled during the free report phase were found between those children having a CI and those having an SI at time 1 or time 2. However, in this phase the CI interviewers asked significantly more questions at time 1 than did the SI interviewers ($t(58) = 8.06$, $p < .0001$, means for CI = 30.18 and for the SI = 12.88). Of these questions 66 per cent were open questions, 22 per cent closed and the remaining 2 per cent fell into the leading or multiple choice category. The same pattern was found at time 2 but here there were no CI/SI differences. The greater number of questions asked by CI interviewers suggests that, when faced with the same amount of free recall information as their SI counterparts, the CI interviewers subsequently adopted a more detailed questioning strategy.

Discussion

At time 1 (two-day delay) the present study found the CI to produce an increase in the amount of correct recall. The effect size ($d = .58$) was somewhat smaller than that reported in earlier studies (see Koehnken *et al.*, 1994) but the control group (the structured interview) is superior to that used in the majority of previous studies. The increase in correct recall with the CI emanated from significantly more accurate object and action details. The increases in correct recall and errors were manifested in the questioning phase of the interview and this raises a number of questions about the effects of techniques used in this stage of the interview.

To what extent is the increase in reporting of details in the questioning phase of the CI due to the use of specific CI techniques? The CI interviewers used a combination of context reinstatement and imagery instructions in the questioning phase. The interviewers actively encouraged the children to generate images of the event and to describe them. They prompted the children with specific questions based on the information the children had given in free recall. The two techniques, activation of images and detailed questioning, could account for the gains in correct and incorrect details. While imagery may be used to facilitate retrieval of information from memory, it may also increase inaccurate reporting as can be seen in the literature on suggestibility and creation of false memories (Ceci, Loftus, Leichtman, & Bruck, 1994; Hyman & Pentland, 1996). Similarly, the use of specific questions with children of the age group sampled in the current study may increase the amount of information that is reported but at the cost of a drop in accuracy (Davies *et al.*, 1989; Dent & Stephenson, 1979; King & Yuille, 1987; Oates & Shrimpton, 1991).

If we look at the absolute numbers of errors compared to correct details, it is clear that the CI produced a greater increase in correct details than in incorrect details. One plausible explanation for this is that the CI technique (which includes 'report everything') shifts the criterion for responding by influencing confidence and willingness to report information (the theoretical basis is illustrated by signal detection theory). Bekerian & Dennett (1993) drew attention to this in a review paper which assessed the theoretical basis of CI. The effect of CI on the response criterion requires further investigation. It is possible that the errors are a result of demand characteristics or social pressure to give a desired response (Cronin *et al.*, 1992). Asking probing questions can have this effect (Davies *et al.*, 1989; Dent, 1991; Oates & Shrimpton, 1991). This study was, however, able to locate the nature of the errors that were being made. The children made more errors about persons than any other type of information. Again previous literature suggests that children have difficulty in describing persons (Davies *et al.*, 1989; Gee & Pipe, 1995).

How should the increase in errors be interpreted by practitioners? Firstly, it should be noted that the CI increases errors but not confabulated details. An increase in confabulated details (e.g. saying the magician wore a cloak when there was no cloak) may have quite different ramifications in a forensic context than a person error (e.g. describing a purple jacket as a blue one). Secondly, if we look at the absolute number of correct details compared to errors in the present study, for every six correct details, there was an error, so the gains appear to outweigh the risks. Thirdly, there is no difference in accuracy rates across cognitive and structured interview conditions. While procedures such as the CI aim to increase the amount of information that is reported, in a forensic context it is the accuracy of the information that is crucial (Koriat & Goldsmith, 1994). In a review, Koriat & Goldsmith (1996) demonstrate how critical it is to separate the measure of quantity of information which fits the 'storehouse metaphor' of traditional research from applied research on everyday memory processes. We suggest that the CI be used with older children (Saywitz *et al.*, 1992) but some caution be exercised when interviewing younger children. Whenever possible external corroboration should be sought for the details reported. Special care should be taken in eliciting person descriptions as several studies have found errors with this type of information in a CI (see also Milne & Bull, 1995; Milne *et al.*, 1995). Finally, it may be the case that the effects obtained here are specific to the eight–nine-year-old age group. We would encourage researchers to test the effectiveness of the CI procedure described in this study with older and younger children.

While the time 1 results were consistent with our hypotheses, the time 2 results were not. In light of the evidence that the CI (at time 1 and time 2) occasions a more extensive memory search, we predicted an increase in additional and repeated information in the CI/CI group at time 2. Similarly, we predicted a carry-over effect boosting performance of the CI/SI group. This was not found; as there was no effect of CI at time 2 (although performance was better if children had been interviewed at time 1). A number of recent studies have obtained similar results (Brock & Fisher, 1994; McCauley & Fisher, 1995). There are several possibilities as to why this may be the case. Taking the position that CI achieves its effect by enhancing interviewer communication and interviewee expectations, perhaps a good first (SI) interview is sufficient to raise performance levels (Roediger & Payne, 1982). It is possible that, over the delay, memory for the event became less context dependent (see Smith, 1988). This would not be incompatible with recent theoretical accounts of memory and forgetting (e.g. Brainerd *et al.*, 1990; Riccio, Rabinowitz, & Axelrod, 1994; Roediger & Challis, 1989). Similarly, Payne, Hembrooke, & Anastasi (1993) maintain that context is a poorer cue at the delayed test than at immediate test either as a consequence of a decrement in context–item association strength, or as a result of changes in the functional context between the two sessions.

The improvements following repeated testing suggest a powerful effect of retrieval practice. If a retrieval attempt in first interview serves to strengthen item-to-context associations sufficiently, such associations would tend to be recovered on the second test (Brainerd *et al.*, 1990). As indicated in the introduction, it is well established in the memory literature that testing shortly after exposure to the to-be-remembered material will attenuate forgetting over a delay (see Brainerd & Ornstein, 1991, for a review). The extent to which quality of the first interview may determine the amount reported upon repeated testing may be explored in future studies by including an untrained control group.

Further research could also be usefully deployed to look at conditions under which repeated interviews are most likely to be effective. From a practical and theoretical perspective, it is important to understand how performance with a CI will vary with longer delays, to examine the patterns of losses and gains (e.g. the frequency with which repeated and new information is reported) and factors that may reduce intertest forgetting. Interviewer credibility, demand characteristics, interviewer instructions and an interviewee's interpretation of the interviewer's requests may also interact in interesting ways with interview technique and these may account for changes in response criteria across repeated tests. Memory theorists have recently developed experimental procedures (e.g. the 'logic of opposition' procedure; see Jacoby, Woloshyn, & Kelley, 1989; Lindsay, Gonzales, & Eso, 1995) which can be applied to address these issues.

Acknowledgements

This research was supported by a grant from the British Economic and Social Research Council (ESRC) R000234290. We are grateful to the staff and pupils of Bassett Green First and Middle School. We thank Angela Holley and Rebecca Milne for their contribution to the research; our interviewers for data collection; Tony Roberts and Chris Colbourn for statistical advice; and Anne Anderson, Ed Geiselman, Mel Pipe, Debra Poole, Steve Lindsay and Sarah Stevenage for their comments on earlier drafts of the paper.

Appendix 1: Sample scored transcript (cognitive condition)

The following is an extract taken from one interview transcript to illustrate the coding and scoring procedure that was used in this study. The data are presented in a table form for illustration purposes only. In actuality, we worked with an entire interview and checked off details against a master list comprising all details reported by all participants. Only *new* information was scored at each stage, i.e. if an item was mentioned in free recall it was not scored again in the question phase (e.g. 'bald').

Free recall. The man looked baldish and I know exactly what happened about the five pound note. He got it behind him the note and just pushed it up.

He done the bird trick and he had a thingy over it and a cover down all round it and um he took it out and there was a bird there, and that's how he done it.

There's me and Matthew and there's the magic man . . . .

Prompt. He had two handkerchiefs and he tied them together and I blowed them and they come undone again. And a pigeon one and a rabbit one . . . .

Questioning. He wore some like a uniform trousers, a tie and he had a bald head. He was pretty tall and was wearing brown shoes and all the children were sitting by the doors. And after we done the tricks, we went and sit down for a while and then Russel came up . . . .

Second retrieval attempt. He said,' Can I have two helpers and that boy over there and that girl over there' and I went up. He says 'Can you hold the string on each side' and his scissors were stiff but the magician cut the rope . . . .

Information	*Correct*[a]	*Error*	*Confabulation*
Free recall			
Man	1		
Baldish	1		
Five pound note	2		
Bird trick	1	1	
Cover	1		
Something appeared	1		
Matthew (not there)			1
Prompt			
Hankies	2		
tied	1		
Blows on hankies	2		
undone	1		
Rabbit	1		
Question			
Trousers	1		
Tie	1		
Brown shoes	1	1	
Russel	1		
Second retrieval			
Asks for helpers	1		

Information	*Correct*[a]	*Error*	*Confabulation*
Two children	2		
Hold string	2		
Scissors	1		
Magician cuts rope	3		

[a]A point was given for every detail based upon how much information was provided. For example, 'five pound note' received two points because it provided more information than the response 'money'.

Notes

1 'Of the 109 children, nine children were absent for testing; in addition, two interviews (one SI, one CI) were discarded without coding on the basis that the children had made no attempt to talk about the event. One further interview (CI) was dropped from the sample because it appeared as an outlier with an extremely unusual number of confabulations ($N = 78$). Several CI and SI interviews from time 1 and time 2 were not transcribed as the tape recordings were of poor sound quality. This reduced the total number of interviews used in the analysis to 87.

2 MANOVAs were not performed on the data as the dependent variables did not always correlate (see Cole, Maxwell, Arvey, & Salas, 1994).

3 Combining all the phases in one repeated measures ANOVA was deemed inappropriate as each phase involved different recall techniques, and recall at each phase was scored on the basis of what was recalled at the earlier phases (additional information). The same principle was adhered to regarding detail types.

References

Bekerian, D. A., & Dennett, J. L. (1993). The cognitive interview: Reviving the issues. *Applied Cognitive Psychology*, *7*, 275–298.

Boggs, S. R., & Eyberg, S. (1990). Interview techniques and establishing rapport. In A. M. La Greca (Ed.), *Through the eyes of the child: Obtaining self-reports from children and adolescents* (pp. 85–108). Boston, MA: Allyn & Bacon.

Brainerd, C., & Ornstein, P. A. (1991). Children's memory for witnessed events. In J. Doris (Ed.), *The suggestibility of children's recollections* (pp. 10–20). Washington, DC: American Psychological Association.

Brainerd, C. J., Reyna, V. F., Howe, M. L., & Kingma, J. (1990). The development of forgetting and reminiscence. *Monographs of the Society for Research in Child Development*, *55*, 3–4.

Brock, P., & Fisher, R. P. (1994). *Effectiveness of the cognitive interview in a multiple testing session*. Paper presented at the Biennial Conference of the American Psychology Law Society, Santa Fe, NM, March.

Bull, R. (1992). Obtaining evidence expertly: The reliability of interviews with child witnesses. *Expert Evidence: The International Digest of Human Behaviour, Science and Law*, *1*, 3–36.

Bull, R. (1995a). Interviewing children in legal contexts. In R. Bull & D. Carson (Eds.), *Handbook of psychology in legal contexts* (pp. 235–246). Chichester: Wiley.

Bull, R. (1995b). Innovative techniques for the questioning of child witnesses especially those who are young and those with learning disability. In M. Zaragoza, J. R. Graham, G. C. N. Hall, R. Hirschman & Y. S. Ben-Porath (Eds.), *Memory and testimony in the child witness* (pp. 179–194). Thousand Oaks, CA: Sage.

Ceci, S., Loftus, E., Leichtman, M., & Bruck, M. (1994). The possible role of source misattributions in the creation of false beliefs among preschoolers. *International Journal of Clinical and Experimental Hypnosis*, *42*, 304–320.

Cole, D. A., Maxwell, S. E., Arvey, R., & Salas, E. (1994). How the power of a MANOVA can both increase and decrease as a function of intercorrelations among the dependent variables. *Psychological Bulletin*, *115*, 465–474.

Clifford, B., & Bull, R. (1978). *The psychology of person identification*. London: Routledge.

Clyde, J. (1992). *The report of the inquiry into the removal of children from Orkney in February 1991*. Edinburgh: HMSO.

Cronin, O., Memon, A., Eaves, R., Küpper, B., & Bull, R. (1992). *The cognitive interview with child witnesses: A child centered approach?* Paper presented at NATO Advanced Study Institute: The child witness in context, Italy, May.

Davies, G., Tarrant, A., & Flin, R. (1989). Close encounters of the witness kind: Children's memory for a simulated health inspection. *British Journal of Psychology*, *80*, 415–429.

Dent, H. R. (1991). Experimental studies of interviewing child witnesses. In J. Doris (Ed.), *The suggestibility of children's recollections* (pp. 138–146). Washington, DC: American Psychological Association.

Dent, H. R., & Stephenson, G. M. (1979). An experimental study of the effectiveness of different techniques of questioning child witnesses. *British Journal of Social and Clinical Psychology*, *18*, 41–51.

Eich, J. E. (1980). The cue dependent nature of state dependent retrieval. *Memory and Cognition*, *8*, 157–173.

Fisher, R. P., & Geiselman, R. E. (1992). *Memory enhancing techniques for investigative interviewing: The cognitive interview*. Springfield, IL: Thomas.

Fisher, R. P., Geiselman, R. E., Raymond, D. S., Jurkevich, L. M., & Warhaftig, M. L. (1987). Enhancing eyewitness memory: Refining the cognitive interview. *Journal of Police Science and Administration*, *15*, 291–297.

Flavell, J. H., & Wellman, E. (1977). Metamemory. In R. V. Kail & J. W. Hagen (Eds.), *Perspectives on the development of memory and cognition* (pp. 3–33). Hillsdale, NJ: Erlbaum.

Flin, R., Boon, J., Knox, A., & Bull, R. (1992). The effects of a five month delay on children's eyewitness memory. *British Journal of Psychology*, *83*, 323–336.

Gee, S., & Pipe, M.-E. (1995). Helping children to remember: The influence of object cues on children's accounts of a real event. *Developmental Psychology*, *31*, 746–758.

Geiselman, R. E., & Fisher, R. P. (1988). The cognitive interview: An innovative technique for questioning witnesses of crime. *Journal of Police and Criminal Psychology*, *2*, 2–5.

Geiselman, R. E., Fisher, R. P., MacKinnon, D. P., & Holland, H. L. (1985). Eyewitness memory enhancement in the police interview: Cognitive retrieval mnemonics versus hypnosis. *Journal of Applied Psychology*, *70*, 401–412.

Geiselman, R. E., Fisher, R. P., MacKinnon, D. P., & Holland, H. L. (1986). Eyewitness memory enhancement in the cognitive interview. *American Journal of Psychology*, *99*, 385–401.

Goodman, G. S., Aman, C., & Hirschman, J. (1987). Child sexual and physical abuse: Children's testimony. In S. J. Ceci, M. P. Toglia & D. F. Ross (Eds), *Children's eyewitness memory* (pp. 1–23). New York, NY: Springer-Verlag.

Goodman, G., & Bottoms, B. (1993). *Child victims, child witnesses: Understanding and improving testimony*. New York, NY: Guilford.

Hudson, J. A. (1990). Constructive processes in children's event memory. *Developmental Psychology*, *26*, 180–186.

Hyman, I. E., & Pentland, J. (1996). The role of imagery in the creation of false childhood memories. *Journal of Memory & Language 35*, 101–117.

Jacoby, L. L., Woloshyn, V., & Kelley, C. M. (1989). Becoming famous without being recognised: Unconscious influences of memory produced by dividing attention. *Journal of Experimental Psychology: General, 118*, 115–125.

King, M., & Yuille, J. (1987). Suggestibility and the child witness. In S. J. Ceci, M. Toglia & D. Ross (Eds.), *Children's eyewitness memory* (pp. 24–35). New York, NY: Springer-Verlag.

Koehnken, G., Finger, M., Nitschke, N., Höfer, E., & Aschermann, E. (1992). *Does a cognitive interview interfere with a subsequent Statement Validity Analysis?* Paper presented at the American Psychology and Law Society meeting, San Diego.

Koehnken, G., Milne, R., Memon, A., & Bull, R. (1994). *A meta-analysis of the effects of the cognitive interview*. Paper presented at the Biennial Conference of the American Psychology Law Society, Santa Fe, NM, March.

Koehnken, G., Schimmossek, E., Aschermann, E., & Höfer, E. (1995). The cognitive interview and the assessment of the credibility of adults' statements. *Journal of Applied Psychology, 80*, 671–684.

Koehnken, G., Thürer, C., & Zorberbier, D. (1994). The cognitive interview: Are interviewers' memories enhanced too? *Applied Cognitive Psychology, 8*, 13–24.

Koriat, A., & Goldsmith, M. (1994). Memory in naturalistic and laboratory contexts: Distinguishing accuracy oriented and quantity oriented approaches to memory assessment. *Journal of Experimental Psychology: General, 123*, 297–315.

Koriat, A., & Goldsmith, M. (1996). Memory metaphors and the everyday laboratory controversy: Comparing the storehouse and correspondence conceptions of memory. *Brain and Behavioural Sciences, 19*, 167–188.

Lindsay, D. S., Gonzales, V., & Eso, K. (1995). Aware and unaware uses of memories of postevent suggestions. In M. Zaragoza, J. R. Graham, G. C. N. Hall, R. Hirschman & Y. S. Ben-Porath (Eds.), *Memory and testimony in the child witness* (pp. 86–108). Thousand Oaks, CA: Sage.

Loftus, E. F., & Fathi, D. C. (1985). Retrieving multiple autobiographical memories. *Social Cognition, 3*, 280–295.

McCauley, M. R., & Fisher, R. P. (1995). Facilitating children's eyewitness recall with the revised cognitive interview. *Journal of Applied Psychology, 80*, 510–517.

MacLeod, M., Frowley, J., & Shepherd, J. (1994). Whole body information and its relevance to eyewitness identification. In D. Ross, J. D. Read & M. Toglia (Eds.), *Adult eyewitness testimony: Current trends and developments* (pp. 125–143). Cambridge: Cambridge University Press.

Mantwill, M., Koehnken, G., & Aschermann, E. (1995). Effects of the cognitive interview on the recall of familiar and unfamiliar events. *Journal of Applied Psychology, 80*, 68–78.

Memon, A., & Bruce, V. (1985). Context effects in episodic studies of verbal and facial memory: A review. *Current Psychological Research and Reviews, Winter 1985–86*, 349–369.

Memon, A., Cronin, Ó., Eaves, R., & Bull, R. (1996). An empirical test of the mnemonic components of the cognitive interview. In G. M. Davies, S. Lloyd-Bostock, M. McMurran & C. Wilson (Eds.), *Psychology and law: Advances in research*. Berlin: De Gruyter.

Memon, A., Cronin, Ó., Eaves, R., & Bull, R. (1993). The cognitive interview and child witnesses. In G. M. Stephenson & N. K. Clark (Eds.), *Children, evidence and procedure* (pp. 3–9). Issues in Criminological & Legal Psychology. No. 20. Leicester: British Psychological Society.

Memorandum of good practice (1992). *Department of health*. London: HMSO.

Milne, R., & Bull, R. (1995). *Interviewing children with mild learning difficulty with the cognitive interview*. Paper presented at the BPS Division of Criminological and Legal Psychology Annual Conference, Rugby, UK, September.

Milne, R., Bull, R., Koehnken, G., & Memon, A. (1995). The cognitive interview and suggestibility. In G. M. Stephenson & N. K. Clark (Eds.), *Criminal behaviour: Perceptions, attributions and rationality* (pp. 21–27). BPS Division of Criminological and Legal Psychology Occasional Papers, No. 22. Leicester: British Psychological Society.

Oates, K., & Shrimpton, S. (1991). Children's memories for stressful and non-stressful events. *Medicine, Science and Law*, *31*, 4–10.

Paivio, A. (1971). *Imagery and verbal processes*. New York, NY: Holt, Rinehart & Winston.

Payne, D. G. (1987). Hypermnesia and reminiscence in recall: A historical and empirical review. *Psychological Bulletin*, *101*, 5–27.

Payne, D. G., Hembrooke, H. A., & Anastasi, J. S. (1993). Hypermnesia in free and cued recall. *Memory and Cognition*, *21*, 48–62.

Poole, D. A., & White, L. T. (1995). Tell me again and again: Stability and change in repeated testimonies of children and adults. In M. Zaragoza, J. R. Graham, G. C. N. Hall, R. Hirschman & Y. S. Ben-Porath (Eds.), *Memory and testimony in the child witness* (pp. 24–43). Thousand Oaks, CA: Sage.

Poole, D. A., & White, L. T. (1993). Two years later: Effects of question repetition and retention interval on the eyewitness testimony of children and adults. *Developmental Psychology*, *27*, 975–986.

Riccio, D. C., Rabinowitz, V. C., & Axelrod, S. (1994). Memory: When less is more. *American Psychologist*, *49*, 917–926.

Roediger, H. L. III & Challis, B. H. (1989). Hypermnesia: Improvements in recall with repeated testing. In C. Z. Izawa (Ed.), *Current issues in cognitive processes: The Tulane Floweree Symposium on cognition* (pp. 175–199). Hillsdale, NJ: Erlbaum.

Roediger, H. L., & Payne, D. G. (1982). Hypermnesia: The role of repeated testing. *Journal of Experimental Psychology: Learning, Memory and Cognition*, *8*, 66–72.

Saywitz, K. J., Geiselman, R. E., & Bornstein, G. K. (1992). Effects of cognitive interviewing and practice on children's recall performance. *Journal of Applied Psychology*, *77*, 744–756.

Scrivner, E., & Safer, M. A. (1988). Eyewitnesses show hypermnesia for details about a violent event. *Journal of Applied Psychology*, *73*, 371–377.

Smith, S. (1988). Environmental context dependent memory. In G. Davies & D. Thomson (Eds.), *Memory in context: Context in memory*, pp. 13–34. London: Wiley.

Tulving, E., & Thomson, D. M. (1973). Encoding specificity and retrieval processes in episodic memory. *Psychological Review*, *80*, 353–370.

Turtle, J., & Yuille, J. (1994). Lost but not forgotten details: Repeated eyewitness recall leads to reminiscence but not hypermnesia. *Journal of Applied Psychology*, *79*, 260–271.

Wark, L., Memon, A., Koehnken, G., & Bull, R. (1995). *Uses and abuses of schematic knowledge*. University of Southampton, Department of Psychology, Working Paper, RWPS/95/1.

Warren, A., & Lane, P. (1995). Effects of timing and type of questioning on eyewitness accuracy and suggestibility. In M. Zaragoza, J. R. Graham, G. C. N. Hall, R. Hirschman & Y. S. Ben-Porath (Eds.), *Memory and testimony in the child witness* (pp. 44–60). Thousand Oaks, CA: Sage.

4 Does the cognitive interview help children to resist the effects of suggestive questioning?

Rebecca Milne and Ray Bull

Introduction

Research examining child witness issues is ever increasing which in itself demonstrates the importance of children within the criminal justice system. However, until relatively recently legal professionals have focused on children's inabilities, and this view has in the past caused children to be seen as incompetent and unreliable. Nevertheless, the psychological literature (see Milne & Bull, 1999; Poole & Lamb, 1998, for reviews) has begun to re-educate the legal profession, as it has been demonstrated on numerous occasions that these negative views have been largely based on unfounded assumptions. As a result, more children are now being afforded access to justice and there is a need to develop non-biasing interviewing techniques to help children to report events. The cognitive interview (CI) is one such technique and the research reported in this paper found the CI to increase the reporting of information by 21% and also helped children to resist the negative effects of suggestive questions.

Children and recall

Young children usually report less information than older children or adults, though they are no less accurate (see Bull, 1996). However, the amount of information reported increases steadily with age, with the number of erroneous details reported remaining relatively stable (Davies, 1994). It has been repeatedly demonstrated that when child witnesses make errors they tend to be errors of omission rather than commission (e.g. Granhag & Spjut, 2001). For example, Steward, Bussey, Goodman, & Saywitz (1993) found that children reported only 25% of the total event. Furthermore, errors of omission tend to be due to retrieval failures as opposed to encoding failures (Hutcheson, Baxter, Telfer, & Warden, 1995). Research therefore needs to develop techniques which target errors of omission and which try to increase the quantity of detail elicited from children, as detail is the currency of the criminal justice system. The more information available, the more likely a case is taken to court, tried, the guilty punished, and the innocent exonerated (Milne & Bull, 2004).

Interviewing children

The use of the phased interviewing approach for investigative interviews of children has been recommended by researchers (e.g. Bull, 1996; Poole & Lamb, 1998) and in governmental guidance given to legal professionals (e.g. *Memorandum of Good Practice*, Home Office and Department of Health, 1992). However, there are limitations to this method of interviewing. For example, young children's free report is often limited; and as a result this leaves little for the interviewer to use for basing their follow-up questions upon (Davies, Wilson, Mitchell, & Milsom, 1995). Thus, memory-enhancing techniques need to be developed to help practitioners elicit the maximum amount of information from children, especially prior to questioning them. The CI may be one such technique which has been recommended by researchers for use with this group (Milne & Bull, 1999) and is mentioned in the new governmental guidelines for interviewing all vulnerable groups including children *(Achieving Best Evidence,* Home Office and Department of Health, 2001).

The CI was initially developed in the USA by Geiselman and Fisher (see Milne & Bull, 1999, for a full description of the CI) and was based on extant theoretical principles concerning memory retrieval (e.g. the encoding specificity principle; Tulving & Thomson, 1973). The CI aims to increase the quantity and quality of information elicited from cooperative witnesses, victims, and suspects of crime, and consists of techniques which aim to improve memory retrieval and dyadic communication. It has been found to increase the recall of correct information by approximately 35–45% for adult witnesses (see Koehnken, Milne, Memon, & Bull, 1999, for a meta-analysis). There are now 14 known studies, published and unpublished, examining the use of the CI with children from the age of 6 years onwards (see Milne & Bull, 1999, for a detailed overview). Only two of these studies found no effect for the CI and both of these involved testing memory performance after longer delays (Memon, Cronin, Eaves, & Bull, 1993; Memon, Wark, Holley, Bull, & Koehnken, 1996b). However, no study, regardless of interviewee type, has found the CI to result in fewer details being reported. In three studies (Finger, Nitschke, & Koehnken, 1992; McCauley & Fisher, 1995; Memon, Wark, Bull, & Koehnken, 1997) there were significantly more incorrect details reported and in two studies more confabulations noted by children interviewed with a CI (Finger *et al.*, 1992; Hayes & Delamothe, 1997). Nevertheless, the percentage accuracy of the elicited information from children interviewed with a CI in all research has been found to be high (ranging from 81 to 93%). In line with this past research it was hypothesized that the CI would aid the reporting of correct recall for children (*hypothesis 1*) without increasing incorrect details or confabulations.

Research has started to unravel which details of an event (e.g. person, object or action) the CI increases the reporting of by children (see Clifford & George, 1996, for detail types and adults). Once this has been determined, one can then concentrate on developing techniques and refinements to enhance all kinds of event information. Two studies have noted detail type and found that the CI increased the correct reporting of details pertaining to actions and objects in the event (Granhag & Spjut, 2001; Memon *et al.*, 1997). In addition, Memon *et al.*'s (1997) research highlighted that the increased reporting of incorrect details sometimes found with the CI concerned persons. Research therefore needs to ascertain whether there is a pattern emerging with respect to the kinds of correct and erroneous information being found with this technique. Thus the first primary aim of this study was to examine which types of detail (person, object, action, or surroundings) the CI increases the reporting of and, if more incorrect details or confabulations are reported, which aspects of the event do they concern? It was hypothesized that the CI would increase the reporting of details pertaining to actions and objects (*hypothesis 2*).

Limited research has found out exactly *where* in the interview the CI superiority effect emanates and where any reported erroneous information is arising. Memon *et al.* (1997) and Granhag & Spjut (2001) examined this and found that the CI enhancement effect came from questioning rather than the free recall or second retrieval phases of the interview. Thus, more research is needed, especially as the CI is to be recommended for use by legal practitioners who are known to rush children into the questioning phase of the interview (Davies *et al.*, 1995). The second primary aim of this study was to determine which phase of the CI (free report, questioning, or reverse order recall) accounts for the increased reporting of correct and erroneous details? It was hypothesized that any enhancement effect found with the CI would emanate from questioning (*hypothesis 3*).

Children and suggestibility

Suggestibility concerns the degree to which an interviewee's encoding, storage, retrieval and/or reporting of events can be influenced by a range of social and psychological factors (Ceci & Bruck, 1993). It has been believed by the legal profession in the past that children are particularly suggestible and easily influenced (e.g. Heydon, 1984). There is no doubt that children do succumb to suggestive questions (see Ceci & Bruck, 1993, 1995, for reviews); however, adults are also susceptible (Milne & Bull, 1999). There have been numerous reasons put forward as to why this occurs (Ceci & Bruck, 1993). Some fall into the cognitive domain, as it is believed that children are especially prone to suggestion due to some form of memory impairment. For example, trace theory, where it is thought that vulnerability to suggestion is negatively correlated to trace strength (Brainerd & Reyna, 1990), and thus more prone to alteration (Loftus & Ketcham, 1991) or co-existence of a competing trace and thus open to source misattribution errors (Lindsay & Johnson, 1989). Indeed, it has been found that suggestibility rates are negatively correlated to memory performance (see Candel, Merckelbach, & Muris, 2000; Ochsner, Zaragoza, & Mitchell, 1999). Other explanations for suggestibility involve social characteristics (see Vrij & Bush, 2000, for an overview). Important here are the specific conditions within an interview that induce compliance to an interviewer's suggestions, a 'social dominance phenomenon' (Gudjonsson & Clark, 1986).

Training should concentrate on reducing the use of poor questioning by practitioners. However, some believe it necessary to use suggestive questions to elicit detail from children concerning abuse (Ceci & Bruck, 1995). Thus, it is crucial to examine ways to inoculate children against the negative effects of such questions (i.e. the false reporting of information). Geiselman, Fisher, Cohen, Holland, & Surtes (1986) found that the CI helped to inoculate adults against misleading questions given *after* a CI (but not before) and Memon, Holley, Wark, Bull, & Koehnken (1996a) found the same effect with 8–9-year-old children who had seen a video clip of a magic show. However, Hayes & Delamothe (1997) did not find this for 5–7-year-olds and 9–11-year-olds who had witnessed a smuggling scenario, though the suggestive questions were presented prior to the CI. The third aim of the research was to examine whether the CI could help children to resist the effects of suggestive questions presented after the interview (compared to being presented before [*hypothesis* 4]; the CI increases resistance to subsequently asked misleading questions).

'Scripts' facilitate memory processing (Davies, 1994) and are defined as temporally organized sequences that specify the actions, actors, and props most and least likely to occur during any given occurrence of an event (Nelson & Gruendel, 1981). Research has started to examine the influence of scripts on the susceptibility of children to suggestion. This is especially important, as children who have been subjected to repeated abuse are likely to have developed 'scripts' of the abuse. Pezdek & Roe (1997) posited that if the suggestive information is script-consistent and the original memory of the event is weak or lost (or not there in the first place) it may be more difficult for witnesses to decide that a detail was not present in the event. Indeed, Endres, Poggenpohl, & Erben (1999) found that children's answers to suggestive questions contained more errors when this suggestive information was script-consistent and the 'empty slots' could be filled in (i.e. there was no competing information available). Dawson & Roberts (1995) also found that children were more accurate in their answers to schema-inconsistent than schema-consistent misleading questions. Thus, the fourth aim of this study was to examine the impact of scripts on susceptibility to suggestion, and it was hypothesized that children would be more resistant to script-inconsistent misleading questions (*hypothesis 5*).

Method

Design

The design was a 2×2×2 mixed factorial design, with interview type (cognitive interview vs. structured interview) and presentation of the suggestive questions (before or after the interview) being between subjects, and script consistency (script-consistent vs. script-inconsistent) being within subjects.

Participants

Eighty-four schoolchildren aged from 8 to 9 years (M = 8 years 10 months), 41 boys and 43 girls, participated in the study (with equal ages and gender across conditions). Only one age group was chosen because previous research had demonstrated that children of this age are old enough to benefit from the CI instructions (Koehnken *et al.*, 1999). Thus, for a good test of whether (or not) the CI induces resistance to suggestion, this age group was chosen.

Interviews

The interviews all consisted of the six phases of rapport, free recall, 'can you remember more?', questioning based on each participant's free recall, second retrieval attempt, and closure (Milne & Bull, 1999). The CI differed from the structured interview (SI) in the use of context reinstatement, instruction to report everything, transfer control of the interview to the interviewee, guided imagery questioning, witness-compatible questioning, and the reverse order recall during the second retrieval attempt. The SI was similar to the phased approach of interviewing recommended in the *Memorandum of Good Practice,* government guidelines for the investigative interviewing of children (Home Office and Department of Health, 1992; see also Bull, 1992, 1996). Further, this control interview (SI) was identical to the CI except for the specific CI techniques. As a result, this was a good control condition from both a theoretical and an applied perspective. (See Appendix A for a comparative outline of the two interview techniques.) It should be noted that the change perspective CI instruction, which research has revealed children of this age may have difficulty using, was omitted from the CI protocol (see Milne & Bull, 2002, for a discussion).

Interviewers and interviewer training

The interviewers consisted of five undergraduates and three graduates, four female and four male ($M = 21$ years; no main or interaction gender effects were found for interviewer or interviewee). The authority/status of the interviewers was kept as equal as possible due to the fact that different authority types can affect the way children comply (Milne & Bull, 1999). This was done by using the same aged interviewers and by the interviewers wearing similar casual clothing.

Each interviewer was only trained to use one of the interviewing strategies, thus ensuring that the CI techniques did not infiltrate the SI condition so that a true comparison could be made between interviewing styles. Furthermore, CI and SI interviewers received the same quality and quantity of training, except that the CI interviewers received training in the 'special' CI techniques. Thus any differences found between interview conditions could not be attributed to only one group receiving training. CI and SI interviewers were trained separately and throughout the study it was ensured that the two groups did not know that the other had been trained differently. All interviewers were also told that they were being trained in an innovative interviewing technique which has been shown to enhance children's accounts of an event. This aimed to equate interviewer motivation across interview conditions. All interviewers (regardless of interview condition) participated in two 4-hour-long interview training sessions, which consisted of lectures (explaining the underlying theory), examples, practice, role-playing with video feedback, and personal comments from the trainers. Each teaching method was used for each of the phases of the interview, culminating in a practice session of the whole interview. The training material consisted of an extensive handout that outlined the material covered in the training days and an accompanying practice booklet. (For more on the content of the training see Memon *et al.*, 1996b; Milne & Bull, 1999) All interviews underwent a quality assurance check (by the first author) to ensure (1) that no CI 'special' instructions were given in the SI condition and (2) that each CI and SI fulfilled the necessary criteria.

The witnessed event

The event consisted of a video recording of a 9-minute magic show. The magic show theme was chosen because it would be of interest to the children, and it included vast amounts of action, person and object details.

Pre-determined list of suggestive questions

The children were also presented orally with a pre-set list of 20 questions, half the children before the interview and half after the interview. This list consisted of eight leading (i.e. leading the child to the correct response) and eight misleading (i.e. leading the child to an incorrect response) questions (four script-consistent and four script-inconsistent). The list also included four neutral, non-leading questions (see Appendix B). All questions were presented in a random order to counteract order effects and there were equivalent numbers of correct yes and no answers to questions to account for response biasing (Rudy & Goodman, 1991). To define questions as script-consistent or inconsistent a questionnaire asking about what usually happens in a magic show was distributed to an independent group of 17 children (14 girls and 3 boys with ages ranging from 7 to 11 years). The questionnaire consisted of open-ended questions asking for information about what usually happens in a magic show (e.g. the appearance of the magician, objects the magician would use, and so on; Wark, Memon, Koehnken, & Bull, 1995).

IQ subtest

Each child also verbally completed, at the end of the interview process, an IQ subtest in order to check that participants' pragmatic and vocabulary abilities did not differ across experimental conditions. The test administered was the similarities or reasoning subtest of the Wechsler Intelligence Scale for Children (WISC).

Procedure

The videotaped event was shown to the participants in small groups of up to eight children, and equal viewing conditions were ensured (as far as possible) for all participants. The individual showing the event was not involved in the subsequent interviews, since this could have affected the 'transfer control' instruction in the CI condition. All were told 'watch carefully as you will be asked what you think about it later'. The participants were then randomly assigned to the CI or SI interview group. Approximately 24 hours later, each participant was individually interviewed by one of the interviewers (randomly allocated) and each interview was audiotaped. To avoid the possibility of spontaneous context reinstatement effects occurring, the interviews were conducted in an environment different from the one in which the participants had seen the video clip. Each audiotaped interview was transcribed into a written format and scored.

Scoring procedure

The video recording of the magic show was put into a skeletal written format and the details were categorized into four groups; person (e.g. what the magician was wearing and looked like), action (e.g. what the magician did), object (e.g. what the magician was carrying), and surrounding (e.g. what the place where the magic show took place looked like). Other research has similarly subdivided details reported in this way (e.g. Hutcheson *et al.*, 1995). An exhaustive list containing all the available details was drawn up with the appropriate weighted scores (according to specificity) next to each detail (e.g. dove=2, bird=1). Any details mentioned which were not in the list were added progressively, subject to confirmation by watching the video clip. The final coding scheme consisted of 771 units of information in the event, which were further subdivided into 120 units of person information, 128 units of object information, 491 units of action information, and 32 units of surrounding information. It is felt that this method of scoring and coding is more sensitive to any erroneous information that may arise in the interview compared with a system that merely examines the central elements of an event. This is because any incorrect details reported about an event tend to concern the peripheral rather than the central themes of an event. It could be that it is a piece of peripheral detail which is the key to solving the whole case. It also tends to be peripheral information which is challenged in court.

The child's free recall, responses in the questioning phase, and responses in the second retrieval attempt were coded and scored separately, with only new information being evaluated (i.e. repeated information was not scored). Given that information at each phase of the interview was related to what had been reported earlier, interview phase was not treated as a repeated measures factor in the analysis. Similarly, the detail types were related, by virtue of the fact that details were recorded in a number of information sections concurrently (e.g. if the child said that the 'magician magicked a dove', one point would be given for magician in the person detail category, and also one point for magician would be given in the action category). Since the detail categories are not unrelated, factorial analysis could not be conducted involving detail type as a repeated measure.

Each detail recalled was coded as being correct, incorrect, or a confabulation within the detail categories. A piece of information was coded as incorrect if the detail was discrepant with the relevant detail in the film (e.g. red jumper instead of black jumper; an error concerning colour). If a detail was mentioned that was not present in the film, it was coded as a confabulation. Coding incorrect details and confabulations separately is important since, in a forensic investigation, the two may have quite different implications. Furthermore, research suggests that these two different measures may reflect different psychological phenomena (Gudjonsson & Clare, 1995). Total correct, incorrect and confabulated details were also calculated. A further score was calculated; the proportion of correct details relative to the total number of details reported (i.e. percentage accuracy).

With regard to the predetermined list of suggestive questions, each child's responses to misleading questions were scored as 'misled' (yield/incorrect response), 'not misled' (resistance/correct response), or 'I don't know'. Responses to leading questions were scored as either 'led' (yield/correct response), 'not led' (resistance/incorrect response) or 'I don't know'. 'Don't know' responses were scored separately because earlier work (e.g. Rudy & Goodman, 1991) has been criticized for erroneously assuming that an 'I don't know' response constitutes resistance. Instead it could be that the 'I don't know' response reflects a child's misunderstanding of the question (Ceci & Bruck, 1993). For those participants who were administered this pre-set list of questions before their interview their subsequent interviews were checked to see if (1) any of the misleading information was incorporated into the child's reports of the event (i.e. intrusions), and (2) if those who were led before their interview recalled the same (or more, or less) amount of information given in the leading questions than did those children who did not receive the questionnaire until after the interview. (For correct responses to leading questions it is, of course, not possible to ascertain whether these represent compliance to the question or memory of the event.) Replies to the non-leading/ neutral questions were scored for accuracy.

Results

The results section will in the first instance examine the recall data and then turn to the effects of suggestion. The effectiveness of the CI compared to the SI for children was examined. The effects of interview type on the total number of (1) correct, (2) incorrect, and (3) confabulated details were evaluated using ANOVA.

Did the CI produce more correct recall than the SI?

Table 4.1 shows that participants interviewed using a CI recalled more correct details ($M = 130$) than those interviewed with an SI ($M = 106$; $F[1,80] = 7.59, p < .01$). There were no significant differences for interview type regarding the number of incorrect or confabulated details reported. Thus, evidence was found to support hypothesis 1 that the CI does increase the volume of correct recall, without increasing the reporting of incorrect details or confabulations. The accuracy of the information (i.e. the proportion of correct details relative to the total number of

Table 4.1 Mean number of correct, incorrect and confabulated details per interview (CI/SI)

Details	*Interview condition*			
	Cognitive interview		*Structured interview*	
	M	*SD*	*M*	*SD*
Correct	129.8	42.4	105.9	39.6
Person	19.6	31.4	11.4	4.3
Objects	24.1	8.0	23.5	8.7
Action	81.9	31.4	65.4	29.8
Surroundings	4.1	3.3	3.5	2.2
Incorrect	17.7	11.3	13.0	7.2
Confabulations	16.2	13.2	13.1	8.6

details reported) was very similar across interview conditions (81% for the CI and 80% for the SI, respectively).

What type of extra details account for the CI enhancement effect?

Given that the CI occasioned significantly more correct recall than did the SI, it was deemed important to determine what type of detail most demonstrated this effect. Thus, the overall total correct details were subdivided into four detail categories of person, object, action and surrounding. As can be seen from Table 4.1, the overall superiority effects found with the CI emanated from significantly more details concerning persons ($F[1,80] = 38.20$, $p < .0001$) and actions ($F[1,80] = 6.45$, $p < .02$) being reported. There were no significant differences found as a function of interview type for details about surroundings and objects. These findings in part support hypothesis 2, as the CI elicited more correct recall about actions (but not objects). The accuracy of the information was very similar across detail types as a function of interview (CI/SI respectively: actions, 84%/82%; objects, 79%/78%; surroundings, 79%/79%; and persons, 65%/72%).

From what phase in the interview did these effects arise?

The interview was subdivided into three recall phases; (1) free recall, (2) questioning, and (3) second retrieval attempt (reverse order recall for the CI, and motivated second retrieval attempt for the SI) to find out which phase(s) demonstrated the enhanced recall of the CI. Children interviewed with a CI recalled significantly more correct information in the questioning phase of the interview ($F[1,80] = 20.78$, $p < .0001$) than those interviewed with an SI. However, the CI had no effect on the free recall or second retrieval attempt phases of the interview. Nevertheless, nearly half of all the correct recall elicited across the whole interview occurred during the free recall phase regardless of interview type (i.e. 43% for the CI and 50% for the SI). These findings support hypothesis 3, as the CI elicited more correct recall in questioning. Percentage accuracy per interview phase was also examined. The free recall phase produced the most reliable information (89% CI; 89% SI) while the questioning phase (72% CI; 70% SI) produced the least reliable information (second retrieval phase; 81% CI; 80% SI).

Further analyses were conducted to examine variables which might explain some of the above findings (i.e. interview length, questions used by the interviewers, and interviewee ability).

Interview measures

The CIs took significantly longer than the SIs (CI $M = 19$ minutes and SI $M = 11$ minutes; $F[1,80] = 48.99$, $p < .0001$). As the duration of the interview increased so did the number of correct details recalled ($r = .55$, $p < .0001$). However, all interviewees, regardless of interview condition, received the same instructions regarding interview time (i.e. as much time as they wanted). Analysis of covariance, with interview length as the covariate, found no significant difference in total correct recall (across the whole interview) as a function of interview type.

The questions asked in both interview conditions were divided into six categories; open-ended, closed, leading, misleading, forced-choice, and multiple questions. Analysis was also carried out on the total number of questions asked. Over the whole interview, interviewers in the CI condition asked significantly more questions than in the SI condition ($F[1,80] = 80.02$, $p < .0001$; CI $M = 38$; SI $M = 14$ questions per interview). (However, the number of questions did not significantly correlate with the amount of correct recall elicited in the CI.) Ninety-one per cent of the questions asked by all interviewers were predominantly good question types (i.e. open-ended and non-biasing closed questions).

Abilities

There were no significant differences across interview type for children's scores on the subtest of WISC. However, these scores were, as expected, significantly correlated across both groups with the amount of correct details recalled ($r = .23$, $p < .04$).

How vulnerable are children to suggestive questions?

We now turn to the results that concern the suggestibility data which examined the vulnerability of children to suggestion, whether the CI helps children to resist the effects of poor questioning, the relation of this to their recall, and whether scripts play a role in susceptibility of children to poor questioning.

Children were misled by 41% of the misleading questions (i.e. gave an incorrect response/yield), actively resisted 38% of these questions (i.e. gave a correct response), and responded with 'I don't know' to 21%. With regard to leading questions, children gave a correct response to 92% of this category of question, actively resisted (i.e. gave an incorrect response) to 7% of these questions, and responded with 'I don't know' to 1% of these questions.

Did the CI help children to resist the effects of suggestive questions?

Misleading questions

When looking at the *misled* variable (i.e. yield), it was found that children were significantly more misled if they answered the questions before an interview of any sort ($F[1,75] = 4.17, p < .04$) with no significant interaction effects with interview type (CI/SI) and presentation place (before or after the interview). However, when examining the *not misled* variable (i.e. resistance) (see Table 4.2), not only were children more resistant after any interview ($F[1,75] = 6.23, p < .01$), there was also a significant interaction effect ($F[1,75] = 6.62, p < .01$) with children interviewed by a CI being more resistant to misleading questions but only when these misleading questions were presented after the CI. Thus, there is evidence to support hypothesis 4, that children will be more resistant to misleading questions presented after a CI. The *'don't know'* responses to misleading questions were also examined and no significant main or interaction effects were present.

Leading questions

No significant effects were found as a function of interview type and presentation place for any of the three dependent variables of led, not led and 'don't know'.

Neutral questions

Children responded correctly to 74% of the neutral questions asked, incorrectly to 10%, confabulated to 12%, and responded 'don't know' to 3%. No significant main or interaction effects for interview type and presentation place were found for neutral questions.

Did children's recall have an effect on their responses to subsequent suggestive questioning?

Since it was found that having an interview (especially a CI) increased children's resistance to the effects of subsequent misleading questions, correlational analyses (Pearson's product moment) were conducted on the association between their interview recall data and their responses to the subsequent pre-set list of questions.

Table 4.2 Percentage resistance to misleading questions as a function of interview type and presentation place

Interview type	*Presentation place*	
	Before interview	*After interview*
Cognitive	34	50
Structured	35	36

(Those children who received their questions before their interview are, of course, not included in this analysis. Relevant analysis for them is presented below.) This analysis was carried out to see if the children's recall in the interview phase of the study had any relationship with their responses to the suggestive questions. The analysis took the form of correlating each type of response to the pre-set list of questions (e.g. 'misled', 'not misled', etc.) with all the interview recall categories (i.e. correct, incorrect and confabulations, etc.). Only the significant correlations are presented.

It was found that the more correct information the child recalled in their initial interview the fewer incorrect responses they gave to subsequent misleading questions ($r = -.33, p < .04$) and the more resistant they were to such misleading information ($r = .31, p < .05$). In addition, the amount of incorrect details reported in the initial interview significantly related to the amount of incorrect responses they gave to subsequent misleading questions ($r = .31, p < .04$). Thus, the child's initial reporting of the event had a relationship with how they responded to subsequently asked misleading questions.

Did script consistency/inconsistency have an effect on children's responses to leading and misleading questions?

Misleading questions

As Table 4.3 shows, for misleading questions children gave more incorrect responses to script-consistent than to script-inconsistent questions ($F[1,77] = 396.13$, $p < .0001$) and were less resistant to script-consistent than to script-inconsistent misleading questions ($F[1,77] = 165.87, p < .0001$). Thus, hypothesis 5 was supported. Children gave more 'don't know' responses to misleading script-inconsistent questions ($F[1,77] = 25.86, p < .0001$). One three-way interaction effect emerged for interview type, presentation place and script consistency for misled responses to misleading questions ($F[1,77] = 5.84, p < .018$), where *post hoc* analysis (Tukey) found that the CI increased resistance to misleading questions effect emanates from higher resistance to script-consistent misleading questions.

Table 4.3 Percentage responses to misleading and leading questions as a function of script consistency

Response	*Script consistency*	
	Consistent	*Inconsistent*
Misled	64	18
Not misled	22	56
'Don't know'	14	27
Led	90	95
Not led	10	4
'Don't know'	1	1

Leading questions

Children gave more correct responses to leading questions that were script-inconsistent than to script-consistent leading questions ($F[1,69] = 5.97$, $p < .02$) and gave fewer incorrect responses to script-inconsistent than to script-consistent leading questions ($F[1,69] = 7.90$, $p < .006$). (See Table 4.3.)

Thus script inconsistency occasioned more resistance to misleading questions. Furthermore, the enhanced CI resistance effect reported above seems to be accounted for by script-consistent misleading questions, which are the very questions children are most vulnerable to.

Did those children who were given the suggestions before the interview intrude any such information into their subsequent interviews?

Misleading questions

It was found that children who received the questions before their interview produced 30 recall errors in their subsequent interviews that could have resulted from the prior misleading questions. The children who received the misleading questions after their interview had 12 errors that 'related' to the misleading questions but could not have been caused by the questions because these children had not yet had the questions (here this latter group is being used as a control group). A binomial test was conducted on these error data and no significant effect of interview place (i.e. before or after the questions) was found. These errors were then subdivided into script-consistent and script-inconsistent intrusions and it was found that there were more script-consistent intrusions for those who received the misleading questions before the interview compared to script-inconsistent ones ($p < .03$). There was no effect of interview type.

Leading questions

It was found for the children who had the leading questions before their interview that there were 147 pieces of correct recall that could have related to the prior questions. For those children who had the questions after their recall there were 95 such pieces of information in their recall. A binomial test was conducted on these data and it was found that children who were given the leading information before the interview did to a significantly greater extent include this information into their subsequent interview compared with the control ($p < .03$). In addition, significantly more script-inconsistent inclusions occurred for those who received the leading questions before the interview compared with the control ($p < .003$). There was one significant effect for interview type, with those children who received the script-inconsistent leading questions before the CI including more of this correct information into their interviews ($p < .03$), compared to those in the SI group.

Thus children did not intrude much information relating to prior erroneous questions into their subsequent interviews (the minority which did tended to intrude script-consistent information). Children did, however, use prior leading information (i.e. correct information) as a memory prompt (i.e. recalled more correct information relating to the prior questions), especially in the CI condition and when the information was script-inconsistent.

Discussion

CI effects

As predicted, it was found that the children who were interviewed using a CI recalled significantly more correct information than those interviewed using an SI. Furthermore, the CI did not significantly increase the reporting of incorrect or confabulated details. The 21% enhancement of correct recall with the CI is similar to that previously found with children when no practice interview was used (e.g. 21% reported by Geiselman & Padilla, 1988; 26% in Saywitz, Geiselman, & Bornstein, 1992). The percentage accuracy of the information obtained with the CI is similar to that which is found in other research, which is typically above 80% for the CI.

All detail types are of investigatory value. However, the fact that the CI in this study increased the reporting of person information is extremely positive as witnesses, especially children, have been found to have difficulty spontaneously reporting such information (e.g. Ochsner *et al.*, 1999). The CI as expected was found to increase the reporting of actions, as has been found by prior research (Granhag & Spjut, 2001; Memon *et al.*, 1997). Whilst the accuracy of reports concerning actions is typically high, it has often been found to be much lower for information about persons (see Memon & Vartoukin, 1996). Again, in the present study, accuracy for person details was lower than that for action details (69% vs. 83%).

As in Memon *et al.* (1997) and Granhag & Spjut's (2001) research the enhancement effect of the CI arose from the questioning phase of the interview. This is an important finding because even if practitioners rush into the questioning phase of an interview (Davies *et al.*, 1995), if the interview is a CI then there may still be enhancement effects found. Nevertheless, it should be noted that approximately half of the total correct recall reported occurred in the free report phase, whereas the majority of the erroneous details were reported in questioning. Overall it was the free report phase which produced the most reliable information, followed by the second retrieval attempt, with questioning producing the least reliable. This parallels the work which has found that the number of details reported increases with cue specificity, but so do the number of incorrect details reported (Lamb *et al.*, 1996).

The present study has also demonstrated that the more recall attempts someone has at remembering an event, the more information is reported. It was found that 12% of all the correct information reported across the interview was reported in the second retrieval attempt (i.e. after free recall and questioning) without significantly increasing the number of incorrect or confabulated details reported. However, the amount of recall in this phase of the interview was not significantly different across interview conditions (i.e. reverse order recall did not elicit more information than a motivated second retrieval attempt). The children, however, did not have difficulty using this CI technique, when prompts were used to avoid the great leaps back in time, and the reverse order recall instruction did not increase the reporting of erroneous information (see Milne & Bull, 2002, for similar findings). Thus, this technique should not be omitted as a matter of course from the CI for use with child witnesses, as it often is (McCauley & Fisher, 1995).

Importantly, and from an applied perspective, we have found that the CI elicits more recall than the interview which is currently being practised in the UK when interviewing children for legal purposes (i.e. the SI used in this study). However, the CI did take significantly longer to conduct and more questions were asked than in the SI. This time and question factor has been found in other research (see Memon *et al.*, 1996b). However, it must be noted that the CI instructions, especially context reinstatement, take longer to administer than the instructions used in the SI condition and, as the CI elicits more recall, there are more probing questions (open and closed) required.

Suggestion

Children were found to answer the majority of leading questions (inferring the correct response) correctly (93%) and these responses were unaffected by interview type. However, we do not know whether we are triggering the interviewee's memory or whether he/she is responding correctly out of compliance. If children are answering these questions primarily out of compliance then this is worrying, as investigators require only what children actually remember about an incident. On the other hand, even if leading questions were predominantly being used to help trigger memory, this could lead to an increased susceptibility to subsequently asked misleading questions. This is because their use could help to compound the view that the interviewer is knowledgeable about the event. Future research needs to examine the cumulative effects of misleading and leading questions.

When presented with misleading questions, children more often than not responded incorrectly. Thus, it is necessary to develop techniques to help inoculate children against these negative effects. In this study, children's susceptibility to misleading questions was less after being interviewed, and especially after being interviewed with a CI. It was also found that there was a relationship between prior recall and the children's responses to subsequently asked misleading questions (see also Candel *et al.*, 2000; Memon *et al.*, 1996a). The reason for the heightened resistance after a CI is as yet unknown. One suggestion is that, if it is assumed that the CI results in more extensive search and more effective retrieval strategies, a child interviewed using a CI may be more able to discriminate original event details from misinformation, through more effective source monitoring (Johnson, Hashtroudi, & Lindsay, 1993). Alternatively, it could be that the CI helps children to realize that an adult is not a reliable source of information, as the 'transfer control' instruction explicitly informs the child that the interviewer has no knowledge and this renders them less vulnerable to social compliance.

Interestingly, those children who were presented with the misleading information prior to their interviews did not tend to intrude this erroneous information into their subsequent interviews. It is believed (Endres *et al.*, 1999) that the interviewee initially accepts the misleading information in order to fill in the gap in memory concerning that particular aspect of the event. Indeed, we found that when children did intrude misleading information into their subsequent interviews it was more likely to be script-consistent. It could be that the children *initially* agree to the misleading information out of compliance either because they want to please the interviewer (Lepore & Sesco, 1994), or because they consider an adult a reliable source of information (Leichtman & Ceci, 1995), or they do not realize that the interviewer has no knowledge of the event and cannot help in answering the questions (Mulder & Vrij, 1996). The fact that children gave more 'I don't know' responses to misleading questions presented prior to the interview, and were more resistant to such questions after the interview, again points to 'social' explanations of suggestibility. After an interview when, perhaps, children have gained some confidence in themselves through recall (see Vrij & Bush, 2000, for a relationship between confidence and suggestibility), have become familiar with the interview situation, and feel more at ease with the interviewer through rapport (i.e. a more equal interviewee–interviewer relationship has been established), they are now more comfortable and thus are more likely openly to resist the interviewer's suggestions.

Children were less resistant and responded less accurately to misleading questions which were consistent with their scripts of a magic show (see Dawson & Roberts, 1995). This parallels research which has found that memory for highly consistent script details seems to be more susceptible to error and distortion (Pezdek & Roe, 1997). It seems reasonable to assume that when presented with a misleading question the child needs to decide how to respond, either with (1) resistance, (2) compliance, or (3) saying 'I don't know'. When the misleading question provides information, though erroneous, which is compatible with the child's script of the event, it is more likely that s/he will decide to comply, especially when there is no competing information available (Endres *et al.*, 1999). Interestingly, the CI was more likely to help children to resist misleading script-consistent questions. The CI therefore helps to inoculate children against the very questions they are most vulnerable to.

In conclusion, the CI has been found to increase the reporting of correct information, concerning persons and actions, particularly in the questioning phase of the interview. The CI has also been found to help children to resist the effects of subsequently asked misleading questions. This is important, as the *Memorandum of Good Practice* (Home Office and Department of Health, 1992) suggests the use of suggestive questions as a last resort, at the end of the interview. If this interview is a CI, resistance to erroneous suggestions is enhanced. Future research should attempt to examine this effect further, as this study is not without its limitations (for instance, using a video clip as an event). Children were found to be most susceptible to misleading script-consistent questions. This is an important finding and leads us to suggest that it is imperative for investigators to be particularly careful in asking such questions of children who are victims/witnesses of scripted events (e.g. long-term abuse). However, more ecologically valid research is now needed in this sphere.

Acknowledgements

The authors would like to thank Prof. Gunter Koehnken and Dr. Amina Memon for their advice and assistance as the first author's second and third PhD supervisors. We are also grateful to all the participants for their help, to the staff at the schools (Wimborne Middle School and Arundel Court Middle School), and to our interviewers. In addition, we would like to thank two anonymous reviewers for their helpful comments on an earlier draft of this paper.

Appendix A: Cognitive and structured interviews (*Italics* = *CI* only)

Phase 1 Greet and establish rapport

Phase 2 Explain the aims of the interview

Report everything
Transfer control
No fabrication or guessing
Concentrate hard
Context reinstatement
Initiate free report

Phase 3 'Remember more' prompt

Phase 4 Questioning

Activate and probe an image
Child-compatible questioning
Report everything
Open and closed questions
No fabrication or guessing
OK to say 'don't know'

Phase 5 Motivated second retrieval/Reverse *order recall*

Phase 6 Closure

Appendix B: Pre-set list of questions

1 The magician said abracadabra didn't he?
2 What colour was the magician's cloak?
3 What was the magician's dog's name?
4 The carpet in the room was red wasn't it?

5 What was your favourite trick?
6 What colour were the flowers that the magician used?
7 The magician didn't make the dolls disappear did he?
8 The magician wasn't wearing a hat was he?
9 What was the magician's face like?
10 What colour was the rabbit that the magician pulled out of the hat?
11 One of the children who helped the magician held the torn playing card didn't he?
12 How many swords did the magician use?
13 What was the last trick the magician did?
14 The magician did a card trick didn't he?
15 The magician didn't have a real gun did he?
16 Was the magician's right or left eye covered with an eye-patch?
17 The magician was wearing a jacket wasn't he?
18 The children in the video were as quiet as mice weren't they?
19 The magician had his tricks on a table didn't he?
20 Where did the magic show take place?

References

Brainerd, C., & Reyna, V. F. (1990). Gist in the grist: Fuzzy-trace theory and the new intuitionism. *Developmental Review*, *10*, 3–47.

Bull, R. (1992). Obtaining evidence expertly: Investigative interviews with child witnesses. *Expert Evidence*, *1*, 5–12.

Bull, R. (1996). Good practice from video recorded interviews with child witnesses for use in criminal proceedings. In G. Davies, S. Lloyd-Bostock, M. McMurran, & C. Wilson (Eds.), *Psychology, law and criminal justice*. Berlin: de Gruyter.

Candel, I., Merckelbach, H., & Muris, P. (2000). Measuring interrogative suggestibility in children: Reliability and validity of the Bonn Test of statement suggestibility. *Psychology, Crime and Law*, *6*, 61–70.

Ceci, S. J., & Bruck, M. (1993). Suggestibility of the child witness: A historical review and synthesis. *Psychological Bulletin*, *113*, 403–439.

Ceci, S., & Bruck, M. (1995). *Jeopardy in the courtroom: A scientific analysis of children's testimony*. Washington, DC: American Psychological Association.

Clifford, B. R., & George, R. (1996). A field investigation of training in three methods of witness/victim investigative interviewing. *Psychology, Crime and Law*, *2*, 231–248.

Davies, G. M. (1994). Children's testimony: Research findings and policy implications. *Psychology, Crime and Law*, *1*, 175–180.

Davies, G. M., Wilson, C., Mitchell, R., & Milsom, J. (1995). *Videotaping children's evidence: An evaluation*. London: HMSO.

Dawson, S., & Roberts, K. P. (1995). *Children's memory for television: Is it script-based?* Paper presented at the British Psychological Society Developmental Section Conference, Glasgow.

Endres, J., Poggenpohl, C., & Erben, C. (1999). Repetitions, warnings, and video: Cognitive and motivational components in pre-school children's suggestibility. *Legal and Criminological Psychology*, *4*, 129–146.

Finger, M., Nitschke, N., & Koehnken, G. (1992). *Criteria based content analysis and the cognitive interview*. Poster presented at the NATO Advanced Study Institute: The child witness in context: Cognitive, social and legal perspectives, La Lucca.

Geiselman, R. E., Fisher, R. P., Cohen, G., Holland, H. L., & Surtes, L. (1986). Eyewitness responses to leading and misleading questions under the cognitive interview. *Journal of Police Science and Administration, 14*, 31–39.

Geiselman, R. E., & Padilla, J. (1988). Cognitive interviewing with child witnesses. *Journal of Police Science and Administration, 16*, 236–242.

Granhag, P., & Spjut, E. (2001). Children's recall of the unfortunate fakir: A further test of the enhanced cognitive interview. In R. Roesch, R. R. Corrado, & R. J. Dempster (Eds.), *Psychology in the courts: International advances in knowledge*. Amsterdam: Harwood Academic.

Gudjonsson, G. H., & Clare, I. C. H. (1995). The relationship between confabulation and intellectual ability, memory, interrogative suggestibility and acquiescence. *Personality and Individual Differences, 19*, 333–338.

Gudjonsson, G. H., & Clark, N. K. (1986). Suggestibility in police interrogation: A social psychological model. *Social Behaviour, 1*, 83–104.

Hayes, B. K., & Delamothe, K. (1997). Cognitive interviewing procedures and suggestibility in children's recall. *Journal of Applied Psychology, 82*, 562–577.

Heydon, J. (1984). *Evidence, cases and materials*. London: Butterworths.

Home Office and Department of Health. (1992). *Memorandum of good practice for video recorded interviews with child witnesses for criminal proceedings*. London: HMSO.

Home Office and Department of Health. (2001). *Achieving best evidence in criminal proceedings: Guidance for vulnerable or intimidated witnesses, including children*. London: HMSO.

Hutcheson, G. D., Baxter, J. S., Telfer, K., & Warden, D. (1995). Child witness statement quality: Question type and errors of omission. *Law and Human Behavior, 19*, 631–648.

Johnson, M. K., Hashtroudi, S., & Lindsay, D. S. (1993). Source monitoring. *Psychological Bulletin, 114*, 3–28.

Koehnken, G., Milne, R., Memon, A., & Bull, R. (1999). The cognitive interview: A meta-analysis. *Psychology, Crime and Law, 5*, 3–28.

Lamb, M. E., Hershkowitz, I., Sternberg, K. J., Esplin, P. W., Hovav, M., Manor, T., & Yudilevitch, L. (1996). Effects of investigative utterance types on Israeli children's responses. *International Journal of Behavioral Development, 19*, 627–637.

Leichtman, M. D., & Ceci, S. J. (1995). The effects of stereotype and suggestions on preschoolers' reports. *Developmental Psychology, 31*, 568–578.

Lepore, S. J., & Sesco, B. (1994). Distorting children's reports and interpretations of events through suggestion. *Journal of Applied Psychology, 79*, 108–120.

Lindsay, D. S., & Johnson, M. K. (1989). The eyewitness suggestibility effect and memory for source. *Memory and Cognition, 17*, 349–358.

Loftus, E. F., & Ketcham, K. (1991). *Witness for the defense*. New York, NY: St. Martin's Press.

McCauley, M. R., & Fisher, R. P. (1995). Facilitating children's recall with the revised cognitive interview. *Journal of Applied Psychology, 80*, 510–516.

Memon, A., Cronin, O., Eaves, R., & Bull, R. (1993). The cognitive interview and child witnesses. In G. M. Stephenson & N. K. Clark (Eds.), *Children, evidence and procedure*. Leicester: British Psychological Society.

Memon, A., Holley, A., Wark, L., Bull, R., & Koehnken, G. (1996a). Reducing suggestibility in child witness interviews. *Applied Cognitive Psychology, 10*, 416–432.

Memon, A., Wark, L., Holley, A., Bull, R., & Koehnken, G. (1996b). Interviewer behaviour in investigative interviews. *Psychology, Crime and Law, 3*, 135–155.

Memon, A., & Vartoukin, R. (1996). The effects of repeated questioning on young children's eyewitness testimony. *British Journal of Psychology, 87*, 403–415.

Memon, A., Wark, L., Bull, R., & Koehnken, G. (1997). Isolating the effects of the cognitive interview techniques. *British Journal of Psychology*, *88*, 179–197.

Milne, R., & Bull, R. (1999). *Investigative interviewing: Psychology and practice*. Chichester: Wiley.

Milne, R., & Bull, R. (2002). Back to basics: A componential analysis of the original cognitive interview mnemonics with three age groups. *Applied Cognitive Psychology*, *16*, 1–11.

Milne, R., & Bull, R. (2004). Interviewing by the police. In D. Carson & R. Bull (Eds.), *Handbook of psychology in legal contexts* (2nd ed.). Chichester: Wiley.

Mulder, M. R., & Vrij, A. (1996). Explaining conversation rules to children: An intervention study to facilitate children's accurate responses. *Child Abuse and Neglect*, *20*, 623–631.

Nelson, K., & Gruendel, J. (1981). Generalised event representations: Basic building blocks of cognitive development. In M. E. Lamb & A. L. Brown (Eds.), *Advances in developmental psychology* (Vol. 1). Hillsdale, NJ: Erlbaum.

Ochsner, J. E., Zaragoza, M. S., & Mitchell, K. J. (1999). The accuracy and suggestibility of children's memory for neutral and criminal eyewitness events. *Legal and Criminological Psychology*, *4*, 79–92.

Pezdek, K., & Roe, C. (1997). The suggestibility of children's memory for being touched: Planting, erasing and changing memories. *Law and Human Behavior*, *21*, 95–106.

Poole, D., & Lamb, M. (1998). *Investigative interviews of children: A guide for helping professionals*. Washington, DC: American Psychological Association.

Rudy, L., & Goodman, G. S. (1991). Effects of participation on children's reports. *Developmental Psychology*, *27*, 527–538.

Saywitz, K. J., Geiselman, R. E., & Bornstein, G. K. (1992). Effects of cognitive interviewing and practice on children's recall performance. *Journal of Applied Psychology*, *77*, 744–756.

Steward, M. S., Bussey, K., Goodman, G. S., & Saywitz, K. J. (1993). Implications for the developmental research for interviewing children. *Child Abuse and Neglect*, *17*, 25–37.

Tulving, E., & Thomson, D. M. (1973). Encoding specificity and retrieval processes in episodic memory. *Psychological Review*, *80*, 353–370.

Vrij, A., & Bush, N. (2000). Differences in suggestibility between 5–6 and 10–11 year olds: The relationship with self-confidence. *Psychology, Crime and Law*, *6*, 127–138.

Wark, L., Memon, A., Koehnken, G., & Bull, R. (1995). *Uses and abuses of schematic knowledge*. University of Southampton, Department of Psychology Working Paper RWPS/1995/1.

5 The enhanced cognitive interview: expressions of uncertainty, motivation and its relation with report accuracy

Rui M. Paulo, Pedro B. Albuquerque and Ray Bull

Introduction

As several researchers (Fisher & Geiselman, 1992; Prescott, Milne, & Clark, 2011) have acknowledged over the years, interviewing witnesses is a key procedure that frequently determines the outcome of a police investigation. However, memory is not so accurate and what witnesses actually report rarely corresponds fully with what they remember (Bower, 1967), particularly when inadequate interviewing techniques are used (Flin, Boon, Knox, & Bull, 1992).

To address this issue, Geiselman et al. (1984) developed the Cognitive Interview (CI). The CI originally included four cognitive mnemonics: report everything, mental reinstatement of context, change order, and change perspective. The report everything mnemonic consists of instructing witnesses to report everything they can remember, whether it seems trivial or not (Fisher & Geiselman, 2010). The mental reinstatement of context consists of asking witnesses to mentally recreate the to-be-recalled event, as well as their physiological, cognitive, and emotional states at the time of the crime. Lastly, the change order (asking the witness to recall the event in a different chronological order – e.g. reverse order) and change perspective mnemonics (to recall the event from a different perspective – e.g. report what the witness saw from another witness' point of view) can be used to try to obtain information that has not yet been recalled. A few years later, this was further developed by Fisher & Geiselman (1992) as the Enhanced Cognitive Interview (ECI). Several social and communicative components, such as rapport building, witness-compatible questioning, transferring control of the interview to the witness and mental imagery, crucial for conducting good investigative interviews, were added (see Fisher & Geiselman, 1992 or Paulo, Albuquerque, & Bull, 2013, for more information about the ECI mnemonics and components, as well as the theory underlying such procedures [Tulving, 1991; Tulving & Thomson, 1973]).

As Paulo et al. (2013) also reviewed, the ECI has been found to be effective in different countries (e.g. the USA, UK, Australia, Brazil), with different types of witness (e.g. children, adults, elderly), with various delays between the crime and the interview (e.g. minutes to weeks), with a variety of events (e.g. crime, traffic accident, phone call), both in laboratory and field studies. These studies consistently showed that this interview technique increases the amount of correct information recalled by witnesses, while maintaining accuracy, i.e. the amount of correct items of information proportionate to all recalled items of information. Such a finding is commonly referred to as the ECI superiority effect (Akehurst, Milne, & Koehnken, 2003; Aschermann, Mantwill, & Koehnken, 1991; Campos & Alonso-Quecuty, 1999; Dando & Milne, 2010; Higham & Memon, 1999; Koehnken, Milne, Memon, & Bull, 1999; Memon, Holley, Wark, Bull, & Koehnken, 1997; Rivard, Fisher, Robertson, & Mueller, 2014; Stein & Memon, 2006). As mentioned above, most of the ECI research is focused on how to increase the amount of produced information without decreasing report accuracy. Nonetheless, actually increasing or evaluating report accuracy, i.e. the proportion of correct details in a given statement, is also crucial for police investigations (Milne & Bull, 1999). It could be very valuable if it could be determined which part of the recalled information is more likely to be correct and which may be incorrect. One of the most promising methods to achieve this goal could be to use metacognitive techniques for monitoring recall (Evans & Fisher, 2010).

Metacognition refers to what we know about our own cognition and how we can use such knowledge to regulate cognition, as well as what we know about our own memory and mnemonic strategies (metamemory), and how we can use such knowledge to improve our memory, particularly, in terms of quality (Metcalfe & Shimamura, 1996). In fact, research on metacognition contributed to researchers changing their focus from improving report quantity to improving report quality (Koriat & Goldsmith, 1996). Subsequently, several studies addressed how metacognitive techniques can be used to improve or evaluate witnesses' accuracy (Higham, Luna, & Bloomfield, 2010; Roberts & Higham, 2002). For the purpose of the present study, we will focus on three of those techniques: confidence judgments; frequency judgments; and report option.

Several studies suggest that in some situations, such as selections from lineups (Brewer, Weber, Wootton, & Lindsay, 2012; Lindsay et al., 2013), cued recall (Luna & Martín-Luengo, 2012), or free recall (Allwood, Ask, & Granhag, 2005), and when using the adequate measures – calibration approach (Luna & Martín-Luengo, 2012), a positive relationship between confidence and accuracy can be found. Therefore, higher accuracy for a given response can be expected when witnesses are more confident that this response is accurate. However, only two studies have focused on how this procedure can be used to evaluate ECI report accuracy (Allwood et al., 2005; Roberts & Higham, 2002). These authors interviewed witnesses with either the ECI or a Structured Interview (SI), which is very similar to the ECI, but does not include some of its cognitive and social components (see 'Methods' section). Afterwards, they asked participants to provide confidence judgments for a small portion of their statements, using a numerical rating scale. Using this procedure, witnesses were able to distinguish between more and less accurate information, regardless of the interview condition. Therefore, the statement portions assigned with high confidence were more accurate than the full set of statements. However, these studies focus on metacognitive procedures that are applied after the interview is conducted. After finishing the interview, a small portion of the witness' report, which is selected by the interviewer, is rated in terms of confidence judgments. From this, two main concerns can be identified. First, numerical confidence judgments, performed after the interview has been conducted do not reflect witnesses' capacity to spontaneously differentiate statements that are less likely to be correct in a natural fashion (O'Hagan et al., 2006). Second, such procedures require a considerable amount of the interviewer's time, for instance, for applying these scales and selecting the limited information which will be evaluated by the interviewee. Therefore, it is difficult to use such procedures, in a holistic manner, in a real police interview setting.

Asking witnesses to predict how many items of information are correct, or wrong, for a given part of their statement (frequency judgments) could be a less time demanding approach to evaluate report accuracy (Gigerenzer, Hoffrage, & Kleinbölting, 1991; Liberman, 2004; Sniezek & Buckley, 1991). However, several studies questioned the accuracy of frequency judgments in interview settings. For instance, Granhag, Jonsson, & Allwood (2004) interviewed participants with either the ECI or an SI, and subsequently asked them to answer 45 forced-choice questions and give a confidence judgment for each question. Participants were then asked to provide a frequency judgment (how many questions they had answered correctly) and the authors found that participants severely underestimated their actual performance. Paulo, Albuquerque, Saraiva, & Bull (2015) evaluated if witnesses were able to perform accurate frequency judgments for each interview phase as well as for overall recall, during an investigative interview. These authors presented the same (mock) crime recording to two groups of participants and interviewed them with either an ECI or an SI. After each interview phase (e.g. free recall, questioning phase, second retrieval, etc.), they asked participants to estimate their error rate for that particular phase (frequency judgment). The same question was asked at the end of the interview for overall recall. Regardless of the interview phase, both groups were unable to successfully evaluate their error rate, there being no association between participants' frequency judgments and participants 'real' error rate.

Other studies (Evans & Fisher, 2010; Koriat & Goldsmith, 1996) suggest that witnesses can improve their accuracy by using other metacognitive control techniques, namely exercising 'report option' or adjusting 'report precision'. Exercising 'report option' refers to giving witnesses an opportunity to withhold information. For instance, if the witness is not sure about her ability to accurately answer a question, or to recall part of the event, she can withhold such information – e.g. say 'I do not remember'. Using this procedure, witnesses seem to be capable of withholding more unreliable information, and maintaining the reliable recall, consequently improving report accuracy. Accordingly, most interview protocols, including the ECI and SI, instruct witnesses not to guess when they do not know the answer to a question or do not recall part of the event. However, there are more levels of confidence between a 'full guess' (e.g. I assume he had a black shirt because robbers always wear black shirts) and a 'full certainty' (e.g. I'm sure the robber had a black shirt). For instance, witnesses commonly use spontaneous verbal expressions of uncertainty (e.g. I think, maybe, I believe, etc.) to report somewhat uncertain information. ECI research (Dando & Milne, 2010; Prescott et al., 2011) usually disregards such expressions in the coding and analysis. Thus, 'I think the robber had a gun' would (for example) simply be coded as 'the robber had a gun'. Instead of disregarding such qualifications, the interviewer could ask witnesses to withhold all 'uncertainties' (e.g. I think the robber had a black shirt) in order to increase report accuracy. However, such an instruction may have several problems: (1) it is somewhat incompatible with the 'report everything' mnemonic. In the same way that 'irrelevant' recall might activate 'relevant' recall (Tulving, 1991), an 'uncertainty' might activate a 'certainty'. Therefore, asking witnesses to withhold such information might undermine report length; (2) even though the participant is not sure about that particular information ('uncertainty') the interviewer might have other methods to verify the accuracy of such information (e.g. other witnesses' reports, crime scene analysis, etc.). This could lead to the omission of very valuable information; and (3) research has not yet evaluated if items of information that are spontaneously preceded, or followed (e.g. the robber had a black shirt, I think), by wording that expresses uncertainty ('uncertainties') differ, in terms of accuracy, from items of information not preceded/followed by such wording ('certainties').

To evaluate if spontaneous verbal expressions of uncertainty can be used to evaluate and improve report accuracy, we decided to treat these two separately, and test: (a) if 'certainties' would involve greater accuracy than 'uncertainties' and (b) if the ECI superiority effect over an SI (in terms of quantity of information) does not affect other parameters, such as the proportion of 'uncertainties' or the accuracy of such information. To date, no study has evaluated if witnesses are able to perform spontaneous real-time memory monitoring for their account. This is crucial because, if witnesses are able to spontaneously discriminate less reliable information while reporting the crime, differentiating 'uncertainties' from 'certainties' can be an easy, intuitive, and time-saving way (O'Hagan et al., 2006) to differentiate less reliable information ('uncertainties') from more reliable information ('certainties').

Another method to improve, and estimate, report accuracy might involve witnesses' perception of their own motivation during the interview. Two studies (Read, Powell, Kebbell, & Milne, 2009; Walsh & Bull, 2011) recently acknowledged that witnesses' perceptions toward the interview process might determine how rapport is established and maintained throughout the interview, which might be crucial during investigative interviews and associated with better recall (Vallano & Compo, 2015). Fisher & Geiselman (2010) also suggested that interviewing witnesses involves more than mere use of cognitive techniques. They recognize the need for more studies addressing witnesses' attitudes toward the interview process and the interviewer, which is a topic that has so far received very little attention from researchers. Recent findings (Ballardin, Stein, & Milne, 2013) suggest that witness' perceptions, such as the perception of interviewer effort and the perception of their own motivation during the interview can have a major influence on the outcome of the investigative interview. However, it is important to understand how these perceptions can influence witnesses' report, for instance, in terms of report accuracy (Fisher & Geiselman, 2010). To our knowledge, such research questions have not yet been addressed. Therefore, the present study examined how witnesses' perceptions can influence their report. We focused on whether witnesses' perception of their own motivation was related to their recall in terms of report accuracy because, as previously mentioned, improving report accuracy is the main focus of our study. If more motivated witnesses achieve better report accuracy, promoting witnesses' motivation can be another possible method to further increase report quality.

Overall, our main goal was to see if report accuracy can be increased, and/or estimated, through two different procedures: (1) witnesses spontaneous metacognitive judgments and (2) witnesses' perception of their own motivation. We established three main hypotheses: (1) uncertainties' will be less accurate than 'certainties', because participants will be able to monitor the information they are providing homogeneously throughout the interview (Allwood et al., 2005; Evans & Fisher, 2010; Koriat & Goldsmith, 1996; Roberts & Higham, 2002). As a result, removing 'uncertainties' from the report will increase accuracy; (2) the ECI superiority effect over an SI (in terms of quantity of information) does not affect other parameters, such as the proportion of 'uncertainties' or, as several studies suggest (Aschermann et al., 1991; Dando & Milne, 2010; Rivard et al., 2014), report accuracy. Therefore, longer reports are expected for the ECI condition as the result of using effective cognitive mnemonics to improve recall; and (3) witnesses who rate themselves as more motivated during the interview will have greater accuracy, because they are more motivated to provide a good report, and possibly will apply more effort to monitor their report through spontaneous metacognitive/metamemory techniques.

Methods

Participants

A total of 44 Portuguese psychology students, 36 females and 8 males, with an age range from 17 to 46 years old (M = 21, SD = 3) participated in this study for course credits. We used G*Power 3.1 (Faul, Erdfelder, Buchner, & Lang, 2009) to conduct power analysis based on the effect sizes reported in a recent ECI meta-analysis review (Memon, Meissner, & Fraser, 2010) to ensure that our sample size was adequate. Both interview groups had 22 participants, 18 females and 4 males each. The ECI group age ranged from 17 to 46 years old (M = 21, SD = 6) and the SI group age ranged from 18 to 34 years old (M = 21, SD = 4).

Design

A between subjects experimental design was used with interview condition as the independent variable with two levels: (1) ECI and (2) SI. The amount of reported information and accuracy was measured in information units and proportion, respectively.

Materials

The participants watched the recording on a Fujitsu L7ZA LCD computer screen. The video recording, which was edited from the second episode of the first season of the 2004 Portuguese television drama *Inspector Max* (Riccó & Riccó, 2004), was 3 minutes and 11 seconds long. This nonviolent video recording shows a male armed subject walking inside a bank and taking several hostages to carry out the robbery. He verbally and physically interacts with them, with the cashier and a police officer that later approaches the robber.

After the interview was conducted, participants were asked to evaluate their motivation during the interview ('How do you evaluate your motivation to testify during the interview?') on a seven-point Likert scale (1 – very low; 2 – low; 3 – slightly low; 4 – moderate; 5 – slightly high; 6 – high; and 7 – very high). All interviews were video and audio recorded.

Procedure

Ethics committee approval was obtained. Participants took part in two sessions. At the first session, they were randomly assigned to one of the two conditions (ECI vs. SI). Having signed a consent form after reading general information about the study, they were shown the video recording. They were asked to pay as much attention as possible to the video recording because they would be later interviewed about it. The second session took place approximately 48 hours later and each participant was interviewed with either the ECI or SI. After the interview, all participants immediately answered the question regarding motivation perception.

Interview conditions

The interview protocols employed were translated and adapted from Milne & Bull (2003) for the Portuguese language. Overall, the only differences between the ECI and SI protocols were the four cognitive mnemonics and the transfer of control instruction and mental imagery (see Table 5.1). Both interview protocols included procedures such as rapport building and appropriate questioning (e.g. witness-compatible questioning) because they are now considered an essential aspect of any investigative interview. Thus, we wanted to focus on the effect that the remaining components, only applied in the ECI condition, would have on recall. All SI procedures were also included in the ECI. Fisher & Geiselman's (1992) guidelines for conducting the ECI were followed. All the cognitive, social, and communicative components described in Fisher & Geiselman (1992) were included in the ECI protocol.

Both interview protocols enclosed seven main phases: (1) preliminary phase; (2) free report; (3) open-ended questioning; (4) second retrieval; (5) third retrieval (for new information only); (6) summary; and (7) closure.

During Phase 1 (preliminary phase), procedures such as greeting, establishing rapport, explaining the instructions, and purpose of the interview to the witness and

Table 5.1 Differences between the two interview protocols: procedures that were only applied in the ECI condition according to the interview phase

	Phase 1 Preliminary	*Phase 2 Free report*	*Phase 3 Open-ended questioning*	*Phase 4 Second retrieval*	*Phase 5 Third retrieval*	*Phase 6 Summary*
ECI	Transfer of control Report everything	Context reinstatement Report everything	Mental imagery	Change order	Change perspective	–

X: no procedure specific to the ECI.

asking not to guess were followed for both interview protocols. However, the ECI condition included the transfer of control instruction: 'you are the only one who saw the video and have the ability to report all the important information [. . .] you can tell me what happened in the order you desire and pause whenever you want'; as well as the report everything instruction: 'please tell me everything that you remember with as much detail as you can [. . .] even the details that might seem irrelevant to you, are very important to me [. . .] tell me everything that pops into your mind'.

During Phase 2 (free report), participants were asked to recall what they could remember about the video in any order and at any pace they desired. In the ECI condition, they were reminded to report everything they could remember with as much detail as possible, and mental reinstatement of context was applied:

> Try to remember the day you have watched the video [. . .] now picture the crime scene in your mind [. . .] as clear as possible [. . .] picture all the sounds [. . .] all the objects [. . .] all the people [. . .] and now focus on what happened and tell me everything you can remember.

During Phase 3 (open-ended questioning), three open-ended questions were asked to each participant according to his/her free report (e.g. Please describe the perpetrator – if the participant previously reported seeing the criminal). However, for the ECI condition, mental imagery instructions were used – e.g.

> You told me that you looked at the perpetrator when he entered the bank, because he looked very anxious. Can you please close your eyes . . ., think about everything that you remember concerning him . . ., his clothes . . ., his face . . ., his behavior . . . and when you have a full picture of him in your mind, describe everything that you can remember about him.

During Phase 4 (second retrieval), participants were asked to report what they could remember about the video once again:

> I know it may seem redundant, but it is actually highly important that you report one more time what happened on the video [. . .] report not only new

information that you might recall, but also all the information you've already reported [. . .].

In both conditions, participants were encouraged to give this second report and the importance of such procedure was explained: 'It is very important that you focus as hard as you can and tell me one more time what happened on the video.' In the ECI condition, participants were asked to recall the video in the reverse order: 'Please tell me what happened in reverse order [. . .] Focus on the last episode that you remember . . . then focus on the previous one . . . and so on [. . .]. What is the last episode that you remember?'

During Phase 5 (third retrieval), participants were asked to focus one more time on the video and try to report any new detail they could remember, if possible. In both interview conditions, the importance of such a procedure was explained and participants were encouraged to do the best they could. In the ECI condition, participants were asked to adopt a different internal perspective in order to try to remember new details: 'please focus on the event as if it was a common event at the bank, instead of a robbery, as you probably assumed before seeing the robber entering the bank'.

On Phase 6 (summary), the interviewer summarized what he understood of the witness account and asked her to correct him if he misheard, or misinterpreted, any part of the statement. He also told her to interrupt him if she/he could remember any new detail while hearing the summary. On the last phase (closure), appreciation for participants' hard work and cooperation was acknowledged and neutral topics were again discussed. These last two phases were exactly alike for both interview conditions.

Interviewer training

An expert in the ECI who had followed several qualified courses on investigative interview techniques, consisting of more than 50 hours of lectures, practice, role-playing exercises, and feedback/evaluation, conducted all the interviews. To assure that the interviewer performance was adequate and consistent across interview conditions, interview protocols were read verbatim whenever possible (e.g. open-ended questioning and summary phase need to be adapted according to the participant' previous recall) and an independent researcher, who is also an expert on human memory and forensic psychology, randomly checked 25% of the interviews, using a structured evaluation grid to evaluate verbal, and nonverbal, behavior.

Coding

Recordings of each interview were coded using the template scoring technique from Memon et al. (1997). A comprehensive list of details in the video recording was compiled and items of information were categorized as referring to: (1) person; (2) action; (3) object; (4) location; (5) conversation; and (6) sound, resulting in 378 items of information. Recalled information was classified as either correct, incorrect (e.g. saying the pistol was brown when it was black), or confabulation (mentioning a detail or event that was not present or did not happen). Also noted was the phase within the interview in which an item of information was recalled. If an item of information (correct or not) was repeated during the same, or a subsequent phase, that information was scored only the first time, it was mentioned (Prescott et al., 2011). We classified items of information as either 'certainties' or 'uncertainties'. As described above, when participants spontaneously used verbal expressions of uncertainty (e.g. I think, maybe, I believe, etc.) to report an item of information they were uncertain about, such item was classified as an 'uncertainty'. Otherwise, items of information were labeled as 'certainties'. Coders were provided with a list of Portuguese words that are commonly used to express uncertainty. They have used their best judgment to verify the intent of the participant when using this kind of expressions of uncertainty, because, in very rare situations, these expressions could be used with other purposes rather than express uncertainty. Therefore, in these exceptional cases, the adjacent information would not be rated as an 'uncertainty'. Inter-rater reliability was assessed to measure agreement on this measure, as discussed in the following section. Subjective statements or opinions were disregarded (e.g. The robber was gorgeous).

Inter-rater reliability

To assess inter-rater reliability, 11 (25%) interviews were selected randomly and scored independently by a researcher who was naive to the aims of the experiment and hypothesis, but familiar with the template method of scoring interviews and had access to the crime video. Intra-class correlation coefficients (ICCs) were calculated for correct information, incorrect information and confabulations, as well as for 'certainties' and 'uncertainties', and for the six information categories (person, action, etc.). High inter-rater reliability was found for all measures in that the values of the ICC ranged between 0.979 and 1.000, with an overall ICC of 0.992.

Results

Bonferroni corrections were applied when multiple statistical tests were conducted on a single data set, to avoid type 1 error (Field, 2013).

General recall and accuracy

It was expected that participants in the ECI condition would provide more correct items of information, in comparison with a control group (SI), without compromising accuracy. Participants in the ECI condition recalled more correct items of information ($M_{ECI} = 76$, SD = 24.71) in comparison with the control group ($M_{SI} = 58$, SD = 13.91), $t(42) = 2.96$, $p = .005$, $d = 0.89$, 95% CI [−30.11, −5.71].

As seen from Table 5.2, no differences were found between the two interviews regarding the proportion values of (i) correct recall (the ratio between the amount

Table 5.2 Proportion values (mean and SD) for correct recall, errors, and confabulations, according to the interview condition

	Correct recall	*Errors*	*Confabulations*
ECI	.86 (.07)	.09 (.04)	.05 (.04)
SI	.87 (.05)	.08 (.05)	.05 (.03)

of correct items of information recalled over all the items of information), t (42) = 0.96, p = .343, d = 0.29; (ii) errors (the ratio between the amount of errors produced over all items of information), t (42) = 1.12, p = .269, d = 0.34; and (iii) confabulations (the ratio between the amount of confabulated information over all items of information), t (42) = 0.80, p = .431, d = 0.24.

Thus, participants interviewed with the ECI were able to provide more information without increasing the proportion of errors and confabulations on their reports.

'Uncertainties' frequency

We first conducted a two-way mixed-design 2 × 5 ANOVA to see if 'uncertainties' proportion (i.e. information units which are preceded, or followed, by expressions of uncertainty over all information units) was stable across interview conditions (ECI vs. SI), and interview phases (Phase 2 vs. Phase 3 vs. Phase 4 vs. Phase 5 vs. Phase 6). Phase 1 (preliminary phase) was not included in this analysis because participants were not asked to recall information at this part of the interview.

We found no main effect of interview condition on uncertainties proportion, F (1, 12) = .09, p = .770, η_2 = 0. Therefore, our results do not suggest that participants in the ECI condition produce a higher 'uncertainties' proportion (M_{ECI} = .14, SD = .08), in comparison to the SI group (M_{SI} = .12, SD = .07). Although we found a main effect of the interview phase on 'uncertainties' proportion, F (4, 48) = 3.43, p = .02, η_2 = .21, pairwise comparisons revealed no significant differences between any of the different interview phases regarding this ($M_{phase\ 2}$ = .04; $M_{phase\ 3}$ = .14; $M_{phase\ 4}$ = .08; $M_{phase\ 5}$ = .03; $M_{phase\ 6}$ = .02). There is also no interaction effect of interview condition and interview phase on 'uncertainties' proportion, F (4, 48) = 1.04, p = .394, η_2 = .06.

Further analysis revealed that report size (total amount of details) is not associated with the proportion of produced 'uncertainties' (proportion of 'uncertainties' in a given report), r = .29, p = .06. Therefore, our study does not support that participants who are providing more information units are more uncertain about such information. There is also no correlation between the proportion of produced 'uncertainties' in a report and proportion of correct recall for the remaining recall (proportion of correct information for 'certainties' only), r = .25, p = .10. Thus, our data do not support that participants who are providing more uncertainties are simultaneously committing more errors/confabulations when recalling 'certainties'.

'Uncertainties' accuracy

The 'uncertainties' constituted a small proportion of the overall recall ($M = .13$, SD = .08). Furthermore, their exclusion from the accuracy analysis raised this proportion value from .86 (overall correct recall: amount of correct items of information over the total amount of produced items of information) to .90 (correct recall for 'certainties' only: amount of correct 'certainties' over all produced 'certainties'). Such difference was statistically significant, $t\,(43) = 7.38, p < .001, d = 1.11$, 95% CI [−.04, −.02]. Error proportion for 'certainties' only was significantly lower than overall error proportion (amount of errors over the total amount of produced items of information), $t\,(43) = 6.65, p < .001, d = 1.02$, 95% CI [−.22, −.11] and confabulation proportion for 'certainties' only was also lower than overall confabulation proportion, $t\,(43) = 3.22, p = .002, d = 0.93$, 95% CI [.03, .11]. Such results occur because, as shown in Table 5.3, correct recall proportion for 'uncertainties' is low and significantly different from correct recall proportion for 'certainties' only, $t\,(43) = 7.99, p < .001, d = 1.21$, 95% CI [.18, .30] in that .65 of 'uncertainties' were correct items of information, in comparison with 'certainties' that have a .90 correct recall rate.

Similar results were found for the ECI and SI conditions alone. The exclusion of 'uncertainties' within the ECI accuracy analysis raised this from .86 (overall proportion of correct recall) to .89 (proportion of correct recall for certainties only), $t\,(21) = 7.01, p < .001, d = 1.49$, 95% CI [−.04, −.02]. The exclusion of 'uncertainties' within the SI accuracy analyses also raised this from .87 (overall correct recall proportion) to .90 (correct recall proportion value for certainties only), $t\,(21) = 4.30, p < .001, d = 0.92$, 95% CI [−.05, −.02].

Witnesses' motivation perception

Out of a seven-point Likert scale (1 – very low; 2 – low; 3 – slightly low; 4 – moderate; 5 – slightly high; 6 – high; and 7 – very high), only the highest four levels of motivation were chosen by participants to rate their motivation, $N_{\text{moderate}} = 4$ ($N_{\text{ECI}} = 2$; $N_{\text{SI}} = 2$); $N_{\text{slightly high}} = 13$ ($N_{\text{ECI}} = 10$; $N_{\text{SI}} = 3$); $N_{\text{high}} = 21$ ($N_{\text{ECI}} = 15$; $N_{\text{SI}} = 6$); $N_{\text{very high}} = 6$ ($N_{\text{ECI}} = 4$; $N_{\text{SI}} = 2$). Procedures such as rapport building and greeting, which were part of both interview conditions, might have precluded lower levels of motivation.

We found no effect of interview condition (ECI or SI) on participants' perception of their own motivation during the interview, $U = 196, p = .245, r = .18$. However,

Table 5.3 Proportion values (mean and SD) for correct recall, errors, and confabulations for 'certainties', 'uncertainties', and both types of information together (overall)

	Correct recall	*Errors*	*Confabulations*
'Certainties'	.90 (.06)	.06 (.04)	.04 (.04)
'Uncertainties'	.65 (.21)	.23 (.19)	.12 (.15)
Overall	.86 (.06)	.09 (.04)	.05 (.04)

participants' perception of their own motivation during the interview was correlated to report accuracy, measured in correct recall proportion, $r_s = .37, p = .026$, 95% CI [.10, .68].

Since 'moderate' and 'very high' motivation levels were chosen by only a few participants ($N = 10$), we merged the two lowest levels of motivation ('moderate' and 'slightly high' motivation) and the two highest levels of motivation ('high' and 'very high' motivation) in order to have more participants in each group: 'lower' motivation ($N = 17$) and 'higher motivation' ($N = 27$). Afterwards, we conducted a *t*-test for independent samples and found that witnesses who perceived themselves as more motivated during the interview had a higher correct recall proportion ($M_{\text{high Mot}} = .88$, SD = .05) than witnesses who reported having lower levels of motivation ($M_{\text{low Mot}} = .84$, SD = .07), $t\ (42) = 2.35, p = .023, d = 0.73$, 95% CI [−.08, −.01].

Discussion

This study examined how use of witnesses' spontaneous metacognitive judgments of 'uncertainty', as well as their perception of their own motivation, could help to increase and/or evaluate report accuracy. Our major findings were that spontaneous 'uncertainties' were less accurate than 'certainties' and thus their exclusion raised overall, ECI, and SI, accuracy values. Also, witnesses who perceived themselves as more motivated during the interview had better recall accuracy.

Since ECI research is mostly focused on how to increase the amount of produced information (Milne & Bull, 1999), we focused on how to increase report accuracy. We found that participants were capable of spontaneously distinguishing more reliable information ('certainties') from less reliable information ('uncertainties'). Our results are supported by previous findings suggesting that witnesses are able to use several metacognitive techniques to monitor their own report (Allwood et al., 2005; Evans & Fisher, 2010; Koriat & Goldsmith, 1996; Roberts & Higham, 2002; Sniezek & Buckley, 1991). However, to our knowledge, this is the first study to reveal that witnesses are able to spontaneously perform real-time memory monitoring while recalling information in an interview setting. Furthermore, such results were stable across both interview conditions (ECI or SI) which is consistent with previous findings suggesting that metacognitive techniques are effective in several different situations and contexts (Allwood et al., 2005; Lindsay et al., 2013; Luna & Martín-Luengo, 2012). Such findings can have major implications for real-life investigations.

Our study is also consistent with previous research (Aschermann et al., 1991; Dando & Milne, 2010; Rivard et al., 2014) that suggests the ECI superiority effect over an SI (in terms of quantity of information) does not affect other parameters, such as the accuracy of such information and, as our study now suggests, the proportion of produced uncertainties. When confronted with consecutive retrieval attempts or instructions such as the 'report everything' mnemonic, participants could provide 'uncertain' information that they might otherwise withhold, therefore explaining the increase in recall on the ECI condition. Our study does not support this, because even though the ECI participants are providing more details, they are not eliciting a higher proportion of 'uncertainties'. Such results are highly important for ECI usage, because they suggest that more detailed reports, typically achieved when using the ECI, may well be the result of indeed using diversified and effective recall strategies (Fisher & Geiselman, 1992; Paulo et al., 2013). Witnesses could also be withholding 'uncertain' information' at the beginning of the interview, and later choosing to reveal it, assuming that, if the interviewer is asking for successive retrieval attempts, he/she expects more information from the witness, regardless of its accuracy. However, our study does not suggest this because pairwise comparisons revealed no differences between interview phases regarding the amount of produced uncertainties, proportion-wise. Lastly, it is important to state that we found no correlation between the proportion of produced 'uncertainties' for a given report and accuracy for the remaining recall. Therefore, our study does not support that 'uncertainties' are the result of inferior memory traces since witnesses who provide more 'uncertainties' do not seem to be providing more errors and confabulations in their remaining recall. We believe that 'uncertainties' are the result of metacognitive monitoring that is homogeneously performed throughout the interview, regardless of interview condition, interview phase, or report length. Such monitoring is effectively performed, since only 65% of the produced 'uncertainties' were correct items of information, in comparison with 'certainties' that have a 90% correct recall rate.

Our study purposely constrained motivation perception variability with procedures such as greeting and establishing rapport (Vallano & Compo, 2015; Walsh & Bull, 2011) that aim, among many other purposes, to preclude low levels of motivation (Read et al., 2009). Even though we focused on the effect that motivation perception could have on report accuracy when only moderate to high levels of motivation were reported, we found that more motivated witnesses were more accurate. Such results are supported by previous research which suggests that witness' perceptions toward the interviewer and the interview process might have an important role on witnesses' report (Ballardin et al., 2013; Walsh & Bull, 2011). However, to our knowledge, this is the first study that assessed the relationship between witnesses' perception of their own motivation and report accuracy, suggesting that promoting witnesses' motivation, for instance, through rapport, might also be another effective procedure to further increasing report accuracy.

One could argue that accuracy is influencing witnesses' motivation: participants who provide a more accurate report consequently feel more motivated. However, as previously discussed, Paulo et al. (2015) found that witnesses were unable to successfully evaluate their accuracy for different interview phases, as well as for the whole interview. Similarly to Granhag et al. (2004), these authors found no association between participants' frequency judgments and participants 'real' error rate. Therefore, if witnesses are unable to accurately evaluate accuracy for large portions of their statement, and for their overall statement, it is very unlikely that our participants who achieved higher accuracy rates were able to perceive so, and consequently felt more motivated. It is our believe that highly motivated witnesses may be applying more effort to successfully provide an accurate report, for instance, by effectively monitoring such information, which, as we previously established, has a major role on increasing report accuracy. However, this requires further testing as discussed in the following section.

Limitations and future directions

Given the size of our sample, two motivation levels had only a few participants (see 'Results' section). This constrained our ability to further test if highly motivated participants are applying more effort to monitor their report, consequently providing a more accurate report. In the future, it would be interesting to develop a study with more participants to test if highly motivated witnesses present more signs of memory monitoring (e.g. elicit more 'uncertainties') than witnesses who report moderate/lower levels of motivation. Furthermore, only one measure of motivation was used in this study. Given that witnesses' motivation could have an effect on report accuracy, it is important to further test this hypothesis with other motivation measures, such as real-time motivation assessments during the interview, as well as by manipulating participants' motivation levels. Lastly, it would be very interesting to separate 'certainties' in two new groups: (a) 'regular recall' – e.g. 'he had a black shirt' and (b) 'full certainty' – e.g. 'I am definitely sure he had a black shirt'. However, participants seldom spontaneously report a 'full certainty'. Therefore, a different research design which encourages participants to tell when they are absolutely sure about a piece of information they have previously reported is necessary.

Conclusion

Our findings support that differentiating spontaneous 'certainties' from 'uncertainties' and promoting witnesses' motivation are key points that researchers and professionals should consider. Taking note of witnesses' motivation and ability to use spontaneous verbal expressions of uncertainty to naturally monitor their own report might be an effective and time-saving procedure to increase or evaluate report accuracy.

Acknowledgements

We express our gratitude to Dr Becky Milne (of the University of Portsmouth) for her help and support.

Disclosure statement

No potential conflict of interest was reported by the authors.

Funding

This work was supported by the Portuguese governmental institution 'Fundação para a Ciência e a Tecnologia' under grant number [SFRH/BD/84817/2012].

References

Akehurst, L., Milne, R., & Koehnken, G. (2003). The effects of children's age and delay on recall in a cognitive or structured interview. *Psychology, Crime & Law*, *9*(1), 97–107. doi:10.1080/1068316021000057686

Allwood, C., Ask, K., & Granhag, P. (2005). The cognitive interview: Effects on the realism in witnesses' confidence in their free recall. *Psychology, Crime & Law*, *11*(2), 183–198. doi:10.1080/10683160512331329943

Aschermann, E., Mantwill, M., & Koehnken, G. (1991). An independent replication of the effectiveness of the cognitive interview. *Applied Cognitive Psychology*, *5*(6), 489–495. doi: 10.1002/acp.2350050604

Ballardin, M., Stein, L., & Milne, R. (2013). Além das técnicas de entrevista: Características individuais em entrevista investigativa com testemunhas. [Beyond the interview techniques: Individual characteristics in investigative interviews with witnesses]. *Revista Brasileira de Segurança Pública*, *7*, 6–16.

Bower, G. (1967). A multicomponent theory of the memory trace. In K. W. Spence & J. T. Spence (Eds.), *The psychology of learning and motivation* (Vol. 1, pp. 229–325). New York, NY: Academic Press.

Brewer, N., Weber, N., Wootton, D., & Lindsay, S. (2012). Identifying the bad guy in a lineup using confidence judgments under deadline pressure. *Psychological Science*, *23*(10), 1208–1214. doi:10.1177/0956797612441217

Campos, L., & Alonso-Quecuty, M. L. (1999). The cognitive interview: Much more than simply 'try again'. *Psychology, Crime & Law*, *5*(1–2), 47–59. doi:10.1080/10683169908414993

Dando, C., & Milne, R. (2010). The cognitive interview. In R. Kocsis (Ed.), *Applied criminal psychology: A guide to forensic behavioral sciences* (pp. 147–169). Sydney, NSW: Charles C. Thomas.

Evans, J. R., & Fisher, R. P. (2010). Eyewitness memory: Balancing the accuracy, precision and quantity of information through metacognitive monitoring and control. *Applied Cognitive Psychology*, *25*(3), 501–508. doi:10.1002/acp.1722

Faul, F., Erdfelder, E., Buchner, A., & Lang, A. G. (2009). Statistical power analyses using G*Power 3.1: Tests for correlation and regression analyses. *Behavior Research Methods*, *41*(4), 1149–1160.

Field, A. (2013). *Discovering statistics using IBM SPSS Statistics* (4th ed.). London: Sage.

Fisher, R. P., & Geiselman, R. E. (1992). *Memory-enhancing techniques for investigative interviewing: The cognitive interview*. Springfield, IL: Charles C. Thomas.

Fisher, R. P., & Geiselman, R. E. (2010). The cognitive interview method of conducting police interviews: Eliciting extensive information and promoting therapeutic jurisprudence. *International Journal of Law and Psychiatry*, *33*(5–6), 321–328. doi:10.1016/j.ijlp.2010.09.004

Flin, R., Boon, J., Knox, A., & Bull, R. (1992). The effect of a five month-delay on children's and adults' eyewitness memory. *British Journal of Psychology*, *83*(3), 323–336.

Geiselman, R. E., Fisher, R. P., Firstenberg, I., Hutton, L., Sullivan, S. J., Avetissian, I. V., & Prosk, A. L. (1984). Enhancement of eyewitness memory: An empirical evaluation of the cognitive interview. *Journal of Police and Science Administration*, *12*, 74–80.

Gigerenzer, G. Hoffrage, U., & Kleinbölting, H. (1991). Probabilistic mental models: A Brunswikian theory of confidence. *Psychological Review*, *98*(4), 506–528. doi: 10.1037/0033-295X.98.4.506

Granhag, P. A., Jonsson, A., & Allwood, C. M. (2004). The cognitive interview and its effect on witnesses' confidence. *Psychology, Crime & Law*, *10*(1), 37–52. doi:10.1080/10683160210000030577

Higham, P. A., Luna, K., & Bloomfield, J. (2010). Trace-strength and source-monitoring accounts of accuracy and metacognitive resolution in the misinformation paradigm. *Applied Cognitive Psychology*, *25*(2), 324–335. doi:10.1002/acp.1694

Higham, P. A., & Memon, A. (1999). A review of the cognitive interview. *Psychology, Crime & Law*, *5*(1–2), 177–196. doi:10.1080/10683169908415000

Koehnken, G., Milne, R., Memon, A., & Bull, R. (1999). The cognitive interview: A meta-analysis . *Psychology, Crime & Law*, *5*(1–2), 3–27. doi:10.1080/10683169908414991

Koriat, A., & Goldsmith, M. (1996). Monitoring and control processes in the strategic regulation of memory accuracy. *Psychological Review*, *103*(3), 490–517.

Liberman, V. (2004). Local and global judgements of confidence. *Journal of Experimental Psychology: Learning, Memory and Cognition*, *30*(3), 729–732. doi:10.1037/0278-7393.30.3.729

Lindsay, R., Kalmet, N., Leung, J., Bertrand, M., Sauer, J., & Sauerland, M. (2013). Confidence and accuracy of lineups selections and rejections: Postdicting rejection accuracy with confidence. *Journal of Applied Research in Memory and Cognition*, *2*(3), 179–184. doi:10.1016/j.jarmac.2013.06.002

Luna, K., & Martín-Luengo, B. (2012). Confidence–accuracy calibration with general knowledge and eyewitness memory cued recall questions. *Applied Cognitive Psychology*, *26*(2), 289–295. doi:10.1002/acp.1822

Memon, A., Holley, A., Wark, L., Bull, R., & Koehnken, G. (1997). Isolating the effects of the cognitive interview techniques. *British Journal of Psychology*, *88*(2), 179–197. doi:10.1111/j.2044-8295.1997.tb02629.x

Memon, A., Meissner, C. A., & Fraser, G. (2010). The cognitive interview: A meta-analytic review and study space analysis of the past 25 years. *Psychology, Public Policy, and Law*, *16*(4), 340–372. doi:10.1037/a0020518

Metcalfe, J., & Shimamura, A. P. (1996). *Metacognition: Knowing about knowing*. Cambridge, MA: MIT Press.

Milne, R. & Bull, R. (1999). *Investigative interviewing: Psychology and practice*. Chichester: Wiley. doi:10.1002/cbm.444

Milne, R., & Bull, R. (2003). Does the cognitive interview help children to resist the effects of suggestive questioning? *Legal and Criminological Psychology*, *8*(1), 21–38. doi:10.1348/135532503762871219

O'Hagan, A., Buck, C. E., Daneshkhah, A., Eiser, J. R., Garthwaite, P. H., Jenkinson, D. J., . . . Rakow, T. (2006). *Uncertain judgements: Eliciting experts' probabilities*. Chichester: Wiley. doi:10.1002/0470033312

Paulo, R. M., Albuquerque, P. B., & Bull, R. (2013). The enhanced cognitive interview: Towards a better use and understanding of this procedure. *International Journal of Police Science & Management*, *15* (3), 190–199. doi:10.1350/ijps.2013.15.3.311

Paulo, R. M., Albuquerque, P. B., Saraiva, M., & Bull, R. (2015). The enhanced cognitive interview: Testing appropriateness perception, memory capacity and error estimate relation with report quality. *Applied Cognitive Psychology*, *29*(4), 536–543. doi:10.1002/acp.3132

Prescott, K., Milne, R., & Clark, J. (2011). How effective is the enhanced cognitive interview when aiding recall retrieval of older adults including memory for conversation? *Journal of Investigative Psychology and Offender Profiling*, *8*(3), 257–270. doi:10.1002/jip.142

Read, J. M., Powell, M. B., Kebbell, M. R., & Milne, R. (2009). Investigative interviewing of suspected sex offenders: A review of what constitutes best practice. *International Journal of Police Science & Management*, *11*(4), 442–459. doi:10.1350/ijps.2009.00.0.143

Riccó, A. (Director), & Riccó, R. (Director). (2004). O Assalto [The robbery] [Television series episode]. In V. Castelo (Producer), *Inspector Max*. Lisbon: Produções Fictícias.

Rivard, J. R., Fisher, R. P., Robertson, B., & Mueller, D. H. (2014). Testing the cognitive interview with professional interviewers: Enhancing recall of specific details of recurring events. *Applied Cognitive Psychology*. doi:10.1002/acp.3026/full

Roberts, W. T., & Higham, P. A. (2002). Selecting accurate statements from the cognitive interview using confidence ratings. *Journal of Experimental Psychology: Applied*, *8*(1), 33–43. doi:10.1037/1076-898X.8.1.33

Sniezek, J. A. & Buckley, T. (1991). Confidence depends on level of aggregation. *Journal of Behavioral Decision Making*, *4*(4), 263–272. doi:10.1002/bdm.3960040404

Stein, L. M., & Memon, A. (2006). Testing the efficacy of the cognitive interview in a developing country. *Applied Cognitive Psychology*, *20*(5), 597–605. doi:10.1002/acp.1211

Tulving, E. (1991). Concepts of human memory. In L. R. Squire, N. M. Weinberger, G. Lynch, & J. L. McGaugh (Eds.), *Memory: Organization and locus of change* (pp. 3–32). New York, NY: Oxford University Press.

Tulving, E., & Thomson, D. (1973). Encoding specificity and retrieval processes in episodic memory. *Psychological Review*, *80*(5), 352–373.

Vallano, J. P., Compo, N. S. (2015). Rapport-building with cooperative witnesses and criminal suspects: A theoretical and empirical review. *Psychology, Public Policy, and Law*, *21*(1), 85–99. doi:10.1037/law0000035

Walsh, D., & Bull, R. (2011). Examining rapport in investigative interviews with suspects: Does its building and maintenance work? *Journal of Police and Criminal Psychology*, *27*(1), 73–84. doi:10.1007/ s11896-011-9087-x

6 Child witnesses in Scottish criminal trials

Rhona Flin, Ray Bull, Julian Boon and Anne Knox

Introduction

Child witnesses are never far from the news. A Scottish judicial inquiry produced a lengthy report on a case centring on allegations of ritualistic child sexual abuse on the Orkney Islands. In the Orkney case, the children did not give evidence in court, but when children are required to attend criminal trials a variety of problems can occur. For example, an English child sexual abuse case collapsed when the Crown said that it could no longer rely on the evidence of the alleged victims, sisters aged 10 and 14 years (*The Times*, 20.11.91). Another alleged sexual abuse case had to be abandoned when a 12 year old boy hid in the lavatories of the Central Criminal Court in London, too frightened to give evidence (*Independent*, 20.11.91). And, charges were dropped against a man accused of sexual abuse when a five year old was deemed not competent after a High Court judge said 'he was not satisfied the girl could tell the difference between truth and lies' *(Aberdeen Press and Journal*, 6.3.93). It appears that despite recent attempts at legal reform, many of the problems relating to children's evidence in criminal cases remain unsolved.

In Britain no official records or statistics are kept of the children who are required to give evidence as witnesses in legal proceedings. There are, however, indications that the number of children involved per annum is not insignificant and that this figure may be increasing. In Scotland, two illustrative samples of data have been collected with the assistance of the Procurator Fiscal Service (public prosecutors) who provided details of all children cited as prosecution witnesses in their jurisdiction for a given period. The first sample showed that in Aberdeen (population 200,000) a total of 226 children under the age of 16 were cited as witnesses for criminal trials in a one year period (Flin, Davies, & Tarrant, 1988). A second study (Flin, Bull, Boon, & Knox, 1990) based in Glasgow (population 700,000) recorded 1,800 children cited for criminal trials in a 15 month period (i.e. 1,440 per annum) (see Table 6.1 for details). Certainly in Scotland, the majority of these witnesses are not victims of sexual abuse. Instead they are more typically bystander witnesses to assaults or breaches of the peace. The frequency with which children are called to give evidence may be higher in Scotland than in other

Table 6.1 Types of charges listed on witness citations by age

Type of charge	*Age range (years)*		
	3 to 8	*9 to 13*	*14 to 15*
RTA[†]	6	70	95
BOP[†]	30	164	273
Theft	22	193	250
Reset[†]	0	2	0
Fraud	0	3	7
MDA[†]	0	1	10
Assault	86	428	676
Sex related	37	95	39
Attempted murder	4	9	2
Murder	7	14	35
Other	69	240	314

[†] Road traffic act; breach of the peace; receiving stolen goods; misuse of drugs act.

Note: More than one charge could be listed for a given child. These figures represent 3,181 charges on citations for 1,800 child witnesses.

parts of the United Kingdom (although no comparable data are available), due to the Scottish legal rule that all evidence in criminal trials be corroborated.

The British criminal justice systems present a number of problems for children who are required to give evidence as victims or bystanders in criminal trials. These include lack of legal knowledge (Flin, Stevenson, & Davies, 1989), long delays waiting to attend court (Flin, Boon, Knox, & Bull, 1992; Plotnikoff, 1990), unsuitable court facilities, and the demands of an adversarial trial (see Morgan & Zedner, 1992; Flin, 1993; Spencer & Flin, 1993, for recent reviews). Such problems are not unique to the United Kingdom (see Dezwirek-Sas, 1992; Sisterman, Amacher, & Kastanakis, 1992; Whitcomb, 1992 for a North American comparison, and Loesel, Bender, & Bliesner, 1992, for a European overview).

Despite widespread concern in Britain about child witnesses being exposed to the demands of a criminal trial, there have been no empirical studies of children's behaviour in the witness box, nor has there been any research into the ability of our courtroom lawyers to present or test children's evidence. This paper contains the first data from an observational study of child witnesses giving evidence in criminal trials in Scotland. It focuses on what is the most critical stage of the legal process – when the child enters the witness box to give evidence. At this point there can be problems not only for the child witness, but also for the lawyers who have the task of presenting the child's evidence to the court or of testing that evidence by cross-examination. The only research to date which has collected systematic observations of children giving testimony was carried out in the USA by Goodman *et al.* (1992). Their study is extremely comprehensive but their research aims were concerned solely with sexual abuse victim witnesses which limits the utility of the findings for researchers interested in the entire spectrum of child witnesses. Moreover, only 17 children in their sample actually testified in füll trial proceedings.

The investigation described in this article was designed to gather as much information as possible with a view to distinguishing and highlighting:

(i) the procedures which children may expect in court,
(ii) the nature and frequency of any special measures adopted for taking evidence from children,
(iii) the emotional and cognitive abilities of children in coping with what was required of them by the court,
(iv) any aspects of the procedure which appeared to cause difficulty for the child or for the court, and
(v) the characteristics of the prosecution and defence examinations and their effects on the children and their evidence.

Research method

The project was based in Glasgow and the research team received notification from the Procurators Fiscal (public prosecutors) of all children under 16 years of age called to give evidence as prosecution witnesses in the criminal courts. An attempt was made to observe as many of these children as possible within a period of 12 months. It should be emphasized that the majority of witnesses cited to give evidence will not actually find themselves in the witness box or even at the court-house: accused persons frequently change their 'not guilty' pleas to 'guilty' in the run up to the trial, not all witnesses cited are required to give evidence, and not all trials listed will run on the first date scheduled. Over the 15 month study period (1988–1989), 366 children were 'tracked' up to their attendance at court and 89 of these children were observed giving evidence in 40 trials. In view of the very large numbers of cases and the location of courts in different parts of the city, it was necessary to adopt a prioritizing policy as to which cases the two research staff should attend in the event of more than one trial going ahead on a given day. The priorities in such instances were to attend the most serious cases and those trials which involved the youngest children. It is therefore important to bear in mind when interpreting the observation data that these may include an inflated proportion (with reference to the total sample) of younger children and cases relating to more serious charges.

The method used to conduct this study was based on experience which had been gained during a pilot study in which observations had been made on 22 children giving evidence in Aberdeen during 1986 and 1987 (Flin *et al.*, 1988). These previous data were purely qualitative and no attempt had been made to standardize the recording of the observations.

In addition, we knew that a very similar exercise was being conducted in Denver, Colorado, where psychologist Gail Goodman and her colleagues were observing children on the witness stand as part of a large scale assessment of the effects of giving testimony on child sexual abuse victims (Goodman *et al.*, 1992). They were tracking a sample of 218 child sexual assault victims referred to District Attorney's offices in Denver between 1985 and 1987. As part of this investigation they recorded interview and observational data on 40 children testifying at preliminary hearings, 8 children testifying at competence hearings and 17 children who testified at trial. The researchers watched each child testifying and recorded their observations on a set of specially designed rating scales. In order to standardize our own comparison, we contacted Gail Goodman, who sent us copies of her observational scales. These were adapted for use in Scotland first by rating adult witnesses giving evidence and then by modifying the scales to suit Scottish terminology, procedures and child witnesses.

At each trial attended, the research staff would consult with the Procurator Fiscal Depute who was handling the case regarding its likelihood of proceeding, of the cited children being called, and the estimated starting time of the trial. In addition, at each trial the presiding judge was presented with a sheet which informed him or her of our presence and requested that in the event of the court being cleared of the public that we would be allowed to remain for research purposes. The researchers were permitted to stay in all but one case involving a four year old girl who was later deemed by the judge not to be competent to give her evidence.

With the permission of the presiding judge, the researcher sat in a discreet position as near to the child as possible to permit unobtrusive observation and data recording using a 'Courtroom Observation Schedule'. This consisted of three subsections designed to record a comprehensive picture of the court, the people present, the case, the examinations, and the demeanour of the child witness. It was subdivided into three parts as follows:

> Part I recorded basic demographic and court details, e.g. the child's age, sex, type of crime, date of incident, type of court, waiting time, presence of accompanying adults.
>
> Part II was used to record court details (e.g. number of people present), procedures (e.g. adjournments) and the use of special practices (e.g. removing wigs and gowns, clearing the court, screening the child, seeing the child outwith the witness box).
>
> Part III consisted of the scales used to rate the child's demeanour and the questioning techniques. A separate set was used for (a) the judge's competency assessment; (b) examination-in-chief by the prosecution; (c) the defence cross-examination/s, and (d) the prosecution's re-examination.

The first six children observed giving evidence were rated by both of the research staff, and inter-rater reliability was assessed on two criteria. The first was based on percentage agreement where the researchers had made identical ratings relating to the children and the lawyers. The mean concordance rate was 95% with a range of 87% to 99%. The second criterion which was adopted was also based on percentage agreement but here agreement was defined on the basis of the researchers' concurring on the polarity of the bipolar scales. This less stringent criterion would, for example, classify two ratings of 'Self-confident' and 'Very self-confident' as being agreement between researchers. It would not however classify two ratings of 'Not self-confident' and 'Self-confident' as being agreement. Under this criterion the mean concordance rate was 97% with a range of 96% to 100%.

In view of the high levels of inter-rater reliability and the time consuming nature of its assessment, only three more child witnesses were jointly rated by the researchers. When the ratings relating to these three witnesses were included in the calculations the mean concordance rates are 92.5% (range 81% to 99%) based on complete agreement, and 98.8% (range 96% to 100%) based on polarity agreement. From this point, observations were recorded by one researcher alone. Agreement between two raters is only a measure of inter-rater reliability and does not measure the validity or accuracy of the rating scales. These are obviously subjective impressions of the child's behaviour and responses and therefore the ratings can only be regarded as indicative of emotional state or linguistic competence. If the rater was unable to judge all the scales for a given child (e.g. if a cross-examination was very brief) then this is recorded as missing data on Tables 6.3–6.8 below.

Details of child witnesses

The 89 children observed gave evidence in all four types of Scottish court:

(i) District Courts (Justice of the Peace = lay magistrate) (3 male, 3 female);
(ii) Sheriff-Court Summary Procedure (judge alone) (26 male, 7 female);
(iii) Sheriff/Court-Solemn Procedure (judge plus jury) (9 male, 7 female);
(iv) High Court (senior judge plus jury) (23 male, 11 female).

Table 6.2 provides a breakdown of the children's ages and the types of charges involved in each case.

These children had waited an average of 193 days (6.5 months) since witnessing the alleged incident (range: 30–718 days; SD = 116). (It should be noted that there can sometimes be a delay between the alleged offence and the initial complaint;

Table 6.2 Age of observed witness and nature of charges

Principal charge type	*Age range (years)*			
	5 to 8	*9 to 13*	*14 to 15*	
RTA	0	1	4	(5.6%)
BOP	0	0	1	(1.1%)
Theft	0	2	3	(5.6%)
Reset	0	0	2	(2.2%)
Assault	2	13	14	(33.7%)
Murder, att. murder	1	3	24	(31.4%)
Sex-related	4	6	6	(16.8%)
Other	3	0	0	(3.4%)
TOTAL	10	25	54	

this is not uncommon for example in sexual assault cases.) The relationship between the child witness and the accused was also noted. This indicated that 34% of the sample were giving evidence against strangers, 9% against a relative, and 56% against known persons (in one case the relationship could not be ascertained). In addition, data were collected concerning the children's involvement in the case: 75% were bystander witnesses and 25% appeared as victim witnesses.

Basic court data

Court delays

Only 64% of the sample were called to give their evidence on the first day they were asked to attend court. Of the remainder, 5% gave their evidence the following day, 31% on a later day still (maximum = 9 days).

Special measures for child witnesses

In Scotland any special measures which are adopted for taking evidence from child witnesses are at the discretion of the presiding judge. There was no provision in Scotland for the use of live videolinked evidence (i.e. closed-circuit TV) at the time of the study, although this is now available at a number of courts and is currently being evaluated by a team of researchers funded by the Scottish Home and Health Department (Murray, 1992).

Of the children observed, 13 (14.6%) gave their testimony from outside the witness box. In most cases these children were seated in the well of the court, but one nine year old girl giving evidence in a serious assault case (involving her uncle), was allowed to sit up on the bench alongside the Sheriff.

Screens

Only two children were giving evidence while the accused was hidden from view behind a screen. This was in an incest, and lewd and libidinous, case involving the accused's 11 year old daughter and her friend. For each of the girls, the screen (a conspicuous hospital type) was in position on their entry into the courtroom. During the testimony, when questioned about the accused, the girls looked apprehensively at the screen; nevertheless, they were able to give their evidence and in one case the child was exceptionally confident. However, at the close of her evidence she became very upset as the screen was taken away and she was required formally to identify her father. In another High Court case, in which there was an overnight adjournment after a 7 year old girl had broken down in the witness box, the prosecution requested the use of a screen which would prevent her from seeing the accused who was known to her. In this instance, after objections from the defence lawyers that to introduce the screen during an examination-in-chief would prejudice the jury, permission for this measure was refused by the judge.

More subtle ways are available to de-emphasize the presence of the accused while children and vulnerable witnesses give evidence. These include advising the child to address the judge in Summary trials and to address the jury in Solemn and High Court cases. Such advice would be especially effective were it facilitated by sitting the child on a chair which is positioned in a direction facing the judge and jury and away from the accused. In our sample, excluding the two girls mentioned above who were provided with a screen, only four children were so seated.

Removing wigs and gowns

One of the most simple expedients by which the courts may try to reduce formality is for the judge to instruct the removal of wigs and/or gowns. However, such measures were not adopted very frequently – for six children, wigs were removed, and for five of these children, gowns were also removed. (In our experience, particularly where older child witnesses are concerned, there were occasions where the weight of the court, and its formality, was required to overcome children's reticence in providing incriminating evidence. However, for young children it may be helpful to reduce the degree of formality in the courtroom.)

Excluding the public

It is at the discretion of the presiding judge as to whether the court is closed to the public; in the case of 18 (20%) of the children the public were excluded. When courts were open to the public there could be large numbers present on the public benches, which for 38 children in our sample meant giving evidence in front of more than 40 people. However, in cases which were tried before a jury, even when the public were excluded, there were still a significant number of adults present: the 15 members of the jury, the judge, the lawyers, the stenographer, the clerk, the uniformed police and court officers, and the accused.

In general, our experience of special measures for children was that their adoption was sporadic. Furthermore, their introduction appeared to be dependent more on the personal views of the presiding judge than on the basis of a coherent set of principles or practices. Since this research was completed, the Lord Justice General has issued a memorandum which offers general guidance for Scottish judges and which will hopefully bring more uniformity to such decisions (see Nicholson & Murray, 1992 for a copy) This lack of consistency in courtroom procedures for child witnesses has also been reported for other jurisdictions. Morgan & Plotnikoff (1990) in an English study of child victims oberved a number of trials and concluded:

> A wide variety of procedures are now available which may ameliorate stress for the child witness and facilitate the giving of testimony, but the way in which they are used is fairly haphazard. There appears to be little shared information and experience among courts about the treatment of child witnesses.
> (1990, p. 192)

Likewise, Goodman *et al.* (1992) reported that in Denver, while some practices were more regularly adopted, such as permitting a victim assistant or non-offending parent to remain in the courtroom, other techniques available such as live closed-circuit television or screens were used relatively infrequently.

Competence assessment and oath administration

In Scotland there is no lower age restriction on competence, and children as young as three years of age have given evidence in criminal trials. The trial judge must be satisfied by appropriate questioning of the child, that he or she can give evidence intelligibly and can understand the difference between truth and falsehood. In practice, children under 12 years of age generally give unsworn evidence while older children and adults usually take the oath. Whether any child gives evidence on oath or not is a matter for judicial discretion.

The children in the sample were assessed as follows and the following outcomes were observed:

(i) being assessed as to their competence and not allowed to testify (1 aged 4 years, not included in the final sample);
(ii) assessed as to their competence and permitted to testify but not asked to take the oath (10 aged 5–8 years; 16 aged 9–13 years; 4 aged 14–15 years);
(iii) assessed as to their competence, allowed to testify and asked to take the oath (7 aged 9–13 years; 6 aged 14–15 years); and finally
(iv) no competency assessment and automatically given the oath on entry into the witness box (2 aged 9–13 years; 44 aged 14–15 years).

Judges usually administered the oath to any child of 14 years and over; there was a wide divergence of practice for children of 9 to 13 years, and the younger children with one exception were all deemed competent but not sworn.

Examinations-in-chief, cross-examinations and re-examinations

After the initial competence assessment and/or administration of the oath by the judge, the children were examined by the prosecution and then usually by the defence lawyer(s). There were wide variations in terms of the number of examinations given, their duration, and the number of adjournments. Following the initial examination-in-chief by the prosecuation lawyer, 65 of the 89 children were cross-examined by one or more defence lawyers. A further examination was then required by the prosecution lawyer for 20 of the children who had been cross-examined. The average duration of the examination-in-chief was 16 minutes, but this mean value disguises large variations (range: 3–92 mins). The average duration of cross-examination was 10 minutes but again there were wide variations around the mean figure (range: 1–59 mins). For those children who were re-examined by the prosecution the average duration was 4.5 minutes (range: 1–18 mins). These data are similar to the findings of Goodman *et al.* (1992) from their observations in Denver, USA. They reported that in preliminary hearings, children spent 4–90 minutes (mean 27 mins) on the stand, in competence examinations the time ranged from 4–21 minutes (mean 10 mins) and in trials from 13–270 minutes (mean 69 minutes). Their data were recorded as overall time on the stand rather than the time taken for each examination.

The number of examinations which the court required of the child witnesses became less predictable where there were multiple accused. Although 52 (58%) of the children appeared in cases which were brought against a sole accused, 26 (29%) gave evidence in cases where there were 5 or more accused. The effect of having multiple accused could be dramatic, since each defence lawyer has the right to cross-examine the witness – the right which would almost certainly be exercised if the witness gave incriminating evidence regarding their client during the examination-in-chief. This meant, for example, that in one case involving eight accused, a child was examined no less than ten times – once with the examination-in-chief, eight cross-examinations by different lawyers, and a final re-examination by the prosecution.

Adjournments

Adjournments could occur for a number of reasons, e.g. when a point of law arose which required consideration outwith the presence of the witness, when a witness was too upset to continue, and at lunch time. The evidence of 15 (17%) of the observed witnesses was interrupted by one adjournment, 5 (6%) witnesses by two adjournments, and in the case of one child, by three adjournments. The duration of adjournments varied considerably according to the reason prompting the break, with most cases being resumed the same day (range: minimum = 1 minute, maximum = 2 hours). Four children were asked to come back to continue their evidence the following day.

The effects of adjournments on the children were not always negative. In a High Court murder case, an overnight adjournment was called when a 15 year old girl's answers were for the most part inaudible. The inaudibility was, in the opinion of the lawyers and research staff alike, a means used by the girl to avoid answering sensitive questions. Overnight, a basic sound amplification system was set up in court, and the following morning the girl gave clear and important evidence. We have also observed cases where the prosecution suggested a short adjournment for a 14 year old girl who became very upset giving evidence regarding a brutal attack on her grandfather. The judge in this instance refused permission for an adjournment concluding instead that a few moments hiatus in the proceedings would be preferable; eventually, and with great distress, the girl was able to give her evidence.

In our opinion there were occasions where breaks in the proceedings had a detrimental effect on testimony. In one instance a seven year old girl was giving evidence in a High Court case against multiple accused including a known acquaintance. Her testimony was proceeding satisfactorily until at a critical point, one of the defence lawyers interrupted the proceedings requesting an adjournment to discuss a point of law. While the request was discussed for some minutes the child was left in the witness box and caught the eye of the accused. Following this the girl burst into tears and the trial was suspended until the following morning. So great was the child's distress that the parents of the other children scheduled to appear refused to allow them to attend. The seven year old girl did return the following morning and eventually gave her evidence with the aid of tranquillizers.

It therefore seems that there is no uniform picture which emerges regarding the impact of adjournments on the quality of children's testimony and their emotional state while giving evidence. But there do appear to be occasions when an unscheduled adjournment has a detrimental effect on the child's evidence, and other cases where a distressed child might benefit from being allowed a brief rest. On balance, it would seem advisable to avoid interrupting the child's examination by unscheduled interruptions if possible.

Demeanour of child witnesses

When a child is a witness for the prosecution the aims of the three stages of legal examination are as follows. The initial examination-in-chief is an interview conducted by the prosecution lawyer in which questions are asked which are designed to elicit from the child the basic facts he or she knows relating to the alleged crime. This may then be followed by a cross-examination in which the defence lawyer attempts to cast doubt on the testimony previously given. In doing so it is usually necessary to ask questions which directly challenge the child such as 'Are you sure that you saw X? I put it to you that what you saw was in fact Y'. However these sorts of questions are not solely the preserve of the defence. If during the cross-examination the child retracts something which was said during the examination-in-chief, the prosecution may wish to exercise its right to conduct a re-examination. If this happens, the prosecution may well need to put questions of an equally challenging nature to those put previously by the defence. It is not therefore simply the defence lawyers who may apply pressure to the child, but both sides, depending on the circumstances of the case and what has been said in the preceding examinations.

The majority of children gave their evidence without becoming so obviously upset that they were reduced to tears. In the 89 examinations-in-chief there were only 5 children who cried. In the 65 cross-examinations, 5 children were seen crying, while only 1 of the 18 children re-examined by the prosecution was moved to tears. Perhaps surprisingly, it was not usually the youngest children who cried but the older ones (aged 8–15 years).

To the extent that it is possible to generalize on the basis of these small numbers, there were three common strands. First, all those who cried were giving evidence in Sheriff or High Court cases; secondly, the evidence they gave was in relation to serious charges (i.e. murder, incest or assault to severe injury); and thirdly, it was at the point that they were questioned about the critical part of the incident that they broke down. However, while children may not in general become tearful in the courtroom, a much higher percentage appeared to be unhappy and tense while giving their evidence.

Table 6.3 Happy–unhappy scale

Ratings	*Examination*		
	Examination-in-chief	*Cross-examination*	*Re-examination*
Very happy	0	0	0
Happy	5 (5.6%)	2 (3.1%)	1 (5%)
Neutral	34 (38.2%)	30 (46.1%)	11 (55%)
Unhappy	46 (51.7%)	31 (48.4%)	6 (30%)
Very unhappy	3 (3.4%)	1 (1.6%)	2 (10%)
Missing value	1	1	0

Table 6.4 Relaxed–tense scale

Ratings	*Examination*		
	Examination-in-chief	*Cross-examination*	*Re-examination*
Very relaxed	0	0	0
Relaxed	6 (6.7%)	1 (1.5%)	0
Neutral	31 (34.8%)	33 (50.8%)	8 (40%)
Tense	48 (53.9%)	30 (46.2%)	12 (60%)
Very tense	3 (3.4%)	1 (1.5%)	0
Missing value	1	0	0

Tables 6.3–6.5 present the rating scores for observations of the children's (a) happiness, (b) tension, (c) self-confidence. Table 6.3 indicates that in the examinations-in-chief, and cross-examinations approximately 50% of the children were rated as being either unhappy or very unhappy, with 40% of the children re-examined by the prosecution appearing unhappy.

Similarly Table 6.4 shows that approximately half the children were rated as being tense or very tense during their examinations. Goodman *et al.* (1992) found that 11 (65%) of 17 child sexual abuse victims observed giving evidence were rated as experiencing some distress or as being very distressed.

Ratings were also made as to the degree of self-confidence the children showed while delivering their evidence. These were made on the basis of the child's demeanour while giving evidence and not the degree of confidence a child expressed in his or her statements to the court. For example, we observed children who seemed very shy and timid in the delivery of their testimony but who were clear and firm as to the sequence and nature of events which they were asked to describe. Conversely, we have also observed children who have shown highly confident and unabashed irritation at being pressed for details which they have already indicated they could not remember clearly. Table 6.5 indicates that the children varied considerably in the degree of self-confidence which they showed. The ratings indicate that in the initial examination-in-chief and the cross-examination, 46% of the sample were able to cope at least to a reasonable extent, with a further 40% showing some degree of confidence. The remaining 14% of children were rated as lacking self-confidence.

Table 6.5 Self-confidence scale

Ratings	*Examination*		
	Examination-in-chief	*Cross-examination*	*Re-examination*
Very self-confident	5 (5.6%)	4 (6.1%)	2 (10%)
Self-confident	31 (34.8%)	22 (30.7%)	4 (20%)
Neutral	39 (43.8%)	30 (46.1%)	12 (60%)
Lacking self-confidence	13 (14.6%)	9 (13.8%)	1 (5%)
Very lacking in self-confidence	0	0	0
Missing value	1	0	1

Fluency of children's evidence and linguistic difficulties

While observing the child giving evidence, the researcher would make ratings of the verbal performance of each child and the appropriateness of the questioning technique used. There were six scales which recorded

(i) fluency;
(ii) amount of detail;
(iii) appropriateness of the vocabulary used by the lawyer;
(iv) age appropriateness of the grammar used by the lawyer;
(v) confidence in their statements; and
(vi) the number of 'don't know' or mute responses.

As can be seen from Table 6.6 the majority of children were relatively fluent and able to provide at least some detail. However, these data are based on ease of speech and the quantity of information provided, and are not necessarily indicative of effective communication between the lawyers and the children.

Table 6.7 shows that difficulties could emerge as a consequence of questions being put by the examining lawyer which were age inappropriate either in terms of vocabulary or grammar. Although the majority of children (85%) were asked age-appropriate questions in terms of grammar, 12% of examinations-in-chief, and 40% of cross-examinations contained some vocabulary that the child appeared not to understand.

The problem of incomprehension includes instances where children have been wrong-footed by questions containing double negatives, language which is unfamiliar, or grammatical constructions which are too difficult. Sometimes children answered with what they thought the lawyer wanted to know rather than asking for the question to be explained. In most cases this was readily apparent from the answer which was given by the child and the question was then rephrased. However, we have seen lines of questioning result from misunderstood questions and answers, the erroneous nature of which has only become evident much later. When this happened it was necessary not only to start the questioning again from the relevant point but to clarify all the confused points.

Table 6.6 Fluent–faltering and detail scales

Ratings	*Examination*		
	Examination-in-chief	*Cross-examination*	*Re-examination*
Fluency			
Very fluent	12 (13.5%)	5 (7.6%)	3 (15%)
Relatively fluent	67 (75.3%)	53 (81.5%)	13 (65%)
Somewhat faltering	7 (10.8%)	7 (10.8%)	3 (15%)
Very faltering	1 (1.1%)	0	0
Missing value	0	0	1
Detail			
A lot of detail	11 (12.4%)	5 (7.7%)	2 (10%)
Some detail	36 (40.4%)	27 (41.5%)	2 (10%)
A little detail	38 (42.7%)	27 (41.5%)	11 (65%)
No detail	4 (4.5%)	5 (7.7%)	1 (5%)
Missing value	0	1	4

Table 6.7 Age appropriateness of lawyers' vocabulary and grammar

Ratings	*Examination*		
	Examination-in-chief	*Cross-examination*	*Re-examination*
Vocabulary			
Virtually all age appropriate	78 (87.6%)	38 (58.5%)	16 (80%)
Some age inappropriate	11 (12.4%)	24 (36.9%)	3 (15%)
Many age inappropriate	0	2 (3.1%)	0
Most age inappropriate	0	0	1
Missing value	0	1	1
Grammar			
Virtually all age appropriate	80 (89.9%)	54 (83%)	17 (85%)
Some age inappropriate	9 (10.1%)	9 (13.8%)	2 (10%)
Most age inappropriate	0	1 (1.5%)	0
Virtually all age inappropriate	0	0	0
Missing value	0	1	1

Children in the witness box may be reluctant to admit ignorance or uncertainty in their answers. At school, children are encouraged to guess if they are not sure but in court an answer to a misunderstood question or a best guess can obviously have serious consequences. Table 6.8 indicates that only a small minority of the children expressed uncertainty in the content of their answers. In a context of generally confident responses, it it difficult to detect when a child is offering a best guess as opposed to a robust answer. Children rarely said that they did not understand the question (although sometimes it later transpired that they had not in fact

Table 6.8 Statement confidence and ability to answer scales

Ratings	*Examination*		
	Examination-in-chief	*Cross-examination*	*Re-examination*
Confidence			
Very confident in statements	10 (11.2%)	7 (10.7%)	3 (15%)
Confident in statements	68 (76.4%)	43 (66.1%)	13 (65%)
Neutral	4 (4.5%)	9 (13.8%)	2 (10%)
Not confident in statements	5 (5.6%)	5 (7.6%)	1 (5%)
Virtually no confidence in statements	0	0	0
Missing value	2	1	1
Answering			
Answered all questions	51 (57.3%)	33 (50.8%)	6 (30%)
Some 'I don't knows'	33 (37.1%)	27 (41.5%)	12 (60%)
Many 'I don't knows'	5 (5.6%)	5 (7.6%)	0
No answer	0	0	0
Missing value	0	0	2

understood the original question). Whether the children did not like to say when they had not properly understood, or whether they thought they had understood well enough to answer, is difficult to assess from an observational perspective. Table 6.8 indicates that relatively high percentages of children would answer 'I don't know' in response. These data at first appear encouraging; however, they also include responses where the children were not, in fact, willing to give answers to sensitive questions which they had probably well understood and could have answered. It is therefore important to exercise caution when interpreting these figures. In any event, children should always be given an explanation of the requirements when answering questions in court and this should be reinforced where examinations are lengthy or following adjournments.

Where problems in understanding did occur they were by no means concentrated upon the younger children. One probable reason for this was that with very young witnesses the lawyers appeared to be conscious of the need to keep questions as simple as they could. We have observed several instances where there has been a sense of frustration for all concerned at the failure to be able to get even questions relating to simple matters understood. The following examples of lawyers' utterances which we have heard in court help to illustrate this:

- 'Did you form an impression about the piece of wood?'
- 'Did he then take offence?'
- 'May I take you back to the evidence you gave earlier?'
- 'What was the nature of the street lighting?'
- '. . . put this line for the sake of this line. . .'

- 'What is your position regarding. . .'
- 'A witness speaks to. . .'
- 'Madam Fiscal'/'Learned friend'/'My Lord'.

However, in concluding this section, we would like to say that we are not unsympathetic to some of the difficulties involved. Questioning a young child in the formal atmosphere of a criminal trial would be a daunting prospect for the most experienced of child interviewers.

The interaction between lawyers and the child witnesses

One of the most prevalent claims of those who believe that children are disadvantaged relative to adults in giving evidence in court is that the problem is particularly accentuated during the cross-examination. Brennan & Brennan (1988; p. 5) suggest 'Cross examination is that part of court proceedings where the interests and rights of the child are most likely to be ignored and sacrificed'. The defence has been characterized as the key source of distress if the child becomes upset in the witness box. This has meant that defence lawyers have been portrayed as being aggressive in their interview style and keen to focus on peripheral details which could call into question the reliability of the child's main evidence. Two scales were used to assess the lawyers' interviewing styles

(i) degree of supportiveness; and
(ii) amount of questioning on peripheral details.

Data from the 'supportiveness' scale, which rated the degree of support the lawyers gave the child during their examinations, indicated that the prosecution during examination-in-chief was perceived as being significantly more supportive than were the defence lawyers during their cross-examinations ($t = 5.69$, $df = 62$, $p < .001$). This is a finding also reported by Goodman *et al.* (1993). This is hardly surprising given that all children were prosecution witnesses. However, the supportiveness shown by the prosecution diminished to the same level as that of the defence when they conducted their re-examinations (ex-in-chief/re-exam $t = 3.35$, $df = 16$, $p < .01$; cross/re-exam $t = 1.10$, $df = 18$, n.s.). There was some evidence that the children's confidence in their statements reflected these changes in interviewing styles. Quite small but significant reductions in the children's confidence in their statements were observed in the cross-examination relative to the examination-in-chief ($t = 2.78$, $df = 63$, $p < .01$). Similarly, there was also a reduction in statement confidence in the re-examination relative to the examination-in-chief ($t = 2.36$, $df = 18$, $p = .03$) with no significant difference between cross-examination and re-examination levels.

Classifying details in terms of being central or peripheral can be very difficult since the distinction is in the eye of the beholder. Our operating definition was to decide if the lawyers' questions pertained to details of perceptual salience or obscurity within the context of the event concerned. Questions about peripheral detail were relatively infrequent. The majority of questions at direct examination (93%), cross-examination (83%) and re-examination (89%) focused on central information. Peripheral questioning was used to some degree by both defence and prosecution lawyers. Whether this happens, and when, appears to be influenced by the circumstances of the case and what the child has already said in evidence (especially where incriminating evidence has been given or retracted).

Comparison of the effects of prosecution and defence questioning

Our ratings showed that the children were no more likely to be rated as being unhappy, tense, faltering or lacking in self-confidence when answering the prosecution's questions, than when answering the questions of the defence. Many defence lawyers would not be surprised that the children appeared to react in the same way to them as to the prosecution lawyers. They argue that it would not be in their interests to be seen putting children under pressure in the witness box since it may well lose them, and therefore their clients, the sympathy of the court. This point, coupled with that made above concerning the need for prosecution lawyers sometimes to apply pressure, might account for the comparability in the ratings during the prosecution and defence examinations.

In terms of the language used, again little difference was found between the prosecution and the defence lawyers. No significant difference was found in the age appropriateness of the vocabulary used in questioning. However, significant differences were found with respect to the age appropriateness of the grammatical structures. These indicated that on average the prosecution lawyers were more successful in putting questions during the examination-in-chief at levels which the children could understand than were the defence lawyers during their cross-examinations (ex-in-chief/cross, $t = 4.07$, df $= 64$, $p < .001$). Interestingly, this trend remains consistent even at the re-examination (cross/re-exam, $t = 2.35$, df $= 18$, $p = .03$). Goodman *et al.* (1992) also found that while most questioning they observed was reasonably age appropriate, defence attorneys used more age-inappropriate wording of their questions than prosecutors.

Overview and conclusions

The above data are from a preliminary investigation which was designed to elicit as much information as possible about children giving evidence in criminal proceedings. The population studied was highly heterogeneous representing a wide range of ages, crimes and types of court, and any conclusions must be of a preliminary nature. At present it is very difficult to generalize concerning the treatment a child may expect when he or she goes to court to give evidence, and this is likely to create difficulties for those attempting to prepare child witnesses for their court experience.

Regarding children's linguistic ability to cope with the quesions which were put to them, we did observe misunderstandings on the part of both the lawyers and the children. This appears to be an obvious areas for legal skills training, which could greatly enhance the effectiveness of taking evidence from young witnesses with limited linguistic capabilities.

Our findings do not provide support for the view that the defence cross-examination is necessarily the most difficult part of the trial. While differences did emerge between defence and prosecution styles and the children's responses to them, they appeared to be a function of the style of examination being conducted rather than a simple distinction between defence and prosecution *per se*. Children's experiences while giving evidence in court are dependent on a host of internal and external factors including the circumstances of the case, the measures taken to help alleviate stress, the personalities of all involved, and what the child has said in evidence at each successive stage in the proceedings.

One of the principal concerns about children as witnesses is that they are disadvantaged compared with adults in terms of their relative ability to cope with this experience. While we do not have any ratings on adult witnesses from which to draw comparisons, our data indicate that the majority of children were able to give their evidence reasonably well in terms of providing at least some detail relatively fluently. Nevertheless, a large percentage of children did appear tense and unhappy while giving their evidence. This problem may be alleviated to some extent by the introduction of the videolink (system) which allows the child to give evidence from outwith the courtroom.

Davies & Noon (1991) have just completed an evaluation of a 'Live Link' TV system which has been provided in a number of English and Welsh courts since 1989. They observed a total of 154 children giving evidence using a version of Goodman's 'Court Observation' scales which were also used in our study. This enabled them to make comparisons between their ratings of 154 children giving evidence in physical and sexual assault cases via the 'Live Link' and 28 subjects from our data set of children giving evidence in open court in similar cases. The two samples were not matched in terms of age, sex or crimes charged, and the cases were being tried under different legal systems. Therefore as Davies & Noon (1991) acknowledge, the comparison needs to be treated with a significant degree of caution. They found that the length of time witnesses gave evidence was longer using the 'Live Link' method ($x = 50$ mins) as opposed to the open court examination ($x = 24$ mins) and that a comparison of observers' ratings for the two samples suggests that 'the Live Link system facilitates the giving of evidence by children, who were happier, more fluent and less likely to given inconsistent testimony' (1991; p. 75).

The 'Live Link' system does not, however, solve the problems of long pretrial delays, inadequate preparation of child witnesses or the potential difficulties of formal examinations and cross-examinations. An alternative solution is to consider seriously the use of pre-recorded videotapes of initial interviews and evidentiary examinations in place of live evidence at trial (see Spencer & Flin, 1993). The admission of videotaped interviews in place of the examination-in-chief, which is now permitted in England and Wales (Criminal Justice Act, 1991), still requires the child to wait many months for the trial, to attend court and to be cross-examined (usually via the Live Link) during the trial proceedings. Whatever procedures are finally adopted for hearing and testing children's evidence, it is now clear that proper preparation of the child is likely to enhance both the quality of their testimony and to protect their emotional well-being (Dezwirek-Sas, 1992; Saywitz & Snyder, 1993). The recent publication of a special information pack for child witnesses (NSPCC, 1993) must be regarded as a welcome step in the right direction. Many adult witnesses, particularly victims, would also benefit from this type of support pre-trial, and the extension of available programmes should be seriously considered.

References

Brennan, M., & Brennan, R. (1988). *Strange language.* Wagga Wagga: Riverina Literacy Centre.

Davies, G., & Noon, E. (1991). *An evaluation of the live link for child witnesses.* Report to the Home Office. London: Home Office.

Dezwirek-Sas, L. (1992). Empowering child witnesses for sexual abuse prosecutions. In H. Dent & R. Flin (Eds.), *Children as witnesses* (pp. 181–199). Chichester: Wiley.

Flin, R. (1993). Hearing and testing children's evidence. In G. Goodman & B. Bottoms (Eds.), *Child victims, child witnesses* (pp. 279–336). New York, NY: Guilford.

Flin, R., Davies, G., & Tarrant, A. (1988). *The child witness.* Report to the Scottish Home and Health Department.

Flin, R., Stevenson, Y., & Davies, G. (1989). Children's knowledge of legal proceedings. *British Journal of Psychology, 80,* 285–297.

Flin, R., Bull, R., Boon, J., & Knox, A. (1990). *Child witnesses in criminal prosecutions.* Report to the Scottish Home and Health Department.

Flin, R., Boon, J., Knox, A., & Bull, R. (1992). The effects of a five months delay on children's and adults' eyewitness memory. *British Journal of Psychology, 83,* 323–336.

Goodman, G., Taub, E., Jones, D., England, P., Port, R, Rudy, L., & Prado, L. (1993). *Testifying in court: Emotional effects of criminal court testimony on child sexual assault victims. SRCD Monograph, 57* (5), Serial No. 229.

Loesel, F., Bender, D., & Bliesner, T. (Eds.) (1992). *Psychology and law: International perspectives.* Amsterdam: Swets & Zeitlinger.

Morgan, J., & Plotnikoff, J. (1990). Children as victims of crime: Procedures at court. In J. Spencer, G. Nicholson, R. Flin, & R. Bull (Eds.), *Children s evidence in legal proceedings* (pp. 189–192). Available from Cambridge University Law Faculty.

Morgan, J., & Zedner, L. (1992). *Child victims.* Oxford: Clarendon Press.

Murray, K. (1992). *Children's evidence and the use of live television links in Scotland.* Paper presented at the Children's Evidence and Technology Conference; University of Glasgow, 25 September, 1992.

Nicholson, G., & Murray, K. (1992). The child witness in Scotland. In H. Dent & R. Flin (Eds.), *Children as witnesses* (pp. 131–150). Chichester: Wiley.

NSPCC. (1993). *The Child Witness Information Pack.* National Society for the Prevention of Cruelty to Children. Headley Library, 67 Saffron Hill, London, EC1N 8RS.

Plotnikoff, J. (1990). Delay in child abuse prosecutions. *Criminal Law Review,* 645–647.

Saywitz, K., & Snyder, L. (1993). Improving children's testimony with preparation. In G. Goodman & B. Bottoms (Eds.), *Child victims, child witnesses* (pp. 117–146). New York, NY: Guilford.

Sisterman, K., Amacher, E., & Kastanakis, J. (1992). The court-prep group: A vital part of the court process. In H. Dent & R. Flin (Eds.), *Children as witnesses* (pp. 201–209). Chichester: Wiley.

Spencer, J., & Flin, R. (1993). *The evidence of children* (2nd ed.). London: Blackstone Press.

Whitcomb, D. (1992). *When the victim is a child.* Washington, DC: National Institute of Justice.

7 A state of high anxiety: how non-supportive interviewers can increase the suggestibility of child witnesses

Jehanne Almerigogna, James Ost, Ray Bull and Lucy Akehurst

The present study examined the effects of state and trait anxiety on 8–11 year old children's susceptibility to misleading post-event information. Participants' state and trait anxiety were measured, after which they watched an extract from a children's movie. They were then individually interviewed using either a supportive or a non-supportive style. During the interviews, the children were asked 14 questions about the movie, seven of which were control and seven contained misleading information. After the interview, their state anxiety was measured again. Results showed that participants interviewed in a non-supportive style were more likely to provide incorrect answers to misleading questions. Furthermore, participants who scored highly on both trait and post-interview state anxiety measures more often responded incorrectly to misleading questions. Also, pre- to post-interview changes in state anxiety were correlated with more incorrect responses to misleading questions.

Typically, researchers looking at the suggestibility of child witnesses have focused their attention on cognitive factors (Ceci & Bruck, 1993) and on the effects of certain questioning styles (Fivush, Peterson, & Schwarzmueller, 2002). However, studies have now started to examine the influence of social and individual factors on the testimony of these witnesses (e.g. Davis & Bottoms, 2002a; Ridley, Clifford, & Keogh, 2002). The present study investigated two such factors: interviewer manner (a social factor) and anxiety (an individual factor). To examine these two factors, it focused on three questions. First, can the behaviour of interviewers affect the quality of the information given by the children they are interviewing? Second, does the level of anxiety experienced by children affect their accuracy or suggestibility? And finally, is there an interaction between the interviewer manner and the child's level of anxiety?

What factors can affect the quality of information provided by child witnesses?

As Ceci & Bruck (1993) noted, cognitive capacities are only one of a number of possible factors that can affect the quality of information children provide in forensic interviews. Other social and situational factors are likely to be equally important. The manner or behaviour of the interviewer is one such factor. During an interview, an interviewer can adopt a generally supportive or non-supportive behaviour. For example, a supportive interviewer might be smiling, making eye contact, sitting with an open body posture and building rapport with the interviewee, whereas a non-supportive interviewer might be cold and distant, avoiding smiles and eye contact. Bull (1998) argued that an interviewer who adopts a negative behavioural manner creates an interpersonal environment in which a child witness may not feel comfortable or at ease. Such non-supportive environments may not really help in obtaining full and accurate reports from child witnesses (Wood, McClure, & Birch, 1996).

One common way of reducing these negative effects would be for the interviewer to behave in a supportive manner (Moston, 1989). Yet, the effect of interviewers' social support on child witnesses is a sensitive subject in eyewitness research because it has generally been thought that supporting children during interviews could actually increase their suggestibility by augmenting their desire to comply with and be agreeable to the interviewer (Moston & Engelberg, 1992). However, several studies have now demonstrated that quite the opposite may be likely to happen (Bottoms, Quas, & Davis, 2007). For example, Carter, Bottoms, & Levine (1996) found that a supportive interviewer actually reduced the suggestibility of child witnesses. In their study, 5–7 year old children were interviewed in either a supportive manner (i.e. the interviewer was friendly, smiled and gazed often at participants, sat in a relaxed manner and attempted to build rapport) or in an intimidating manner (i.e. the interviewer was cold and distant, did not smile or gaze much and did not attempt to build rapport with the children). Their results showed that whilst interviewer manner had no effect on the children's free recall, it did have an effect on their level of suggestibility. Those children who were interviewed in the supportive manner demonstrated an increased resistance to misleading questions compared to those interviewed in the intimidating manner. Carter et al. (1996) hypothesised that the positive effect on suggestibility of an interviewer who behaved in a supportive manner could be due to this style of interviewing making children less anxious. Davis & Bottoms (2002a) conducted an experiment to test this assumption directly. They showed that social support in the form of positive reinforcement and behaviours displayed by the interviewer during an interview might, as previously demonstrated, increase children's resistance to misleading suggestions. Positive reinforcements were defined by the interviewer building rapport, smiling and gazing often, speaking with a warm tone of voice and sitting closely and in a relaxed manner. Their results also indicated that the interviewer-provided social support served to reduce children's level of anxiety. That is, children interviewed by the supportive interviewer felt less anxious during the interview than children interviewed by the intimidating interviewer. Although Davis and Bottoms did not find any effect of anxiety on children's suggestibility, they suggested that anxiety might be a mediating factor between interviewers' behaviours and suggestibility.

What are the effects of anxiety on the accuracy and suggestibility of child witnesses?

Goodman, Rudy, Bottoms, & Aman (1990) observed that child witnesses often give only short accounts of the events they have witnessed. Part of the reason why this happens, they noted, might be the anxiety-inducing nature of interviews. That is, interviews may be experienced by children as anxiety-inducing situations (Moston & Engelberg, 1992). In the present study, we were therefore interested in the effect of both trait and state anxiety at the retrieval phase, that is, during the interview. Trait anxiety is a stable and enduring personality dimension, which is said to remain constant across different situations. State anxiety, on the other hand, is the anxiety a person experiences in a certain situation (Spielberger, 1972). It is therefore directly linked to the specific characteristics of a situation (Rachman, 2004). In the present study, it was predicted that the two distinct interviewing styles should differently affect children's state anxiety.

Research has shown that the performance of anxious people is usually inferior to that of non-anxious individuals on a variety of cognitive tasks (Eysenck, 1992). Eysenck (1997) proposed that at event-recall, high-trait anxious individuals are more likely to be concerned about failure and self-presentation than low-trait anxious ones. This could increase their suggestibility by using cognitive resources which would otherwise be applied to retrieval strategies and memory monitoring (Williams, Watts, MacLeod, & Mathews, 1988). For state anxiety, Farber & Spence (1953) argued that high levels of state anxiety at retrieval reduce performance on complex tasks while having facilitating effects on more simple exercises. High-state anxious persons are more likely to misinterpret a question or to feel unable to access an answer they are confident they know (Sarason, 1980). Accordingly, highly anxious individuals should perform more poorly in suggestibility studies than low anxious participants (Wolfradt & Meyer, 1998). Gudjonsson (1988) found support for this hypothesis in a study with adults in which he demonstrated that high levels of both state and trait anxiety, as measured by the Spielberger State–Trait Anxiety Inventory (Spielberger, Gorsuch, & Lushene, 1970), were related to high scores on his scale of interrogative suggestibility (the Gudjonsson Suggestibility Scale: Gudjonsson, 1984). However, Ridley & Clifford (2004) found that adult participants scoring higher on a state anxiety measure were actually less likely to answer incorrectly to misleading questions. Yet, by only measuring state anxiety, Ridley and Clifford may have missed the possible interaction of pre-existing trait anxiety with state anxiety. They also might have overlooked the possibility that anxiety acts as a mediator between suggestibility and other factors (e.g. interviewer manner).

How could the interaction between the interviewers' behaviour and child witnesses' anxiety affect their suggestibility?

The present study attempted to extend Carter et al.'s (1996) study by manipulating interviewer manner and measuring both state and trait anxiety. The present study's aim was to examine the interacting effects of interviewing manner and anxiety on the suggestibility and memory accuracy of child witnesses. Participants first watched a short film after which their trait and state anxiety were measured. They were then individually interviewed in either a supportive or a non-supportive manner and asked seven control and seven misleading questions. After the interview, each child completed a second state anxiety questionnaire. In line with previous research (e.g. Carter et al., 1996; Davis & Bottoms, 2002a), it was predicted that a non-supportive interviewer would lead children to answer more of the misleading questions incorrectly. Furthermore, it was predicted that children with higher state and trait anxiety scores would exhibit a higher tendency to answer misleading questions incorrectly compared to children with lower anxiety scores. Finally, it was predicted that the state anxiety of participants would differ depending on which interviewing style they experienced. Children interviewed in a supportive manner should show a decrease in state anxiety whereas those interviewed in a non-supportive manner should demonstrate an increase in state anxiety. Furthermore, whether these changes in levels of pre- to post-interview state anxiety were related to participants' suggestibility scores was also examined.

Method

Participants

Seventy-four children participated in the experiment. Following cleaning and screening, data from five children were removed due to large numbers of missing values which, because of the nature of analysis, could not be replaced with a measure of central tendency such as a median or a mean. Of the remaining 69 children, there were 35 girls and 34 boys. The mean age for this sample was 9.27 years (range = between 8 years and 11.5 years, $SD = 0.72$ years). The participants were all pupils from a primary school. Four classes took part in the experiment, 2 year three classes (ages 8–10 years) and 2 year four classes (ages 9–11 years). One class from each year was assigned to either the supportive or the non-supportive interview style conditions. Children's age did not differ as a function of whether they were interviewed by a supportive or non-supportive interviewer ($p > 0.05$).

Materials

Anxiety questionnaire

The questionnaire used to measure trait and state anxiety was Spielberger, Edwards, Lushene, Montuori, & Platzek's (1973) State–Trait Anxiety Inventory for Children (STAI-C). It comprised 40 questions printed on two sheets. The first part of the questionnaire consisted of 20 questions designed to measure children's trait anxiety. It included statements such as 'I am shy', 'I notice my heart beats fast' and 'I worry about what others think of me'. These questions were answered by indicating 'hardly ever', 'sometimes' or 'often'. The other 20 questions measured their state anxiety with statements like 'I feel very calm, calm or not calm', 'I feel very nervous, nervous or not nervous' and 'I feel very terrified, terrified or not terrified'. The instructions were written on top of the questionnaire. The same questionnaire was distributed to all participants.

Movie

The clip shown to the participants was an extract from the U-rated movie *Madeline*. It was 5 minutes and 17 seconds long. All pupils saw the same clip. An outline of the event is appended.

Interviewer manner manipulation

In line with previous research (e.g. Carter et al., 1996; Davis & Bottoms, 2002a), the two interviewing styles (supportive and non-supportive) were distinguished by the interviewer's use of different verbal and non-verbal behaviours. In the non-supportive interviews, the interviewer adopted a formal and stern attitude. She was sitting with her legs crossed and arms folded, leaning back in her chair. Her behaviour was serious and she did not smile. She made very little attempt to build rapport with her interviewees. She was wearing black formal clothes and spectacles. For the supportive interviews, the same interviewer appeared a lot more relaxed. She adopted an open body posture. She tried to build rapport with the children, looked at them more and acted in a friendlier manner. She was wearing coloured casual clothes and did not wear spectacles.

Structure of the interview and interview questions

For the purpose of the study, 14 questions were designed based on the movie clip. In order to control for item-specific confounds in the ease with which participants might be misled about certain aspects of the movie, each question was designed to have both a control and a misleading form. For example, a question asking children what was on the kitchen table would in its control form be '*Was there anything on the table*'? and in its misleading form '*Were there eggs on the table*'? Children were presented with either the control form of a question or the misleading form of it. No child was presented with the same question in different forms (i.e. control and misleading). Each question was presented in its control and misleading version the same number of times.

Each child was asked 14 questions, seven control and seven misleading. The questions were presented to the children orally by the interviewer. Questions were asked once and followed the sequence of the movie. The answers to the seven control questions were used to measure children's memory accuracy (thus giving a 'memory accuracy' score of 0–7). Their responses to the seven misleading questions measured their level of susceptibility to misinformation (thus giving a 'suggestibility' score of 0–7).

Procedure

For the first part of the experiment, the children were tested in groups. First, the STAI-C was distributed to them. The instructions, which were written at the top of the sheets, were read aloud by the investigator. They were also told that they were free to ask questions at any time if there was something they did not comprehend in the questionnaire. There was no time limit for the completion of the STAI-C although none of the participants took more than 15 minutes to finish it. The children then watched the movie in groups of 14 to 23 after which they were individually interviewed. After each interview, participants were presented with a second state anxiety questionnaire which comprised the same 20 questions which formed the state anxiety part of the STAI-C. The children were then thanked and returned to their usual class activities. Interviews lasted between 7 and 15 minutes. Once all pupils had participated, the experimenter debriefed them in groups as to the aims of the study and answered any questions they had.

Results

Effects of interviewing style on memory accuracy and suggestibility scores

A MANOVA was performed with interviewing style (supportive or non-supportive) as the independent variable, and the memory accuracy and suggestibility measures as dependent variables. To verify whether the results could have been influenced by either the age or the gender of participants, these two variables were entered as covariates. There was an effect of interviewer manner for suggestibility scores (i.e. incorrect responses to misleading questions) ($F_{1, 65} = 27.21, p < 0.001$, partial $\eta^2 = 0.29$). The mean scores indicated that participants interviewed in a non-supportive manner gave significantly more incorrect responses to misleading questions ($M = 2.03$, $SD = 1.05$) than those being interviewed in a supportive manner ($M = 0.86$, $SD = 1.06$). There was no effect of interviewing style on accuracy scores ($p > 0.05$) and there was no effect of age or gender on either the accuracy or suggestibility scores (both $p > 0.05$).

Effects of state and trait anxiety on memory accuracy and suggestibility scores

In order to investigate the effect of state and trait anxiety on children's memory accuracy and suggestibility, median-splits were performed on participants' trait anxiety scores and post-interview state anxiety scores. For trait anxiety, the median score was 36 and for post-state anxiety the median score was 29. Participants with scores under the median were categorised as low-state or low-trait anxious whereas scores above the median were categorised as high-state or high-trait anxious. This resulted in a combined anxiety variable with four levels (i.e. high-trait/high-state, high-trait/low-state, low-trait/high-state, low-trait/low-state). Table 7.1 shows the means and standard deviations of the memory accuracy and suggestibility scores for each of these groups.

Table 7.1 Means and standard deviations for the number of correct answers on control questions and the number of incorrect answers on misleading questions for the four levels of anxiety groups

	Correct control		*Incorrect misleading*	
	Mean	*SD*	*Mean*	*SD*
High-trait/high-state ($N = 21$)	4.33	1.28	1.95	1.16
High-trait/low-state ($N = 14$)	4.86	1.17	1.5	1.02
Low-trait/high-state ($N = 11$)	3.91	1.45	1.36	0.81
Low-trait/low-state ($N = 23$)	4.35	1.3	0.91	0.9

A MANOVA was performed with the four levels of anxiety as the independent variable, and accuracy and suggestibility scores as the dependent variables. There was a main effect of anxiety on the suggestibility scores ($F_{3, 65} = 4.19$, $p < 0.01$, partial $\eta^2 = 0.02$). *Post hoc* Tukey tests revealed that only the difference between the low-trait/low-state and the high-trait/high-state anxiety groups for the suggestibility scores was significant ($p < 0.005$). The means revealed that participants with high scores on both the state and trait anxiety measures gave more incorrect responses to misleading questions ($M = 1.95$) than children with low-state and -trait anxiety scores ($M = 0.91$). It should be noted that the same combination of high-trait and high post-interview state anxiety did not have a significant effect on the number of correct responses to control questions.

Relationship between interviewing styles and anxiety

In order to observe the possible effects of the supportive and non-supportive styles of interviewing on the level of state anxiety of participants, the difference between pre- and post-state anxiety for the two interviewing style groups was examined with an independent *t*-test. A significant difference between the two groups in terms of pre-interview state anxiety was observed ($t_{67} = 4.04$, $d = 1.00$, $p < 0.0001$; supportive $M = 33.22$, non-supportive $M = 27.88$). As the groups were similar in terms of age and gender, the reason for this pre-interview state anxiety difference is unclear. *t*-tests were also performed to compare the means of the pre- and post-interview state anxiety scores, which found that the changes between the pre-interview state anxiety and post-interview state anxiety were significant for both the supportive group ($t_{35} = 5.66$, $d = 0.98$, $p < 0.001$; pre-interview state anxiety $M = 33.22$, post-interview state anxiety $M = 28$) and the non-supportive group ($t_{32} = 3.84$, $d = 0.74$, $p = 0.001$; pre-interview state anxiety $M = 27.88$, post-interview state anxiety $M = 31.88$). These results suggest that the two different interviewing styles did have an effect on the state anxiety of participants, with the supportive manner decreasing it and the non-supportive one increasing it. No significant difference in terms of trait anxiety scores was observed between the supportive group ($M = 36.72$) and the non-supportive one ($M = 36.48$).

Relationship between state anxiety variations and memory and suggestibility

To further investigate the possible relationship between anxiety and suggestibility, a new variable was calculated from participants' pre- and post-interview state anxiety measures. The post-interview state anxiety scores were subtracted from the pre-interview state anxiety scores so as to give a pre- to post-interview change in the state anxiety scores of each participant. A positive score on this variable therefore showed that the participant became less anxious during the interview (e.g. a pre-state anxiety score of 30 minus a post-state anxiety score of 25 equals a difference of +5) whereas a negative score indicated a rise in state anxiety (e.g. a pre-state anxiety score of 30 minus a post-state anxiety score of 35 equals a difference of −5). Correlations between this new 'change' variable and the performance on control and misleading questions demonstrated that there was no relationship between the state anxiety 'change' variable and number of correct answers to control questions ($r = 0.16$, $p = 0.18$) but there was a significant negative relationship between the 'change' scores and the number of incorrect answers to misleading questions ($r = -0.46$, $p < 0.001$). That is, participants who reported feeling less anxious after the interview than before gave less incorrect answers to the misleading questions and those who were more anxious after the interview than before it provided a greater number of incorrect responses to misleading questions (only two of those children feeling more anxious post- than pre-interview had been interviewed by the supportive interviewer). However, their pre- to post-state anxiety differences were very low (−2 and −3, respectively) and both children made no incorrect answers to the misleading questions).

Trait anxiety, memory and suggestibility

The correlation between trait anxiety and the number of correct responses to control questions was significant ($r = 0.26$, $p < 0.05$). That is, children with higher trait anxiety scores were more likely to give correct answers to control questions than children with lower trait anxiety levels. The correlation between trait anxiety and the number of incorrect responses to misleading questions was also significant ($r = 0.34$, $p < 0.005$). Children with higher trait anxiety scores were more likely to answer misleading questions incorrectly than children with lower trait anxiety scores.

Discussion

The aim of the present study was to examine the possible effects of interviewing style and levels of state and trait anxiety on children's eyewitness testimony. The results showed that the two different interviewing styles (supportive and non-supportive) had a significant effect on children's suggestibility, with children in the non-supportive group answering significantly more of the misleading questions incorrectly than children in the supportive condition. Furthermore, participants scoring highly on measures of both state and trait anxiety were more prone to give incorrect responses to misleading questions than participants having low scores on these measures. Moreover, the two different interviewing methods appeared to create environments that were, as measured by their post-interview state anxiety scores, experienced differently by children.

Interviewing styles and suggestibility

The present study demonstrated that an interviewer adopting a non-supportive demeanour could increase children's suggestibility. This is in accordance with Gudjonsson's (1992) argument that interviewer authority would lead children to comply more with whatever an interviewer says thus augmenting their suggestibility. In a similar vein, Goodman, Bottoms, Schwartz-Kenney, & Rudy (1991) noted that an interviewer providing social support, such as smiles and verbal encouragements, to child interviewees significantly lessened incorrect free recall and subsequent errors in response to misleading questions.

Engelberg & Christianson (2002) contended that interviewees have to be provided with an environment of safety and support in order to make them feel more comfortable and secure, and to this we can add 'less anxious'. In this way, adult and child interviewees alike may be more able to talk about their memories in a more articulate and complete manner. However, too much support may also decrease performance as interviewers may become too persistent and coercive (Garven, Wood, Malpass, & Shaw, 1998) and, as Bain, Baxter, & Fellowes (2004) have highlighted, a balance between support and focus on the matter under discussion may be needed. Therefore, for improved forensic practice, variables which could possibly influence interviewees and their account of the witnessed event need to be better identified and understood. As demonstrated by the present study, the behaviour of the interviewer plays a key role (Carter et al., 1996). However, more research is needed to further investigate these issues. For example, are there specific aspects of an interviewer's non-verbal or verbal behaviour that have more, or less, of an effect on the accuracy of what child witnesses recall and report?

Anxiety and suggestibility

Clark & Wells (1995) argued that an anxious person's performance can be diminished by anxiety because of processes such as intrusive thoughts and worry. They stated that anxious people are so preoccupied with their internal sensations and their meanings that they become relatively inattentive to whatever is going on around them. These anxious individuals, their mind full of interfering negative thoughts about themselves and their capacities, with both their self-confidence and their efficacy undermined, would be expected to perform poorly on a cognitively demanding task such as answering questions (Wells, 2005). The findings of the present study are also in line with the processing efficiency theory (Eysenck & Calvo, 1992), suggesting that highly anxious children might have had fewer cognitive resources available to allocate to the more difficult aspects of the task at hand (i.e. dealing with misleading questions).

The present study found that anxiety was related to suggestibility, but not to accuracy scores. This, too, may be best explained in terms of differences in levels of cognitive resources required to answer misleading and non-misleading questions. According to the discrepancy detection principle (Tousignant, Hall, & Loftus, 1986), memories are less likely to be transformed when one directly detects discrepancies between the original memory and the misinformation (Schooler & Loftus, 1986). Undetected discrepancies may lead to source misattribution errors, that is, recalling items that were only suggested (Zaragoza & Lane, 1994). Retrieving answers to non-misleading questions should therefore be, cognitively speaking, a less demanding task than undertaking a memory search to compare misleading information provided by an interviewer with what was initially witnessed. The difference in difficulty and hence cognitive resources required, may explain the finding that anxiety was only related to participants' suggestibility scores and not their memory accuracy scores.

Interviewing styles and anxiety

The present study found an effect of interviewing style on state anxiety with supportive interviewer behaviours decreasing children's level of state anxiety and non-supportive manners increasing it. Because state anxiety is sensitive to changes in the immediate context (Spielberger, 1972), it was influenced by interviewer behaviours. The more pleasant environment created in the supportive condition may have put children more at ease and, as a consequence, made them feel less nervous. On the contrary, in the non-supportive interviews, participants, feeling more vulnerable and oppressed, became more anxious. This is in line with Carter et al.'s (1996) hypothesis which stated that children should be less anxious when an interviewer behaves in a supportive, as opposed to a non-supportive, manner. This finding is important for applied procedures. It is recognised that forensic interviews are unpleasant experiences for children. Simply by adopting certain behaviours, the interviewer can affect the interviewees' feelings of the situation (Davis & Bottoms, 2002b). That is, by being more supportive, the interviewer can make children feel more comfortable and less anxious. In this more positive environment, they are likely to report more information of better quality (Goodman et al., 1990) and, as the present study demonstrated, to be better able to resist misleading information.

Limitations of the present study

The present study measured anxiety with the STAI-C and, although this test has good validity and reliability (Spielberger et al., 1970), its construct has been questioned. Kelly (2004) argued that the trait scale of the STAI comprised a 'worry' component which should actually be considered separately from trait anxiety (Davey, Hampton, Farrell, & Davidson, 1992). To overcome such problems, previous studies have sometimes measured arousal using participants' physiological responses like heart rate, blood pressure or palm sweating. For example, Quas & Lench (2006) measured children's heart rate while encoding and retrieving information from a fear eliciting video clip. Children with higher heart rate at encoding answered fewer questions incorrectly while those with higher heart rate at retrieval answered more questions incorrectly but only when interviewed by a non-supportive interviewer. Such measures may be more appropriate and accurate to investigate the relationship between witnesses' arousal and suggestibility.

The to-be-remembered event used in the present study was a movie clip. As has been argued, movie clips, although rich in information and easily controllable, are not very ecologically valid (Saywitz, Goodman, Nicholas, & Moan, 1991). They are also rather impersonal and insignificant for the participating children. With such events, children are passive observers and they may therefore feel little concern to put all of their attention in the task (Thierry & Spence, 2004). Several studies (e.g. Krackow & Lynn, 2003; Nathanson & Saywitz, 2003) have demonstrated that it is quite possible to involve children in a meaningful activity while remaining ethical. For example, Gilstrap & Papierno (2004) staged an event with a magician visiting the children at school. The children watched and participated in magic tricks, sang and danced. In Krackow and Lynn's study, children were involved in a game of Twister. Such events are both salient and exciting for children. For a better application of laboratory studies and to better mimic the actions of children's memory about a real-life event, it would be better not to use movie clips as the to-be-remembered event.

Conclusion

Situational factors influencing people's memory and suggestibility in forensic interviews have seldom been studied. However, the present study demonstrated that such factors can have a great influence on child interviewees. It was shown that both the behaviour the interviewer adopts while trying to gather information and children's level of anxiety during an interview do affect the quality of the children's answers. Factors such as interviewing manner can be controlled and manipulated in interviews more easily than can individual or cognitive factors (Roberts, Lamb, & Sternberg, 2004). Future research should therefore focus on these dynamic situational aspects of interviews in order to develop more appropriate procedures for interviewing child witnesses.

Acknowledgements

The authors would like to thank Dr. Michael Fluck, Prof. Graham Davies and two anonymous reviewers for their constructive comments which improved the quality of this paper. The authors would also like to thank the headmaster, teachers, parents and children who participated in this study.

Appendix

Summary of the movie clip

The clip showed girls sneaking out of their bedroom at night to find something to eat in the kitchen while the headmistress and the cook are playing cards in the living room. While gathering ingredients to make a cake, the neighbour's boy comes screaming at the kitchen window which scares the girls. Some of the girls drop the eggs, flour and water they were holding, making a mess. Having heard the noise, the headmistress and the cook come running into the kitchen to find the mess and telling the girls to clean everything.

References

Bain, S. A., Baxter, J. S., & Fellowes, V. (2004). Interacting influences on interrogative suggestibility. *Legal and Criminological Psychology*, *9*, 239–252.

Bottoms, B. L., Quas, J. A., & Davis, S. L. (2007). The influence of interviewer-provided social support on children's suggestibility, memory, and disclosures. In M. E. Pipe, M. Lamb, Y. Orbach, & A. C. Cederborg (Eds.), *Child sexual abuse: Disclosure, delay and denial* (pp. 135–147). Mahwah, NJ: Erlbaum.

Bull, R. (1998). Obtaining information from child witnesses. In A. Memon, A. Vrij, & R. Bull (Eds.), *Psychology and law: Truthfulness, accuracy, and credibility* (pp. 188–209). Maidenhead: McGraw-Hill.

Carter, C. A., Bottoms, B. L., & Levine, M. (1996). Linguistic and socioemotional influences on the accuracy of children's reports. *Law and Human Behavior*, *20*, 335–358.

Ceci, S. J., & Bruck, M. (1993). Suggestibility of the child witness: A historical review and synthesis. *Psychological Bulletin*, *113*, 403–439.

Clark, D. M., & Wells, A. (1995). A cognitive model of social phobia. In R. G. Heimberg, M. R. Liebowitz, D. A. Hope, & F. R. Schneier (Eds.), *Social phobia: Diagnosis, assessment and treatment* (pp. 69–93). New York, NY: Guilford Press.

Davey, C. L., Hampton, J., Farrell, J., & Davidson, S. (1992). Some characteristics of worrying: Evidence for worrying and anxiety as separate constructs. *Personality and Individual Differences*, *13*, 133–147.

Davis, S. L., & Bottoms, B. L. (2002a). Effects of social support on children's eyewitness reports: A test of the underlying mechanism. *Law and Human Behavior*, *26*, 185–215.

Davis, S. L., & Bottoms, B. L. (2002b). Social support and children's eyewitness testimony. In M. L. Eisen, J. A. Quas, & G. S. Goodman (Eds.), *Memory and suggestibility in the forensic interview* (pp. 437–457). Mahwah, NJ: Erlbaum.

Engelberg, E., & Christianson, S.-A. (2002). Stress, trauma, and memory. In M. L. Eisen, J. A. Quas, & G. S. Goodman (Eds.), *Memory and suggestibility in the forensic interview* (pp. 143–163). Mahwah, NJ: Erlbaum.

Eysenck, M. W. (1992). *Anxiety: The cognitive perspective*. Hove: Lawrence Erlbaum Associates.

Eysenck, M. W. (1997). *Anxiety and cognition: A unified theory*. Hove: Psychology Press.

Eysenck, M. W., & Calvo, M. (1992). Anxiety and performance: The processing efficiency theory. *Cognition and Emotion*, *6*, 409–434.

Farber, I. E., & Spence, K. W. (1953). Complex learning and conditioning as a function of anxiety. *Journal of Experimental Psychology*, *45*(2), 120–125.

Fivush, R., Peterson, C., & Schwarzmueller, A. (2002). Questions and answers: The credibility of the child witnesses in the context of specific questioning techniques. In M. L. Eisen, J. A. Quas, & G. S. Goodman (Eds.), *Memory and suggestibility in the forensic interview* (pp. 331–354). Mahwah, NJ: Erlbaum.

Garven, S., Wood, J. M., Malpass, R. S., & Shaw, J. S. (1998). More than suggestion: The effect of interviewing techniques from the McMartin Preschool case. *Journal of Applied Psychology, 83*, 347–359.

Gilstrap, L. L., & Papierno, P. B. (2004). Is the cart pushing the horse? The effects of child characteristics on children's and adults' interview behaviours. *Applied Cognitive Psychology, 18*, 1059–1078.

Goodman, G., Bottoms, B., Schwartz-Kenney, B., & Rudy, L. (1991). Children's testimony for a stressful event: Improving children's reports. *Journal of Narrative and Life History, 1*, 69–99.

Goodman, G. S., Rudy, L., Bottoms, B., & Aman, C. (1990). Children's concerns and memory: Issues of ecological validity in the study of children's eyewitness testimony. In R. Fivush, & J. Hudson (Eds.), *Knowing and remembering in young children* (pp. 249–284). New York: Cambridge University Press.

Gudjonsson, G. H. (1984). A new scale of interrogative suggestibility. *Personality and Individual Differences, 5*, 303–314.

Gudjonsson, G. H. (1988). Interrogative suggestibility: Its relationship with assertiveness, social-evaluative anxiety, state anxiety and method of coping. *British Journal of Clinical Psychology, 27*, 159–166.

Gudjonsson, G. H. (1992). *The psychology of interrogations, confessions and testimony*. Chichester: Wiley.

Kelly, W. E. (2004). Examining the relationship between worry and trait anxiety. *College Student Journal, 38*, 370–373.

Krackow, E., & Lynn, S. J. (2003). Is there touch in the game of Twister? The effects of innocuous touch and suggestive questions on children's eyewitness memory. *Law and Human Behavior, 27*(6), 589–604.

Moston, S. (1989). *Social support and the quality of children's eyewitness testimony*. Unpublished Ph.D. thesis, University of Kent.

Moston, S., & Engelberg, T. (1992). The effects of social support on children's eyewitness testimony. *Applied Cognitive Psychology, 6*, 61–75.

Nathanson, R., & Saywitz, K. J. (2003). The effects of the courtroom context on children's memory and anxiety. *Journal of Psychiatry and Law, 31*, 67–98.

Quas, J. A., & Lench, H. C. (2006). Arousal at encoding, arousal at retrieval, interviewer support, and children's memory for a mild stressor. *Applied Cognitive Psychology, 19*, 1–17.

Rachman, S. (2004). *Anxiety* (2nd ed.). Hove: Psychology Press.

Ridley, A. M., & Clifford, B. R. (2004). The effects of anxious mood induction on suggestibility to misleading post-event information. *Applied Cognitive Psychology, 18*, 233–244.

Ridley, A. M., Clifford, B. R., & Keogh, E. (2002). The effects of state anxiety on the suggestibility and accuracy of child eyewitnesses. *Applied Cognitive Psychology, 16*, 547–558.

Roberts, K. P., Lamb, M. E., & Sternberg, K. J. (2004). The effects of rapport-building style on children's reports of a staged event. *Applied Cognitive Psychology, 18*, 189–202.

Sarason, I. G. (1980). Introduction to the study of test anxiety. In I. G. Sarason (Ed.), *Test anxiety: Theory, research and applications* (pp. 3–14). Hillsdale, NJ: Erlbaum.

Saywitz, K. J., Goodman, G. S., Nicholas, E., & Moan, S. F. (1991). Children's memories of a physical examination involving genital touch: Implications for reports of child sexual abuse. *Journal of Consulting and Clinical Psychology*, *57*, 682–691.

Schooler, J., & Loftus, E. F. (1986). Individual differences and experimentation: Complementary approaches to interrogative suggestibility. *Social Behaviour*, *1*, 105–112.

Spielberger, C. D. (1972). Anxiety as an emotional state. In C. D. Spielberger (Ed.), *Anxiety: Current trends in theory and research* (Vol. 1). New York: Academic Press.

Spielberger, C. D., Edwards, C. D., Lushene, R., Montuori, J., & Platzek, D. (1973). *STAI-C preliminary manual for the State–Trait Anxiety Inventory for children*. Palo Alto, CA: Consulting Psychologists Press.

Spielberger, C. D., Gorsuch, R. L., & Lushene, R. E. (1970). *Manual for the State–Trait Anxiety Inventory*. Palo Alto, CA: Consulting Psychologists Press.

Thierry, K. L., & Spence, M. J. (2004). A real-life event enhances the accuracy of preschoolers' recall. *Applied Cognitive Psychology*, *18*, 297–309.

Tousignant, J. P., Hall, D., & Loftus, E. F. (1986). Discrepancy detection and vulnerability to misleading postevent information. *Memory and Cognition*, *14*, 329–338.

Wells, A. (2005). Worry, intrusive thoughts, and generalized anxiety disorder: The metacognitive theory and treatment. In D. A. Clark (Ed.), *Intrusive thoughts in clinical disorders: Theory, research and treatment* (pp. 119–144). New York, NY: Guilford Press.

Williams, J. M. G., Watts, F. N., MacLeod, C., & Mathews, A. (1988). *Cognitive psychology and emotional disorders*. Chichester: Wiley.

Wolfradt, U., & Meyer, T. (1998). Interrogative suggestibility, anxiety and dissociation among anxious patients and normal controls. *Personality and Individual Differences*, *25*, 425–432.

Wood, J. M., McClure, K. A., & Birch, R. A. (1996). Suggestions for improving interviews in child protection agencies. *Child Maltreatment*, *1*, 223–230.

Zaragoza, M. S., & Lane, S. M. (1994). Source misattributions and the suggestibility of eyewitness memory. *Journal of Experimental Psychology: Learning, Memory and Cognition*, *20*, 934–945.

8 The investigative interviewing of children and other vulnerable witnesses: psychological research and working/professional practice

Ray Bull

What is meant by 'vulnerable' witnesses?

Around the world, there is no generally agreed definition of the word 'vulnerable' as it applies to witnesses in the investigative setting. In the last 20 years a growing number of countries have realized, largely based on psychological research, that children (because of their vulnerabilities) may well have special needs in investigative and legal procedures which heretofore had been designed for ordinary adult witnesses. In a few countries governments and/or other agencies have tried to come to grips with the needs of vulnerable adult witnesses (e.g. those with what used to be called 'mental handicap' or 'mental retardation'), especially since, such adults may be at greater risk of victimization (Knutson & Sullivan, 1993; Sabsey & Varnhagen, 1991; Turk & Brown, 1992; Williams, 1995; Wilson & Brewer, 1992). To readers it may seem obvious that a critical component of law enforcement is the ability of police officers to obtain accurate and detailed information from such witnesses. However, until fairly recently police organizations around the world have not invested much time and effort in assisting their officers to be effective at this critical task. Why is this so? There are probably several reasons, but a crucial one is that until around 25 years ago the discipline of greatest relevance, that is psychology, had little to say on this topic because relevant research had not yet been conducted. However, since then, an ever-increasing amount of high-quality psychological research has been conducted regarding how best to conduct actual investigative interviews of children and vulnerable adults. A challenge for the police has been to translate 'what works' in research studies with witnesses into their own interviews. A very relevant research topic has been that of what constitutes an effective account from witnesses.

Effective accounts

Twenty years ago, in a seminal article, Bell & Loftus (1989) found that the amount of detail provided by witnesses can have a substantial effect on mock jurors' decisions. More recently, Kulkofsky, Wang, & Ceci (2008) found that the narrative cohesion of (child) witnesses' accounts was significantly related to the accuracy of the accounts. Thus, given what has become known via psychological research about what constitutes effective witness accounts, one might expect that investigative interviewers, for example, police officers, would interview witnesses in ways that are likely to produce effective accounts.

Beliefs concerning vulnerable witnesses

Another relevant research topic is the beliefs people have about the competence of vulnerable witnesses. Stobbs & Kebbell (2003) asked jury-eligible adults all to read the same transcript of a witness for the prosecution giving evidence in a robbery case. The transcript was based on a real-life case in which the actual witness did have a learning disability. Some of the adults were informed that the witness was from the general population (i.e. they were not informed about learning disability), whereas others were informed that he had a learning disability. Having read the transcript, all of the adults filled in a questionnaire concerning their assessments of factors relating to the witness' evidence. Those participants who were informed that the witness had a learning disability rated his guilt as higher and evidence as significantly less competent, less credible, and less accurate than did those who were led to believe that the witness was from the general population. Thus, this study suggests that those who read/listen to the information/evidence provided by witnesses/victims with learning disability may (probably unwittingly) allow their negative expectations about such witnesses to bias their assessment of the quality of that information. As a consequence, of this, it is essential that such witnesses are interviewed in a way that allows them to provide high-quality information so as to (hopefully) overcome to some extent the prejudice (Aarons & Powell, 2003).

Access to justice

Over 15 years ago in the USA, Valenti-Hein & Schwartz (1993) stated that 'Throughout history various groups have been excluded from the legal system because they have been deemed incompetent to provide accurate and valid testimony' (p. 287). They noted that whereas 'people with mental retardation' (p. 291) may be more at risk of sexual victimization, only a very small proportion of such victimizations seemed to make progress through investigative and court procedures (Sabsey & Doe, 1991; Tharinger, Horton, & Millea, 1990). Such a state of affairs (Spencer & Flin, 1990) also used to apply to abused children, but in some countries governments and/or relevant agencies have taken major steps to address this (at least for children – see below). In England and Wales in the late 1980s the government set up a committee (chaired by Judge Thomas Pigot QC) to make recommendations regarding *children* giving evidence. Members of this committee (Home Office, 1989) were minded to make (what was then) the radical recommendation that investigative interviews with child witnesses in serious cases should routinely be video recorded but they were very concerned as to whether there existed sufficient research on which to base guidance on how such now 'publicly' available interviewing should be conducted. They were assured by several people, including myself, that such psychological research did exist. (For more on this see below.)

The lack of access to justice for vulnerable *adult* witnesses (see Sanders, Creaton, Bird, & Weber, 1997) led the government in England and Wales to publish in 2000 the document *No secrets: Guidance on developing and implementing multi-agency policies and procedures to protect vulnerable adults from abuse* which made the point that in order to communicate with vulnerable adults interviewers may well need specific training (government again having checked that sufficient psychological and other research was available upon which to base such training). This 2000 document also stated that the *Independent Longcare Inquiry* (Bergner, 1998) had noted the importance of 'communication and the best use of skill'. (We were involved in assisting the police in the Longcare case to interview to the best of their ability – for more on this see Milne & Bull, 1999.)

A comprehensive review of some of the provisions in *other* countries for gathering information from vulnerable witnesses was published in by the Scottish Executive Central Research Unit (2002). This review pointed out that few jurisdictions around the world had begun to face up to this issue. Several pages of the report deal with the vexed issue of the questioning of vulnerable people and it noted that 'A general point to arise consistently in the literature . . . is that many . . . professionals are relatively poor, and often untrained in questioning . . . "vulnerable" witnesses' (p. 65). However, as will be mentioned below, there are many examples of good interview practice arising from the findings of psychological research.

Special measures

With regard to access to justice for vulnerable adults, the 1999 *Youth justice and criminal evidence act* in England and Wales is among the most important pieces of legislation in the world. It enables a range of 'special measures' to be used to assist the provision of testimony/evidence/information from vulnerable people (which had hitherto been a problem – Bull & Cullen, 1992, 1993).

Among the 'special measures' are the use of:

- screens (so that the witness in court cannot see the defendant),
- live TV link (from the court to where the witness is),
- video recorded evidence-in-chief (e.g. the previously video recorded investigative interview with the police, so long as the interviewing was of an appropriate, 'best evidence' standard),
- use of an intermediary (either at court or during the police interview to assist communication, it having been noticed by government that psychological research had made it clear that communicating with vulnerable people requires considerable skill – for reviews see Milne & Bull, 1999, 2001, 2006), and
- aids to communication to enable such witnesses to give their best evidence (e.g. by the use of communication boards, particularly by the use of skilled investigative interviewing).

What does skilled interviewing consist of? Official guidance

To assist interviewers to be skilled in 2002 the government (for England and Wales) published *Achieving best evidence (ABE) in criminal proceedings: Guidance for vulnerable and intimated witnesses, including children* (Home Office, 2002, 2008). This extensive document has a large section on the interviewing of vulnerable *adults* (written by myself) which was informed by relevant research (conducted largely by psychologists). It also has a substantial section regarding children which updated the government's 1992 document entitled *Memorandum of good practice on video recorded interviews with child witnesses for criminal proceedings* (Home Office, 1992). Psychological research in the 10 years preceding 1992 had demonstrated that even young children are usually able to give a worthwhile report of what happened if they are interviewed appropriately (Bull, 1988, 1992, 2001; Davies, Stevenson-Robb, & Flin, 1986; Fivush & Hudson, 1990; Murray & Gough, 1991). However, children (and indeed adults) rarely provided a full account (Flin, Boon, Knox, & Bull, 1992) and so questioning was necessary to gather more information from them (Dent & Flin, 1992; Perry & Wrightsman, 1991). Psychological research had also demonstrated that inappropriate interviewing, especially that with a suggestive style, can bias children's accounts (Baxter, 1990; Ceci & Bruck, 1993, 1995; Doris, 1991). This 1992 *Memorandum* was based on drafts commissioned from a psychologist (i.e. myself – on interviewing) and a law professor (e.g. relevant legislation).

Since, the 1992 publication of the *Memorandum* a large number of 'laboratory' and school based studies have been conducted that have underlined the value of the detailed guidance given within it. These include the effects of:

(i) variations in the types of questions asked (e.g. Carter, Bottoms, & Levine, 1996; Hardy & Van Leeuwen, 2004; Hughes-Scholes & Powell, 2008; Peterson & Biggs, 1997),
(ii) interviewer misunderstandings/distortions of what the child has just said on what the child subsequently says (Roberts & Lamb, 1999),
(iii) interviewer praise on what children subsequently say (Billings *et al.*, 2007),
(iv) warning children that some of the interviewer's questions might be misleading (Endres, Poggenpohl, & Erben, 1999).

The 1992 *Memorandum* was probably the world's first governmental guidance on this topic and its large section on interviewing was extensively informed by psychological research (for more on this see Bull & Barnes, 1995; Milne & Bull, 1999). The interviewing advice described in detail in the *Memorandum* and in *ABE* (for interviewing *children* and *vulnerable adult* witnesses) employs the 'phased approach' (Jones & McQuiston, 1988), involving the four consecutive phases of:

1 establish good rapport,
2 then obtain as much free narrative as possible,

3 then ask questions of the right type in the right order, and
4 then have meaningful closure.

The *rapport phase* involves setting up good communication with the witness and helping her/him to relax (e.g. by talking about topics of interest to the witness that are 'neutral' regarding the aims of the interview). This communication will supplement the interviewer's prior knowledge (if any) of relevant witness skills/limitations. During this time witnesses should be informed that it is important and indeed acceptable that they say 'Don't understand', 'Don't know', 'Can't remember' (when appropriate).

The *free narrative* phase involves encouraging witnesses to provide spontaneously an account in their own words (free from interruptions/questions, but prompts such as 'Tell me more about that' can be used if necessary). Research has demonstrated that young children and some vulnerable adults spontaneously provide less information in free narrative than other/ordinary people, though this information may be no less accurate. Thus, a questioning phase is even more likely to be needed.

In the *questioning phase* interviewers must bear in mind that psychological research has demonstrated that some types of questioning are more likely to unduly influence witnesses' replies. This phase should always begin with *open questions* (that are initially based on what the witness has just said in free narrative). For example, if a witness had earlier said in free narrative that 'A man in the park frightened me', an open question could be 'What did the man in the park look like?'. Once open questions have been asked, then *specific questions* can be employed. These remain 'open' in style but they (i) seek extension/clarification of information already provided and (ii) help witnesses understand what is relevant from the interviewer's point of view by, for example, asking 'What. . .?', 'Who. . .?', 'Where. . .?', and 'When. . .?'. Only after these questions should *forced-choice* (sometimes referred to as closed or option-posing) questions be asked. These provide the witness with a limited number of alternatives to choose from and, as long as they do contain a number of sensible and equally likely alternatives, should not be suggestive (i.e. imply an answer). *Leading questions* imply the answer and should only be used as a last resort and only when necessary (e.g. to immediately safeguard a person). If a leading question is used and the witness provides an answer such a question should not immediate be followed by another leading question but by an open, or specific, or a forced-choice question.

In the *closure phase* the interviewer should (i) summarize the important information provided by the witness as much as possible in the witness' own words, having told the witness to intervene if any summarizing is incorrect, (ii) answer any questions the witness has, (iii) thank the witness and try to assist the witness to leave the interview in as positive a frame of mind as possible (e.g. by returning to the neutral topics discussed in the rapport phase), and (iv) provide the witness with the interviewer's contact details (e.g. in case the witness decides later to provide more information).

Thus, psychological research also played a major role in assisting government to decide what may well work in interviews with vulnerable *adults* as well as *children* (Westcott, Davies, & Bull, 2002).

Studies of the investigative interviewing of child witnesses

While these positive contributions from psychological research concerning how best to interview have been incorporated into 'official' guidance documents (such as *ABE*), psychologists have also conducted studies of how well police officers do actually interview children in investigative interviews (i.e. in the 'field'). Among the first of these examined whether police officers in England and Wales were able to follow the 1992 *Memorandum*'s guidance having received some relevant training (Davies, Wilson, Mitchell, & Milsom, 1995). This study found that the recommended first phase of rapport was generally well conducted and that the second phase involving trying to obtain from the child a free narrative account was present in the majority of the (video recorded) interviews assessed. However, the third phase involving questioning was not well conducted (e.g. in only 30% off the 40 interviews did the interviewers first employ open questions), and the final closure phase was too brief. A later study by Sternberg, Lamb, Davies, & Westcott (2001) used 119 transcripts of (video recorded) interviews conducted between 1994 and 1997 (i.e. when relevant training had become more established) also found a mixture of interviewer strengths and weaknesses. For example, many conducted the closure phase in a way that could encourage the child to say more if she/he wished to do so (Bull, 1996), but only half of the interviewers empowered the children to reply 'Don't know' (the advice to do this being based on relevant psychological research and theory – Milne & Bull, 1999).

Using 70 of the transcripts analysed by Sternberg, Lamb, Davies, & Westcott (2001) and Sternberg, Lamb, Orbach, Esplin, & Mitchell (2001), Westcott & Kynan (2006) found that the interviewers (who had received relevant training) were able to deliver the four phases in the recommended order and to have in the initial rapport phase some discussion of non-investigation topics. However, relatively few conducted the free narrative phase appropriately (e.g. they moved too quickly on to the questioning phase). In connection with the weaker aspects of interviewer performance, these researchers raised the important question of 'Is it a matter of resourcing, or is the task in *Memorandum* interviews almost impossible to achieve?' (p. 378). It seems that the national court of appeal for England and Wales is of the opinion that interviews which adhere to the relevant government guidance are possible to achieve in that not following such guidance can relate to whether a conviction is to be quashed (see the case all of R v H (CA) on June the 27, 2005 – cite: BLD 2806052805).

The training in England and Wales of child witness interviewers involving investigative psychology may well recently have improved. For example, an extensive training pack (written by our small group of psychologists) was a few years ago disseminated by government (Welsh Assembly Government, 2004).

Unfortunately, no comprehensive study has yet been published on what more recently trained interviewers are able to achieve in England and Wales.

In the USA in 1996 a pioneering study of the transcripts of 42 visually recorded interviews with children in routine sexual abuse investigations took place (Warren, Woodall, Hunt, & Perry, 1996). Whereas the majority of interviewers did first of all attempt to establish rapport with the children, they failed to commence the questioning with open-ended questions or to explain to the children that 'Don't know', Don't understand', and 'Don't remember' can be appropriate answers. Also in the USA the important relationship between police interviewer performance and children's accounts began to be examined. For example, Craig, Scheibe, Raskin, Kircher, & Dodd (1999) found (in 48 transcripts of real-life interviews) that interviewers who encouraged free narrative and used open questions obtained in the children's accounts more of the content criteria thought to be indicative that the children were recounting a genuinely experienced event (also see Wood & Garven, 2000).

The findings of these field studies have now been replicated in several other countries. For example, in Sweden (Cederborg, Orbach, Sternberg, & Lamb, 2000) and Norway (Thoresen, Lonnum, Melinder, Stridbeck, & Magnussen, 2006) interviewers rarely used open questions, but relied very much on a closed questioning style, even when the children responded well to open questions. Interestingly, Thoresen *et al.* (2006) noted from their 91 police interviews conducted between 1985 and 2002 that the proportionate use of open questions had increased across the years. Recently, in Finland Korkman, Santilla, Westeraker, & Sandnabba (2008) found that even when in investigative interviews child witnesses responded to open questions with judicially significant information, the next questions posed to them were nevertheless closed questions. (Also see Korkman, Santilla, Drzewiecki, & Sandnabba, 2008.) In Estonia, we found a similar pattern in (relatively untrained) police video recorded interviews with child witnesses (Kask & Bull, 2009). During these interviews (conducted in 2004/5) the proportion of open questions decreased over time even though the children produced longer answers to open questions and more judicially relevant information emerged in response to open questions. Clearly, such interviewers are likely to benefit from a greater awareness of relevant psychological research that should be achieved via their training.

Studies of investigative interviews of vulnerable adult witnesses

Only a limited number of studies are currently available on how police officers actually interview vulnerable adult witnesses. Stacey (1999) reported her Australian study of the interviewing of people with intellectual disability about a short film clip she had shown to them. Although most of the police officers who volunteered to take part in this study had many years of police experience, they had received little or no prior training on how best to communicate with such witnesses (this was very typical of policing around the world at the time – that is, only 10 years ago). Stacey found that 30% of the information the witnesses provided was incorrect and that this was in large part due to the police interviewers' use of suggestive and multiple-choice questions. Those interviews which allowed/encouraged the witnesses firstly to provide free recall of the event contained very few errors in such free recall. The police officers with more years of service conducted interviews which contained less incorrect recall and confabulations.

A study that examined how well *specially trained* police officers interviewed children with intellectual disabilities was conducted by Agnew, Powell, & Snow (2006). These 28 officers had all previously completed a training course on interviewing children that included a day on intellectual disability. The training included mention of useful findings from relevant psychological research. The 28 children with intellectual disability were interviewed (one per officer) about a staged event that they had participated in at their school several days earlier. Analyses of the interviews revealed that these *trained* police interviewers only very rarely used leading or suggestive questions (in contrast to Stacey's finding – see above) and their questioning was better than caregivers who also were interviewers in this study. The police officers did commence the interview with free narrative prompts. However, they began employing specific questions in order to clarify information while the children were still supplying free narrative.

Given that in the above studies those interviewers who had received minimal or no relevant training were generally rather poor at interviewing vulnerable witnesses in ways in line with the findings of basic and applied psychological research, we should ask why this is so? One largely ignored, yet rather obvious reason is that the existence of training implies that people do not naturally do what the training involves because if they did it, there will be no need for the training. The need for training implies that people should stop doing what they normally, naturally do, and instead do something different (Powell, 2002). Awareness of this reason makes it much clearer why in the above 'field' studies investigative interviewer performance was a mixture of appropriate and inappropriate behaviours.

An outstanding example

An outstanding example of how to combine the findings of research from investigative (and other aspects of) psychology with what is known about making training effective has recently been achieved by Lamb and his colleagues. This shining example is eloquently overviewed in their book (Lamb, Hershkowitz, Orbach, & Esplin, 2008). Several years ago Lamb and Sternberg realized that the USA (and many other countries) did not, unlike England and Wales, have available nationally a comprehensive child witness investigative interviewing protocol. They also noted that in many places training is very basic or non-existent. They, therefore, rightly decided to develop a protocol that is quite prescriptive in its advice (i.e. more prescriptive than the *Memorandum* and *ABE* were designed to be in England and Wales).

Sternberg, Lamb, Esplin, & Baradaran (1999) published the results of their pilot study of the use of the scripted protocol which they had developed, based extensively on prior research on children's abilities and interviewers' limitations (e.g. Poole & Lamb, 1999; Sternberg *et al.*, 1996). This crucial pilot study was followed up by several studies of the use of the protocol in the field by official youth investigators in Israel (Orbach *et al.*, 2000) and by police officers in the USA (Sternberg *et al.*, 2001), in England (Lamb *et al.*, 2006), and in Canada (Cyr, Lamb, Pelletier, Leduc, & Perron, 2006; Dion & Cyr, 2008; in this latter, some interviewers were social workers).

These studies produced convincing evidence for the effectiveness of the protocol (plus its related training), including (among other things):

- a greater use of open questions,
- fewer option-posing questions (though these still constituted 20% of interviewer utterances – these are questions that include a limited number of alternatives, none of which may actually be correct, but the question implies that the interviewee should choose one of the alternatives),
- fewer suggestive questions (these are questions that imply the answer), and
- more details being provided by the children before the first option-posing question was asked.

However, protocol interviews did not elicit more details than did the comparison, non-protocol interviews. However, we know from other research that the information provided by children in response to open questions is usually more reliable and accurate than in response to option-posing questions.

It should be noted that in Canada though Dion & Cyr (2008, p. 150) found that a small number of interviewers seemed unable to interview in a way that followed the protocol even though they had participated in a 5 day intensive training programme in which current knowledge about children's memory and developmental capacities, as well as factors influencing suggestibility were presented and discussed, 'role-plays were filmed . . . feedback was analysed and discussed in detail'.

Lamb's team is aware that the protocol has potential that has not yet been realized and that some further issues need to be addressed. These include:

- demonstrating that the information the protocol elicits from children in real-life investigations is indeed more accurate (Lamb *et al.*, 2008) and produces investigative leads (Darwish, Hershkowitz, Lamb, & Orbach, 2008) and
- developing a version of the protocol that is effective with particularly vulnerable children (and adults).

Some other issues

Two other issues that would benefit from more research being conducted on them include (i) the effects of how the interviewer behaves and (ii) the effects of long delays.

The effect of interviewer manner

Since 1992 I have regularly been asked to write expert reports on video recorded investigative interviews with children. In the early days I noticed that whereas some interviewers adopted a supportive style (often these were social workers), others were more businesslike (often these were the police officers who may have moved into child protection after years of interviewing adult suspects). Such variations in manner, style, behaviour have not been as extensively investigated as the effects of variations in the content of what interviewers say. This is surprising given that the few relevant studies have found significant effects (e.g. Almerigogna, Ost, Bull, & Akehurst, 2007; Goodman, Bottoms, Schwartz-Kenney, & Rudy, 1991). In one of our studies, for example, young children significantly more often went along with misleading questions if the interviewer adopted an authoritative style of behaviour (Bull & Corran, 2003). In another (Paterson, Bull, & Vrij, 2002) the interviewer behaved in a 'supportive' or in a 'formal' manner (by varying clothing – informal/formal; demeanour – lot/little smiling + eye-contact; introduction of self to child using 'first name'/'family' name).

The supportive style resulted in significantly more correct:

- free recall,
- recall to open questions,
- recall to 'reflection' questions (these are questions that repeat back to the child, in the form of a question, what the child has just said, for example, the child says 'then he hurt me', and the interviewer follows this with 'he hurt you?' perhaps adding 'what can you tell me about that?'), and
- recall to final prompt for 'any more information?'.

The effect of long delays

One of the greatest weaknesses in psychological research on memory over the decades has been to assume that since, short-term memory lasts only some seconds or a few minutes, studies purporting to study long-term memory can merely employ delays of hours or a few days. Within the realm of investigative psychology, studies (and the relevant theories) need to involve delays of months or years (and, of course, stimuli that are large, complex, dynamic, and meaningful rather than pointless lists of words and the like used in many laboratory studies). Fortunately, a few enterprising and realistic researchers have studied children's memory for meaningful events after very long delays (these I overviewed in Memon, Vrij, & Bull, 2003). For example, one of the studies involving the longest delay (Quas *et al.*, 1999) examined the recall of young children of an intimate and distressing medical test procedure that took place between 7 and 2 years prior. The researchers found that while the children who are only 2 years old at the time of the test later provided no clear evidence of remembering it, children aged three or older at the time of the event did delay to demonstrate some memory object. Furthermore, while age at the time of the event did relate to how much of it the children could remember when minimally prompted, it did not relate to the accuracy of the children's responses to direct questions about it. In Peterson & Whalen (2001) reported a study of children's recall of an event that took place several years earlier. Children who had been aged between 2 and 13 years at a time of having a medical emergency (that is, experiencing an injury serious enough to require going to the hospital emergency department) were interviewed 5 years later. A large proportion of what the children recalled was correct. In discussing their findings these researchers stated that 'children as young as 3 or 4 at the time of event occurrence had impressive recall' (p. S21) and 'Even after 5 years children who are at least 3 years of age recalled over 80% of injury central components, with an accuracy rate of over 80%' (p. S19).

From such studies of long delays it does seem that even relatively young children can produce comprehensive and accurate accounts of what they experienced years ago. These long delay studies counter the view that children's accounts of what (allegedly) happened years before should not be relied upon to secure criminal convictions. Clearly, we know from psychological research that if one purposely questions or interviews children in ways designed to produce errors (e.g. studies of the 'misinformation effect' and of 'false memory') that, indeed, inaccuracies will result.

Particularly vulnerable witnesses

Children with learning disability

Although the research literature regarding 'ordinary' child witnesses is now vast, that concerning particularly vulnerable children is sparse. However, there is a growing research literature regarding the questioning/interviewing of children with learning disability.

Henry & Gudjonsson (1999, p. 491) emphasized that 'there is little research on child witnesses with mental retardation'. They reviewed the pioneering study by Dent (1986) and our study of the usefulness of the cognitive interview for children with mild learning disabilities (Milne & Bull, 1996). In their own study children with average or low intelligence (mean IQ = 60) witnessed a staged event and the next day were interviewed about it in line with the government's *Memorandum of good practice.* With regard to the amounts of free recall of the witnessed event, children with mental retardation did not differ from the other children, nor did they differ with regard to open questions. However, with regard to misleading questions (of the 'yes/no' type) the lower intelligence children were more often misled than were similarly aged children of average intelligence. Misleading questions are ones which imply an incorrect answer, for example, saying (as in one case I was involved in) 'I bet that really hurt you?' when the child had not yet mentioned being hurt (and it later turned out that she was not, even though she went along with the misleading question).

Henry & Gudjonsson (2007) conducted a further study in which children also witnessed a real-life event. They found that children with intellectual disabilities (i) freely recalled less of the event than did ordinary children of similar ages and (ii) produced more errors in response to misleading questions. Thus, it could be that children with intellectual disability do recall less than do ordinary children. This lesser recall will cause interviewers to ask questions, but these questions need to be appropriate (e.g. as advised in 'official' guidance documents and in the book by Lamb *et al.* (2008)).

In a study by Agnew & Powell (2004) children participated at school in a magic show. A large number of children with mild and moderate intellectual disabilities took part as did two comparison groups of ordinary children, one group matched for actual age with the children with intellectual disabilities, and another group matched with these children for 'mental age'. All of the children were first interviewed 3 days after the magic show. The major purpose of this interview was to question the children in a suggestive way. Then, 1 day later, a 'proper' interview was conducted that followed best practice guidelines (e.g. Bull, 1996). In the first interview, the children with intellectual disabilities (spontaneously) mentioned fewer items from within the magic show. Therefore, in order to obtain more information from these children about the non-recalled items the interviewer (who was the same for all children) asked them 'specific' questions (as defined earlier in this article). With regard to the specific questions, the percentage accuracy of the children with intellectual disabilities was significantly lower than the other two groups. Such a result is not surprising. However, a very surprising finding was that the children with intellectual disabilities were no more affected in this second interview by the seven 'false detail' questions asked in the prior, first interview than were the other children. With the benefit of hindsight, this surprising result could be explained by the possibility that 'The poorer memory and receptive and expressive language skills of the children with intellectual disabilities may have reduced the likelihood that the children remembered the interviewer suggestions' (p. 290). Indeed, these children also were no more affected by the 'true detail' questions from the first interview. The greater error responses made by these children to the specific questions 'tended to be "external intrusion" errors (feasible details that did not occur in the event . . .). Many of these errors were stereotypical responses' (p. 291; i.e. what typically happens in a magic show). Thus, the children with intellectual disabilities were able to use their own general knowledge to answer the questions (incorrectly). Agnew & Powell (2004) concluded by highlighting the importance of *not* underestimating what some vulnerable children could achieve if interviewed properly.

Elderly adults

There is a growing recognition that some very elderly witnesses may require skilled interviewing if their communication and cognitive functioning have declined. However, research suggests that people hold beliefs that all elderly witnesses are more suggestible and less accurate (e.g. Brimacombe, Jung, Garrioch, & Allison, 2003; Ross, Dunning, Toglia, & Ceci, 1990). Indeed, Wright & Holliday (2005) found that a majority of police officers in England indicated (on a questionnaire) that they believed older witnesses (i.e. over 60 years of age) to be less reliable and less thorough than younger adult witnesses (even though many of these officers rarely dealt with older witnesses). Again, this research on beliefs suggests that the information gained from such (older) witnesses/victims may need to be particularly impressive to overcome people's negative expectations.

In 2007 when overviewing the available research on older witnesses, Bartlett & Memon (2007) stated that 'research on the older eyewitness is in its infancy' (p. 311). In their own research younger adults (average age 22 years) and older adults (71 years) were interviewed about an encounter they had experienced 1 month earlier (as part of the experiment). The older participants recalled only half as much information as did the younger adults, and the older adults' recall was also less accurate (77 vs. 89%). Similarly, Wright & Holliday (2007) found that young adults recalled significantly more of an event than did either 'old-old' adults (average age 82 years) or 'young-old' adults (average age 67 years), and with greater accuracy. However, the actual number of errors in recall was not affected by age (probably because the interviews were conducted in line with the relevant guidance documents – *ABE*). Clearly, effective questioning of older witnesses is necessary to obtain fuller accounts and this should be based on the findings of relevant psychological research.

Guidance on interviewing particularly vulnerable witnesses

This section will provide brief examples of the additional advice given, and the research underpinning it, regarding that part of *ABE* that focuses on *particularly* vulnerable witnesses.

Coping with the unfamiliar

Many investigative interviewers will not be very familiar with various types of particularly vulnerable witness (e.g. those with communicative and physical disabilities). This is important not only in terms of interviewers trying to understand what it is a witness wishes to convey and interviewers being understood by witnesses, it is also important in terms of interviewers' reactions to vulnerable people. Research has made it clear that when people meet others with whom they are unfamiliar their own behaviour may well become abnormal (Heinemann, 1990). This unusual behaviour is often noted by vulnerable people who may view it as a sign of our discomfort (Coleman & DePaulo, 1991). Interviewers also need to be aware that while they may intentionally try to act in a friendly and helpful way to vulnerable witnesses, they may at the same time unwittingly be giving off contradictory signals of unease and/or embarrassment, anxiety, insecurity, and so on, including feelings about their own incompetence. Interviewers should also be aware that for many disabled people their disability is not central to their self concept (Coleman & DePaulo, 1991). They should try to focus on the vulnerable witness as a person rather than on the vulnerability.

The pace of the interview

A considerable proportion of particularly vulnerable witnesses will require that their interviews go at a much slower pace than do other witnesses. Psychological research (summarized in Milne & Bull, 1999) strongly suggests that interviewers will need:

- to slow down their speech rate,
- to allow extra time for the witness to take in what has just been said,
- to provide time for the witness to prepare a response,
- to be patient if the witness replies slowly, especially if an intermediary is being used,
- to avoid immediately posing the next question, and
- to avoid interrupting.

The rapport phase

Vulnerable witnesses can spend much of their lives trying to appear competent (Perske, 1994) and, therefore, may be especially unwilling to admit 'I don't know' unless they are assisted in the rapport phase to realize how good it is to say this (when appropriate, of course). Communication (on neutral topics) in this phase should guide the interviewer concerning this particularly vulnerable witness' relevant competencies. Establishing rapport is likely to decrease the gap between what the witness can remember and that he/she chooses to say to the interviewer (Leander, Granhag, & Christianson, 2009).

The free narrative phase

Only the most general, open-ended questions should be asked in this phase as guidance to the witness concerning the general area of life experience relevant to the investigation. Research findings consistently have shown that improper questioning of vulnerable people is a greater source of distortion of their accounts than are memory deficits (Bull, 1995) and that the accuracy of their free recall is greater than their accuracy in response to questions (Kebbell & Hatton, 1999; Porter, Yuille, & Bent, 1995).

The questioning phase

Some vulnerable interviewees may be particularly compliant in that they will try to be helpful by going along with much of what they believe the interviewer 'wants to hear' and/or is suggesting to them. This is particularly so for witnesses who believe the interviewer to be an authority figure (Ericson, Perlman, & Isaacs, 1994).

Research has often found that some particularly vulnerable witnesses acquiesce to 'yes/no' questions. That is, they answer such questions affirmatively with 'Yes' regardless of question content (Matikka & Vesala, 1997). This can even occur even when an almost identical 'yes/no' question is asked subsequently but this time with the opposite meaning. Similarly, sometimes 'nay-saying' (repeatedly responding with 'No') will occur, particularly for questions dealing with matters that are socially disapproved of/social taboos (Shaw & Budd, 1982). Questions that have a 'yes/no' format can very often be transformed into questions that have an 'either/or' format. (For example, 'Did he touch you over your clothes or under your clothes?' rather than 'Did he put his hand under your clothes?'). Such 'either/or' questions, by avoiding 'yea-saying' or 'nay-saying', more frequently elicit reliable responses from vulnerable people than do 'yes/no' questions (Heal & Sigelman, 1995).

Some vulnerable witnesses may not seem able to provide any free narrative, and thus, some interview protocols focus on maximizing the number of open-ended questions used. For a small proportion of vulnerable witnesses use of specific questions may be necessary to elicit a disclosure, but such questions should not bias the witness' response and they should wherever possible be followed up by the use of open questions.

Ignoring of unwanted information

Investigative interviewers should be aware of the common human frailty of ignoring information contrary to one's own view. This ignoring of 'unwanted' information may be even more likely to affect interviewers of particularly vulnerable people if they believe such witnesses to be less competent than ordinary witnesses (Antaki & Rapley, 1996).

Some remaining issues

So far, this article has overviewed, in the limited space available, some of the important psychological research findings that can serve to have an impact on investigative interviewers, such as the police, and upon legal processes. However, a number of other topics need to be researched/resolved. For example, almost no published research has examined the role that interviewee or interviewer ethnicity is likely to play (e.g. witnesses from various ethnicities may well differ in their willingness to talk about sexual/familial matters) nor the related issue of the use of interpreters (Powell, 2003). Also needed are studies which are able to compare (i) the actual sexual abuse vulnerable witnesses experienced with (ii) their recall of it. Of course, conducting such studies requires the highest standards of the researcher (e.g. in terms of ethics, of obtaining access to 'records' of the actual abuse, of interviewing such witnesses skilfully). It was impressive to note that Lina Leander did just this for her 2007 doctorate (see Leander, Christianson, & Granhag, 2007, 2008; Leander, Granhag, & Christianson, 2005, 2009).

Psychological research thus has discovered much that can inform good interviewing practice, and in some countries *investigators* (e.g. the police) have attempted to improve their practice accordingly. Now it is clearly time that those who interview/question such witnesses in *court proceedings* (e.g. legal 'professionals') brought themselves up to date. Pioneering psychological research in England (by Kebbell), in Australia (by Cashmore & Trimboli, 2005), and in New Zealand (by Zajac, 2009; Zajac, Gross, & Hayne, 2003; Zajac & Hayne, 2003, 2006) has made it clear that most of those who question vulnerable witnesses *during court proceedings* largely seem to be unaware of the constructive findings of relevant psychological research and seem presently to be rather poor at this task.

References

Aarons, N., & Powell, M. (2003). Issues related to the interviewer's ability to elicit reports from children with an intellectual disability: A review. *Current Issues in Criminal Justice*, *14*, 257–268.

Agnew, S., & Powell, M. (2004). The effect of intellectual disability on children's recall of an event across different question types. *Law and Human Behavior*, *28*, 273–294.

Agnew, S., Powell, M., & Snow, P. (2006). An examination of the questioning styles of police officers and caregivers when interviewing children with intellectual disabilities. *Legal and Criminological Psychology*, *11*, 35–53.

Almerigogna, J., Ost, J., Bull, R., & Akehurst, L. (2007). A state of high anxiety: How unsupportive interviewers can increase the suggestibility of child witnesses. *Applied Cognitive Psychology*, *21*, 963–974.

Antaki, C., & Rapley, M. (1996). Questions and answers to psychological assessment schedules: Hidden troubles in quality of life interviews. *Journal of Intellectual Disability Research*, *40*, 421–437.

Bartlett, J., & Memon, A. (2007). Eyewitness memory in young and older adults. In R. Lindsay, D. Ross, J. D. Read, & M. Toglia (Eds.), *Handbook of eyewitness psychology* (Vol. 2, pp. 309–338). Mahwah, NJ: Erlbaum.

Baxter, J. (1990). The suggestibility of child witnesses: A review. *Applied Cognitive Psychology*, *4*, 393–407.

Bell, B., & Loftus, E. (1989). Degree of detail of eyewitness testimony and mock juror judgments. *Journal of Applied Social Psychology*, *18*, 1171–1192.

Bergner, T. (1998). *Independent Longcare inquiry*. London: Department of Health.

Billings, F. J., Taylor, T., Burns, J., Corey, D., Garven, S., & Wood, J. (2007). Can reinforcement induce children to falsely incriminate themselves? *Law and Human Behavior*, *31*, 125–139.

Brimacombe, C. A., Jung, S., Garrioch, L., & Allison, M. (2003). Perceptions of older adult eyewitnesses: Will you believe me when I'm 64? *Law and Human Behavior*, *27*, 507–522.

Bull, R. (1988). Children as witnesses. *Policing*, *4*, 130–143.

Bull, R. (1992). Obtaining evidence expertly: The reliability of interviews with child witnesses. *Expert Evidence*, *1*, 5–12.

Bull, R. (1995). Interviewing people with communication disabilities. In R. Bull & D. Carson (Eds.), *Handbook of psychology in legal contexts*. Chichester: Wiley.

Bull, R. (1996). Good practice for video recorded interviews with child witnesses for use in criminal proceedings. In G. Davies, S. Lloyd-Bostock, M. McMurran, & C. Wilson (Eds.), *Psychology, law and criminal justice*. Berlin: de Gruyter.

Bull, R. (2001). *Children and the law*. An edited volume plus commentaries, Blackwell series of essential readings in developmental psychology, Oxford: Blackwell.

Bull, R., & Barnes, P (1995). Children as witnesses. In D. Bancroft & R. Carr (Eds.), *Influencing children's development*. Oxford: Blackwell.

Bull, R., & Corran, E. (2003). Interviewing child witnesses: Past and future. *International Journal of Police Science and Management*, *4*, 315–322.

Bull, R., & Cullen, C. (1992). *Witnesses who have mental handicaps*. Edinburgh: Document prepared for the Crown Office.

Bull, R., & Cullen, C. (1993). Interviewing the mentally handicapped. *Policing, 9*, 88–100.

Carter, C., Bottoms, B., & Levine, M. (1996). Linguistic and socio-emotional influences on the accuracy of children's reports. *Law and Human Behavior, 20*, 335–358.

Cashmore, J., & Trimboli, L. (2005). *An evaluation of the NSW child sexual assault special jurisdiction pilot*. Sydney: NSW Bureau of Crime Statistics and Research.

Ceci, S., & Bruck, M. (1993). Suggestibility of the child witness: A historical review and synthesis. *Psychological Bulletin, 113*, 403–439.

Ceci, S., & Bruck, M. (1995). *Jeopardy in the courtroom: A scientific analysis of children's testimony*. Washington, DC: American Psychological Association.

Cederborg, A., Orbach, Y, Sternberg, K., & Lamb, M. (2000). Investigative interviews of child witnesses in Sweden. *Child Abuse and Neglect, 24*, 1355–1361.

Coleman, L., & DePaulo, B. (1991). Uncovering the human spirit: Moving beyond disability and 'missed' communications. In N. Coupland, H. Giles, & J. Wiemann (Eds.), *Miscommunication and problematic talk* (pp. 61–84). Newbury Park, CA: Sage.

Craig, R., Scheibe, R., Raskin, D., Kircher, R., & Dodd, D. (1999). Interviewer questions and content analysis of children's statements of sexual abuse. *Applied Developmental Science, 3*, 77–85.

Cyr, M., Lamb, M., Pelletier, J., Leduc, P., & Perron, A. (2006, July). *Assessing the effectiveness of the NICHD investigative interview protocol in francophone Quebec*. Paper presented at the Second International Investigative Interviewing Conference, Portsmouth.

Darwish, T., Hershkowitz, I., Lamb, M., & Orbach, Y. (2008). *The effect of the NICHD protocol on the elicitation of investigative leads in child sexual abuse investigations*. Paper presented at the American Psychology-Law Society Conference, Jacksonville, Fl.

Davies, G., Stevenson-Robb, Y., & Flin, R. (1986). The reliability of children's testimony. *International Legal Practitioner, 11*, 95–103.

Davies, G., Wilson, C., Mitchell, R., & Milsom, J. (1995). *Videotaping children's evidence: An evaluation*. London: Home Office.

Dent, H. (1986). An experimental study of the effectiveness of different techniques of questioning mentally handicapped child witnesses. *British Journal of Clinical Psychology, 25*, 13–17.

Dent, H., & Flin, R. (1992). *Children as witnesses*. Chichester: Wiley.

Dion, J., & Cyr, M. (2008). The use of the NICHD protocol to enhance the quantity of details obtained from children with low verbal abilities in investigative interviews: A pilot study. *Journal of Child Sexual Abuse, 17*, 144–162.

Doris, J. (1991). *The suggestibility of children's recollections: Implications for eyewitness testimony*. Washington, DC: American Psychological Association.

Endres, J., Poggenpohl, C., & Erben, C. (1999). Repetitions, warnings, and video: Cognitive and motivational components in preschool children's suggestibility. *Legal and Criminological Psychology, 4*, 129–146.

Ericson, K., Perlman, N., & Isaacs, B. (1994). Witness competency, communication issues and people with developmental disabilities. *Developmental Disabilities Bulletin, 22*, 101–109.

Fivush, R., & Hudson, J. (1990). *Knowing and remembering in young children*. New York: Cambridge University Press.

Flin, R., Boon, J., Knox, A., & Bull, R. (1992). The effect of a five month delay on children's and adults' eyewitness memory. *British Journal of Psychology, 83*, 323–336.

Goodman, G., Bottoms, B., Schwartz-Kenney, B., & Rudy, L. (1991). Children's testimony about a stressful event. *Journal of Narrative and Life History*, *1*, 69–99.

Hardy, C., & Van Leeuwen, S. (2004). Interviewing young children: Effects of probe structures and focus of rapport-building talk on the qualities of young children's eyewitness statements. *Canadian Journal of Behavioural Science*, *36*, 155–165.

Heal, L., & Sigelman, C. (1995). Response bias in interviews of individuals with limited mental ability. *Journal of Intellectual Disability Research*, *39*, 331–340.

Heinemann, W. (1990). Meeting the handicapped: A case of affective–cognitive inconsistency. *European Review of Social Psychology*, *1*, 323–338.

Henry, L., & Gudjonsson, G. (1999). Eyewitness memory and suggestibility in children with mental retardation. *American Journal of Mental Retardation*, *104*, 491–508.

Henry, L., & Gudjonsson, G. (2007). Individual and developmental differences in eyewitness recall and suggestibility in children with intellectual disabilities. *Applied Cognitive Psychology*, *21*, 361–381.

Home Office. (1989). *Report of the advisory group on video evidence*. London: Author.

Home Office. (1992). *Memorandum of good practice for video recorded interviews with child witnesses for criminal proceedings*. London: Her Majesty's Stationery Office.

Home Office. (2002). *Achieving best evidence in criminal proceedings: Guidance for vulnerable or intimidated witnesses, including children*. London: Author.

Home Office. (2008). *Achieving best evidence in criminal proceedings: Guidance for vulnerable and intimidated witnesses, including children (updated)*. London: Author.

Hughes-Scholes, C., & Powell, M. (2008). An examination of the types of leading questions used by investigative interviewers of children. *Policing: An International Journal of Police Strategies and Management*, *31*, 210–225.

Jones, D., & McQuiston, M. (1988). *Interviewing the sexually abused child*. London: Gaskell.

Kask, K., & Bull, R. (2009). *Estonian investigators' questioning styles with child witnesses*. Manuscript submitted for publication.

Kebbell, M., & Hatton, C. (1999). People with mental retardation as witnesses in court: A review. *Mental Retardation*, *37*, 179–187.

Knutson, J., & Sullivan, P. (1993). Communicative disorders as a risk factor in abuse. *Topics in Language Disorders*, *13*, 1–14.

Korkman, J., Santilla, P., Drzewiecki, T., & Sandnabba, N. K. (2008). Failing to keep it simple: Language use in child sexual abuse interviews with 3–8-year-old children. *Psychology, Crime and Law*, *14*, 41–60.

Korkman, J., Santilla, P., Westeraker, M., & Sandnabba, N. K. (2008). Interview techniques and follow-up questions in child sexual abuse interviews. *European Journal of Developmental Psychology*, *5*, 108–128.

Kulkofsky, S., Wang, Q., & Ceci, S. (2008). Do better stories make better memories? Narrative quality and memory accuracy in preschool children. *Applied Cognitive Psychology*, *22*, 21–38.

Lamb, M., Hershkowitz, I., Orbach, Y., & Esplin, P. (2008). *Tell me what happened: Structured investigative interviews of child victims and witnesses*. Chichester: Wiley.

Lamb, M., Sternberg, K, Orbach, Y., Aldridge, J., Bowler, L., Pearson, S. *et al.* (2006, July). *Enhancing the quality of investigative interviews by British police officers*. Paper presented at the second international investigative interviewing conference, Portsmouth.

Leander, L., Christianson, S. A., & Granhag, P. A. (2007). A sexual abuse case study: Children's memories and reports. *Psychiatry, Psychology, and Law*, *14*, 120–129.

Leander, L., Christianson, S. A., & Granhag, P. A. (2008). Internet initiated sexual abuse: Adolescent victims' reports about on- and off-line sexual activities. *Applied Cognitive Psychology*, *22*, 1260–1274.

Leander, L., Granhag, P. S., & Christianson, S. A. (2005). Children exposed to obscene phone calls: What they remember and tell. *Child Abuse and Neglect*, *29*, 871–888.

Leander, L., Granhag, P. S., & Christianson, S. A. (2009). Children's reports of verbal sexual abuse: Effects of police officers' interviewing style. *Psychiatry, Psychology, and Law*, *16*(3), 340–354.

Matikka, L., & Vesala, H. (1997). Acquiescence in quality of life interviews with adults who have mental retardation. *Mental Retardation*, *35*, 75–82.

Memon, A., Vrij, A., & Bull, R. (2003). *Psychology and law: Truthfulness, accuracy and credibility* (2nd ed.). Chichester: Wiley.

Milne, R., & Bull, R. (1996). Interviewing children with mild learning disability with the cognitive interview. In N. Clark & G. Stephenson (Eds.), *Investigative and forensic decision making: Issues in Criminological Psychology*. Leicester: British Psychological Society.

Milne, R., & Bull, R. (1999). *Investigative interviewing: Psychology and practice*. Chichester: Wiley.

Milne, R., & Bull, R. (2001). Interviewing witnesses with learning disabilities for legal purposes. *British Journal of Learning Disabilities*, *29*, 93–97.

Milne, R., & Bull, R. (2006). Interviewing victims of crime, including children and people with intellectual disabilities. In M. Kebbell & G. Davies (Eds.), *Practical psychology for forensic investigations*. Chichester: Wiley.

Murray, K., & Gough, D. (1991). *Interviewing in child sexual abuse*. Edinburgh: Scottish Academic Press.

Orbach, Y., Hershkowitz, I., Lamb, M., Sternberg, K, Esplin, P., & Horowitz, D. (2000). Assessing the value of structured protocols for forensic interviews of alleged abuse victims. *Child Abuse and Neglect*, *24*, 733–752.

Paterson, B., Bull, R., & Vrij, A. (2002). *The effects of interviewer style on children's event recall*. Paper presented at the 25th Congress of Applied Psychology, Singapore.

Perry, N., & Wrightsman, L. (1991). *The child witness: Legal issues and dilemmas*. Newbury Park, CA: Sage.

Perske, R. (1994). Thoughts on the police interrogation of individuals with mental retardation. *Mental Retardation*, *32*, 377–380.

Peterson, C., & Biggs, M. (1997). Interviewing children about trauma: Problems with specific questions. *Journal of Traumatic Stress*, *10*, 279–290.

Peterson, C., & Whalen, N. (2001). Five years later: Children's memory for medical emergencies. *Applied Cognitive Psychology*, *15*, 7–24.

Poole, D., & Lamb, M. (1999). *Investigative interviews of children: A guide for helping professionals*. Washington, DC: American Psychological Association.

Porter, S., Yuille, J., & Bent, A. (1995). A comparison of the eyewitness accounts of deaf and hearing children. *Child Abuse and Neglect*, *19*, 51–61.

Powell, M. (2002). Specialist training in investigative and evidential interviewing: Is it having any effect on the behaviour of professionals in the field? *Psychiatry, Psychology and Law*, *9*, 44–55.

Powell, M. (2003). Interviewing and assessing clients from different cultural backgounds: Guidelines for all forensic professionals. In D. Carson & R. Bull (Eds.), *Handbook of psychology in legal contexts* (2nd ed., pp. 625–643). Chichester: Wiley.

Quas, J., Goodman, G., Bidrose, S., Pipe, M.-E., Craw, S., & Ablin, D. (1999). Emotion and memory: Children's long-term remembering, forgetting and suggestibility. *Journal of Experimental Child Psychology*, *72*, 235–270.

Roberts, K., & Lamb, M. (1999). Children's responses when interviewers distort details during investigative interviews. *Legal and Criminological Psychology*, *4*, 23–31.

Ross, D., Dunning, D., Toglia, M., & Ceci, S. (1990). The child in the eyes of the jury: Assessing mock jurors' perceptions of child witnesses. *Law and Human Behavior*, *14*, 5–23.

Sabsey, D., & Doe, T. (1991). Patterns of sexual abuse and assault. *Sexuality and Disability*, *9*, 243–259.

Sabsey, D., & Varnhagen, C. (1991). Sexual abuse, assault and exploitation of Canadians with disabilities. In C. Bagley & R. Thomlinson (Eds.), *Child sexual abuse: Critical perspectives on prevention, intervention and treatment* (pp. 203–216). Toronto, ON: Wall & Emerson.

Sanders, A., Creaton, J., Bird, S., & Weber, L. (1997). *Victims with learning disabilities: Negotiating the criminal justice system*. Oxford: Centre for Criminological Research, University of Oxford.

Scottish Executive Central Research Unit. (2002). *Vulnerable and intimidated witnesses: Review of provisions in other jurisdictions*. Edinburgh: Stationery Office.

Shaw, J., & Budd, E. (1982). Determinants of acquiescence and naysaying of mentally retarded persons. *American Journal of Mental Deficiency*, *87*, 108–110.

Spencer, J., & Flin, R. (1990). *The evidence of children: The law and the psychology*. London: Blackstone.

Stacey, H. (1999). *Investigation into the skills used by the police officers when interviewing intellectually disabled witnesses*. Unpublished Master's dissertation. School of Psychology, University of Leicester, Leicester.

Sternberg, K., Lamb, M., Davies, G., & Westcott, H. (2001). The memorandum of good practice: Theory versus application. *Child Abuse and Neglect*, *25*, 669–681.

Sternberg, K., Lamb, M., Esplin, P., & Baradaran, L. (1999). Using a scripted protocol to guide investigative interviews: A pilot study. *Applied Developmental Science*, *3*, 70–76.

Sternberg, K., Lamb, M., Hershkowitz, I., Esplin, P., Redlich, A., & Sunshine, N. (1996). The relation between investigative utterance types and the informativeness of child witnesses. *Journal of Applied Developmental Psychology*, *17*, 439–451.

Sternberg, K., Lamb, M., Orbach, Y., Esplin, P., & Mitchell, S. (2001). Use of a structured investigative protocol enhances young children's responses to free recall prompts in the course of forensic interviews. *Journal of Applied Psychology*, *86*, 997–1005.

Stobbs, G., & Kebbell, M. (2003). Jurors' perception of witnesses with intellectual disabilities and the influence of expert evidence. *Journal of Applied Research in Intellectual Disabilities*, *16*, 107–114.

Tharinger, D., Horton, C., & Millea, S. (1990). Sexual abuse and exploitation of children and adults with mental retardation and other handicaps. *Child Abuse and Neglect*, *14*, 301–312.

Thoresen, C., Lonnum, K., Melinder, A., Stridbeck, U., & Magnussen, M. (2006). Theory and practice in interviewing young children: A study of Norwegian police interviews 1985–2002. *Psychology, Crime and Law*, *12*, 629–640.

Turk, V., & Brown, H. (1992). Sexual abuse and adults with learning disabilities: Preliminary communication of survey results. *Mental Handicap*, *20*, 56–58.

Valenti-Hein, D., & Schwartz, L. (1993). Witness competency in people with mental retardation: Implications for prosecution of sexual abuse. *Sexuality and Disability*, 11, 287–294.

Warren, A., Woodall, C., Hunt, J., & Perry, N. (1996). 'It sounds good in theory, but. . .': Do investigative interviewers follow guidelines based on memory research? *Child Maltreatment, 1*, 231–245.
Welsh Assembly Government. (2004). *Training pack: Achieving best evidence in criminal proceedings for vulnerable and intimidated witnesses including children*. Cardiff: Author.
Westcott, H., Davies, G., & Bull, R. (Eds.), (2002). *Children's testimony: Psychological research and forensic practice*. Chichester: Wiley.
Westcott, H., & Kynan, S. (2006). Interviewer practice in investigative interviews for suspected child sexual abuse. *Psychology, Crime and Law, 12*, 367–382.
Williams, C. (1995). *Invisible victims: Crimes and abuse against people with learning disabilities*. London: Jessica Kinglsey.
Wilson, C., & Brewer, N. (1992). The incidence of criminal victimisation of individuals with an intellectual disability. *Australian Psychologist, 27*, 114–117.
Wood, J., & Garven, S. (2000). How sexual abuse interviewers go astray: Implications for prosecutors, police and child protection services. *Child Maltreatment, 5*, 109–118.
Wright, A., & Holliday, R. (2005). Police officers' perceptions of older eyewitnesses. *Legal and Criminological Psychology, 10*, 211–223.
Wright, A., & Holliday, R. (2007). Enhancing the recall of young, young-old, and old-old adults with the cognitive interview. *Applied Cognitive Psychology, 21*, 19–43.
Zajac, R. (2009). Investigative interviewing in the courtroom: Child witnesses under cross-examination. In R. Bull, T. Valentine, & T. Williamson (Eds.), *Handbook of the psychology of investigative interviewing*. Chichester: Wiley.
Zajac, R., Gross, J., & Hayne, H. (2003). Asked and answered: Questioning children in the courtroom. *Psychiatry, Psychology and Law, 10*, 199–209.
Zajac, R., & Hayne, H. (2003). I don't think that's what really happened: The effect of cross-examination on the accuracy of children's reports. *Journal of Experimental Psychology: Applied, 9*, 187–195.
Zajac, R., & Hayne, H. (2006). The negative effects of cross-examination style questioning on children's accuracy. *Applied Cognitive Psychology, 20*, 3–16.

9 True lies: police officers' ability to detect suspects' lies

Samantha Mann, Aldert Vrij and Ray Bull

Overview

Police manuals give the impression that experienced police detectives make good lie detectors (Inbau, Reid, Buckley, & Jayne, 2001), though this claim has not been supported by previous research. The present study is unique, as we tested police officers' ability to distinguish between truths and lies in a realistic setting (during police interviews with suspects), rather than in an artificial laboratory setting. This provides us with a more valid test of Inbau et al.'s claim. Apart from testing truth and lie detection ability, we also examined what characterizes good and poor lie detectors. On the basis of the available deception research, we argue that paying attention to cues promoted in police manuals (gaze aversion, fidgeting, etc.) actually hampers ability to detect truths and lies.

Accuracy rates and their relationships with background characteristics

In scientific studies concerning the detection of deception, observers are typically given videotaped or audiotaped statements from a number of people who are either lying or telling the truth. After each statement, observers are asked to judge whether the statement is true or false. In a review of all the literature available at the time, Kraut (1980) found an accuracy rate (percentage of correct answers) of 57%, which is a low score because 50% accuracy can be expected by chance alone. (Guessing whether someone is lying or not gives a 50% chance of being correct.) Vrij (2000a) reviewed an additional 39 studies that were published after 1980 (the year of Kraut's publication) and found an almost identical accuracy rate of 56.6%. In a minority of studies, accuracy in detecting lies was computed separately from accuracy in detecting truth. Where this did occur, results showed a *truth bias*; that is, judges are more likely to consider that messages are truthful than deceptive and, as a result, truthful messages are identified with relatively high accuracy (67%) and deceptive messages with relatively low accuracy (44%). In fact, 44% is below the level of chance, and people would be more accurate at detecting lies if they simply guessed. One explanation for the truth bias is that in daily life, most people are more often confronted with truthful than with deceptive statements and so are therefore more inclined to assume that the behavior they observe is honest (the so-called availability heuristic; O'Sullivan, Ekman, & Friesen, 1988).

Both reviews (Kraut, 1980; Vrij, 2000a) included studies in which college students tried to detect lies and truths in people they were not familiar with. It could be argued that college students are not habitually called on to detect deception. Perhaps professional lie catchers, such as police officers or customs officers, would obtain higher accuracy rates than laypersons. In several studies, professional lie catchers were exposed to videotaped footage of liars and truth tellers and their ability to detect lies was tested (see Vrij & Mann, 2001b, for a review). Three findings emerged from these studies. First, most total accuracy rates were similar to those found in studies with college students as observers, falling in the 45%–60% range. DePaulo & Pfeifer (1986), Meissner & Kassin (2002), and Vrij & Graham (1997) found that police officers were as (un)successful as university students in detecting deception (accuracy rates around 50%). Ekman & O'Sullivan (1991) found that police officers and polygraph examiners obtained similar accuracy rates to university students (accuracy rates around 55%). Second, some groups seem to be better than others. Ekman's research has shown that members of the Secret Service (64% accuracy rate), Central Intelligence Agency (73% accuracy rates), and sheriffs (67% accuracy rates) were better lie detectors than other groups of lie detectors (Ekman & O'Sullivan, 1991; Ekman, O'Sullivan, & Frank, 1999). Third, the truth bias, consistently found in studies with students as observers, is much less profound, or perhaps even lacking, in studies with professional lie catchers (Ekman et al., 1999; Meissner & Kassin, 2002; Porter, Woodworth, & Birt, 2000). Perhaps the nature of their work makes professional lie catchers more wary about the possibility that they are being lied to.

In summary, even the accuracy rates for most professional lie catchers are modest, raising serious doubt about their ability to detect deceit. However, these disappointing accuracy levels may be the result of an artifact. In typical deception studies, including those with professional lie catchers, observers detect truths and lies told by college students who are asked to lie and tell the truth for the sake of the experiment in university laboratories. Perhaps in these laboratory studies the stakes (negative consequences of being caught and positive consequences of getting away with the lie) are not high enough for the liar to exhibit clear deceptive cues to deception (Miller & Stiff, 1993), which makes the lie detection task virtually impossible for the observer.

To raise the stakes in laboratory experiments, participants are offered money if they successfully get away with their lies (Vrij, 1995), or participants (e.g., nursing students) are told that being a good liar is an important indicator of success in a future career (Ekman & Friesen, 1974; Vrij, Edward, & Bull, 2001a, 2001b). In some studies, participants are told that they will be observed by a peer who will judge their sincerity (DePaulo, Stone, & Lassiter, 1985b). In a series of experiments in which the stakes were manipulated, researchers found that such "high-stakes" lies were easier to detect than low-stakes lies (Bond & Atoum, 2000; DePaulo, Kirkendol, Tang, & O'Brien, 1988; DePaulo, Lanier, & Davis, 1983; DePaulo, LeMay, & Epstein, 1991; DePaulo et al., 1985b; Feeley & deTurck, 1998; Forrest & Feldman, 2000; Heinrich & Borkenau, 1998; Lane & DePaulo, 1999; Vrij, 2000b; Vrij, Harden, Terry, Edward, & Bull, 2001).

In an attempt to raise the stakes even further, participants in Frank & Ekman's (1997) study were given the opportunity to "steal" $50. If they could convince the interviewer that they had not taken the money, they could keep all of it. If they took the money and the interviewer judged them as lying, they had to give back the $50 in addition to their $10 per hour participation fee. Moreover, some participants faced an additional punishment if they were found to be lying. They were told that they would have to sit on a cold metal chair inside a cramped, darkened room ominously labeled *XXX*, where they would have to endure anything from 10 to 40 randomly sequenced, 110-decibel starting blasts of white noise over the course of 1 hr.

A deception study like this probably borders on unethical, and yet the stakes are still not comparable with the stakes in real-life situations in which professional lie catchers operate, such as during police interviews. Therefore, one might argue that the only valid way to investigate police officers' true ability to detect deceit is to examine their skills when they detect lies and truths that are told in real-life criminal investigation settings. Vrij & Mann (2001a, 2001b) were the first researchers to do this. Vrij & Mann (2001a) exposed police officers to fragments of a videotaped police interview with a man suspected of murder. However, that study had two limitations. First, fragments of only one suspect were shown, and second, the police officers could not understand the suspect because he spoke a foreign language (suspect and police officers were of different nationalities). Vrij & Mann (2001b) later exposed judges to videotaped press conferences of people who were asking the general public for help in finding either their missing relatives or the murderers of their relatives. They all lied during these press conferences, and they were all subsequently found guilty of having killed the "missing person" themselves. This study had limitations as well. First, the judges were only subjected to lies, and, second, again the lie detectors and liars spoke in different languages, as they were from different nationalities.

We overcame these limitations in the present experiment. We exposed British police officers to fragments of videotaped real-life police interviews with English-speaking suspects and asked them to detect truths and lies told by these suspects during these interviews. We expected truth and lie accuracy rates to be significantly above the level of chance (which is 50%), and, as a consequence of this, expected lie accuracy rates to be significantly higher than those typically found in previous research (44%; Hypothesis 1). In view of the fact that police officers in the present study were assessing the veracity of suspects, a group that is likely to arouse heightened skepticism in a police officer (Moston, Stephenson, & Williamson, 1992), a truth bias is unlikely to occur.

We also expected individual differences, with some police officers being more skilled at detecting truths and lies than others. We predicted that the reported experience in interviewing suspects would be positively correlated with truth and lie accuracy (Hypothesis 2). This background characteristic has not been examined in deception research before, but we expected it to be related to accuracy, as it is this particular aspect of police work that gives police officers experience in detecting lies and truths. Previous research has focused on the relationship between length of service/years of job experience and accuracy, and a significant relationship between the two was not found (Ekman & O'Sullivan, 1991; Porter et al., 2000; Vrij & Mann, 2001b). This is not surprising, as an officer who has served in the police force for many years will not necessarily have a great deal of experience in interviewing suspects, and vice versa. Other background characteristics, such as age and gender, have generally not been found to be related to accuracy (DePaulo, Epstein, & Wyer, 1993; Ekman & O'Sullivan, 1991; Ekman et al., 1999; Hurd & Noller, 1988; Koehnken, 1987; Manstead, Wagner, & MacDonald, 1986; Porter et al., 2000; Vrij & Mann, 2001b).

Cues used to detect deceit

We asked lie detectors to indicate which verbal and nonverbal cues they typically use to decide whether someone is lying, so-called beliefs about cues associated with deception (DePaulo, Stone, & Lassiter, 1985a; Zuckerman, DePaulo, & Rosenthal, 1981). We expected good lie detectors to mention speech-related cues significantly more often than poor lie detectors (Hypothesis 3). In part, this is because research has shown that the intellectual ability of suspects who are interviewed by the police is often rather low. Gudjonsson (1994) measured intellectual functioning with three subtests of the Wechsler Adult Intelligence Scale—Revised (WAIS–R; Wechsler, 1981)—Vocabulary, Comprehension, and Picture Completion—and found a mean IQ of 82, with a range of 61–131. It might well be that people with a low IQ will find it hard to tell a lie that sounds plausible and convincing (Ekman & Frank, 1993). Moreover, in their review of detection of deception research, DePaulo et al. (1985a) found that lie detectors who read transcripts only (and are therefore "forced" to focus on story cues) are typically better lie detectors than those who are exposed to the actual person (speech, sound, and behavior; see also Wiseman, 1995).

Stereotypical views typically held among professional lie catchers (and also laypersons) are that liars look away and fidget (Akehurst, Koehnken, Vrij, & Bull, 1996; Vrij & Semin, 1996). These cues, however, are unrelated to deception (see DePaulo, Lindsay, Malone, Muhlenbruck, Charlton, & Cooper, 2003; Vrij, 2000a, for reviews about nonverbal and verbal cues to deceit). We therefore expected negative correlations between mentioning such cues and accuracy rates; in other words, the more of these cues the officers reported to look at, the lower their accuracy rates would become (Hypothesis 4).

In their influential manual about police interviewing, *Criminal Interrogation and Confessions*, Inbau, Reid, & Buckley (1986; a new edition was published: Inbau et al., 2001) described in detail how, in their view, liars behave. As evidence, the authors included showing gaze aversion, displaying unnatural posture changes, exhibiting self-manipulations, and placing the hand over the mouth or eyes when speaking. None of these behaviors have been found to be reliably related to lying in deception research. It is therefore not surprising that participants in a deception detection study by Kassin & Fong (1999), who were trained to look at the cues Inbau and colleagues claim to be related to deception, actually performed worse than naive observers who did not receive any information about deceptive behavior. In the present study, we expected negative correlations between reporting "Inbau cues" and accuracy. In other words, the more of these Inbau cues that police officers mentioned that they use to detect deceit, the worse we expected them to be at distinguishing between truths and lies (Hypothesis 5).

We also examined whether the cues lie detectors used to make their veracity judgments were related to the behaviors shown by the suspects in the videotape (so-called cues to perceived deception; Zuckerman et al., 1981).[1] We predicted that poor lie detectors would be significantly more guided by invalid cues, such as gaze aversion, than good lie detectors (Hypothesis 6).

Accuracy–confidence relationship

Studies investigating lie detectors' confidence in their decision making typically reveal three findings. First, there is usually no significant relationship between confidence and accuracy (see DePaulo, Charlton, Cooper, Lindsay, & Muhlenbruck, 1997, for a meta-analysis). Second, confidence scores among professional lie catchers are typically high (Allwood & Granhag, 1999; DePaulo & Pfeifer, 1986; Strömwall, 2001; Vrij, 1993), and police officers are sometimes found to be more confident than laypersons (Allwood & Granhag, 1999; DePaulo & Pfeifer, 1986). Furthermore, DePaulo et al. (1997) found an "overconfidence effect"; that is, judges' confidence is typically higher than their accuracy. Third, observers tend to have higher levels of confidence when judging truthful statements than when judging deceptive statements, irrespective of whether they judge the statement as a truth or a lie (DePaulo et al., 1997).

In the present study, confidence was investigated in two different ways. First, it was investigated in the traditional way, by asking observers after each veracity judgment how confident they were of their decision. Second, we also asked participants at the end of the lie detection experiment how well they thought they had done at the task. This latter method of measuring confidence may well result in more accurate confidence levels (less prone to an overconfidence effect), because at that stage lie detectors have insight into their overall performance and are asked to judge this overall performance. For this reason the latter method may even result in a positive relationship between accuracy and confidence. This issue was explored in the present study.

Method

Participants

Ninety-nine Kent County police officers (Kent, England) participated. Of these, 24 were women and 75 were men. Ages ranged from 22 years to 52 years, with a mean average of 34.3 years (*SD* = 7.40 years). Seventy-eight participants were from the Criminal Investigation Department (CID), 8 were police trainers, 4 were traffic officers, and the remaining 9 were uniform response officers. Although different groups of police officers participated, none of these groups are the specialized groups that are identified by Ekman and his colleagues as particularly good lie detectors (Ekman & O'Sullivan, 1991; Ekman et al., 1999). As some of the group sizes are rather small, differences between groups are not discussed in the main text.

Length of service on the job ranged from 1 year to 30 years, with a mean average of 11.2 years ($SD = 7.31$ years). The distribution of this variable differed significantly from a normal distribution ($z = 1.83$, $p < .01$, skewness = .94, Mdn = 9 years).

Materials

Participants in this study were asked to judge the veracity of people in real-life high-stakes situations. More specifically, participants saw video clips of 14 suspects (of whom 12 were men, 4 were juvenile, and 2 were women) in their police interviews. The interview rooms were fitted with a fixed camera, which produces the main color picture and is aimed at the suspect's chair, and a small insert picture, produced by a wide lens camera. The picture in the small insert was not of good quality and displayed the whole interview room from the view taken at the back of the suspect. The purpose of the wide lens insert is to show how many people are present in the room and any larger movements made by any person present (therefore proving or disproving that the officers might have physically threatened or coerced the suspect in some way).[2] The quality of the main picture was good enough to code the occurrences of eye blinks, but not good enough to see subtler facial changes. Sound quality was good in all interviews. The positioning of the cameras varied slightly, depending on which interview room the interview was conducted, but in all cases the suspect's upper torso could be seen. However, in some cases the lower torso could not be seen, hence leg and foot movements were not analyzed.[3] In the main picture only the suspect was visible. Crimes about which the suspects were being interviewed included theft (9), arson (2), attempted rape (1), and murder (2). Cases had been chosen in which other sources (reliable, independent witness statements and forensic evidence) provided evidence that the suspect told the truth and lied at various points within the interview. Once a case had been selected, only those particular clips in which each word was known to be a truth or a lie were selected. The truths that were selected were chosen so as to be as comparable as possible in nature to the lies (e.g., a truthful response to an easy question such as giving a name and address is not comparable to a deceitful response regarding whether the suspect had committed a murder. Video footage about names and addresses were therefore not included as truths in this study). The following account is an example of one of the cases used: The suspect (a juvenile) spent the night in a derelict building with a friend. With the friend, he shot at windows of a neighboring house with his air rifle and then stole items from a local shop. The suspect denied involvement in any of those activities and provided an alibi. His friend (the alibi), however, immediately admitted to both his and the suspect's part in the offenses. The suspect's alibi fell through, and so the suspect confessed to the crimes and told police of the whereabouts of the stolen goods, his gun, and from where he purchased it. The suspect admitted guilt and was charged accordingly. Lies included in clips were the initial denials of any involvement in the crimes. It is important to point out that, rather than take the form of a straightforward "No, I didn't do it" and "Yes, I did do it," all clips used in this study contained story elements that were true and false. So in the above example, in the denial the suspect gave an alternative story of the events of the day to those that actually occurred (that he went over to another friend's house, etc.), and in the confession he gave a true version of events, not all of which was necessarily incriminating. Therefore, a participant watching the clips, who does not know the facts of the case, would not easily be able to tell what are snippets of denial and what are snippets of confession. See Mann, Vrij, & Bull (2002) for further details.[4]

The length of each clip unavoidably varied considerably (from 6 s to 145 s). There were 54 clips total (23 truthful clips and 31 deceptive clips), and the number of clips for each suspect varied between a minimum of 2 and a maximum of 8 clips (each suspect with at least one example of a truth and a lie). The total length of the video clips of all 14 suspects was approximately 1 hr. Clearly it would be impossible to show each participant all the clips because of logistical constraints and fatigue. Therefore, the clips were divided between four tapes of roughly equal length, and 24–25 participants saw each clip. As mentioned above, the length of the clips varied, and so each of the four tapes contained between 10 and 16 clips (Clip 1: $n = 15$, 6 truths and 9 lies; Clip 2: $n = 16$, 6 truths and 10 lies; Clip 3: $n = 10$, 5 truths and 5 lies; Clip 4: $n = 13$, 6 truths and 7 lies). Those suspects for whom there were several clips may have had clips spread over several of the tapes. However, for each suspect there was always at least one example of a lie and a truth present on each tape on which they appeared. Clips were presented on the tapes in random order so that the same suspect did not appear in consecutive clips. Two analyses of variance (ANOVAs), with tape as the between-subjects factor and lie accuracy and truth accuracy as dependent variables were conducted to examine possible differences in accuracy between the four tapes. Neither of the two ANOVAs were significant for truth accuracy, $F(3, 95) = 0.20$, *ns*, $\eta^2 = .00$; or for lie accuracy, $F(3, 95) = 1.57$, *ns*, $\eta^2 = .05$. Hence, the fact that participants did not all judge exactly the same clips was not considered an issue, and accuracy scores were collapsed over the four tapes in all subsequent analyses.

Procedure

Permission to approach police officers was granted by the Chief Constable in the first instance, and then by appropriate superintendents. Participants were recruited on duty from either the training college where they were attending courses or various police stations within Kent. Participants were approached and asked whether they would participate in a study about police officers' ability to detect deception and informed that their participation would be anonymous. Participants completed the deception detection task individually. Before attempting the task, participants filled out a questionnaire. This included details such as age, gender, length of service, division, perceived level of experience in interviewing suspects (1 = *totally inexperienced*, 5 = *highly experienced*; $M = 3.75$, $SD = 0.85$), and the verbal or nonverbal cues they use to decide whether another person is lying or telling the truth. After completion of this section, each participant was then read the following instructions: "You are about to see a selection of clips of suspects who are either lying or telling the truth. The clips vary considerably in length, and the suspects may appear on several occasions. This is irrelevant. They will be either lying the whole length of the clip or truth-telling for the length of the clip. After viewing each clip I would like you to indicate whether you think the suspect is lying or telling the truth (measured with a dichotomous scale), and how confident you are of your decision, on a seven-point scale. If you recognize any of the suspects please bring it to my attention." (This latter point was not an issue.) Participants were not informed of how many clips they were going to see, or of how many instances of lies and truths they would see.

After completing the task, participants answered a remaining few questions on the questionnaire. These included questions about what behaviors they had used to guide them in making veracity judgments and questions measuring their confidence. Depending on the participant, participation time lasted between 45 and 90 min. After each veracity judgment, participants were shown each clip again and were asked several questions about the clip. This (time-consuming) part of the experiment is beyond the scope of this article and is therefore not addressed further (see Mann, 2001, for further details about this aspect of the study). The variation in participation time was the result of several factors. Some participants took longer than others to complete their forms; some participants took slightly longer to reach a decision, but the largest time range was in the amount of time taken, and detail given, in responding to the questions that were asked about each clip after the veracity judgment had been given.

Dependent variables

The dependent variables for this study were the accuracy scores, the behaviors that participants associated with deception before and after the task, cues to perceived deception, and their confidence scores during and after the task.

Accuracy was calculated by assigning a score of 1 when the participant correctly identified a truth or a lie, and assigning a score of 0 when the participant was incorrect. The lie accuracy score was calculated by dividing the number of correctly classified lies by the number of lies shown on the tape, and the truth accuracy score was calculated by dividing the number of correctly classified truths by the number of truths shown on the tape.

The behaviors that participants typically use to detect deception were investigated with the open-ended question, "What verbal or nonverbal cues do you use to decide whether another person is lying or telling the truth?" The behaviors that participants said they used in the present lie detection task were investigated with the open-ended question, "What verbal or nonverbal cues did you use in this task to decide whether the people on the screen were lying or telling the truth?" In other words, cues to deception both prior to and after the deception task were investigated. A similar procedure was used by Ekman & O'Sullivan (1991). Asking this question twice enabled us to explore whether, in our deception task, the police officers paid attention to cues they typically consider they pay attention to. In case they did, the answers they would give to the "prior" and "after" questions would be similar, whereas the answers would be different in case they did not. We expected similar responses. We had no reason to believe that the police officers would find the responses of the suspects atypical (they were a random sample of suspects' responses in connection with serious crimes), nor did we think that officers would change their mind about beliefs about deception on the basis of a single lie detection task. We return to this issue in the Discussion section. These two open-ended questions were coded by two coders into 30 different cues. Appendix A shows the list of 30 cues.

This list was the result of sorting and tallying all participants' comments into various groups and combining them as much as possible within specific headings to make the system as manageable as possible. Once the coding system was created, the creator coded for each participant every behavior that they mentioned on the questionnaire before and after the task. Another independent coder then used the coding system also to code each behavior mentioned by participants on the questionnaires to determine the reliability of the coding system. For each participant, each code was used a maximum of one time before the task and one time after the task. So, for example, if a participant said before the task "eyes looking up, looking away from interviewer, high-pitched voice, vocally loud," then just the codes gaze and voice would be recorded, even though, in effect, the participant mentioned two aspects of gaze and two aspects of voice. For the 99 participants, 677 behaviors mentioned on the questionnaires before and after completing the task were coded. Hence, each participant mentioned a mean of 6.84 behaviors. In 651 (96.2%) of the 677 mentioned behaviors, the two coders agreed; any disagreements were resolved by discussion. Twenty-nine of those categories could be clustered into four categories: story, vocal, body, and conduct (see the second column of Appendix A). Those four categories have been introduced by Feeley & Young (2000). The total number of times each participant mentioned behaviors in each group was calculated. So, for example, if a participant mentioned gaze aversion and movements, that participant would obtain a score of 2 for the body category. As a result, the scores for story cues could range from 0 to 6, the scores for vocal cues from 0 to 5, the scores for body cues from 0 to 14, and the scores for conduct cues from 0 to 4. One cue, gut feeling, could not be included in any of these categories, and we therefore analyze the data for this cue separately.

To compare good and poor lie detectors, we followed Ekman & O'Sullivan's (1991) procedure and divided the lie detectors into two ability groups. Good lie detectors ($n = 27$) were those who had scored above the mean for lie clips (66.16%, see the Results section) and above the mean for truth clips (63.61%, see the Results section). Poor lie detectors ($n = 72$) were those who remained, who may well have scored very well on either truth clips or lie clips, but did not score above the mean for both.

To test Hypothesis 4, we constructed new variables: "popular stereotypical beliefs" (one variable was created for cues mentioned before the task and one for cues mentioned after the task). These variables included three cues (gaze, fidget, and self-manipulation) and could range from 0 to 3.

To test Hypothesis 5, two further new variables were created: Inbau cues (again, separate variables were created for cues mentioned before the task and cues mentioned after the task). Inbau cues included the following five cues: posture, cover, gaze, fidget, and self-manipulation; they could range from 0 to 5.

To examine cues to perceived deception, 13 behaviors of the suspects in the clips were scored by two independent coders with a coding scheme used previously by Vrij and colleagues (Vrij, 1995; Vrij et al., 2001a, 2001b; Vrij, Edward, Roberts, & Bull, 2000; Vrij, Semin, & Bull, 1996; Vrij & Winkel, 1991). An overview of these behaviors and the interrater agreement rates between the two coders (Pearson correlations) are reported in Appendix B. Differences between truth tellers and liars regarding these behaviors have been discussed elsewhere in detail (Mann et al., 2002). To summarize the findings, liars blinked less and included more pauses in their speech.

Confidence was measured in two ways. First, participants indicated after each veracity judgment how confident they were in their decision (1 = *not at all confident*, and 7 = *very confident*). Second, after completing the lie detection task, the participants were also asked to answer the open-ended question, "What percentage of answers do you think you answered correctly?".

Results

Accuracy rates and their relationships with background characteristics

For the whole sample, the mean lie accuracy was 66.16% (SD = 17.0), and the mean truth accuracy was 63.61% (SD = 22.5). The difference between lie and truth accuracy was not significant, $t(98) = 0.87$, *ns*, $d = 0.09$; neither were lie and truth accuracy significantly correlated with each other, $r(99) = .08$, *ns*.[5]

Both accuracy rates were significantly higher than the level of chance, which is 50%; truth accuracy, $t(98) = 6.02$, $p < .01$, $d = 0.60$; lie accuracy, $t(98) = 9.43$, $p < .01$, $d = 0.95$. (See Clark-Carter, 1997, for conducting *t* tests when the standard deviation of the sample is unknown.) Moreover, the lie accuracy rate was significantly higher than the average lie accuracy rate that was found in Vrij's (2000a) review of previous research (lie accuracy: M = 66.16% vs. 44.00%), $t(98) = 12.93$, $p < .01$, $d = 1.30$. Truth accuracy did not differ significantly from what has previously been found (63.61% vs. 67.00%), $t(98) = 1.50$, *ns*, $d = 0.15$. This supports Hypothesis 1.

Pearson correlations revealed that experience in interviewing, however, was significantly correlated with truth accuracy, $r(99) = .20$, $p < .05$. The correlation with lie accuracy was $r(99) = .18$, $p = .07$. These positive correlations indicate that the more experienced the police officers perceived themselves to be in interviewing suspects, the better they were in the lie detection task. This supports Hypothesis 2.

Age and length of service were unrelated to lie accuracy, $r(99) = -.09$, *ns*, and $r(99) = -.04$, *ns*, respectively; and truth accuracy, $r(99) = .01$, *ns*, and $r(99) = -.07$, *ns*, respectively. Age and length of service were strongly correlated, $r(99) = .80$, $p < .01$; whereas age and experience in interviewing, $r(99) = .34$, $p < .01$, and experience in interviewing and length of service, $r(99) = .46$, $p < .01$, were moderately correlated.

Men were significantly better at detecting truths ($M = 66.61\%$, $SD = 21.9$) than women ($M = 54.22\%$, $SD = 22.3$), $t(97) = 2.40$, $p < .05$, $d = 0.56$; but no differences were found for detecting lies, $t(97) = .41$, *ns*, $d = 0.09$ ($M = 66.56\%$, $SD = 17.0$ vs. $M = 64.92\%$, $SD = 17.7$).[6]

Cues used to detect deceit

Appendix A shows how many police officers mentioned that they use the cues to detect deceit before and after the task. The most frequently mentioned cue was gaze, with 73% of the officers ($n = 72$) mentioning the cue before the task and 78% ($n = 77$) after the task. The second most frequently mentioned cue was movements, which was mentioned by 25 police officers before the task and by 31 officers after the task. Also vagueness, contradictions, miscellaneous speech (a category for speech-related cues that does not fit into other categories, e.g., pleading/minimizing offense or uncertain replies; all story cues), and fidgeting were relatively frequently mentioned.

ANOVAs comparing how many cues were mentioned in each category (ANOVA, with cue category—story, vocal, body, and conduct—as the single within-subjects factor) showed significant differences in the number of cues mentioned, both before the task, $F(3, 96) = 58.56$, $p < .01$, $\eta^2 = .65$; and after the task, $F(3, 96) = 85.61$, $p < .01$, $\eta^2 = .73$. Before the task, police officers mentioned a mean of 1.84 body cues ($SD = 1.05$; see also Table 9.1). Tukey's honestly significant difference test revealed that this is significantly more than any of the other three categories of cues. They also mentioned significantly more story cues than conduct and vocal cues before the task. The latter two categories did not differ significantly from each other. Exactly the same pattern emerged for cues mentioned after the task.

Table 9.1 Overview of the total number of times each participant mentioned story, vocal, body, and conduct cues before and after the task

Cue	*Before the task*		*After the task*	
	M	*SD*	*M*	*SD*
Story	0.68_b	0.62	0.78_b	0.72
Vocal	0.40_a	0.59	0.48_a	0.61
Body	1.84_c	1.05	2.01_c	0.96
Conduct	0.32_a	0.49	0.28_a	0.50

Note: Only mean scores in the columns with a different subscript differ significantly from each other.

To compare the number of cues mentioned before and after the task, we conducted a multivariate analysis of variance (MANOVA),with time (before or after) as the within-subjects factor and the four categories of cues as dependent variables. At a multivariate level, the test revealed a nonsignificant effect, $F(4, 95) = 1.91$, *ns*, $\eta^2 = .07$. In other words, the lie detection task did not influence the police officers' ideas about which cues to attend to in order to detect deceit. However, if we look at individual cues (see Appendix A), rather than the categories, differences emerged regarding some cues. Sharp increases in cues mentioned (between before and after the task) occurred for self-corrections, miscellaneous speech, hand movements and head movements; and sharp decreases were found for contradictions, evidence, facial cues and physiological cues; the latter findings might be the result of the experimental setting. For example, noticing physiological cues might be difficult when watching a tape, hence, in this lie detection task, participants did not look for such cues to detect deceit.

To investigate and compare behaviors mentioned by good and poor lie detectors, we conducted ANOVAs, with skill (good or poor lie detector) as the between-subjects factor and the four cue categories as dependent variables. As predicted in Hypothesis 3, good lie detectors were more inclined to claim that they focused on story cues ($M = .89$, $SD = .60$) than poor lie detectors ($M = .60$, $SD = .60$), $F(1, 97) = 4.50$, $p < .05$, $\eta^2 = .04$; although this effect only occurred for the story cues mentioned before the task. All other effects were not significant.[7]

For the remaining cue, gut feeling, we used chi-square analyses to compare responses from good and poor lie detectors. After the lie detection task, none of the 72 poor lie detectors said that they had relied on gut feeling, whereas 11% ($n = 3$) of the good lie detectors claimed to have relied on such intuitive feelings, $\chi^2(1, N = 99) = 8.05$, $p < .01$, $\phi = .29$. The analysis for mentioning gut feeling before the task was not significant, $\chi^2 (1, N = 99) = 2.63$, *ns*, $\phi = .17$.[8]

ANOVAs further revealed that good and poor lie detectors did not differ significantly from each other on the newly created variables, popular stereotypical beliefs and Inbau cues. A disadvantage of using a dichotomization procedure (i.e., dividing the lie detectors into two groups) is a loss in data measurement, because many participants are treated alike in a dichotomy when in fact they are different. An alternative method is to keep the continuous lie and truth accuracy scores. Pearson correlations (see Table 9.2) revealed that mentioning popular stereotypical beliefs and Inbau cues (both before and after the task) were negatively correlated with accuracy. This supports Hypotheses 4 and 5.[9]

To investigate cues to perception, we conducted multiple stepwise regression analyses. The units of analysis were the 54 different clips. The criterion was the percentage of police officers who judged the suspect in the clip as lying. The predictors were the behaviors displayed by the suspects (13 behaviors were entered, see the Method section), the veracity of the suspects' statements, and age (adult or juvenile) and gender of the suspects. Different analyses were carried out for good and poor lie detectors. The analysis for good lie detectors revealed two predictors, which explained 61% of the variance, $F(2, 51) = 40.16$, $p < .01$; these were veracity of the clip ($R = .76$, $\beta = .74$), $t(53) = 8.48$, $p < .01$, and illustrators ($R = .02$,

Table 9.2 Pearson correlations between popular stereotypical beliefs and Inbau cues with truth accuracy and lie accuracy

Variable	*Before the task*		*After the task*	
	Truth accuracy	*Lie accuracy*	*Truth accuracy*	*Lie accuracy*
Stereotypical beliefs	−.21*	−.02	−.22*	−.08
Inbau cues	−.23*	−.06	−.23*	−.05

Note: * $p < .05$.

$\beta = -.19$), $t(53) = 2.18$, $p < .05$. Participants were most likely to judge the clip as deceptive if the clip was in fact a lie, and the fewer illustrators the suspects made, the more likely it was that they were judged as deceptive.

The analysis for poor lie detectors revealed four predictors, which explained 51% of the variance, $F(4, 49) = 12.60$, $p < .01$. These were gender of the suspect ($R = .38$, $\beta = .57$), $t(53) = 5.14$, $p < .01$; veracity of the clip ($R = .18$, $\beta = .42$), $t(53) = 4.06$, $p < .01$; gaze aversion ($R = .10$, $\beta = .41$), $t(53) = 4.02$, $p < .01$; and head nods ($R = .04$, $\beta = .25$), $t(53) = 2.28$, $p < .05$. Participants were most likely to judge the clip as deceptive if the suspect was a man and if the clip was in fact a lie. Moreover, the more gaze aversion and the more head nods the suspects made, the more likely it was that they were judged as deceptive.

The correlation between displaying gaze aversion and judging the person as deceptive was significant for poor lie detectors, $r(54) = .39$, $p < .01$, but not significant for good lie detectors, $r(54) = .06$, *ns*. These two correlations differed significantly from each other ($z = 1.78$, $p < .05$, one-tailed). This supports Hypothesis 6 (poor lie detectors would be more guided by gaze aversion than good lie detectors).

Accuracy–confidence relationship

Participants were significantly more confident after they saw a truthful clip ($M = 4.55$, $SD = 0.92$) than after watching a deceptive clip ($M = 4.38$, $SD = 0.95$), $t(98) = 3.08$, $p < .01$, $d = 0.18$. Those two confidence measures were significantly correlated with each other, $r(99) = .82$, $p < .01$. The police officers estimated their percentage of correct answers ("posttask estimated accuracy," measured after the lie detection task) very modestly ($M = 49.98\%$, $SD = 15.08$). This percentage was significantly lower than the actual truth accuracy ($M = 63.61$, $SD = 22.50$), $t(98) = 5.65$, $p < .01$, $d = 0.52$, and lie accuracy ($M = 66.16$, $SD = 17.05$), $t(98) = 7.05$, $p < .01$, $d = 0.74$, obtained in the lie detection task.

Neither the truth accuracy–truth confidence correlation, $r(99) = .10$, nor the lie accuracy–lie confidence correlation, $r(99) = .03$, were significant. Neither was the posttask estimated accuracy significantly correlated with the actual lie accuracy, $r(99) = -.07$, or actual truth accuracy, $r(99) = .17$. Age, length of service, and experience in interviewing suspects were not significantly correlated with truth confidence, lie confidence, or posttask estimated accuracy. Neither were there significant differences found between men and women on any of these three variables, although the difference between men and women for posttask estimated accuracy was marginally significant, $t(97) = 1.93$, $p = .056$, $d = 0.47$ (women were more skeptical about their performance, $M = 44.38\%$, $SD = 13.21$, than men, $M = 51.12\%$, $SD = 15.35$).[10]

Discussion

Accuracy rates and their relationships with background characteristics

In the present study, 99 police officers, who did not belong to a group that has been identified as specialized in lie detection, attempted to detect lies and truths told by suspects during their police interviews. Regarding accuracy, two main findings emerged. First, truth accuracy and lie accuracy were both around 65% in this study, which was higher than was found in most previous deception detection studies. It is also the highest accuracy rate ever found for a group of "ordinary" police officers. The accuracy rates found in this sample of ordinary police officers were comparable to those found among specialized groups of lie detectors in previous studies (Ekman & O'Sullivan, 1991; Ekman et al., 1999). In other words, ordinary police officers might well be better at detecting truths and lies than was previously suggested. Although the accuracy rates were significantly higher than the average accuracy scores obtained by laypersons (mostly college students) in previous research, we cannot conclude that police officers are actually better lie detectors than laypersons, because the latter were not included in this study. Had they been included as participants, it is possible that laypersons would have scored similarly to police officers. Unfortunately, inclusion of a group of laypersons was not possible, as (understandably) the police would not give us permission to show the highly sensitive stimulus material (fragments of real-life police interviews) to laypersons.

Second, findings showed a modest but significant relationship between experience in interviewing suspects and truth accuracy, with the more experience police officers reported in interviewing suspects (a self-report measure), the higher truth accuracy scores they obtained. This finding suggests that experience does make police officers better able to distinguish between truths and lies, a finding typically not found in deception studies with professionals as observers (DePaulo & Pfeifer, 1986; Ekman & O'Sullivan, 1991; Porter et al., 2000). We believe that this finding is affected by the way we measured experience. Other researchers use length of service/years of job experience as a measurement for experience (DePaulo & Pfeifer, 1986; Ekman & O'Sullivan, 1991; Porter et al., 2000). Such a measurement is unfortunate, as it says little about the officers' actual experience in situations in which they will attempt to detect deceit such as interviewing suspects. There is little reason to suggest that a police officer who had worked for many years in a managerial or administrative position within the police force would be a better lie detector than someone with a similar position outside the police force. Therefore, perhaps unsurprisingly, the present study also did not reveal significant correlations between length of service and accuracy. In other words, experience may benefit truth and lie detection only if the relevant experience is taken into account. Perhaps a weakness of our experience measure is that it is a self-report rather than an objective measure. It would be interesting to see whether an objective measure of experience in interviewing suspects (e.g., the number of suspect interviews a police officer has conducted) would correlate with accuracy as well. This would strengthen our argument. Unfortunately, the police do not record objective measures of experience with interviewing suspects.

The findings further revealed that men were better at detecting truths than women. We discuss this further below.

Theoretically, the higher than usual accuracy rates obtained in this study could be explained in several ways. First, as previously discussed in the introduction, the stakes for liars and truth tellers were higher in this study than in previous studies, and high-stakes lies were easier to detect than low-stakes lies. Second, the police officers were exposed to truths and lies told by the sort of people they are familiar with, namely police suspects, and familiarity with this group of people might have increased the accuracy rates. Third, police officers were exposed to truths and lies in a setting that is familiar to them, namely during police interviews, and familiarity with the setting might have increased accuracy rates. Probably all three factors contributed to the high accuracy rates found in this study. Therefore, these explanations have two theoretical implications. First, the obtained findings might well be situation and person specific and we therefore cannot guarantee that exposing police officers to high-stakes lies in situations that they are not familiar with (such as lies told by businesspeople in negotiations, by salespersons to clients, by politicians during interviews, or between romantic partners, etc.) would lead to similar accuracy rates to those found in this study. Similarly, we cannot guarantee that police officers will be any good at detecting low-stakes lies told by suspects. Second, to obtain insight into police officers' skills to detect deceit, exposing them to ecologically valid material (high-stakes lies told by suspects in police interviews) is crucial. This ecologically valid argument also applies to the measurement of relevant background variables, such as measuring police officers' experience with interviewing suspects.

Cues used to detect deceit

The majority of police officers claimed that looking at gaze is a useful tool to detect deceit. This discovery was in agreement with previous findings (Akehurst et al., 1996; Vrij & Semin, 1996). On the one hand, this finding is surprising given that deception research has convincingly demonstrated that gaze behavior is not related to deception (DePaulo et al., 2003; Vrij, 2000a). Nor was gaze related to deception in the present stimulus material (Mann et al., 2002). On the other hand, this finding is not so surprising given that police manuals, including Inbau's manual, which is widely used, claim that suspects typically show gaze aversion when they lie (Gordon & Fleisher, 2002; Hess, 1997; Inbau et al., 1986, 2001). In other words, police officers are taught to look for these incorrect cues.

Several (modest) relationships occurred between cues mentioned by the officers as useful to detect deceit and their accuracy in truth and lie detection. First, good lie detectors mentioned story cues more often than poor lie detectors. Second, the more popular stereotypical belief cues participants mentioned (gaze, fidget, and self-manipulations), and the more they endorsed Inbau's view on cues to deception (liars show gaze aversion, display unnatural posture changes, exhibit self-manipulations, and place the hand over the mouth or eyes when speaking), the worse they became at distinguishing between truths and lies. In other words, looking at Inbau et al.'s (1986, 2001) cues is counterproductive. This is not surprising, as deception research has not supported Inbau's views (DePaulo et al., 2003; Vrij, 2000a). Female participants claimed to look more at Inbau cues than male participants, which might explain why female participants were poorer at detecting truths than male participants.

When we, by means of a regression analysis, compared the veracity judgments made by good and poor lie detectors with the behaviors actually shown by the suspects in the stimulus material (so-called cues to perceived deception), we found that poor lie detectors associated an increase in gaze aversion and an increase in head nods with deception. However, good lie detectors associated a decrease in illustrators with deception. Research has demonstrated that a decrease in illustrators is a much more valid cue to deception than gaze aversion or head nods (Ekman & Friesen, 1972; see DePaulo et al., 2003, and Vrij, 2000a, for reviews of such literature). The regression analysis further showed that poor lie detectors were guided by the gender of the suspect: Female suspects were considered less suspicious than male suspects. Obviously, such a generalized approach has nothing to do with sophisticated truth and lie detection.

Police officers were asked both prior to and after the lie detection task which cues they pay attention to in order to detect deceit. The results revealed that, with a few exceptions, the officers mentioned the same cues before and after the task. The exceptions are easy to explain. For example, officers mentioned physiological cues more often prior to the task. This is unsurprising, as such cues are difficult to notice when someone watches a videotape. Moreover, they mentioned looking for facts more often prior to the task than after. This is also unsurprising, as facts about the cases were not made available to the lie detectors in this study. The fact that a big overlap emerged between cues mentioned before and after the task has a theoretical implication. It suggests that the cues police officers rely on are more general rather than idiosyncratic. Moreover, these general views could then be used to predict police officers' lie detection ability in future situations. Our results support this idea. Mentioning popular stereotypical beliefs and mentioning Inbau's cues prior to the task was negatively correlated with accuracy.

Finally, apart from relying on different cues, the results revealed one further difference between poor and good lie detectors. For poor lie detectors, a significant negative correlation emerged between lie and truth accuracy, whereas such a significant correlation did not emerge for good lie detectors. This implies that for poor lie detectors, increased success at one aspect of the task (success at either lie detection or truth detection) hampers success at the other aspect of the task.

Accuracy–confidence relationship

Our analyses regarding the accuracy–confidence relationship revealed three major findings. First, as many researchers before us (see DePaulo et al., 1997, for a review), we did not find a significant relationship between accuracy and confidence. Even our alternative method of measuring confidence (measuring confidence after completing the whole lie detection task instead of after each veracity judgment) did not lead to any significant relationships. Second, participants were more confident when they were rating actual truths compared with when they were rating actual lies. This same effect has been found before (DePaulo et al., 1997), including in several recent studies (Anderson, Ansfield, & DePaulo, 1999; Vrij & Baxter, 2000; Vrij et al., 2001). However, the reason for this is unclear. Possibly, when judges observe lies, there is something going on in the presentation that raises their doubts. Perhaps there is not enough to indicate the person as a liar, but enough to raise doubts about their subsequent judgment.

Most important, participants' estimated performance in the lie detection task (investigated after the task was completed) was significantly lower than their actual performance. This contradicts the overconfidence effect typically found in deception studies (DePaulo et al., 1997). Perhaps the overconfidence is an artifact.

People are typically asked to express their confidence after each veracity judgment they make. One might argue that this is a very difficult task that could easily lead to overconfidence. Participants may believe that some veracity judgments they make during a lie detection task are correct. They then will probably give themselves confidence levels of above 50% for these judgments. For each judgment in which they are uncertain, they will probably give themselves a 50% chance of being correct, because why would they think that they have less than a 50% chance of being correct for each individual judgment? A confidence score above 50% is the likely result of this strategy.

Methodological issues

Two methodological issues merit attention. First, police officers were exposed to an unbalanced number of truths and lies. This made it impossible to calculate a total accuracy score (accuracies of truths and lies combined) in this study, as that score cannot be unambiguously interpreted. For example, if an observer thinks that everyone was lying, that person would have a high total accuracy score in the event that he or she watched Tape 1 because that tape included nine lies and six truths. However, in this example, there would be no lie detecting ability, only a lie bias. We overcame this problem in two different ways, first by calculating truth and lie accuracy scores separately. The results showed that the difference between lie and truth accuracy was not significant, indicating that the sample as a whole did not show a truth or lie bias. We found that experience in interviewing was positively correlated with both truth accuracy and lie accuracy (although the latter correlation was only marginally significant). The fact that both correlations were positive indicates that experienced officers were most accurate and rules out the consideration that they were more biased. If they had a lie bias, then the experience–truth accuracy correlation would have been negative and vice versa; if they had a truth bias, then the experience–lie accuracy correlation would have been negative. The same reasoning applies to the other correlational findings. For example, mentioning Inbau et al.'s (1986, 2001) cues was negatively correlated with both truth and lie accuracy (although the latter correlation was not significant), hence, looking at those cues makes observers less accurate and not more biased. Moreover, we found that men were significantly better at detecting truths than women, whereas no significant gender difference emerged for detecting lies. Again, this demonstrates that men were more accurate at detecting truths and not more biased. In other analyses, in which the group of police officers were divided into two ability groups (poor lie detectors and good lie detectors), good lie detectors were those who scored both above the mean for lie clips (66.16%) and above the mean for truth clips (63.61%). This rules out that any of the good lie detectors could have been biased, as a lie bias would have resulted in a low truth accuracy score and a truth bias would have resulted in a low lie accuracy score.

Second, although the lie detection task was very realistic, it still differs in some aspects from real-life lie detection in police interviews. For example, normally the police officers would conduct the interview, and not just watch it. However, research has shown that conducting the interview is not necessarily advantageous in lie detection. Several researchers compared the accuracy scores of observers who actually interviewed potential liars with those who passively observed the interviews but did not actually interview the potential liars (Buller, Strzyzewski, & Hunsaker, 1991; Feeley & deTurck, 1998; Granhag & Strömwall, 2001). In all three studies, researchers found that passive observers were more accurate in detecting truths and lies than were interviewers. These findings suggest that merely observing is actually an advantage, not a disadvantage, in detecting deceit.

Moreover, ordinarily the police officer would see a much larger section, if not the whole interview(s), than they were exposed to in this experiment. Showing the whole interview would not have worked in this experiment, because without cutting out the majority of the interview, the footage would contain a huge amount of information that the experimenter could not be sure was true or false. Additionally, the experimenters were not asking participants to determine whether the suspect was guilty, as the truth–lie did not necessarily specifically relate to whether the suspect committed the crime under investigation, as mentioned earlier.

Also, in real life, officers may know some facts of the case. Although we could have provided our participants with the available evidence facts, we found this undesirable, as it would have made detecting some lies (those of which the suspect's statement contradicts the available evidence) too easy.

Finally, although participants on the whole were very willing to participate in the task, and keen to achieve high accuracy levels, this experiment does not have the same motivating consequences for them that judging the veracity of suspects in real life has. However, DePaulo, Anderson, & Cooper (1999) demonstrated that motivation does not improve performance in a lie detection task.

Conclusion

Police manuals typically give the impression that police officers who are experienced in interviewing suspects are good lie detectors (Inbau et al., 1986, 2001). Although previous research could not support this view whatsoever, our study, superior in terms of ecological validity over previous research, revealed that these claims are true to a limited extent. Police officers can detect truths and lies above the level of chance, and accuracy is related to experience with interviewing suspects. However, the results also revealed serious shortcomings in police work. First, accuracy rates, although above the level of chance, were far from perfect, and errors in truth–lie detection were frequently made. Second, police officers had a tendency to pay attention to cues that are not diagnostic cues to deceit, particularly body cues, such as gaze aversion. There may be various reasons why these nondiagnostic cues are so popular, one of which may be the discussion of these cues as diagnostic cues to deception in popular police manuals, such as the manual published by Inbau and colleagues. In fact, our research revealed that the more police officers followed their advice, the worse they were in their ability to distinguish between truths and lies.

Appendix A

Cue categories, descriptions and frequency of cues mentioned before and after the task, and number of participants to mention each cue

Cue	*Group*	*Examples (including antonyms)*	*Before task*	*After task*
Vagueness	Story	Vague reply/lots of detail	19	20
Contradictions	Story	Contradictions in story/consistent	18	10
Speech content	Story	Story content/specific words	9	15
Self-corrections	Story	Corrected self/corrected officer	0	7
Repetitions	Story	Repeating the question/buying time	3	1
Misc. speech	Story	Anything about speech that does not fit into "speech content," e.g., pleading/minimizing offense or "uncertain replies"	10	22
Evidence	Story	Facts of the case	8	2
Hesitance/pauses	Vocal	Hesitation/pauses in speech/fluent speech	16	27
Voice	Vocal	Voice pitch/volume/harshness/soft	15	16
Stammering	Vocal	Stammered/stuttered	4	0
Speech fillers	Vocal	Lots of "ems" and "ahs"/no "ems"	2	1
Response length	Vocal	Lengthy reply/one-word reply	3	4

(Continued)

Appendix A (continued)

Cue	*Group*	*Examples (including antonyms)*	*Before task*	*After task*
Gaze	Body	Averting gaze/eye contact	72	77
Movements	Body	Body language and movements	25	31
Posture	Body	Upright posture/slouched	6	13
Fidgeting	Body	Fidgeting/nervous movements/twiddling	19	11
Covering face	Body	Hands over face/hiding mouth	6	8
Hands	Body	Hand movements/still hands	9	28
Self-manipulation	Body	Touching/fiddling with self—excluding nails	7	6
Facial	Body	Facial expression/smiling/frowning	5	1
Props	Body	Playing with other things, e.g., cup/cigarette	3	2
Nail-biting	Body	Biting the nails/chewing fingers	2	2
Head movements	Body	Shaking/nodding/moving head	0	9
Physiological	Body	Sweating/blushing/blinking	15	5
Emotion	Body	Crying/upset/happy	6	1
Changes	Body	Changes in behavior/attitude	7	5
Demeanor	Conduct	Demeanor/relaxed/attitude	9	10
Defensive	Conduct	Sitting defensively/legs or arms crossed	12	9
Confidence	Conduct	Confidence/nervousness	11	9
Gut feeling	Other	Gut feeling/intuition	1	3
Total			322	355

Note: Misc. = miscellaneous.

Appendix B

Descriptions of the coded behaviors displayed by the suspects in the stimulus material and the interrater agreement scores between the two coders (Pearson correlations)

1 Gaze aversion: number of seconds in which the participant looked away from the interviewer (two coders, $r = .86$).
2 Smiles: frequency of smiles and laughs ($r = .98$).
3 Blinking: frequency of eye blinks ($r = .99$).
4 Head nods: frequency of head nods for which each upward and downward movement was counted as a separate nod ($r = .93$).
5 Head shakes: frequency of head shakes. Similar to head nods, each sideways movement was counted as a separate shake ($r = .98$).

6 Other head movements: head movements that were not included as head shakes or head nods (e.g., tilting the head to the side, turning the face, etc.; $r = .95$).
7 Shrugs: frequency of where one or both shoulders is briefly raised in an "I don't know" type gesture ($r = .99$).
8 Self-manipulations: frequency of scratching the head, wrists, etc. (touching the hands was counted as hand/finger movements rather than self-manipulations; $r = .99$).
9 Illustrators: frequency of arm and hand movements which were designed to modify and/or supplement what was being said verbally ($r = .99$).
10 Hand and/or finger movements: any other movements of the hands or fingers without moving the arms ($r = .99$).
11 Speech fillers: (speech fillers and speech errors were scored on the basis of a typed verbatim text) frequency of saying "ah" or "mmm," etc., between words ($r = .98$).
12 Speech errors: frequency of word and/or sentence repetition, sentence change, sentence incompletion, stutters, etc. ($r = .97$). Deviations from the official English language (e.g., local dialects such as saying "it weren't me" rather than "it wasn't me") were not included as speech errors.
13 Pauses: number of seconds in which there is a noticeable pause in the monologue of the participant ($r = .55$).

Notes

1 Investigating *beliefs about cues associated with deception* provides insight into which cues people think they use when detecting deceit, but it does not necessarily mean that they actually use these cues when they try to detect deceit. For example, people may indicate that they use gaze aversion as a cue for deceit, but it still may be the case that they subsequently judge someone who shows gaze aversion to be truthful. Investigating *cues to perceived deception* provides insight into which cues lie detectors actually use to indicate deception, but it is not certain whether they actually realize this. For example, when there is a tendency among lie detectors to judge those who moved a great deal as more deceptive than those who made few movements, it can be concluded that they used making movements as a cue to detect deception. It is, however, unclear whether lie detectors realized that they used making movements as a cue to detect deceit. The combination of those two methods therefore provides the most complete insight.
2 The picture in the small insert was not clear enough to enable the viewer to see any detail like, for example, the expressions of the interviewer. It is therefore unlikely that the participants paid any attention to this small insert picture (nobody mentioned that they did), and so it is unlikely that participants have been guided by the behavior or demeanor of the interviewer when judging the veracity of the suspects. (When the participants were asked afterward to indicate what made them decide whether the suspect on the screen was lying, nobody mentioned that they had been influenced by the interviewer.)
3 Although it is unfortunate that sometimes the lower torso could not be seen, this is not atypical for detection of deception research, as in many studies, including Ekman et al. (1999), only the head and shoulders are visible.
4 Mann et al. (2002) examined the behaviors of 16 suspects. However, 2 of those suspects were omitted for the purpose of this study. Those 2 were too well-known to show the

clips to participants, as they were higher profile cases that received some media attention. We did not want participants to know the cases that they were seeing, as obviously this would give them an advantage, and they may score high accuracy, not on the merits of the task, but purely on facts that they already knew.

5 Separate analyses for poor and good lie detectors showed that the truth–lie accuracy correlation was significant for poor lie detectors, $r(72) = -.35, p < .01$, but not for good lie detectors, $r(27) = -.21$, *ns*. A negative correlation means that the better poor lie detectors were at detecting truths, the worse they were at detecting lies, and vice versa. However, truth and lie accuracy did not differ significantly from each other for poor lie detectors (truth accuracy: $M = 57.61$, $SD = 22.7$; lie accuracy: $M = 61.37$, $SD = 16.6$), $t(71) = 0.97$, *ns*, and good lie detectors (truth accuracy: $M = 79.61$, $SD = 11.5$; lie accuracy: $M = 78.94$, $SD = 10.4$), $t(26) = 0.20$, *ns*.

6 A 2 (veracity) × 2 (gender of suspect) × 2 (gender of observer) ANOVA, with a mixed factorial design (the first two factors were within-subjects factors), was carried out to investigate the gender issue in more detail. In this analysis, only 74 participants (58 men and 16 women) were included because on one tape, no female suspects appeared. Apart from a significant gender of observers effect, $F(1, 72) = 5.51, p < .05, \eta^2 = .07$ (indicating that male accuracy was superior, $M = 68\%$, $SD = .13$, to female accuracy, $M = 58\%$, $SD = .20$), a deception × gender of suspect effect occurred, $F(1, 72) = 15.09$, $p < .01, \eta^2 = .17$. In male suspects, lies ($M = 72.00$, $SD = 19.11$) were more easily detected than truths ($M = 59.73$, $SD = 24.44$), whereas in female suspects, truths ($M = 79.73$, $SD = 40.48$) were more easily detected than lies ($M = 52.03$, $SD = 43.44$). However, participants only saw three deceptive clips of female suspects (and six truthful clips), so conclusions have to be drawn with caution. A significant difference between the four groups was found for detecting lies, $F(3, 95) = 4.44, p < .01, \eta^2 = .12$.

The 4 traffic officers who participated were highly accurate ($M = .95$, $SD = .58$), and Tukey's honestly significant difference test revealed that they were more accurate than any of the other three groups of participants (which did not differ significantly from each other). Because only 4 traffic officers participated, it would be presumptuous to assume that this sample is representative of all traffic officers and claim that all officers in this area of specialty would be more accurate at detecting deception. However, reasons why traffic officers may be more accurate than officers from other divisions include that they are more used to making snap judgments (e.g., highway patrol officers) about whether a person is drinking, or is lying about their involvement in a crash, and so on. Also they may speak to more people on a daily basis, because many traffic offenses are fairly quick to deal with, and hence traffic officers are more practiced in making veracity judgments than officers in other departments.

7 These findings are available from Aldert Vrij.

8 Following Anderson, DePaulo, Ansfield, Tickle, & Green (1999), who found gender differences in cues mentioned, we conducted ANOVAs and chi-square analyses, with gender as the between-subjects factor and the four categories and gut feeling as dependent variables. We only found one significant difference: Before the task, female participants mentioned more body cues ($M = 2.21$, $SD = 1.18$) than male participants ($M = 1.72$, $SD = .98$), $F(1, 97) = 4.08, p < .05, r^2 = .04$.

9 To explore gender differences in how often popular stereotypical beliefs and Inbau cues were mentioned, ANOVAs were carried out, with gender as the between-subjects factor and popular stereotypical beliefs and Inbau cues as dependent variables. Before the task, women mentioned popular stereotypical beliefs significantly more often ($M = 1.29$, $SD = 0.69$) than men ($M = 0.89$, $SD = 0.65$), $F(1, 97) = 6.65, p < .05, r^2 = .06$. Also after the task, women mentioned these cues more often ($M = 1.17$, $SD = 0.76$) than men ($M = 0.88$, $SD = 0.59$); although the difference was borderline significant, $F(1, 97) = 3.69, p = .058, r^2 = .03$.

Before the task, women mentioned Inbau cues significantly more often ($M = 1.46$, $SD = 0.78$) than men ($M = 1.00$, $SD = 0.72$), $F(1, 97) = 7.13, p < .01, r^2 = 07$. No gender differences emerged regarding the mention of Inbau cues after the task (men: $M = 1.09$, $SD = 0.74$; women: $M = 1.38$, $SD = 0.82$), $F(1, 97) = 2.50$, *ns*, $r^2 = 03$.

10 Differences between the four groups (Criminal Investigation Department, police trainers, traffic officers, and uniform response officers) were not found on any of the three (truth confidence, lie confidence, and posttask estimated accuracy) confidence scores (all $ps > .32$).

References

Akehurst, L., Koehnken, G., Vrij, A., & Bull, R. (1996). Lay persons' and police officers' beliefs regarding deceptive behaviour. *Applied Cognitive Psychology, 10*, 461–471.

Allwood, C. M., & Granhag, P. A. (1999). Feelings of confidence and the realism of confidence judgments in everyday life. In P. Juslin & H. Montgomery (Eds.), *Judgment and decision making: Neo-Brunswikian and process-tracing approaches* (pp. 123–146). Mahwah, NJ: Erlbaum.

Anderson, D. E., Ansfield, M. E., & DePaulo, B. M. (1999). Love's best habit: Deception in the context of relationships. In P. Philippot, R. S. Feldman, & E. J. Coats (Eds.), *The social context of nonverbal behavior* (pp. 372–409). Cambridge, England: Cambridge University Press.

Anderson, D. E., DePaulo, B. M., Ansfield, M. E., Tickle, J. J., & Green, E. (1999). Beliefs about cues to deception: Mindless stereotypes or untapped wisdom? *Journal of Nonverbal Behaviour, 23*, 67–89.

Bond, C. F., & Atoum, A. O. (2000). International deception. *Personality and Social Psychology Bulletin, 26*, 385–395.

Buller, D. B., Strzyzewski, K. D., & Hunsaker, F. G. (1991). Interpersonal deception II: The inferiority of conversational participants as deception detectors. *Communication Monographs, 58*, 25–40.

Clark-Carter, D. (1997). *Doing quantitative psychological research: From design to report.* Hove, England: Psychology Press.

DePaulo, B. M., Anderson, D. E., & Cooper, H. (1999). *Explicit and implicit deception detection.* Paper presented at the Society of Experimental Social Psychologists, St. Louis, MO.

DePaulo, B. M., Charlton, K., Cooper, H., Lindsay, J. L., & Muhlenbruck, L. (1997). The accuracy–confidence correlation in the detection of deception. *Personality and Social Psychology Review, 1*, 346–357.

DePaulo, B. M., Epstein, J. A., & Wyer, M. M. (1993). Sex differences in lying: How women and men deal with the dilemma of deceit. In M. Lewis & C. Saarni (Eds.), *Lying and deception in everyday life* (pp. 126–147). New York: Guilford Press.

DePaulo, B. M., Kirkendol, S. E., Tang, J., & O'Brien, T. P. (1988). The motivational impairment effect in the communication of deception: Replications and extensions. *Journal of Nonverbal Behavior, 12*, 177–201.

DePaulo, B. M., Lanier, K., & Davis, T. (1983). Detecting the deceit of the motivated liar. *Journal of Personality and Social Psychology, 45*, 1096–1103.

DePaulo, B. M., LeMay, C. S., & Epstein, J. A. (1991). Effects of importance of success and expectations for success on effectiveness at deceiving. *Personality and Social Psychology Bulletin, 17*, 14–24.

DePaulo, B. M., Lindsay, J. L., Malone, B. E., Muhlenbruck, L., Charlton, K., & Cooper, H. (2003). Cues to deception. *Psychological Bulletin, 129*, 74–118.

DePaulo, B. M., & Pfeifer, R. L. (1986). On-the-job experience and skill at detecting deception. *Journal of Applied Social Psychology, 16*, 249–267.

DePaulo, B. M., Stone, J. L., & Lassiter, G. D. (1985a). Deceiving and detecting deceit. In B. R. Schenkler (Ed.), *The self and social life* (pp. 323–370). New York: McGraw-Hill.

DePaulo, B. M., Stone, J. I., & Lassiter, G. D. (1985b). Telling ingratiating lies: Effects of target sex and target attractiveness on verbal and nonverbal deceptive success. *Journal of Personality and Social Psychology*, *48*, 1191–1203.

Ekman, P., & Frank, M. G. (1993). Lies that fail. In M. Lewis & C. Saarni (Eds.), *Lying and deception in everyday life* (pp. 184–201). New York, NY: Guilford Press.

Ekman, P., & Friesen, W. V. (1972). Hand movements. *Journal of Communication*, *22*, 353–374.

Ekman, P., & Friesen, W. V. (1974). Detecting deception from the body or face. *Journal of Personality and Social Psychology*, *29*, 288–298.

Ekman, P., & O'Sullivan, M. (1991). Who can catch a liar? *American Psychologist*, *46*, 913–920.

Ekman, P., O'Sullivan, M., & Frank, M. G. (1999). A few can catch a liar. *Psychological Science*, *10*, 263–266.

Feeley, T. H., & deTurck, M. A. (1998). The behavioral correlates of sanctioned and unsanctioned deceptive communication. *Journal of Non-verbal Behavior*, *22*, 189–204.

Feeley, T. H., & Young, M. J. (2000). The effects of cognitive capacity on beliefs about deceptive communication. *Communication Quarterly*, *48*, 101–119.

Forrest, J. A., & Feldman, R. S. (2000). Detecting deception and judge's involvement: Lower task involvement leads to better lie detection. *Personality and Social Psychology Bulletin*, *26*, 118–125.

Frank, M. G., & Ekman, P. (1997). The ability to detect deceit generalizes across different types of high-stake lies. *Journal of Personality and Social Psychology*, *72*, 1429–1439.

Gordon, N. J., & Fleisher, W. L. (2002). *Effective interviewing and interrogation techniques*. San Diego, CA: Academic Press.

Granhag, P. A., & Strömwall, L. A. (2001). Detection deception based on repeated interrogations. *Legal and Criminological Psychology*, *6*, 85–101.

Gudjonsson, G. H. (1994). Psychological vulnerability: Suspects at risk. In D. Morgan & G. M. Stephenson (Eds.), *Suspicion and silence: The right to silence in criminal investigations* (pp. 91–106). London: Blackstone.

Heinrich, C. A., & Borkenau, P. (1998). Deception and deception detection: The role of cross-modal inconsistency. *Journal of Personality*, *66*, 687–712.

Hess, J. E. (1997). *Interviewing and interrogation for law enforcement*. Reading, England: Anderson.

Hurd, K., & Noller, P. (1988). Decoding deception: A look at the process. *Journal of Nonverbal Behavior*, *12*, 217–233.

Inbau, F. E., Reid, J. E., & Buckley, J. P. (1986). *Criminal interrogation and confessions* (3rd ed.). Baltimore: Williams & Wilkins.

Inbau, F. E., Reid, J. E., Buckley, J. P., & Jayne, B. C. (2001). *Criminal interrogation and confessions* (4th ed.). Gaithersburg, MD: Aspen.

Kassin, S. M., & Fong, C. T. (1999). "I'm innocent!": Effects of training on judgments of truth and deception in the interrogation room. *Law and Human Behavior*, *23*, 499–516.

Koehnken, G. (1987). Training police officers to detect deceptive eyewitness statements. Does it work? *Social Behaviour*, *2*, 1–17.

Kraut, R. E. (1980). Humans as lie detectors: Some second thoughts. *Journal of Communication*, *30*, 209–216.

Lane, J. D., & DePaulo, B. M. (1999). Completing Coyne's cycle: Dysphorics' ability to detect deception. *Journal of Research in Personality*, *33*, 311–329.

Mann, S. (2001). *Suspects, lies and videotape: An investigation into telling and detecting lies in police/suspect interviews*. Unpublished doctoral dissertation, University of Portsmouth, Portsmouth, England.

Mann, S., Vrij, A., & Bull, R. (2002). Suspects, lies, and videotape: An analysis of authentic high-stake liars. *Law and Human Behavior, 26*, 365–376.

Manstead, A. S. R., Wagner, H. L., & MacDonald, C. J. (1986). Deceptive and nondeceptive communications: Sending experience, modality, and individual abilities. *Journal of Nonverbal Behavior, 10*, 147–167.

Meissner, C. A., & Kassin, S. M. (2002). "He's guilty!": Investigator bias in judgments of truth and deception. *Law and Human Behavior, 26*, 469–480.

Miller, G. R., & Stiff, J. B. (1993). *Deceptive communication*. Newbury Park, CA: Sage.

Moston, S., Stephenson, G. M., & Williamson, T. M. (1992). The effects of case characteristics on suspect behaviour during police questioning. *British Journal of Criminology, 32*, 23–40.

O'Sullivan, M., Ekman, P., & Friesen, W. V. (1988). The effect of comparisons on detecting deceit. *Journal of Nonverbal Behaviour, 12*, 203–216.

Porter, S., Woodworth, M., & Birt, A. R. (2000). Truth, lies, and videotape: An investigation of the ability of federal parole officers to detect deception. *Law and Human Behavior, 24*, 643–658.

Strömwall, L. A. (2001). *Detecting deception: Moderating factors and accuracy*. Unpublished doctoral dissertation, University of Gothenburg, Gothenburg, Sweden.

Vrij, A. (1993). Credibility judgments of detectives: The impact of nonverbal behavior, social skills, and physical characteristics on impression formation. *Journal of Social Psychology, 133*, 601–610.

Vrij, A. (1995). Behavioral correlates of deception in a simulated police interview. *Journal of Psychology, 129*, 15–28.

Vrij, A. (2000a). *Detecting lies and deceit: The psychology of lying and the implications for professional practice*. Chichester, England: Wiley.

Vrij, A. (2000b). Telling and detecting lies as a function of raising the stakes. In C. M. Breur, M. M. Kommer, J. F. Nijboer, & J. M. Reijntjes (Eds.), *New trends in criminal investigation and evidence II* (pp. 699–709). Antwerp, Belgium: Intersentia.

Vrij, A., & Baxter, M. (2000). Accuracy and confidence in detecting truths and lies in elaborations and denials: Truth bias, lie bias and individual differences. *Expert Evidence: The International Digest of Human Behaviour, Science and Law, 7*, 25–36.

Vrij, A., Edward, K., & Bull, R. (2001a). People's insight into their own behaviour and speech content while lying. *British Journal of Psychology, 92*, 373–389.

Vrij, A., Edward, K., & Bull, R. (2001b). Stereotypical verbal and nonverbal responses while deceiving others. *Personality and Social Psychology Bulletin, 27*, 899–909.

Vrij, A., Edward, K., Roberts, K. P., & Bull, R. (2000). Detecting deceit via analysis of verbal and nonverbal behaviour. *Journal of Nonverbal Behaviour, 24*, 239–263.

Vrij, A., & Graham, S. (1997). Individual differences between liars and the ability to detect lies. *Expert Evidence: The International Digest of Human Behaviour, Science and Law, 5*, 144–148.

Vrij, A., Harden, F., Terry, J., Edward, K., & Bull, R. (2001). The influence of personal characteristics, stakes and lie complexity on the accuracy and confidence to detect deceit. In R. Roesch, R. R. Corrado, & R. J. Dempster (Eds.), *Psychology in the courts: International advances in knowledge* (pp. 289–304). London: Routledge.

Vrij, A., & Mann, S. (2001a). Telling and detecting lies in a high-stake situation: The case of a convicted murderer. *Applied Cognitive Psychology, 15*, 187–203.

Vrij, A., & Mann, S. (2001b). Who killed my relative? Police officers' ability to detect real-life high-stake lies. *Psychology, Crime, & Law*, *7*, 119–132.

Vrij, A., & Semin, G. R. (1996). Lie experts' beliefs about nonverbal indicators of deception. *Journal of Nonverbal Behaviour*, *20*, 65–80.

Vrij, A., Semin, G. R., & Bull, R. (1996). Insight into behavior displayed during deception. *Human Communication Research*, *22*, 544–562.

Vrij, A., & Winkel, F. W. (1991). Cultural patterns in Dutch and Surinam nonverbal behavior: An analysis of simulated police/citizen encounters. *Journal of Nonverbal Behavior*, *15*, 169–184.

Wechsler, D. (1981). *Manual for the Wechsler Adult Intelligence Scale—Revised (WAIS–R)*. New York, NY: Psychological Corporation.

Wiseman, R. (1995). The megalab truth test. *Nature*, *373*, 391.

Zuckerman, M., DePaulo, B. M., & Rosenthal, R. (1981). Verbal and nonverbal communication of deception. In L. Berkowitz (Ed.), *Advances in experimental social psychology* (Vol. 14, pp. 1–57). New York, NY: Academic Press.

10 Helping to sort the liars from the truth-tellers: the gradual revelation of information during investigative interviews

Coral J. Dando, Ray Bull, Thomas C. Ormerod and Alexandra L. Sandham

Introduction

Worldwide, face-to-face interviews are the primary method for collecting verbal information from those suspected of wrongdoing, and the resultant data are fundamental in assisting criminal justice systems and other government organizations (e.g., revenue and customs; benefit fraud investigations; medical negligence) to make veracity judgements of guilt or innocence. The interviewer's task is not to make veracity judgements, but to uncover *all* of the event-relevant information in such a manner that decision-makers (ACPO, 2004; Blair, 2009; Shepherd, 2007: e.g., prosecutors, judges, magistrates, and juries) are best able to make veracity judgements. In pursuit of this goal, interviewers strive to maximize effective information gathering when interviewing suspected perpetrators. But, how *should* interviewers use information (which may or may not be potentially incriminating) to maximize opportunities to showcase the veridicality of a verbal account? In particular, *how* and *when* should information be revealed to the interviewee to best assist decision-makers in making accurate veracity judgements? This research addresses these questions, examining three approaches to revealing event information during interviews to maximize the cognitive load for deceivers, while being cognizant of minimizing load for interviewers and end users of interview data.

Where interviews with suspected wrongdoers are not routinely audio or video recorded (e.g., in the United States and many European and South Asian countries), it is vital that interview techniques are developed and empirically investigated to better support interviewers, observers (e.g., legal advisors; lay observers; government representatives; fraud investigators, etc.) and other end-users of the interview data to make real-time veracity judgements. Equally, the routine recording of interviews in some countries (e.g., the United Kingdom) does not negate the need to showcase the veridicality of an account, albeit veracity judgements are supported by the existence of an accurate record of the interview (see Ministry of Justice, 2012). Although recordings allow an observer to revisit portions of an interview, the first viewing of any interview is likely to be highly influential in forming an observer's judgement. Thus, it is important to optimize the conditions under which observers initially take in information imparted during an interview.

The psychological literature highlights differences between deceivers' and truth-tellers' verbal behaviours in interview settings. Deceivers typically provide shorter and less detailed statements and answers than truth-tellers (see Sporer & Schwandt, 2006), which is thought to emanate from increased demands on working memory associated with constructing, verbalizing, and maintaining a deceptive account (e.g., Sporer & Schwandt, 2006). Differences of length and detail between deceivers' and truth-tellers' verbal accounts may also be strategically motivated. Deceptive interviewees often provide less detail to reduce the likelihood of contradicting themselves as evidence emerges during an interview (e.g., Bull, 2012; Dando & Bull, 2011), and because they may have to create more complex lies to account for new evidence as an interview progresses and ensure that new lies are consistent with previous deceptions (e.g., Cody, Marston, & Foster, 1984). Hence, 'keeping it simple' provides opportunities for verbal manoeuvring, allowing flexibility to add detail if requested by the interviewer, and thinking time should additional explanation of behaviours become necessary. In contrast, truthful interviewees typically give more detailed accounts of events, believing as they have nothing to hide that their innocence will be apparent (e.g., Colwell, Hiscock-Anisman, Woods, Memon, & Michlik, 2006; Gilovich, Savitsky, & Medvec, 1998; Lerner, 1980).

Despite differences in the verbal behaviours of truth-tellers and deceivers, making veracity judgements is difficult in legal settings since cues to verbal deception are not readily discernible. Indeed, professionals (e.g., judges, customs officers, civil servants, and police officers) generally perform no better than laypersons, at around chance (Ekman, O'Sullivan, & Frank, 1999; Vrij, 2004; but see Mann, Vrij, & Bull, 2004, for an exception). One common approach to interviewing, specifically included within some techniques (Inbau, Reid, & Buckley, 1986) is to reveal all the known information/evidence early in an interview. Early revelation of evidence is intended to persuade guilty interviewees to confess at the outset. However, in addition to early revelation being linked with false confessions (Bull & Soukara, 2012; Huff, Ratner, & Sagarin, 1986), confessions are rare unless the evidence is overwhelming (Bull, Valentine, & Williamson, 2009). Early revelation of evidence may also support another deceiver strategy, which is to plan how to respond to questioning by developing a 'lie script', a narrative intended to explain potential incriminating pieces of evidence that arise as the interview proceeds (Hines *et al.*, 2010; Porter & Yuille, 1996).

Alternative approaches have sought to amplify verbal deception cues by withholding information (known to the interviewer) until the end of the interview process (e.g., Granhag & Hartwig, 2008). Disclosing information later in an interview may highlight inconsistencies, when the evidence revealed by the interviewer is at odds with the verbal account previously provided by the interviewee. However, late disclosure may have disadvantages because truth-tellers can also display inconsistencies, resulting from forgetting or failing to account for behaviour or information believed by them to be insignificant. Consequently, observers may erroneously conclude that a truth-teller is being deceptive, and may experience a *recency* effect, whereby interviewees' verbal conduct in the closing stages of an interview becomes the most salient behaviour when making veracity judgements. Moreover, observers are likely to experience increased cognitive load as a result of the late revelation of evidence, since they must simultaneously assess the consistency of multiple items of evidence with an interviewee's account (see Beckmann, 2010).

Assessing the consistency of a story is a complex cognitive task that imposes demands upon both long-term memory, in terms of remembering the details of an account (Erdelyi, 2010), and working memory, in terms of drawing inferences to assess the consistency of the evidential statements and the interviewee's account (Johnson-Laird & Byrne, 2002). Consistent with these concerns, when lay observers were asked to make veracity judgements following interviews with mock suspects, where information had been revealed late, they showed only modest improvements in their overall ability to discriminate between liars and truth-tellers versus a control interview where information was revealed early (62%, against a chance level of 50%; Hartwig, Granhag, Strömwall, & Vrij, 2005). Moreover, their accuracy improved only when detecting deceivers (67%), and not truth-tellers (54%).

The literature pertaining to the revelation of information during interviews is not well advanced, and little is known about how best to protect innocent interviewees. Rather, researchers have generally been concerned with detecting deceivers. Moreover, laboratory research has typically concerned itself with managing small amounts of information during interviews (typically three items), which is at odds with the task faced by professional investigators. Low truth-teller detection rates by observers are of particular concern. Innocent interviewees may choose not to disclose information, believing it to be insignificant, or may simply misunderstand the importance of fully accounting for their involvement in an event. Typically, users of interview data in the criminal justice system, effectively equivalent to observers, do not undergo training in specific interview techniques nor do they conduct the interviews. Thus, an effective interview technique must support the requirements of observers, and consider how to protect the innocent while being cognizant of the demands placed upon the interviewer and deceptive interviewees.

Here, we evaluate a 'drip feed' approach to using evidence during interviews, in which revelation occurs gradually throughout the questioning phase of an interview rather than right at the beginning or end (see Bull, 2012; Dando & Bull, 2011). Using this approach, interviewers are supported to continuously assess how best to determine whether an interviewee's account is veridical, by incrementally revealing items of information/evidence. We suggest that incremental evidence utilization maximizes opportunities to detect verbal cues to deception, because it exploits gaps in a deceiver's account immediately inconsistencies begin to emerge, while at the same time providing innocent interviewees an early opportunity to convey their honesty (see Bull *et al.*, 2009; Dando & Bull, 2011). Limiting a deceptive interviewee's verbal options from the very start of the questioning phase may heighten the investigative value of the available evidence, as well as signalling to innocent interviewees the need to account for each item of evidence. Equally, a drip-feed approach is more likely to protect truth-tellers because they are quickly made aware of the knowledge and expectations of the interviewer.

Recently, Granhag, Strömwall, Willén, & Hartwig (2013) have followed up the use of a gradual revelation of evidence initially introduced by Dando & Bull (2011, also see Bull, 2012; Bull & Dando, 2010), described as a 'tactical' use of evidence, by employing a procedure of rating the strength of evidence, using an evidence-framing matrix, in which evidence is ranked according to strength of source and relevance to the investigation. Having compared the incremental revelation approach against Early and Late revelation, they once more replicated the findings of Dando & Bull (2011). Experienced police interviewers showed greater accuracy in identifying both deceivers and truth-tellers when using incremental rather than blocked (Early or Late) revelation, a result replicated by Sorochinski *et al.* (2011). However, in their incremental condition, interviewers revealed evidence in a specified order: The weakest was revealed early and strongest towards the end of the interview. This procedure is problematic for two reasons. First, in real investigations it is not possible *a priori* to specify the strength or potential impact of a piece of evidence. Moreover, an information-gathering approach to interviewing, as adopted in the United Kingdom and elsewhere, does not advocate distinguishing between evidence and information, as the latter might become the former during the course of an interview or later in an investigation. Rather, investigators are duty bound to keep an open mind (see Milne & Bull, 1999; NPIA, 2009; Shepherd, 2007). Second, by revealing the strongest evidence towards the end of the interview, Granhag *et al.* have effectively transmuted the incremental revelation of evidence to a late revelation of strong evidence, and because observer veracity data were not reported the efficacy of their techniques for non-expert observers is not known. Thus, an effective test of the tactical approach to evidence revelations remains to be completed.

Here, we report an experiment comparing *Early*, *Late*, and *Gradual* approaches to information use. The experiment tested the following hypotheses:

(i) Both late and gradual revelation will enhance untrained observers' deception detection performance compared with early revelation, as they prevent deceivers from implementing lie scripts and thus block opportunities for verbal manoeuvring.
(ii) Gradual revelation will be more effective in deception detection than late revelation because incremental use of information provides more opportunities for deceptive interviewees' accounts to be challenged as the interview proceeds.
(iii) Gradual revelation will increase the cognitive demands experienced by deceptive interviewees compared with early and late revelation, because opportunities for verbal manoeuvring are limited when the interviewee does not have the full set of information at any one time with which to construct a lie script, either prospectively (as with early revelation) or retrospectively (as with late revelation).

Method

Participants

Game players

A total of 151 graduate and postgraduate students participated, comprising 69 men and 82 women, *M* = 21.3 years (*SD* = 4.56), ranging from 18 to 54 years. All participants were naïve to the experimental aims and hypotheses.

Interviewer

Interviews were conducted by one interviewer (to limit interviewer variability) with 10 years' specialist police investigative interviewing experience, using strict interview protocols (available from the first author). The interviewer completed additional training that explained in detail the three interview procedures (early, late, and gradual), how each procedure should be applied (using interview protocols and written examples), and the rules of the game. The game rules explained only the truth-tellers' task, thereby increasing the realism of the investigative role. The researchers held two interactive sessions with the interviewer during which the game and interview procedures were verbally explained. The interviewer undertook several practice interviews, and received feedback. The experimental manipulations were not explained, and no information about the existence of 'terrorist' players was provided.

Observers

Thirty laypersons (with no investigative/interviewing experience: 15 men and 15 women) participated as observers. All were blind to interview condition. The mean age of the observers was 37.9 years (*SD* = 3.81), ranging from 24 to 44 years.

Procedure

The study comprised four phases: (i) participants competed in the game in groups of four (each participant competing to win against the other participants); (ii) each participant was afterwards interviewed about their game activities; (iii) participants then completed a post-interview questionnaire concerning their interview experience; (iv) a random selection of recorded interviews were viewed by laypersons, each of whom then gave a veracity judgement.

Phase 1

Upon arrival, participants were assigned to either builder (truth-teller) or terrorist (deceiver) roles. First, they were shown role-specific training videos, which they listened to through headphones and viewed individually, explaining the game software, objectives, and rules, and each player's individual role. Participants were also provided with instruction cards, which could be referred to during the game. They then took part in the game, competing against three other players to traverse a game board presented individually on laptop computers. Randomly generated dice throws determined the number of squares each player could move on each turn. To complete their role-specific tasks, participants purchased materials from virtual shops on the board and delivered them to a virtual Olympic site. The first player to complete his/her tasks was the winner and the game finished.

The builder's goal was to build part of an Olympic stadium. The terrorist's goal was to blow up the stadium. The tasks were differentiated such that deceivers had to mask their activities by trying to appear as legitimate builders. For example, while builders had to purchase small amounts of explosive to clear the site, terrorists were required to purchase much larger amounts, and thus had to find ways to hide their purchases.

Terrorists were provided with an outline of the builders' tasks to allow them to devise ways of masking their true identity by appearing to be a builder. Examples of how terrorists might mask their identity included the following: (i) mirroring purchasing behaviour by repeatedly buying smaller amounts of materials as might be required by builders; (ii) visiting shops at the same time as other players so that the investigator could not tell which player made a purchase; (iii) purchasing items not required for their terrorist task and carrying them as decoys; (iv) visiting shops but not actually purchasing any items.

Each participant was paid a total of £23 for participating, of which £18 was given on completion of the game and £5 was given after the interview phase. To enhance motivation, participants were informed that this final amount would be given only if he/ she were able to convince the interviewer that they were builders. In fact, all participants were paid irrespective of their interview performance. All players were naïve to the roles of others, and truth-tellers were unaware that others were playing with a deception agenda. The number of deceivers per game ranged from zero to three (with a mean of 2 per game).

Phase 2

A 3 (interview: early; late; gradual) × 2 (group: truth-teller; deceiver) experimental design was employed. Approximately 45 min after game completion, participants were interviewed individually about their game activities. This delay ensured sufficient time: (i) for participants to consider the post-game/pre-interview instructions; and (ii) for the interviewer to consider the appropriate game-playing information in readiness for the interviews. Prior to the interview, all participants were instructed 'Your task is to convince the interviewer that you are a builder and that you were not involved in any illegal activity during the game'. No guidance was given to participants as to how they should carry out these instructions in terms of how they might act, what strategies they might use, or what they might say.

Information selection

Upon completion of each game, the interviewer was presented with four case files (one for each player), each documenting a limited amount of game information. Games were sub-divided into four phases (every fourth dice roll signalled the end of a phase and the commencement of a new one), at which point each participant's game-playing information was recorded by the game administrator. Accordingly, there were four game sections within each case file. The information included in each game phase section was limited to the following: (i) where an individual player had been during each of the game phases, such as the shop/s he or she may have visited, and whether he/she had been to the Olympic site and/or builder's depot; (ii) the total stock sold within that phase, but not who bought the stock (this information was common across all case files); (iii) whether a participant's virtual van had been weighed during that phase, and the weight of that van, and (iv) if a participant's virtual van had been inspected, the two items selected for inspection. The mean number of information items presented to the interviewer in each case file was 11.7 ($SD = 1.09$), ranging from 8.61 to 13.09. The interviewer stochastically selected five information items from each case file relevant to the information space of the game. From thereon, these items are referred to as potentially incriminating information. In line with the information-gathering approach to interviewing, *a priori*, the strength or potential impact of each piece of information was not considered. Rather, because the interviewer was unaware of the presence of 'terrorist' players, this information was selected to allow the interviewer to understand and probe participants' accounts of their gaming behaviour in a manner dictated by each interview condition. *Post-hoc* examination of participant game play revealed that the numbers of deceptive participants in each interview condition adopting each of the four strategies for masking their identity did not differ significantly, $p > .15$ (for more detail on how deception strategies were coded, see Ormerod, 2010).

Interview conditions

Each interview, irrespective of condition, comprised (in line with the relevant British police training) the same number of phases in the same order, namely *introduction*, *explain*, *free recall*, *questioning*, and *closure*. Interviews differed according to condition in terms of the phase and the manner in which potentially incriminating information was presented (i.e., revealed in a batch, or incrementally).

EARLY DISCLOSURE

In this condition, interviews commenced with an *introduction* and *explain* phase. The interviewer then disclosed each of the five pieces of potentially incriminating information in a batch, followed by an explanation as to why the information was thought to be incriminating. The interviewee was instructed not to respond at this point, but was asked using an open-ended invitation to provide a *free recall* account of his/her gaming behaviour in as much detail as possible (uninterrupted by the interviewer). Once the account had finished, the interviewer explained that some questions concerning each of the pieces of information presented earlier would be asked (the *questioning* phase). Each piece of information was again presented in a batch, following which the interviewee was then asked to explain/ account for each piece of potentially incriminating gaming behaviour. Where appropriate, participants' replies/ explanations were challenged to clarify their version of events, that is, discrepancies were pointed out and an explanation was invited. Interviews concluded with a *closure* phase.

LATE DISCLOSURE

The *introduction* and *explain* phases of the interviews in this condition were as above. Immediately after these phases, interviewees were asked to provide a free recall account of their game-playing behaviour. The interviewer then commenced the *questioning* phase by asking one question concerning each of the five pieces of potentially incriminating information (one after another) without revealing the nature of that evidence. For example, the builder's task dictated that participants might follow a certain buying pattern: that due to the nature of the task demands, it appears sensible to visit the electrical shop first. If the interviewee had not visited the electrical shop the investigator might ask the question 'Which shop did you visit first?' thereby questioning the interviewee concerning the potentially incriminating information without revealing the nature of that information. The interviewer then provided the participant with an opportunity to add/alter anything he/she had said. At this point (towards the end of the questioning phase) the interviewer disclosed all five pieces of information together, in a batch, followed by an explanation as to why they were potentially incriminating. The interviewee was invited to explain/account for each. Where appropriate, the participant's account was then challenged and the interviewee was invited to explain all discrepancies/contradictions. The *closure* phase concluded the interview.

GRADUAL DISCLOSURE

The *introduction, explain,* and *free recall* phases of the interviews were as described in the late disclosure condition. The interviewer then commenced the *questioning* phase by revealing the potentially incriminating information one piece at a time. The first piece was revealed followed by an explanation as to why this was viewed as suspicious. The interviewee was then asked to account for that particular information. If appropriate (i.e., when the account provided by the interviewee contradicted what the investigator knew, or what the interviewee had said in the free account) the interviewer challenged the participant's account. Each piece of information was similarly presented, incrementally, piece by piece, and challenged accordingly until the interviewee had addressed each in turn. The *closure* phase concluded the interview.

Phase 3

Following the interview, participants immediately completed a questionnaire (see Materials below), were paid for their participation, and then debriefed about the aims of the project.

Phase 4

Thirty randomly selected video recordings of the interviews (10 from each condition, 5 truth-tellers and 5 liars) were viewed by 30 laypersons (each viewing all 30 videos in a counterbalanced order of presentation). Observers viewed the entire recording of each interview. They were not provided with any information about the three different interview conditions, nor were they provided any base rate information concerning the number of deceptive/truth-teller interviewees. They were simply instructed to watch and listen to each video, thus (verbatim), 'You will now be shown several video clips of interviews conducted with people who took part in trials to test a new interactive board game. Each player was given a game task, and set of game rules, and was instructed to complete their task as quickly as possible, according to those rules. Players competed against each other to complete their task first. The first player to complete their task won the game, and was rewarded financially for doing so. Your task is to watch and listen to each of the interviews and to decide who is telling the truth and who is lying'. Observers were also told that any information presented to interviewees (about their game-playing activities) during the interview was correct. Having viewed each interview, the observers were asked to complete a short questionnaire (see Materials below).

Materials

Interviewee questionnaire

This questionnaire collected quantitative data, and comprised questions inviting participants to provide answers on a Likert style scale ranging from 1 (e.g., *very easy/not at all motivated/I was not at all deceptive*) to 7 (e.g., *very difficult/very motivated/I was deceptive throughout*).

Observer questionnaire

This questionnaire comprised six questions, of which three collected participant demographic information. The remaining three questions concerned the observer's task: two collected data pertaining to two qualitatively different veracity judgements, first (dichotomously) whether observers thought interviewees were being deceptive or not, and second the strength of their veracity judgements (on a 7-point scale, ranging from 1 = *definitely lying* to 7 = *definitely telling the truth*). The third question asked observers to rate the difficulty of the veracity task (on a 7-point scale, ranging from 1 = *very easy* to 7 = *extremely difficult*).

Results

Interviewer training

To examine the interviewer's implementation of training across the three conditions (early, late, and gradual), performance was rated using a scale (ranging from 1 to 5, where 1 = *revealed information according to condition and training/managed responses according to condition and training*; 5 = *did not reveal information/manage responses according to condition and training*). The scale was developed to assess the manner in which the case file information was used, and how participants' replies to questions pertaining to that information were either accepted or challenged (see Dando & Bull, 2011). From here on, for the purposes of this analysis, use of game information is referred to as information revelation, and how participants' replies were accepted or challenged is referred to as response management (the scoring rubric and scales are available from the first author). Two independent raters, who were naïve to the experimental hypotheses, scored each interview for information revelation and response management, using the aforementioned rating scale. Cohen's kappa analysis revealed an excellent level of agreement between raters, kappa = 0.89, p = .005 (Landis & Koch, 1977). No significant main effects, or interactions emerged for interviewer's information revelation behaviour or response management as a function of interview condition ($M_{\text{Late Use}} = 1.52$, $SD = 0.57$; $M_{\text{Gradual Use}} = 1.64$, $SD = 0.66$; $M_{\text{Early Use}} = 1.68$, $SD = 0.65$; $M_{\text{Late How}} = 1.46$, $SD = 0.54$; $M_{\text{Gradual How}} = 1.68$; $SD = 0.62$; $M_{\text{Early How}} = 1.54$, $SD = 0.61$), all Fs < 1.366, ps > .175, or group ($M_{\text{Deceiver Use}} = 1.59$, $SD = 0.62$; $M_{\text{Truth-teller Use}} = 1.54$, $SD = 0.76$; $M_{\text{Deceiver How}} = 1.45$, $SD = 0.74$; $M_{\text{Truth-teller How}} = 1.44$, $SD = 0.86$), all Fs < 1.496, ps > .344.

Deceptiveness and motivation

A series of between groups ANOVAs were conducted (employing Bonferroni's correction) for participants' ratings of how deceptive they had been (during the post-game interviews) and their motivation (to comply with the pre-interview instructions) are displayed in Table 10.1. There was a significant main effect of group for deceptiveness, $F(1, 145) = 243.116$, $p < .001$, $\eta^2 = .63$. Participants in the terrorist group reported being more deceptive than those in the builder group. There was a non-significant effect of interview $F(2, 145) = 1.445$, $p = .239$, $\eta^2 = .20$. However, a significant Group × Interview interaction emerged, $F(2, 145) = 4.046$, $p = .002$, $\eta^2 = .53$. Participants in the terrorist group reported having been more deceptive in the early and late conditions than in the gradual condition. No difference emerged between the former two conditions. Participants in the builder group did not differ on their ratings of truthfulness/deceptiveness across interview conditions. Non-significant main effects or interactions emerged for motivation between the groups, $F(1, 145) = 0.002$, $p = .562$ or across interview conditions, $F(2, 145) = 3.621$, $p = .029$, $\eta^2 = .369$.

Table 10.1 Means and standard deviations interviewees' ($N = 151$) post-interview ratings of deceptiveness, cognitive demand, and motivation

	Deceptiveness	*Cognitive demand*	*Motivation*
	M(SD)	*M(SD)*	*M(SD)*
Gradual	2.76 (1.75)	4.31 (0.75)	5.33 (1.64)
Builder gradual	1.67 (1.01)	3.44 (1.22)	5.23 (1.55)
Terrorist gradual	3.99 (210)	5.43 (1.01)	5.49 (1.33)
Late	3.23 (2.09)	3.90 (1.08)	5.49 (1.38)
Builder late	1.32 (0.99)	3.42 (1.12)	5.61 (1.19)
Terrorist late	4.84 (2.01)	4.68 (0.89)	5.70 (1.48)
Early	3.38 (1.45)	3.08 (1.14)	5.48 (1.39)
Builder early	1.77 (0.79)	2.58 (0.99)	5.68 (1.29)
Terrorist early	5.10 (1.98)	3.81 (1.20)	5.19 (1.33)

Table 10.2 Observers' percentage deception detection accuracy rate across interview conditions (Early, Late, and Gradual) and groups (truth-tellers and liars)

% Accuracy	*Interview conditions*		
	Early	*Late*	*Gradual*
Liars	50	54	66
Truth-tellers	48	44	76
Overall	49	50	68

Observers' veracity judgements

Observers' performance, as a function of interview (early; late; gradual) and veracity (truth-teller and liar) is displayed in Table 10.2. A 3 (interview) × 2 (veracity) repeated measures ANOVA was conducted on these data followed by Games–Howell *post-hoc* tests (in each condition participants were awarded a score ranging from 0 to 5 according to the number of correct judgements made).

This revealed a significant main effect of both interview, $F(2, 58) = 9.596$, $p < .001$, $\eta^2 = .97$, and group $F(1, 29) = 22.002$, $p < .001$, $\eta^2 = .99$. The Interview × Group interaction was non-significant, $F = 0.705$, $p = .499$. Observers' performance was significantly better in the gradual ($M = 3.60$, $SD = 1.59$) than in both the late ($M = 2.99$, $SD = 1.35$) and early ($M = 3.13$, $SD = 1.77$) conditions, with non-significant difference between the latter two conditions. Observers were significantly better at judging deceivers ($M = 3.92$, $SD = 1.47$) than truth-tellers ($M = 2.83$, $SD = 1.32$).

Observers' confidence and task difficulty ratings

A series of 3 (interview: late; early; gradual) × 2 (group: builder; terrorist) × 5 (video: 1; 2; 3; 4; 5) repeated measures ANOVAs were carried out on observers'

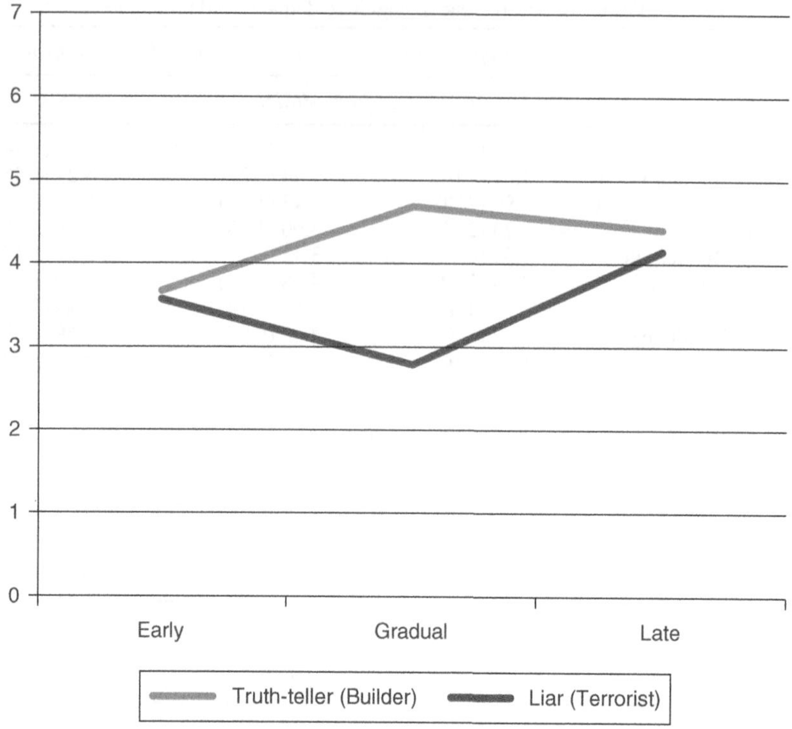

Figure 10.1 Observers' deception/truth confidence ratings (on a scale of 1–7: 1 = *definitely lying*; 7 = *definitely telling the truth*) as function of interview condition (Early; Late; Gradual) and group (truth-tellers; liars).

confidence and task difficulty ratings, followed by a series of planned comparisons. Significant main effects of interview, $F(2, 58) = 12.604$, $p < .001$, $\eta^2 = .30$, and group, $F(2, 58) = 84.767$, $p < .001$, $\eta^2 = .74$, emerged. The main effect of video was non-significant, $F(5, 58) = 1.164$, $p = .330$. Analysis revealed a significant interaction between Interview × Group, $F(2, 58) = 85.673$, $p < .001$, $\eta^2 = .44$ (see Figure 10.1).

On the confidence scale (where 1 = *definitely lying*, 7 = *definitely telling the truth*, and 4 = *indeterminate*), observers' ratings differed significantly for terrorists (M = 3.61, SD = 1.13) and builders (M = 4.26, SD = 1.32), $p < .001$. Also, observers judged interviewees in the late condition as being more truthful (M = 4.28, SD = 0.98) than in both the gradual (M = 3.75, SD = 1.03) and early (M = 3.69, SD = 1.18), $p < .001$, with a non-significant difference between the latter two conditions $p = .297$. The Interview × Group interaction was explored using planned comparisons that compared gradual and late conditions against the early, and the gradual against the late. When judging deceivers (terrorists), the late and gradual conditions (M = 3.70, SD = 1.47) did not differ overall from the early (M = 3.57, SD = 1.30), $p < .420$. However, veracity judgements of deceivers (terrorists) in the gradual condition ($M = 2.99$, $SD = 0.94$) were significantly stronger than the late judgements ($M = 4.15$, $SD = 1.09$), $F(1, 29) = 49.825$, $p < .001$, $\eta^2 = .63$. When judging truth-tellers, the late and gradual conditions ($M = 4.46$, $SD = 1.22$) differed significantly from the early ($M = 3.67$, $SD = 1.69$), $F(1, 29) = 37.583$, $p < .001$, $\eta^2 = .56$. There was a non-significant difference between the late ($M = 4.41$, $SD = 1.07$) and gradual conditions ($M = 4.51$, $SD = 1.20$), $p = .64$.

A significant main effect of interview also emerged for ratings of task difficulty, $F(2, 58) = 33.697$, $p < .001$, $\eta^2 = .43$. Observers rated the veracity task as significantly more difficult in the late ($M = 4.97$, $SD = 1.58$) and early ($M = 5.17$, $SD = 1.15$) than in the gradual interviews ($M = 3.58$, $SD = 1.07$). The main effects of group and video were non-significant, all $Fs < 1.264$, all $ps > .299$. All interactions were non-significant, all $Fs < 1.661$, all $ps > .246$.

Interviewees' cognitive demands

Analysis of interviewees' ratings as to how demanding they found the post-game interviews and how deceptive/truthful they had been (means and standard deviations are displayed in Table 10.1) revealed a significant main effect of both interview, $F(2, 145) = 11.010$, $p < .001$, $\eta^2 = .13$, and group, $F(1, 145) = 44.847$, $p < .001$, $\eta^2 = .24$. Overall, participants reported finding both the gradual and late interviews significantly more demanding than the early interviews with no difference between the former two conditions. Interviewees in the builder group reported both the late and gradual interviews as more demanding than the early, with no difference between the former two conditions. Terrorist participants reported the gradual interviews as significantly more demanding than both the early and late, and the late more demanding than the early. There was no significant interview/group interaction, $F = 1.398$, $p = .250$.

Discussion

This article reports a study that compares the effectiveness, in terms of supporting observer veracity judgements, of a gradual disclosure technique in which possibly incriminating information is disclosed incrementally during an interview against early and late techniques. In addition, we implemented a novel methodology that bridges the gap between experimental and applied approaches to detecting deception, to facilitate a robust investigation of the efficacy of both the late and gradual techniques.

A number of hypotheses were formulated concerning the possible advantages of the gradual disclosure technique compared to the late and early. Our first, that both the gradual and late techniques would enhance the detection of deception by lay observers relative to the early, and our second, that a gradual approach would enhance performance versus a late approach, were both supported. Both gradual and late disclosure improved the detection of deception accuracy compared to the early conditions. However, performance gains were modest in the late condition (4%), whereas the gradual technique improved deception detection performance by 16%.

When observers were asked to indicate the strength of their judgements, they made stronger judgements when judging deceivers in the gradual condition than in both the other disclosure conditions. Furthermore, terrorist participants in the gradual interview condition rated themselves as having been less deceptive, despite having been equally motivated to be so and having devised numerous verbal strategies. We contend that this enhanced observer performance arose due to the manner in which information was revealed and challenged incrementally, thereby disrupting the ability of deceptive interviewees to construct and verbalize a coherent and unchallenged account of the evidence set. Those interviewed using the gradual procedure were asked to account for each piece of information prior to being alerted to its nature, and where appropriate are immediately challenged. As a consequence, deceivers become encircled in such a manner that weaknesses/discrepancies in their verbal armature are highlighted from the outset.

Furnishing interviewees with all the incriminating evidence at the start affords deceivers time to consider and then create an account to 'fit' the evidence, which they are able to present unchallenged until the closing stages of the interview. The late technique differs in that participants are asked to account for their behaviour during questioning without the interviewer revealing what the evidence is until near the end of the interview. Like the early technique, the challenge to the account does not arise until very late in the procedure. We argue that, in common with the early condition, interviewees are again able to create what might appear to observers to be a coherent explanation of all the evidence.

The incremental nature of our gradual approach limits a deceptive interviewees' opportunities to verbally outmanoeuvre investigators, and does not allow them to remain true to any consciously created lie scripts (Hines *et al.*, 2010; Porter & Yuille, 1996). Therefore, deceptive interviewees are *forced* to relinquish control over verbal performance, resulting in increased cognitive load that we suggest maximizes observers' deception detection opportunities in terms of observing inconsistent and contradictory verbal accounts (see Dando & Bull, 2011).

Above, we have suggested two explanations to account for previous findings where a late approach had resulted in poor observer versus interviewer truth-teller accuracy performance. First, there may be a recency effect, in which the revelation of incriminating evidence late in a strategic interview might leave an observer with the impression that failing to account for behaviour previously had been a deliberate verbal strategy. However, recency would increase lie strength judgements for truth-tellers in the strategic condition, which was not the case here.

The second explanation concerns cognitive load, where observers may be disadvantaged by a late approach in terms of the late and block-mode presentation of evidence necessitating several concurrent cognitive operations (e.g., working memory, decision-making, and long-term memory). Loads were likely to be particularly high in the current study, which represents an attempt to replicate real world conditions in the laboratory (as best one can). Inevitably this has resulted in increased complexity in terms of the type and amount of evidence to be considered, and the fact that each participant's account is participant specific, rather than a more generic account, as has been the case in much of the previous research (e.g., Hartwig, Granhag, Strömwall, & Kronkvist, 2006). Observers rated the veracity task as least difficult in the gradual interviews, which supports this view and the suggestion that sequential processing of verbal performance in our gradual procedure reduces observer task demands, thereby enhancing observer performance. It may also explain the positive relationship between observer confidence and accuracy found in the gradual condition.

Our hypothesis was that the gradual procedure would retain the increased cognitive load imposed by the late technique on interviewees, which is important in impacting upon deceptive verbal behaviour. Indeed, interviewee self-ratings of cognitive demand revealed that the gradual and late conditions were far more demanding than the early. Importantly, deceptive interviewees (the 'terrorist' group) found the gradual procedure to be substantially more demanding than both the early and late techniques, suggesting that a gradual approach amplifies the difficulties deceptive interviewees face in developing and maintaining a coherent and believable response to incriminating information: the incremental nature of evidence disclosure limiting opportunities for verbal manoeuvring. As one might expect, the terrorists reported being more deceptive than builders overall. However, their reported deceptiveness was greater in both the early and late conditions, providing further support for our earlier assertion that a gradual approach limits opportunities for deceptive interviewees to construct and/or maintain deceptive accounts.

Despite the positive findings of the current research, there are a number of limitations which future studies should seek to address. First, all the interviews were conducted by a single interviewer, albeit an experienced and trained police investigator (for reasons outlined earlier). In another study (Dando & Bull, 2011), multiple police investigators were trained and used as interviewers, with a similar pattern of encouraging results, pointing to the efficacy and applicability of our gradual procedure across interviewers, and for professional observers (as is often the case where interviews are not recorded, see Dando & Bull, 2011). Second, we used observers who were unaware of the conditions. In many countries, there are numerous aspects of justice systems which render interviews open to scrutiny by those with no awareness of various information disclosure techniques (e.g., juries), so we are of the opinion that the technique *must* be appropriate for such audiences. Nonetheless, future research should also consider using observers trained in each of the three interview techniques discussed.

Finally, we consider why the late approach performed so poorly here compared with previous research. Previously in the relevant published research, limited information sets have been used, interview duration was short (typically 10 min or less), and interviews were truncated. Importantly, participants were often given the deceptions, thus they did not have to construct their own, and the scenarios lacked individual complexity. Here, we used a more realistic and immersive environment in which participants constructed their own deceptions, where interviews were longer and more challenging in terms of the individual nature of every interviewee's behaviour, and more items of evidence were used by the investigator.

A late approach clearly has value as one of a repertoire of interviewing techniques, and indeed the literature pertaining to the procedure has had a role in guiding our approach. Our proposal is that the late technique can usefully be extended by moving away from presenting evidence in a batch manner towards a more gradual approach.

Acknowledgements

This research was supported by funding from the Engineering and Physical Sciences Research Council (Grant Nos EP/F006500/1 and EP/F008600/1).

References

ACPO. (2004). *National Investigative Interviewing Strategy (NIIS)*. London, UK: Author.

Beckmann, J. F. (2010). Taming a beast of burden: On some issues with the conceptualisation and operationalisation of cognitive load. *Learning & Instruction*, *20*, 250–264. doi:10.1016/j.learninstruc.2009.02.024

Blair, J. P. (2009). Interviewing and interrogation. In D. T. Wilcox (Ed.), *The use of the polygraph in assessing, treating and supervising sex offenders* (pp. 243–266). Chichester, UK: Wiley-Blackwell.

Bull, R. (2012). The interviewing/interrogation of suspects: Some contributions from psychological research. *Archbold Review*, *6*, 7–9.

Bull, R., & Dando, C. J. (2010). *Strategy and tactics: Detecting deception and the use of information during interviews with suspects*. Paper presented at the American Association of Psychology and Law Conference, March 18–20, Vancouver.

Bull, R., & Soukara, S. (2012). A set of studies of what really happens in police interviews with suspects. In G. D. Lassiter & C. Meissner (Eds.), *Interrogations and confessions* (pp. 98–113). Washington, DC: American Psychological Association.

Bull, R., Valentine, T., & Williamson, T. (Eds.) (2009). *Handbook of psychology of investigative interviewing*. Chichester, UK: Wiley-Blackwell.

Cody, M. J., Marston, P. J., & Foster, M. (1984). Deception: Paralinguistic and verbal leakage. In R. Bostrom (Ed.), *Communication yearbook 8* (pp. 464–490). Beverly Hills, CA: Sage.

Colwell, K., Hiscock-Anisman, C. K., Woods, D., Memon, A., & Michlik, M. (2006). How liars attempt to convince: Strategies of impression management and deception regarding a simulated theft. *American Journal of Forensic Psychology*, *24*, 31–38. doi:10.1002/jip.73

Dando, C. J., & Bull, R. (2011). Maximising opportunities to detect verbal deception: Training police officers to interview tactically. *Journal of Investigative Psychology and Offender Profiling*, *8*, 189–202. doi:10.1002/jip.145

Ekman, P., O'Sullivan, M., & Frank, G. M. (1999). A few can catch a liar. *Psychological Science*, *10*, 263–266. doi:10.1111/1467-9280.00147

Erdelyi, M. H. (2010). The ups and downs of memory. *American Psychologist*, *65*, 623–633. doi:10.1037/a0020440

Gilovich, T., Savitsky, K., & Medvec, V. H. (1998). The illusion of transparency: Biased assessments of others' ability to read our emotional states. *Journal of Personality and Social Psychology*, *75*, 332–346.

Granhag, P. A., & Hartwig, M. (2008). A new theoretical perspective on deception detection: On the psychology of instrumental mind-reading. *Psychology, Crime & Law*, *14*, 189–200. doi:10.1080/10683160701645181

Granhag, P. A., Strömwall, L. A., Willén, R. M., & Hartwig, M. (2013). Eliciting cues to deception by tactical disclosure of evidence: The first test of the evidence framing matrix. *Legal and Criminological Psychology*, *18*, 341–355. doi:10.1111/j.2044-8333.2012.02047.x

Hartwig, M., Granhag, P. A., Strömwall, L. A., & Kronkvist, O. (2006). Strategic use of evidence during police interrogations: When training to detect deception works. *Law and Human Behavior*, *30*, 603–619. doi:10.1007/s10979-006-9053-9

Hartwig, M., Granhag, P. A., Strömwall, L. A., & Vrij, A. (2005). Deception detection via strategic disclosure of evidence. *Law and Human Behavior*, *29*, 469–484. doi:10.1007/s109709-005-5521-x

Hines, A., Colwell, K., Hiscock-Anisman, C., Garrett, E., Ryan, A., & Montalvo, L. (2010). Impression management strategies of deceivers and honest reporters in an investigative interview. *European Journal of Psychology Applied to Legal Context*, *2*, 73–90.

Huff, C. R., Ratner, A., & Sagarin, E. (1986). Guilty until proven innocent: Wrongful conviction and public policy. *Crime & Delinquency*, *32*, 518–544. doi:10.1177/0011128786032004007

Inbau, F. E., Reid, J. E., & Buckley, J. P. (1986). *Criminal interrogations and confessions*. Baltimore, MD: Williams & Walkins.

Johnson-Laird, P. N., & Byrne, R. M. J. (2002). Conditionals: A theory of meaning, inference, and pragmatics. *Psychological Review*, *109*, 646–678. doi:10.1037/0033-295X.109.4.646

Landis, J. R., & Koch, G. G. (1977). The measure of observer agreement for categorical data. *Biometrics*, *33*, 159–174.

Lerner, M. J. (1980). *The belief in a just world: A fundamental delusion*. New York: Plenum Press.

Mann, S., Vrij, A., & Bull, R. (2004). Detecting true lies: Police officers' ability to detect suspects' lies. *Journal of Applied Psychology*, *89*, 137–149.

Milne, R., & Bull, R. (1999). *Investigative interviewing*. Chichester, UK: Wiley.

Ministry of Justice. (2012). *Evidence and practice review of support for victims and outcome measurement*. London, UK: Author.

NPIA. (2009). *National investigative interviewing strategy*. Wyboston: Association of Chief Police Officers.

Ormerod, T. C. (2010). *Making and modifying plans to commit criminal acts* (unpublished master's thesis). University of Leicester, UK.

Porter, S., & Yuille, J. C. (1996). The language of deceit: An investigation of the verbal cues to deception in the interrogation context. *Law and Human Behaviour*, *20*, 443–459.

Shepherd, E. (2007). *Investigative interviewing, the conversation management approach*. Oxford, UK: Oxford University Press.

Sorochinski, M., Hartwig, M., Osborne, J., Wilkins, E., Marsh, J. J., Kazakov, D., & Granhag, P. A.. (2011). *Interviewing to detect deception*. Paper presented at the 10th International Academy of Investigative Psychology Conference, London, UK.

Sporer, S. L., & Schwandt, B. (2006). Moderators of nonverbal indicators of deception: A meta analytic synthesis. *Psychology, Public Policy, and Law*, *13*, 1–34. doi:10.1037/1076-8971.13.1.1

Vrij, A. (2004). Invited article: Why professionals fail to catch liars and how they can improve. *Legal and Criminological Psychology*, *9*, 159–181. doi:10.1348/1355325041719356

11 Maximising opportunities to detect verbal deception: training police officers to interview tactically

Coral J. Dando and Ray Bull

Introduction

When investigating wrongdoing, contradistinguishing liars and truth tellers has long exercised practitioners and researchers alike. This is particularly so during formal interviews with those suspected of wrongdoing (from here on referred to as suspects), during which interviewees are asked to provide an explanation of their involvement in an event and investigators are tasked with gathering information to assist criminal justice systems to decide whether an interviewee's account is veridical.

The research reported here concerns just such situations, with three objectives. First, to provide a further empirical evaluation of our 'tactical' interview procedure, which employs a drip feed approach to the revelation of information items during an interview to maximise opportunities to detect verbal deception. Second, to investigate how well, or otherwise, this technique is applied by professional police interviewers. Finally, to report interviewers' performance in terms veracity judgements, each having undergone training to use (i) our tactical technique, (ii) a strategic technique, where information is not revealed until the end of the interview and (iii) an early technique, where information is revealed at the beginning of an interview.

Detecting deception

The literature reveals that deciding veracity is a complex task, with most people including professional lie catchers performing at around chance levels (e.g. Ekman, O'Sullivan, & Frank, 1999; Vrij, 2004, 2008; Vrij & Mann, 2001, but also see Mann, Vrij, & Bull, 2004 for an example of above chance performance). Although in the UK (and many other countries) police investigators are not concerned with deciding veracity, they are tasked with maximising the efficacy of each interview situation to uphold the rule of law and support natural justice. Accordingly, they must consider how best to manage the flow of information between interviewer and interviewee during these complex social interactions. Indeed, the current UK investigative interview model PEACE (an acronym for the stages of an investigative interview: Planning and preparation; Engage and explain; Account; Closure; Evaluate) advocates that interviewers plan and prepare for every interview, which includes considering how to manage 'evidence that suggests that he/she [suspect] might have committed an offence' and handle 'information/evidence that emerges from the interview' (Centrex, 2004, p. 86).

There exists a significant body of empirical research suggesting how cognitive effort and working memory can influence verbal indicators of deception in interview situations. In brief, deceivers often provide less detailed accounts and shorter answers than truth tellers (see Sporer & Schwandt, 2006, for a meta-analysis), behaviours thought to emanate from the increased demands on working memory associated with constructing, verbalising and maintaining a deceptive account during an interview (e.g. DePaulo, Lindsay, Malone, Muhlenbruck, Charlton, & Cooper, 2003; Sporer & Schwandt, 2006; Vrij, 2000, 2008; Vrij, Mann, & Fisher, 2006; Zuckerman, DePaulo, & Rosenthal, 1981). This is particularly so when a liar has had little time to prepare, when providing less detail can be a deliberate strategy (Vrij, 2008). By revealing as little information as possible, liars are able reduce the likelihood of contradicting themselves and/or the facts known to the interviewer and hence hope to appear truthful (Bull & Dando, 2010; Granhag, Andersson, Strömwall, & Hartwig, 2004; Hartwig, Granhag, & Strömwall, 2007).

When able to prepare, liars may formulate a lie script, believing that by planning what they are going to say they can reduce contradictions. Liars are also aware that as an interview progresses, they may have to create more complex lies in order to account for new information presented and to ensure that new lies are consistent with any previous deception (e.g. Cody, Marston, & Foster, 1984). By keeping it simple at the outset, deceivers believe that this introduces opportunities for verbal manoeuvring, thereby allowing 'flexibility' to add detail only when requested by the interviewer, and 'thinking time' should the inclusion of additional detail and/or explanations of certain behaviour become necessary (Bull & Dando, 2010). It has also been argued that because deceptive interviewees will usually be unaware of all of the information available to interviewers, providing a less detailed account reduces the risk of contradictions (e.g. Strömwall, Hartwig, & Granhag, 2006; Vrij, 2000).

In contrast, truthful interviewees typically just 'tell the truth', believing that, as they have nothing to hide (e.g. Colwell, Hiscock-Anisman, Memon, Woods, & Michlik, 2006), their innocence will be apparent (Gilovich, Savitsky, & Medvec, 1998; Lerner, 1980). This has been found to manifest itself in a more detailed account of the event and the inclusion of event information that is probably consistent with that known by the investigator.

Taking account of these differences, previous research in this domain has considered how best to use potentially incriminating information during an interview, advocating the revelation of this evidence in its entirety at the end of the interview, as follows: 'interrogations started with the Introduction step, followed by a free recall . . . after which the interrogator posed a number of specific questions . . . the final specific question concerned whether the suspect confessed to the crime. After this the evidence against the suspect was presented' (Hartwig, Granhag, Strömwall, & Vrij, 2005, p. 475; see also Hartwig, 2005 for a more complete description of the procedure). The intended effect is to maximise the cognitive load experienced by the suspect and help investigators plan an interview strategy based on assumptions concerning suspects' strategies (see Granhag & Hartwig, 2008).

Indeed, when asked to judge the veracity of mock suspects, 41 police recruits (trainee police officers) trained to reveal information as described previously (and who had also conducted the interviews) were remarkably accurate, obtaining an overall accuracy rate of 85.4% (truth accuracy 85%; lie accuracy 85.7%) compared with an overall accuracy rate of 56.1% (truth accuracy 57.1%; lie accuracy 55%) obtained by police officers who had not been trained (Hartwig, Granhag, Strömwall, & Kronkvist, 2006).

The current research

This paper extends the information-gathering deception detection literature in a number of ways. First, we compare the aforementioned 'late' approach to revealing information with a novel procedure that is tactical in nature and an 'early' approach. Our tactical approach constitutes an important evolution of that currently offered in the literature in that it differs markedly in its approach to the actual revelation of the information and does not solely concern itself with potentially incriminating evidence. Second, rather than using police trainees or researchers as interviewers, we utilised experienced serving police investigators to conduct our interviews with mock suspects, a necessary progression aimed at answering questions pertaining to training, practicability and forensic application. Finally, that our mock suspects all took part in an immersive, interactive computer game designed to elicit complex deceptive verbal behaviour in a laboratory setting resulted in our interviewers being in the position of having to contend with large amounts of information. Previous published research has considered just a small number of items of potentially incriminating evidence (typically 3), which we would argue falls far short of that encountered by real investigators in complex cases.

To address these concerns, we have previously introduced a tactical interview procedure (Bull & Dando, 2010; Dando & Bull, 2009) employing a 'drip feed, gradual' approach to revealing information, in which revelation occurs throughout the questioning phase of an interview rather than at the very end. Thus, it dictates that interviewers continuously evaluate the means to optimise their objective (to conduct an effective and ethical interview) and in doing so demands that the revelation of items of information (whether incriminating or not) is managed both independently and incrementally throughout the interview. Previous *strategic* techniques, however, appear to only consider how to use potentially incriminating evidence (this being information-concerning behaviour that has the potential to reveal deception) and moreover only evidence 'known' to the investigator, apparently viewing it as a whole, it being presented in bulk at the end of the interview, (e.g. '*the evidence was disclosed right at the end of the interrogation*', Hartwig, 2005, p. 30).

This strategic approach does not consider how best to handle information that may emerge during the interview or how large amounts of information items might be managed in such a manner as to assist investigators during an interview. In the UK immediate electronic assistance (i.e. real time digital streaming of interviews for use whilst an interview is in progress) is not available to interviewers. Hence, a strategic approach is likely to place considerable cognitive demands upon the interviewer, in terms of necessitating several concurrent cognitive operations. Interviews are dynamic situations that evolve quickly, and in the absence of any immediate assistance, officers have to recall what an interviewee has stated, in both the free account and questioning phases, and retain this information until the closing stages of the interview process. By using the strategic approach, it is not until this point that they reveal all the incriminating evidence (in bulk) and then challenge any discrepancies between (i) the interviewee's free account and questioning performance and/or (ii) an interviewee's account and the revealed information. In addition, during a strategic interview, investigators are also required to construct and pose appropriate questions concerning event information/evidence, prior to revealing that evidence, whilst also being cognisant of the information provided earlier in order to appropriately and productively challenge any discrepancies.

The distinction between strategic and tactical cognition was introduced by Miller, Galanter & Pribram (1960): 'The molar units in the organization of behaviour will be said to comprise the behavioural strategy, and the molecular units, the tactics' (p. 17). In the context of suspect interviewing, the molar units of an interview protocol constitute a strategic decision to withhold information for as long as possible. The molecular units constitute tactical decisions as to the precise time and order in which to optimise the revelation of individual pieces of evidence to the suspect. Our tactical approach inherits the strategic objective laid down as previously described, but it introduces a tactical layer of incremental evidence utilisation. It is our contention that this maximises opportunities to detect verbal deception by exploiting gaps in a liar's scripts, at the same time providing innocent interviewees early opportunity to convey their honesty.

To date, the mock suspect paradigm used to test suspect interviewing approaches has involved short crime scenarios, during which the event behaviours of the deceptive and truth telling mock suspects are usually experimentally matched apart from minor crime actions and participants' behaviour is controlled by the experimenter in terms of being instructed how to behave or what to say (Hartwig et al., 2006, 2007; Hartwig, Granhag, Strömwall, & Vrij, 2004). In most investigative settings, police and other agencies encounter complex events (e.g. multiple suspects, different patterns of deceptive and innocent behaviour, embedded lies and large quantities of information). Thus, a new mock suspect paradigm was required that is sensitive to the demands of complex deceptive behaviours and multiple items of information/evidence.

Accordingly, we used an approach in which participants created their own deceptions, rather than maintaining deceptive statements and actions presented by an experimenter. In brief, interviewees (hereafter referred to as *mock suspects)* first play an interactive virtual computer game called Dodgy Builders Ltd, in groups of four. Each player competed individually as either a 'builder' or a 'terrorist' and was striving to complete their role-specific task before the other three players did so. The builder's task was to build part of an Olympic stadium, whereas the terrorists' was to blow up the Olympic stadium. Terrorists were provided with a brief outline of the builders' global task in order to allow them to devise ways of appearing to be a builder, thus masking their true identity. The first player to complete his/her task wins the game.

The current study provides a test of the proposition that tactical interviewing increases overall accuracy by enhancing the detection of liars and truth tellers: that limiting a deceptive interviewee's verbal options from the very start of the questioning phase may heighten the investigative value of the available information, as well as signalling to innocent interviewees the need to account for each item of evidence/information.

Method

Participants

One hundred and fifty graduate and post-graduate students, with a mean age of 27.3 years (standard deviation [SD] = 2.69), participated as mock suspects (78 male and 102 female participants). Interviews were conducted by five experienced police investigators from three large UK police forces (two women and three men, with a mean length of service of 19.2 years, ranging from 6 to 26 years), each of whom were advanced investigative interviewers having undergone extensive specialist police interview training (ranging from 6 months to 9 years prior to their participation in this research). Interviewers underwent 4-day training prior to participation. In brief, interviewers were initially sent a DVD (featuring example interviews) and an instruction manual, outlining each of the three interview techniques (tactical, strategic and early). Interviewers then attended a 2-day face-to-face training course run by the research team, which included numerous practice interviews and extensive performance feedback.

Design and procedure

The study comprised three phases: (i) participants played an interactive, immersive computer game as either truth tellers (mock builders) or deceivers (mock terrorists); (ii) 1 hour after the game had finished players were interviewed (individually) about their gaming by one of the five interviewers; and (iii) interviewers then completed a post-interview questionnaire, which not only asked them to make a veracity judgement but also collected qualitative and quantitative information about their interview experience.

Phase one

Upon arrival, groups of four participants self-selected where they wished to sit (the role of either a 'builder' or a 'terrorist' having previously been allocated by the experimenter to each of the four seats positioned around a large table). Each participant was shown a training video on their individual laptop computer, which they listened to through headphones. These video recordings introduced the players to the software and gave instructions on how to operate it, outlined the game objectives, explained each player's individual role and the game rules. Participants were also provided with instruction cards, which could be referenced during the game. Participants competed against each other to finish their role-specific task (builder or terrorist), taking turns to traverse the game board using dice throws to determine the number of squares they could move. Players were free to travel anywhere on the board: to the shops (electricians and builders' merchant) to purchase materials as necessary, the Olympic site and their own depots to deliver purchased materials when they saw fit. Games took approximately 1 hour. Players received a financial incentive of £24 for this phase.

Phase two

Having completed the game (when any one of the players had successfully completed their tasks), participants were individually interviewed about their gaming behaviour. Interviews commenced approximately 1 hour after the game had concluded, thereby allowing sufficient time (i) for participants to consider the post-game/pre-interview instructions and (ii) for the interviewer to plan and prepare in readiness for the interviews. Prior to interview, all participants were instructed verbatim 'Your task is to convince the interviewer that you are a builder and that you were not involved in any terrorist activity during the game'. No guidance was given to participants as to how they should carry out the aforementioned instructions in terms of how they might act, what strategies they might use or what they might say. Players received an additional financial incentive of £8 for this phase of the research.

All interviews were digitally video and audio recorded. Each interviewer conducted a total of 30 (counterbalanced for both interview condition and group) interviews over a 1-week period, 10 from each *interview* condition (tactical, strategic and early), with five participants from each *group* (deceiver and truth teller). Interviewers were blind to the experimental hypotheses and were given no base rate information about the number of deceptive or truthful interviewees they would encounter.

Interview conditions

Interviews in each of the three conditions comprised the same number of phases in the same order, differing only when (during which phase) and how information about participants' gaming (known to the investigator) was presented and where appropriate challenged.

Control (early disclosure of evidence)

An *early* interview condition was included because prior research (Milne & Bull, 1999) had revealed that many investigators often reveal all of the incriminating evidence near the beginning of an interview (e.g. in the hope that a suspect will confess). Interviews commenced with the *introduction* and *explain* phase (contact first author for full interview protocols) and moved (seamlessly) through each of the phases, as follows. In the *free recall* phase, the interviewer first disclosed all of the available 'gaming' information, listing them one piece at a time. The interviewee was instructed not to respond at this point but was instead asked (using an open-ended invitation—see Oxburgh, Myklebust, & Grant, 2010 for more on question types) subsequently to provide a *free recall* account of his/her gaming behaviour in as much detail as possible (uninterrupted by the interviewer).

Having provided a *free recall* account, the interviewer explained that some questions concerning each of the information items presented earlier in the interview would be asked. Each item/behaviour was presented (one after another), following which the interviewee was then asked to explain/account for each. Where appropriate, their replies/explanations were either (i) challenged (i.e. any discrepancies were pointed out and an explanation was invited) in order to clarify their version of events or (ii) accepted as being consistent with the information known to the investigator. Interviews concluded with the *closure* phase.

Strategic (late disclosure of information)

The *introduction* and *explain* phases of the interviews in the strategic condition are as previously described. However, in this condition, interviewees were asked to provide a freely recalled account of their game playing (the game information was not presented at this point). The investigator then commenced the *questioning* phase by asking one question concerning each of the information items (one after another) without revealing the nature of that information. For example, the builder's task dictated that participants might follow a certain buying pattern: that because of the nature of the task demands, it appears sensible to visit the electrical shop first. If the interviewee had not visited the electrical shop, the investigator might ask the question, 'Which shop did you visit first?', thereby questioning the interviewee concerning known information without revealing what that information was or that it was known by the interviewer. The interviewer then provided the participant with an opportunity to add/alter anything he/she has stated. At this point (towards the end of the questioning phase), the interviewer disclosed all of the information known to him/her, together in bulk. The interviewee was then invited to explain/account for each. Where appropriate, the participant's account was then challenged, and the interviewee was invited to explain all discrepancies/contradictions. The *closure* phase concluded the interview.

Tactical (gradual disclosure of information)

The *introduction, explain and free recall* phases of the interviews in the tactical condition were as previously described in the strategic condition. The interviewer then commenced the *questioning* phase by explaining that some questions would now be asked about the information he/she knew concerning the manner in which the game had been played, and in addition, some of the information offered by the interviewee in the previous free recall phase (which may not have been known to the interviewer prior to the interview) might also be questioned. The information was then revealed one piece at a time. Each individual revelation was followed by an invitation to the interviewee to account for that particular information. If appropriate (i.e. when the account provided by the interviewee contradicted what the investigator knew or what the interviewee had previously stated in the free account), the interviewer challenged separately the participant's explanation/account. Each piece of evidence was similarly presented, incrementally, piece-by-piece and challenged/accepted accordingly until the interviewee had addressed each in turn. The *closure* phase concluded the interview.

Information selection

Prior to interview, investigators were presented with a printout that documented a limited amount of game information (we refer to these as case files). Games were sub-divided into a number of separate phases, (every fourth dice roll signalled the end of a phase and the commencement of a new one), at which point each participant's game-playing information was recorded by the game administrator. The game phase information, included in the case files, was strictly limited to the following: (i) where an individual player had been during each of the game phases; for example, it was listed the places that he/she may have visited on the virtual game board (i.e. shops, building sites, builder's depots, etc.); (ii) the shop stock sold within that phase, allowing the investigator to calculate how many items had been purchased from each of the shops during that phase, although not by whom; (iii) the weight of any one participant's virtual van, selected to be weighed during that phase by the administrator and (iv) a subset of information pertaining to what was being carried in two of the four players' virtual van, where that player themselves selected two items to reveal during a van inspection. In preparation for each interviews, the investigator considered the information presented in the case files, making interview planning notes where appropriate, according to condition.

Following each interview, investigators immediately completed a questionnaire (see materials), were paid for their participation and then debriefed about the aims of the project.

Materials

The investigator (interviewer) post-interview questionnaire collected quantitative data and comprised one dichotomous veracity question and four Likert style questions inviting interviewers to provide fixed answers on a scale ranging from 1 (e.g. definitely not telling the truth/not at all confident/what the interviewee said/not difficult etc.) to 7 (e.g. definitely telling the truth/very confident/how the interviewer behaved/extremely difficult).

Results

Interview training check

To examine interviewers' implementation of their training across the three conditions (tactical, strategic and early), performance was rated using a scale (ranging from 1 to 5, where 1 = revealed information according to condition and training/managed responses according to condition and training; 5 = did not reveal information/manage responses according to condition and training). The scale was developed to assess the manner in which the gaming information was *used* (i.e. when it was disclosed and whether it was disclosed appropriately according to condition: either early in the interview, individually and incrementally throughout the questioning phase or in bulk at the end of the questioning phase), and *how* participants' replies to questions pertaining to that information was either accepted or challenged (i.e. whether replies managed according to interview condition: immediately accepted/challenged individually and incrementally or not accepted/challenged until the end of the interview, in bulk). From here on, for the purposes of this analysis, 'use' of gaming information is referred to as *information revelation,* and 'how' participants' replies were accepted or challenged is referred to as *response management* (the scoring rubric and scales are available from the first author).

Two independent raters, who were naive to the experimental hypotheses, scored each interview for information revelation and response management, using the aforementioned rating scale. Analysis revealed a substantial level of agreement between raters, kappa = 0.81, $p = 0.003$. Overall mean scores as a function of interviewer, for both the aforementioned measures, indicated that all had applied their training satisfactorily (see Table 11.1).

To further examine interviewers' performance, a mixed analysis of variance (ANOVA), with interviewer as the between subjects factor (interviewers 1, 2, 3, 4 and 5) and interview condition (tactical, strategic and early) and veracity (deceiver and truth teller) as the within subjects factors, was conducted on ratings for (i) information revelation and (ii) response management. A significant main effect of information revelation emerged for veracity, $F(1, 20) = 7.624, p = 0.012, \eta^2 = 0.16$ ($M_{\text{revelation deceivers}} = 1.73$; $M_{\text{revelation truth tellers}} = 1.97$). As expected, there was no significant main effect

Table 11.1 Interviewers' mean overall information revelation and response management ratings

	Information revelation	*Response management*
	Mean (SD)	
Interviewer 1	1.90 (0.712)	1.43 (0.679)
Interviewer 2	1.80 (0.801)	1.50 (0.679)
Interviewer 3	2.01 (0.788)	1.40 (0.874)
Interviewer 4	1.98 (0.812)	1.67 (0.711)
Interviewer 5	1.67 (0.768)	1.89 (0.788)

of interview condition. There were no significant interview/veracity/interviewer interactions (all Fs < 0.810, all ps > 0.455). Hence, irrespective of interview condition and/or interviewer, the manner in which information was revealed during interviews with deceivers was less in accordance with training than during interviews with truth tellers.[1] There were no significant main effects or interview/veracity/interviewer interactions for response management (all Fs < 5.51, all ps > 0.089).

Information items

The number of information items in each case file represents individual mock suspects' game playing behaviour; therefore, the number of information items was dictated by the manner in which each participant played the virtual game. Nonetheless, it may have been that interviewers' performance was influenced by the number of information items they used from the case file during each interview: it being sensible to assume that the fewer the information items interviewers were asked to manage, the less cognitively demanding their task and/or that if participants across the groups had played the game differently (in terms of number of movements, etc.), they might reveal their group membership (truth teller and deceiver) by virtue of marked differences in information items.

Analysis of the number of information items used during interviews as a function of (i) interview ($M_{\text{tactical info items}} = 11.42$, $SD = 2.07$; $M_{\text{strategic info items}} = 10.74$, $SD = 2.15$; $M_{\text{control info items}} = 10.54$, $SD = 2.24$), (ii) interviewer ($M_{\text{interviewer 1 items}} = 11.03$, $SD = 2.76$; $M_{\text{interviewer 2 items}} = 10.89$, $SD = 2.04$; $M_{\text{interviewer 3 items}} = 10.09$, $SD = 1.96$; $M_{\text{interviewer 4 items}} = 11.24$, $SD = 1.71$; $M_{\text{interviewer 5 items}} = 10.80$, $SD = 2.76$) and (iii) veracity ($M_{\text{deceiver items}} = 11.64$, $SD = 1.59$; $M_{\text{truth teller items}} = 10.01$, $SD = 1.82$) revealed no significant main effects or interactions (all Fs < 0.920, all ps > 0.439).

Veracity analysis

Using the dichotomous truth/lie judgement, when conducting interviews using the new tactical technique, interviewers obtained an overall accuracy rate of 67% for deceivers and 74% for truth tellers. Having conducted interviews using the strategic and early techniques, interviewers obtained an accuracy rate of 54% and 53% respectively for deceivers and 42% and 47% respectively for truth tellers. To fully analyse interviewer performance, a series of mixed ANOVAs, with interviewer as the between subjects factor (interviewers 1, 2, 3, 4 and 5) and interview condition (tactical, strategic and early) and veracity (deceiver and truth teller) as the within subjects factors, were conducted on interviewers' post-interview questionnaire responses (employing Bonferroni's correction). Because of the exploratory nature of this research, significant findings were investigated employing Games–Howell post hoc tests.

Lie scale

Interviewers were asked to indicate on a lie scale of 1 to 7 whether they believed each mock suspect was telling the truth or being deceptive during the interview (where 1 = definitely telling the truth and 7 = definitely not telling the truth). A significant main effect of veracity emerged, $F(1, 20) = 15.615$, $p = 0.001$, $\eta^2 = 0.43$, and interviewers rated deceivers as more deceptive ($M_{\text{deceivers truth scale}} = 4.48$) than truth tellers ($M_{\text{truth tellers truth scale}} = 3.45$). There was also a significant veracity/interview interaction, $F(1, 20) = 18.87$, $p < 0.001$, $\eta^2 = 0.43$. Interviewers were more accurate in their ratings for both deceivers ($M_{\text{tactical deceivers}} = 5.88$) and truth tellers ($M_{\text{tactical truth tellers}} = 2.48$) in the tactical interview conditions than in both the strategic ($M_{\text{strategic deceivers}} = 3.40$; $M_{\text{strategic truth tellers}} = 4.08$) and early ($M_{\text{early deceivers}} = 4.14$; $M_{\text{early truth tellers}} = 3.80$) conditions, with no significant difference between the latter two conditions. There were no significant interview or interviewer main effects or interactions (all *F*s < 0.820, all *p*s > 0.139).

Confidence

Interviewers indicated how confident they were that their truth scale ratings were correct, on Likert style confidence scale (where 1 = absolutely confident and 7 = not at all confident). A significant main effect of interview type emerged, $F(1, 20) = 15.458$, $p < 0.001$, $\eta^2 = 0.47$; interviewers were more confident having conducted tactical interviews ($M_{\text{tactical confidence}} = 2.08$) than in both the strategic ($M_{\text{strategic confidence}} = 3.78$) and early ($M_{\text{early confidence}} = 4.01$) interview conditions with no difference between the latter two. There was a significant interviewer/veracity interaction, $F(4, 20) = 3.895$, $p = 0.016$, $\eta^2 = 0.43$. Interviewer three was less confident when rating deceivers ($M_{\text{deceiver confidence 3}} = 3.89$) versus the other four interviewers ($M_{\text{deceiver confidence 1}} = 2.80$; $M_{\text{deceiver confidence 2}} = 3.08$; $M_{\text{deceiver confidence 4}} = 2.40$; $M_{\text{deceiver confidence 5}} = 2.69$), with no significant differences between the latter four interviewers. No additional significant main effects or interactions emerged (all *F*s < 4.358, all *p*s > 0.139).

Behaviour

Interviewers were asked to indicate what type of interviewee behaviour they had used to inform their lie scale decision, again using a Likert type scale ranging from 1 to 7 (1 = only verbal behaviour; 4 = both verbal and physical behaviour; 7 = only physical behaviour). A significant main effect of interview emerged, $F(2, 20) = 6.595$, $p = 0.003$, $\eta^2 = 0.23$. When interviewing tactically, interviewers indicated that they used verbal behaviour more when making their lie scale decisions ($M_{\text{behaviour scale}} = 2.81$) compared with when interviewing strategically ($M_{\text{behaviour scale}} = 4.89$) and when interviewing using the early approach ($M_{\text{behaviour scale}} = 4.04$). There were no further significant main effects or interactions (*F*s < 2.018, all *p*s > 0.131).

Difficulty

Interviewers were asked to indicate how difficult (demanding) they had found it to conduct each interview on a Likert type scale ranging from one to seven (1 = not at all difficult; 7 = extremely difficult).Two significant main effects emerged, that of veracity and interview type, $F(1, 20) = 19.615$, $p = 0.007$, $\eta^2 = 0.33$ and $F(2, 20) = 7.873$, $p = 0.011$, $\eta^2 = 0.24$, respectively. Interviewers rated deceivers as more demanding to interview than truth tellers ($M_{\text{difficulty deceiver}} = 4.30$; $M_{\text{difficulty truth teller}} = 3.10$) and rated the tactical and early interviews ($M_{\text{tactical difficulty}} = 3.80$; $M_{\text{early difficulty}} = 4.20$) as less demanding than the strategic ($M_{\text{strategic difficulty}} = 6.10$), with no differences between the former two conditions. No further significant main effects or interactions emerged (*F*s < 3.719, all *p*s > 0.231).

Discussion

This study investigated the efficacy of a new tactical approach to conducting investigative interviews with those suspected of wrongdoing versus a strategic and an early technique. Of our three objectives, the first and the third were to provide an empirical evaluation of our 'tactical' technique with professional investigators and to report their performance when deciding whether a mock suspect was being veridical.

Our results provide empirical support for our contention that interviewing tactically, where the revelation of event information occurs during the questioning phase using a drip feed gradual approach, could enhance trained professional investigators' performance, both in terms of increasing their detection of deceitful senders and assisting them to appreciate when a sender was being truthful.

The dichotomous truth/lie data revealed superior percentage accuracy performance in the tactical condition for both deceivers and truth tellers versus the strategic and early conditions. Additionally, the lie scale and confidence data revealed that tactical interviewing not only enhanced veracity performance *per se* but also strengthened lie judgements and interviewers' confidence in these judgements, for both deceivers and truth tellers alike. Conversely, in the strategic and early conditions, interviewers' strength of veracity judgements for both deceivers and truth tellers were reduced. Moreover, they were much less confident, and their judgements apparently not sufficiently polarised to allow them to discriminate reliably between deceivers and truth tellers (as indicated by the mean lie scale and confidence scale scores that hovered around the midpoint of the scale). That there were no interviewer interactions for strength of veracity judgement indicates that the lie scale task was more pronounced for *all* of our investigators in these latter two conditions.

An interviewer interaction did emerge when analysing the confidence data. However, this interviewer was significantly less confident when rating deceivers only, irrespective of interview condition. This particular police officer was the least experienced investigator (with just 6 years service), who had only completed specialist interview training 6 months previously. Nonetheless, despite finding the task of judging deceivers more demanding, this appeared not to affect her veracity performance, suggesting that this lack of confidence may emanate from less investigative expertise and reduced levels of post-training interviewing experience versus the other interviewers.

The question arises as to why the current pattern of results may have emerged when there exists empirical support for the notion that a strategic approach to conducting interviews is an effective method of enhancing veracity performance (e.g. Hartwig et al., 2004, 2005, 2006). We have previously argued that the tactical approach serves to limit a deceptive interviewee's verbal options from the very start of the questioning phase. Consequently, the investigative value of the available information is heightened because of the manner in which evidence was revealed and challenged incrementally, thereby disrupting the ability of deceptive interviewees to construct and verbalise a coherent and unchallenged account of the evidence/information set. Participants interviewed using the tactical procedure are asked to account for each piece of information/evidence prior to being alerted to the nature of that evidence and where appropriate are immediately challenged. Hence, deceivers are unable to remain true to any consciously created lie scripts (Hines et al., 2010; Porter & Yuille, 1996), becoming encircled in such a manner that weaknesses/discrepancies in their verbal armature are highlighted. Indeed, previous research conducted using the aforementioned paradigm, with multiple information/evidence items, revealed that mock suspects who had devised a lie script prior to being interviewed were less able to implement that script when interviewed using our tactical approach versus a strategic and early technique. Furthermore, deceivers reported finding the tactical technique significantly more cognitively demanding than both the strategic and early interviews (Bull & Dando, 2010).

Furnishing interviewees with all of the evidence/information at the start affords deceivers time to consider and then create an account to 'fit' the evidence, which they are able to present unchallenged until the closing stages of the interview. The strategic technique differs in that the evidence is not revealed early and the participants are asked to account for each behaviour during questioning without the interviewer revealing what the evidence/information is. Nonetheless, the technique does not advocate challenging an account until very late in the procedure. We argue that in common with the early condition, interviewees are again able to create and maintain what might appear to be a coherent account. Moreover, where there exists large amounts of information (be it incriminating or otherwise), a strategic approach is likely to make the interviewers' task more difficult; as was evidenced here, interviewers having rated the strategic and early techniques as being more demanding.

The incremental nature of our tactical approach, in contrast, severely limits deceptive interviewees' opportunities to verbally outmanoeuvre investigators. Therefore, deceptive interviewees are *forced* to relinquish control over verbal performance, resulting in increased cognitive load that we suggest maximises interviewers' deception detection opportunities in terms of inconsistent and contradictory verbal accounts.

In the current research, each interviewer had to manage an average of 11 items of information, a significant increase versus that utilised in the previous literature. In contrast to our tactical technique, the strategic and early approaches are such that the interviewers' primary task elements are not independent, instead having to process multiple evidence explanations simultaneously rather than sequentially, demanding high levels of interactivity that may have served to reduce task performance (see Beckmann, 2010). In addition, a tactical approach to interviewing signals to innocent interviewees the need to account for each item of information presented. Thus far, researchers have paid scant attention to truth teller detection performance. We would argue that this aspect of managing investigative interviews in forensic settings is of equal importance to that of detecting deceivers.

Turning to the type of behaviour, interviewers used to make their veracity judgements. Our data revealed that when interviewing tactically, participants' reported using verbal behaviour to inform their veracity judgements, whereas in the other interview conditions, interviewers indicated that their judgements were at least equally informed by physical behaviour. This may also account, in part, for reduced performance in the strategic and early conditions, it being accepted that physical, non-verbal behaviour is not a reliable indicator of deception (see Vrij, 2008). Conversely, there is much to suggest that monitoring verbal behaviour, by which we mean *what* the interviewee says throughout the interview, provides some of the more reliable cues to deception (see Bull, 2011; Vrij, 2008).

Finally, we were interested in whether professional investigators could be trained to interview tactically, in terms of unlearning old behaviour quickly. Our findings indicate that each of our investigators did implement all of the newly introduced interview techniques satisfactorily, after fairly brief training (far less than is currently afforded police officers in the UK). That stated, all had undergone previous professional interview training, which does comprise some of the elements we introduced across all of the conditions (also see Vander Sleen, 2010). Certainly, our protocols were based on the current UK investigative interview model and were delivered by a researcher who has much experience of training UK police officers at an advanced level. However, that officers were able to learn and apply our technique quickly leads us to offer its suitability for all experienced investigators.

As with all research of this nature, there are a number of limitations that should be addressed in the future. In addition to further independent replications of our findings, a larger sample of police investigators of varying levels of experience are required as participants to progress further the suitability of the technique in applied settings. A more representative sample of mock suspects would allow us to infer the efficacy of our tactical technique across wider population. As we have argued elsewhere, it is important that we assume able opponents when conducting research of this nature. Hence, despite the obvious ethical considerations, in our opinion, it is now important to conduct research using practised deceivers.

In sum, our findings indicate the efficacy of a strategic approach to conducting suspect interviews. The criminal justice system is poorly served by less than effective interviewing; it is of little value to anyone. Interviews are complex social interactions, which are pivotal to the process of upholding the rule of law and perceptions of natural justice. Accordingly, they should always be conducted with integrity and sound judgement, and it is important that we provide investigators with the tools to do just that. We would suggest that our tactical approach is one such tool, which our research clearly indicates has value as one of a repertoire of techniques suitable for use.

Note

1 Despite a significant main effect of veracity, all interviewers conducted interviews across each of the conditions and as a function of group in line with the training, as indicated by overall ratings <2.01 on the training scale. Hence, veracity was excluded as a covariate.

References

Beckmann, J. F. (2010). Taming a beast of burden: On some issues with the conceptualisation and operationalisation of cognitive load. *Learning and Instruction*, *20*, 250–264.

Bull, R. (2011). *Interviewing to detect deception.* Invited lecture at the Western Australian Police Academy, Perth, May.

Bull, R., & Dando, C. J. (2010). *Detecting verbal deception: Strategy versus tactics*. Paper presented at the Annual American Psychology and Law Society, 18–20 March 2010, Vancouver, Canada.

Centrex. (2004). *Core investigative doctrine*. Cambridgeshire: ACPO.

Cody, M. J., Marston, P. J., & Foster, M. (1984). Deception: Paralinguistic and verbal leakage. In R. Bostrom (Ed.), *Communication yearbook 8*. Beverly Hills, CA: Sage.

Colwell, K., Hiscock-Anisman, C., Memon, A., Woods, D., & Michlik, P. M. (2006). Strategies of impression management among deceivers and truth-tellers: How liars attempt to convince. *American Journal of Forensic Psychology*, *24*, 31–38.

Dando, C. J., & Bull, R. (2009). *Interviewing strategically to detect verbal deception*. Paper presented at the 19th Annual Conference of the European Association of Psychology and Law, 2–5 September, Sorrento.

DePaulo, B. M., Lindsay, J. J., Malone, B. E., Muhlenbruck, L., Charlton, K., & Cooper, H. (2003). Cues to deception. *Psychological Bulletin*, *129*, 74–118.

Ekman, P., O'Sullivan, M., & Frank, G. M. (1999). A few can catch a liar. *Psychological Science*, *10*, 263–266.

Gilovich, T., Savitsky, K., & Medvec, V. H. (1998). The illusion of transparency: Biased assessments of others' ability to read our emotional states. *Journal of Personality and Social Psychology*, *75*, 332–346.

Granhag, P. A., & Hartwig, M. (2008). A new theoretical perspective on deception detection: On the psychology of instrumental mind reading. *Psychology, Crime, & Law*, *14*, 189–200.

Granhag, P. A., Andersson, L. O., Strömwall, L. A., & Hartwig, M. (2004). Imprisoned knowledge: Criminal's beliefs about deception. *Legal and Criminological Psychology*, *9*, 103–119.

Hartwig, M. (2005). *Interrogation to detect deception and truth*. PhD thesis, University of Gothenburg, Department of Psychology.

Hartwig, M., Granhag, P. A., Strömwall, L. A., & Vrij, A. (2004). Police officers' lie detection accuracy: Interrogating freely versus observing. *Police Quarterly*, *7*, 429–456.

Hartwig, M., Granhag, P. A., Strömwall, L. A., & Vrij, A. (2005). Deception detection via strategic disclosure of evidence. *Law and Human Behavior*, *29*, 469–484.

Hartwig, M., Granhag, P. A., Strömwall, L. A., & Kronkvist, O. (2006). Strategic use of evidence during police interrogations: When training to detect deception works. *Law and Human Behavior*, *30*, 603–619.

Hartwig, M., Granhag, P. A., & Strömwall, L. A. (2007). Guilty and innocent suspects' strategies during interrogations. *Psychology, Crime, & Law*, *13*, 213–227.

Hines, A., Colwell, K., Hiscock-Anisman, C. L., Garrett, E., Ansarra, R. L., & Montalvo, L. (2010). Impression management strategies of deceivers and honest reporters in an investigative interview. *European Journal of Psychology Applied to Legal Context, 2*, 73–90.

Lerner, M. J. (1980). *The belief in a just world: A fundamental delusion*. New York: Plenum Press.

Mann, S., Vrij, A., & Bull, R. (2004). Detecting true lies: Police officers' ability to detect deceit. *Journal of Applied Psychology, 89*, 137–149.

Miller, G. A., Galanter, E., & Pribram, K. H. (1960). *Plans and the structure of behavior*. New York: Holt, Rinehart & Winston.

Milne, R., & Bull, R. (1999). *Investigative interviewing, psychology and practice*. Chichester: Wiley.

Oxburgh, G., Myklebust, T., & Grant, T. (2010). The question of question types in police interviews: A review of the literature from a psychological and linguistic perspective. *International Journal of Speech Language and the Law, 17*, 45–66.

Porter, S., & Yuille, J. C. (1996). The language of deceit: An investigation of the verbal cues to deception in the interrogation context. *Law and Human Behaviour, 20*, 443–459.

Sporer, S. L., & Schwandt, B. (2006). Moderators of nonverbal indicators of deception: A meta analytic synthesis. *Psychology, Public Policy, and Law, 13*, 1–34.

Strömwall, L. A., Hartwig, M., & Granhag, P. A. (2006). To act truthfully: Non-verbal behavior and strategies during a police interrogation. *Psychology, Crime, & Law, 12*, 207–219.

Vander Sleen, J. (2010). A structured model for the investigative interviewing of suspects. In R. Bull, T. Valentine, & T. Williamson (Eds.), *Handbook of psychology of investigative interviewing*. Chichester: Wiley.

Vrij, A. (2000). Telling and detecting lies as a function of raising the stakes. In C. M. Breur, M. M. Kommer, J. F. Nijboer, & J. M. Reijntjes (Eds.), *New trends in criminal investigation and evidence*. (Vol. 2). Antwerp: Intersentia.

Vrij, A. (2004). Why professionals fail to catch liars and how they can improve. *Legal and Criminological Psychology, 9*, 159–181.

Vrij, A. (2008). *Detecting deceit and lies: Pitfalls and opportunities*. Chichester: Wiley.

Vrij, A., & Mann, S. (2001). Who killed my relative? Police officers' ability to detect real-life high-stakes lies. *Psychology, Crime, & Law, 7*, 119–132.

Vrij, A., Mann, S., & Fisher, R. (2006). An empirical test of the behaviour analysis interview. *Law and Human Behavior, 30*, 329–345.

Zuckerman, M., DePaulo, B. M., & Rosenthal, R. (1981). Verbal and nonverbal communication of deception. In L. Berkowitz (Ed.), *Advances in experimental social psychology*. New York, NY: Academic Press.

12 What really happens in police interviews of suspects? Tactics and confessions

S. Soukara, Ray Bull, Aldert Vrij, Mark Turner and Julie Cherryman

Introduction

Police interviews with suspects are of utmost importance to society. They have, therefore, attracted extensive attention worldwide from the general public and the media as well as from professionals, such as lawyers and a few psychologists. Their nature, however, has rarely been scrutinised in detail in published research because such interviews are not usually made available by the police to 'outside' researchers (Davis & O'Donohue, 2003). Until fairly recently there has been little constructive interaction between psychologists and the police concerning how best to interview suspects. This is still the case in most countries. This lack of interaction created a 'vacuum' that drew police around the world to guidance on suspect interviewing that has not had the benefit of being informed by published psychological research and theory (Gudjonsson, 2003; Kassin, 2006; Vrij, 2002; Williamson, 2006a). However, in England and Wales the last two decades (i.e. since the implementation of the Police and Criminal Evidence Act 1984 usually referred to as PACE) have seen gradual but extensive changes in the interrogation/interviewing manuals and training used, and this has been well informed by psychology (Bull & Milne, 2004; Milne & Bull, 1999).

One of the world's most influential suspect interrogation manuals, now in its fourth edition (Inbau, Reid, Buckley, & Jayne, 2001), recommends the 'Reid Approach' that suggests nine essential steps to the effective interrogation of suspects. Aspects of this approach were also recommended in Walkley's book published in the UK in 1987. However, aspects of the tactics involved in some of these steps has been criticised by several psychologists in the UK (e.g. Gudjonsson, 1992, 2003, 2006; Memon, Vrij, & Bull, 1998, 2003) and in the USA (e.g. Kassin, 2006), as well as by courts in the UK (Williamson, 2006b). Some police forces employing this approach seemed to have overlooked the crucial point made by Inbau, Reid and colleagues that their interrogation procedure was designed for interviewers to use with denying suspects whom the interviewers had already deemed to be 'guilty'. However, Inbau and colleagues' advice concerning how to decide if the suspect is 'guilty' for example, by observing their behaviour in a preceding interview seems not to be in line with published research on valid behavioural cues to lying (Davis, Markus, Walters, Vorus, & Connors, 2005;

De Paulo et al., 2003; Kassin & Fong, 1999; Vrij, 2000, 2004). Furthermore, when Kassin & Fong (1999) examined the effects of training people to use the cues to deception advocated by the Reid Approach they found that such training did not improve lie/truth detection performance, which remained at chance level, but it did increase the number of reasons cited for the decisions. Additionally, Mann, Vrij, & Bull (2004) found those officers citing most of these (supposed) cues were the poorest lie/truth detectors. (But for support for the Reid Approach see Blair & McCamey, 2002; Horvath & Jayne, 1994.)

Partly in the light of consistent media and Appeal Court criticism of police interrogation tactics that could lead to false confessions, the Government in England and Wales brought in over 20 years ago the Police and Criminal Evidence Act 1984. This legislation involved rules governing the way in which suspects are arrested, detained, and interviewed by police officers. It acts (or at least, it is intended to act) as a safeguard for suspects as well as police officers, ensuring that all interviews with suspects are contemporaneously recorded (e.g. audio or video taped) and that suspects are not subjected to undue police pressure that might result in confessions that are not deemed (e.g. by courts) to have been made voluntarily.

However, while PACE sought to 'outlaw' coercive police tactics, in the late 1980s and early 1990s police officers in England and Wales had not yet been equipped with appropriate skills for the interviewing of suspects. In one of the first studies of police interviewing of suspects post-PACE (conducted for the Royal Commission on Criminal Justice), Baldwin (1992, 1993) found that such interviews were not well conducted. For example, he reported that 'Officers were rather tentative in putting allegations to suspects . . . in almost two-thirds of all cases . . . no serious challenge was made by the interviewers to what the suspect was saying' (1993, p. 331). Baldwin also noted from his analysis of tape-recorded interviews that, while over a third of the suspects admitted culpability, almost all of these did so very early on in their interview. Only 3% of suspects actually changed their story in the major course of the interview (i.e. from denial to confession). Furthermore, for only half of this small percentage was Baldwin of the opinion that this had anything to do with the skills of the interviewers. (When suspects confess at the beginning of an interview, reasons for this could include their beliefs about the likely strength of evidence against them and/ or a desire to 'get it off their chest'; see below.)

McConville & Hodgson (1993) also noted a lack of skill. They found that the most common procedure used by the police interviewers was at the outset to tell the suspects that because of the evidence against them they might as well confess. The next most common procedure took place when this was met with denial and it involved the officers resorting to 'accusations and abuse' (p. 127). The third most frequent procedure involved endeavouring to affect the suspects' assessments of the consequences of confessing. Moston, Stephenson, and Williamson (then a senior police officer) also found that police interviewers devoted most of their interviewing time to telling the suspects about the evidence against them and then accusing the suspects of the offences and asking for their responses to such accusations (Moston, Stephenson, & Williamson, 1992). When the majority of suspects resisted these accusations the interviewers seemed not to know what to do. Rarely did the interviewers try to obtain the suspects' accounts. Pearse (then a senior police officer) and Gudjonsson analysed tape-recorded interviews conducted in London in 1991/2 (Pearse & Gudjonsson, 1996). They also noted that the most common procedure was to begin by telling the suspects of the evidence against them (without lying) and accuse them of involvement. Around half the suspects confessed but almost all did so very near to the beginning of the interviews. As found in Baldwin's study, only very few suspects changed their 'position' from denial to confession as the interview further progressed. Challenging the suspect about inconsistencies between (i) what the suspect was saying and (ii) the evidence rarely occurred, partly because suspects were not usually given the opportunity to provide an account. Challenges about inconsistencies within the suspect's account(s) were also rare.

Largely as a consequence of his findings, Baldwin proposed a quite different approach to the interviewing of suspects in which interviewing is seen as an information-gathering exercise requiring certain skills in order to elicit relevant and accurate information. The use of trickery was not recommended, and the supposed nonverbal cues to deception (which so many people seem to believe in Bull, 2004; Vrij, 2000) were to be totally disregarded. That is, the two-phased approach recommended by Walkley and by Inbau, Reid and colleagues (among others) of (i) interview for signs of deception and then (ii) interrogate, was not supported. Instead, preparation/planning, rapport building, and the social skills of the interviewer were deemed to be of central importance in a one-phase approach that is now termed 'investigative interviewing' (Milne & Bull, 1999; Williamson, 2006a).

Partly in light of the above research studies (which were actually conducted at the turn of the decade), in England and Wales the Home Office (i.e. the relevant government department) with the Association of Chief Police Officers formed a working party to develop ethical investigative interviewing principles and practices to be used by all officers, aiming to improve the quality of the interviewing of suspects (and of witnesses). The term 'investigative interviewing' replaced 'interrogation'. A five-stage model was produced, summarised by the mnemonic PEACE (i.e. (i) Planning and preparation; (ii) Engage and explain; (iii) Account; (iv) Closure; (v) Evaluate; for more on this model and psychology's contribution to it, see Milne & Bull, 1999). The new model was explained in a specially produced 1992 booklet called 'A Guide to Interviewing' supported by a second booklet 'The Interviewer's Rule Book'. These were issued to all 127,000 police officers in England and Wales, and most subsequently (i.e. since 1993) have attended a PEACE training course on investigative interviewing of at least a week's duration. In 1996 an updated version of the PEACE model was issued, with increased emphasis on suspect interviewing, published in 'Investigative Interviewing: A Practical Guide'. The Guide provided guidance and explanation of 'best practice', mentioned essential psychological issues, and emphasised that the purpose of interviews with suspects is to gather relevant information and not merely a confession (e.g. to obtain information to assist the determination of whether a confession is a valid one). A further version was produced by the National Crime Faculty (2000). Among the tactics/skills emphasised by the PEACE model are

- the use of open questions to assist suspects to provide their own account;
- then emphasising inconsistencies/contradictions within the suspect's account;
- then disclosing to the suspect the evidence the police have; and
- then challenging the suspect's account using evidence that counters what the suspect has said.

Although an early study on the effectiveness of PEACE produced results that seemed promising (McGurk, Carr, & McGurk, 1993), Clarke & Milne's (2001) detailed national evaluation of PEACE found poor planning and communication skills on the part of the interviewers, exhibiting difficulty in putting into practice some of the contents of the new training course. Their government-funded study did not have the aim of examining the tactics used in interviews with suspects, nor did Bull & Cherryman (1996) in their government-funded project to identify the skills gaps in specialist investigative interviewing of suspects.

Soukara, Bull, & Vrij's (2002) examination of experienced detectives' views on the ways in which interviews with suspects in England should now be conducted revealed that the majority believed in the high importance of (a) specialised training, (b) preparation of the interview, and (c) the social skills of the interviewer. Also, the overwhelming majority said that the search for the truth rather than the search for a confession should be the aim of interviews with suspects, and that trickery should not be used no matter how difficult the case or the suspect might be. The present study was designed partly to examine whether interviews are actually conducted in line with most of these experienced detectives' comments and the PEACE model.

It may, however, be difficult for police officers to adapt to and adopt the ethos of 'new' training. Indeed, if officers already interviewed in the way advocated by the new ethos, they would not need training! While the actual use of various tactics in real-life police interviews has rarely been researched (Leo, 2004), the very few published studies of such tactic usage have found, at least in a small sample of British special cases (Pearse & Gudjonsson, 1999), that coercive tactics have sometimes been used.

In 'experimental' studies (i.e. not of real-life police interviewing) problematical tactics such as 'minimisation' have been found to increase the confession rate (Russano, Meissner, Narchet, & Kassin, 2005). Kassin & Kiechel (1996) designed an ingenious way to investigate (false) confessions in the laboratory setting. While in such a setting it is difficult to mirror real-life police interviewing of suspects largely for moral and ethical reasons, it can nevertheless, under certain circumstances, be stressful for participants (Horselenberg et al., 2006) and it allows for the purposive manipulation of some tactics (e.g. minimisation and maximisation Klaver, Rose, & Lee, 2003) that are advocated in some countries by widely publicised procedures such as the Reid Approach.

In their review Kassin & Gudjonsson (2004) described the Reid Approach as essentially an interplay of the three processes of (i) custody and isolation, (ii) confrontation (involving accusing and blocking denial), and (iii) minimisation ('in which a sympathetic interrogator morally justifies the crime, leading the suspect to infer he or she will be treated leniently and to see confession as the best possible means of escape' p. 43). However, they pointed out that 'It is difficult to know the frequency with which these methods of interrogation are used or what effects they have' (p. 43). The present study was specifically designed to provide information on this, especially since Walkley's (1987) book recommended aspects of such an approach to British police officers.

In the present study interviews were evaluated for the presence of tactics (described in the Method section) commonly mentioned in the previously published literature on the police interviewing of suspects and those mentioned in the PEACE model. The main aims of the present study were

1 to examine how frequently the tactics were used across a sample of interviews; and
2 to determine whether there were any positive correlations between (a) suspects' extent of shift from denial to confession and (b) the degree of usage of each tactic.

Method

Materials

This study involved the examination of audio-tape interviews with suspects, provided by random selection by a relatively large police force in England. (At the time of conducting these interviews the interviewers were not aware that they would a few years later be used in a research study). Details about the interviewers (e.g. their rank, the exact nature of the training courses they had attended) were not available, but it is very likely that all of them had attended some form of 'PEACE' training course as this had been national policy for several years. Similarly, information was not available concerning the suspects (e.g. prior convictions). Due to the sensitive nature of the material, an agreement was made with the police force to ensure confidentiality and use of the data only for the duration of the research and by specific individuals. A sample of 80 audio-tape interviews formed the basis of the present study. Twenty-two different types of offences were identified from these tapes: assault resulting in bodily harm, indecent assault, cruelty, criminal damage, sexual offences against children, motor-vehicle thefts, drug-related thefts, physical assault against children, physical assault against adults, drug dealing, grievous bodily harm, arson, burglary, handling of stolen goods, possession of firearms, public order offences, fraud, shoplifting, reckless driving, homicide, rape, and neglect. Out of the 80 suspects involved in these cases, 72 were male and 8 were female. Some of those interviews were lengthy (lasting up to 4 h), whereas a few were relatively brief (e.g. 10 min). Most were longer than 30 min. To be given research access to these tape-recorded interviews the police organisation stated that all of the interviews had to involve investigations/cases that were no longer 'current'. (No information was available concerning the outcome of each investigation.) Thus, the interviews had been conducted around the turn of the century.

Coding

Five coders, experienced with the topic of the interviewing of suspects through their academic work and research, independently listened to and coded the interviews. One of the coders listened to all 80 interviews, and the other four listened to five different interviews each, these 20 being randomly selected from the 80; the reason for this was to examine inter-coder reliability. All coders were provided with an instruction sheet, which involved the following:

a. Before starting to listen to the interviews the coders were asked to read through the coding sheet to familiarise themselves with the tactics to be coded (e.g. their descriptions see Table 12.1) and the other information to be obtained from the tapes.
b. The coders were asked to listen carefully to each interview and fill in the coding sheet immediately after they had listened to the whole tape. They could stop the tape as often as they needed to and they could make provisional coding judgements as each interview progressed.
c. For each of the 17 tactics the coders were asked to indicate for each interview (i) whether or not the tactic was used in that interview and if so (ii) the degree to which it was used in that interview (on a five-point scale where 1'rarely' and 5'very often'); ('strength of evidence' is not a tactic and was not assessed in this study).
d. For each interview the coders were asked to indicate (i) whether the suspect confessed and if so (ii) whether this occurred in the first, second, or final third of the interview.
e. The coders were also asked to indicate how far the suspect shifted from denial towards confession (on a five-point scale where 1'very little shift' and 5 'total shift' that is, from clear denial to clear confession).

The coding sheets were designed to incorporate the major tactics most commonly mentioned in previous publications on the interrogating/interviewing of suspects. In addition to the publications cited above, these publications included Kalbfleisch (1994), Kassin (1997), Kassin & McNall (1991) and Leo (1992, 1996). The 17 tactics that were the focus of the present study are listed in Table 12.1 along with brief descriptions of each (that were provided to the coders).

Table 12.2 presents information concerning the inter-coder agreement (for the 20 interviews that were evaluated both by the main coder and by one of the other four coders who coded five interviews each) for (i) whether each tactic was used or not in each of these interviews this is expressed in terms of Cohen's kappa and

Table 12.1 The tactics and their descriptions

Tactics	*Descriptions*
T1. Disclosure of evidence	Revealing evidence regarding the offence.
T2. Maximisation of offence	Exaggerating the significance/seriousness of an action, in order to facilitate an admission.
T3. Minimisation of offence	Reducing the significance of an action in order to facilitate admission.
T4. Emphasising contradictions	Pointing out inconsistencies in the suspect's account.
T5. Positive confrontation	Directly accusing the suspect regarding his/her involvement in the crime.
T6. Gentle prods	Trying to make the suspect reveal information by encouraging him/her to continue speaking.
T7. Concern	Showing concern/empathy towards the suspect.
T8. Interruptions	Keep interrupting the suspect when he/she tries to answer the questions.
T9. Silence	Maintaining silence after the suspect has said something.
T10. Repetitive questioning	Repeating the same questions over and over again.
T11. Leading questions	Asking questions in a way in which the answer is suggested.
T12. Open questions	Asking the suspect to give his/her account of events.
T13. Intimidation	Accusing the suspect of being a liar, and/or laughing at the person.
T14. Suggest scenario	Interviewer tries to give his/her side of the story, suggesting possible scenarios of what happened.
T15. Handling the suspect's mood	Recognising changes in the suspect's mood and reacting accordingly.
T16. Challenging the suspect's account	Revealing evidence which counters what the suspect has said, implying that it is not the truth.
T17. Situational futility	Telling the suspect that the truth will come out one day, pointing out negative consequences resulting from continuous denial.

(ii) if the tactic was used, the degree to which in each interview it was used this is expressed in terms of Spearman's rho.

Table 12.2 also presents the percentage of the 80 interviews in which the main evaluator decided whether each tactic was used or not. Some tactics were never used and so Cohen's kappa and Spearman's rho could not be calculated, and some were overall used rarely (and therefore in the inter-coder sub-sample could result in unusually high correlations, for example tactic 15).

Spearman's rho involved data when a tactic was present (to some degree) in some of the 20 interviews that were independently evaluated by two coders. Thus, because the number of interviews that contained a particular tactic varied within the sample, the size of the correlation required for significance varies across tactics (**$p < 0.01$, *$p < 0.05$, one-tailed, because inter-coder agreement was hypothesised).

Table 12.2 Inter-rater agreement and percentage of the 80 interviews in which each tactic was present (to some extent)

Tactic	*Cohen's kappa*	*Percentage present*	*Spearman's rho*
T1. Disclosure of evidence	1.00	99	0.75**
T2. Maximisation	1.00	01	
T3. Minimisation	1.00	00	
T4. Emphasising contradictions	1.00	75	0.78**
T5. Positive confrontation	0.92	74	0.42*
T6. Gentle prods	0.94	43	0.72*
T7. Concern	1.00	19	0.25
T8. Interruptions	1.0	21	0.00
T9. Silence	0.89	15	0.35
T10. Repetitive questioning	1.00	84	0.86**
T11. Leading questions	1.00	91	0.51**
T12. Open questions	1.00	99	0.77**
T13. Intimidation	1.00	00	
T14. Suggest scenario	1.00	29	0.64**
T15. Handling suspect's mood	0.84	33	1.000***
T16. Challenging suspect's account	1.00	71	0.66**
T17. Situational futility	1.00	00	

*p = 50.5; **p = 50.01; *** p = 50.001.

Results

Table 12.2 demonstrates that there was inter-coder agreement (except for the degree of usage of 'concern', 'interruptions' and 'silence'). It also demonstrates (based on the main coder's data) that

(i) the tactics that were most frequently used (at least to some degree) in the sample of 80 interviews were: (a) disclosure of evidence, (b) open questions, (c) leading questions, and (d) repetitive questioning;
(ii) the (other) tactics used in at least half of the interviews were: (a) emphasising contradictions, (b) positive confrontation, and (c) challenging the suspect's account;
(iii) the tactics that were used in less than half of the interviews were: (a) gentle prods, (b) handling suspect's mood, (c) suggest scenario, (d) interruptions, (e) concern, and (f) silence; and
(iv) the tactics that were never or almost never used were (a) maximisation, (b) minimisation, (c) intimidation, and (d) situational futility.

Confessions

As stated above, previous research involving analysis of audio-taped British police interviews with suspects had found (post-PACE) that very few suspects in their interviews actually moved from maintaining denial to eventually confessing. Instead, the majority of those who confessed did so at or very near the beginning of their interview. The PEACE training focuses not on the obtaining of confessions but on the obtaining from suspects of information that could be used to support/verify a confession should one occur in the interview. (Thus it can often be appropriate to continue with the interview once a suspect has confessed.) In the present study suspects confessed in 31 of the 80 interviews. However, only five of these confessions occurred in the first third of the interviews. Fifteen of the confessions occurred in the middle third of the interviews and 11 in the final third.

The data also enable analysis of the possible correlations between (a) the degree of usage of each tactic per interview and (b) how far the suspect shifted from denial toward confession. Table 12.3 presents the Spearman correlations between the degree of usage in each interview of each tactic and how far the suspect shifted. Table 12.3 also presents information concerning in how many of the confession (and no-confession interviews) the tactic was used and, if a tactic was used, the mean degree of usage (on the five-point scale mentioned above).

Some of the tactics did not occur in some of the confession interviews, therefore the size of the correlation required for statistical significance varies across tactics. The tactics used in most of the confession interviews included

- 'disclosure of evidence' and 'open questions' (used in all 31 confession interviews)
- 'leading questions' (used in 30)
- 'positive confrontation' (used in 28)
- 'challenging suspect's account' (used in 26)
- 'emphasising contradictions' and 'repetitive questioning' (used in 25).

Almost all of the positive correlations are smaller than the critical value required (which are lower for one-tailed tests). Only for the tactics of (a) use of open questions and (b) disclosure of evidence are the positive correlations statistically significant (at $p < 0.05$ and $p < 0.01$, respectively one-tailed) and these are small (at 0.20 and 0.27).

For two of the tactics the correlations were actually negative (i.e. for 'emphasising contradictions' and for 'challenging the suspect's account') and these would have been statistically significant had we initially formed a two-tailed hypothesis (at $p < 0.02$ and $p < 0.01$, respectively). These two negative correlations indicate greater degree of tactic usage when less shift from denial toward confession occurred. Indeed, Table 12.3 also demonstrates that for nine of the tactics the degree of usage was greater in the no-confession interviews. (Only four tactics were used more in the confession interviews). The only tactic usage that significantly differentiated between confession and no-confession interviews were (i) 'emphasising contradictions' ($t = 4.01$, $p < 0.01$), (ii) 'repetitive questioning' ($t = 1.97$, $p < 0.05$), and (iii) 'challenging suspect's account' ($t = 2.32$, $p < 0.05$), each of which was used more in the interviews during which suspects did not confess.

Table 12.3 Correlations between degree of tactic usage and amount of shift to confession; plus tactic usage in confession and no-confession interviews

Tactic	*Correlation*	*Number of confession interviews in which tactic was used*	*Number of non-confession interviews in which tactic was used*	*Mean (SD) degree of usage in confession interviews*	*Mean (SD) degree of usage in non-confession interviews*
T1. Disclosure of evidence	0.27	31	48	3.96 (0.77)	4.16 (1.70)
T2. Maximisation	–	0	1	–	4.00 (–)
T3. Minimisation	–	0	0	–	–
T4. Emphasising contradictions	−0.33	25	35	2.71 (1.02)	3.76 (0.92)
T5. Positive confrontation	0.11	28	31	2.90 (0.91)	2.75 (0.97)
T6. Gentle prods	0.25	18	17	2.70 (0.85)	3.22 (1.11)
T7. Concern	0.19	10	5	2.00 (0.71)	2.30 (0.95)
T8. Interruptions	0.26	11	6	1.84 (0.41)	1.91 (0.70)
T9. Silence	0.11	06	06	2.33 (1.03)	2.00 (0.63)
T10. Repetitive questioning	0.14	25	42	2.35 (1.01)	2.84 (0.89)
T11. Leading questions	0.04	30	43	2.23 (1.08)	1.04 (1.03)
T12. Open questions	0.20	31	48	3.60 (0.89)	3.96 (0.75)
T13. Intimidation	–	00	00	–	–
T14. Suggest scenario	0.29	15	8	2.75 (0.70)	2.40 (0.63)
T15. Handling suspect's mood	0.32	15	11	2.45 (0.68)	2.60 (0.91)
T16. Challenging suspect's account	−0.36	26	31	2.25 (0.96)	2.88 (1.07)
T17. Situational futility	–	00	00	–	–

Discussion

One of the main aims of the present study was to identify the actual tactics most commonly used during modern interviews with police suspects in England and Wales. Irving (1980), as well as Softley (1980), concluded that at that time manipulative and persuasive tactics prevailed in UK interviews with suspects. The results of the present study, which largely revealed 'ethical' interviewing tactics, do not concur with their views. The tactics deemed by several psychologists to be the most problematic (i.e. intimidation, minimisation, situational futility, and maximisation) never or almost never occurred. On the other hand, the tactics emphasised in the 'new' British ethos and training were often used; that is, those designed (i) to obtain information from the suspect (e.g. open questions, repetitive questions although the frequent use of leading questions is not in line with the training) and (ii) then to test this information (e.g. emphasising contradictions, challenging the suspect's account, positive confrontation, disclosure of evidence). Future research should try to establish when during typical interviews with suspects various tactics are used.

The data regarding the degree of tactic usage (i.e. if a tactic was used in an interview, the extent/strength with which it was used) are also largely in line with the 'new' ethos in that disclosure of evidence, open questions, and positive confrontation scored highest in this respect. The proportion of the interviews in which the suspects confessed was 39%, which is similar, if a little lower, than that reported in the studies of British policing cited above. However, contrary to the (few) previous studies that have taken the trouble to note when in the interviews the confessions occurred, few of the confessions in the current study occurred at or near the beginning of the interviews. This finding allowed the possible relationship between each tactic's usage and the extent of each suspect's shift from denying to confessing to be examined. A reason for anticipating such a relationship is the understandable expectation that tactic usage influences confessions. However, few such positive relationships were found. Only for 'use of open questions' and 'disclosure of evidence' were statistically significant positive correlations found, which at values of $r = 0.20$ and $r = 0.27$ are not strong. Nevertheless, the emphasis in the British PEACE training model on developing these particular tactics/skills seems well placed.

To our (initial) surprise, two of the correlations were negative. That is, 'emphasising contradictions' and 'challenging the suspect's account' had greater degrees of usage in interviews in which there was less shift from denial toward confession. However, with the benefit of hindsight one can understand why interviewers might persevere in the usage of tactics (contained within their training) with suspects who continue to deny. (It is also possible that some suspects may not shift from denial because of the use of certain tactics.) For the majority of tactics the degree of usage was greater in the no-confession interviews. The tactics of 'emphasising contradictions' and 'challenging the suspect's account' had the largest difference in mean degree of usage between no-confession and confession interviews. Kassin, Goldstein, & Savitsky (2003) similarly found in their mock study that the most pressurising interviews were actually with innocent suspects (who are likely to continue denying) rather than guilty ones (who may be more likely to confess), especially when conducted by (student) interviewers who had expectations that the suspect was guilty (also see Mortimer & Shepherd, 1999).

The present study's findings concerning which were the most frequently used tactics and those employed with the greatest degree of usage concur with a number of suggestions made in Kassin and Gudjonsson's comprehensive overview (2004). For example, that 'the practice of confronting suspects with real evidence, or even their own inconsistent statements, should increase the diagnosticity of the confessions that are ultimately elicited' (p. 60).

Within the North American context, Meissner & Russano (2003) discussed 'a novel alternative approach to the interrogation process that has recently been implemented in Britain' (p. 53). They noted that 'Although the Reid Technique has . . . recently received tacit approval by the Supreme Court of Canada . . . Great

Britain has recently restricted the use of the Reid Technique based on various instances of false confessions and research on the coercive nature of certain techniques' (p. 54). They pointed out that in Britain 'the likelihood of obtaining a confession from a suspect was not inhibited by the application of noncoercive techniques' (p. 60). Having reviewed some of the relevant literature they recommended with regard to false confessions that 'investigators should also be mindful of . . . the implications of leniency inherent to "minimisation" themes' (p. 61). (The present study found that British police officers now do not use this tactic.) Meissner and Russano also noted that 'At the heart of this [British] approach is an "ethical" and "inquisitorial" framework' (p. 60). The present study supports this.

Indeed, Kassin & Gudjonsson (2004) suggested that some offenders (e.g. 'child molesters') may be more likely to confess if the interviewers adopt 'a sensitive approach' (p. 48). However, the human beings who commit other serious crimes may also be more likely to tell the police 'about it' if they are interviewed in the ways that modern psychology could suggest. In Sweden Holmberg & Christianson (2002) invited male prisoners (found guilty of serious crimes) to fill in an extensive questionnaire about how they had been interviewed by the police. Two major styles of interviewing were reported, one described by Holmberg (a former police officer) and Christianson as 'humane', the other as 'dominating'. More of those prisoners who indicated that their interviewers had demonstrated the humane style confessed/ admitted to the (serious) crimes during the interviews (whereas those who reported experiencing the dominating style continued during their interviews to deny). This could be taken to support the PEACE model.

Kassin & Gudjonsson (2004) also suggested that 'the time is ripe for a true collaborative effort among law-enforcement professionals, district attorneys, defense lawyers, judges, social scientists, and policymakers to evaluate the methods of interrogation' (p. 59). To a considerable extent such collaboration has been taking place in Britain over the last 20 years. What the present study discovered concerning the tactics used in real-life police interviews with suspects in England is likely to have been greatly influenced by such collaboration. However, more such studies are necessary across the world. In Britain we must not be complacent, and other countries seriously need to consider where they stand on this issue. The grave consequences of basing the interviewing of suspects on little-researched notions should not be minimised.

References

Baldwin, J. (1992). *Video-taping of police interviews with suspects: An evaluation*. Police Research Series Paper No. 1. London: Home Office.

Baldwin, J. (1993). Police interview techniques. Establishing truth or proof? *British Journal of Criminology*, *33*, 325–352.

Blair, J., & McCamey, W. (2002). Detection of deception: An analysis of the behavioural analysis interview technique. *Illinois Law Enforcement Executive Forum*, *2*, 165–170.

Bull, R. (2004). Training to detect deception from behavioural cues. In P.A. Granhag, & L. Stromwall (Eds.), *The detection of deception in forensic contexts* (pp. 251–268). Cambridge: Cambridge University Press.

Bull, R., & Cherryman, J. (1996). *Helping to identify skills gaps in specialist investigative interviewing*. London: Home Office Police Department.

Bull, R., & Milne, R. (2004). Attempts to improve the police interviewing of suspects. In G.D. Lassiter (Ed.), *Interrogations, confessions and entrapment* (pp. 181–196). New York: Kluwer.

Clarke, C., & Milne, R. (2001). *National evaluation of the PEACE investigative interviewing course*. Police Research Award Scheme. London: Home Office.

Davis, D., & O'Donohue, W. (2003). The road to perdition: Extreme influence tactics in the interrogation room. In W. O'Donohue, & E. Levensky (Eds.), *Handbook of forensic psychology: Resource for mental health and legal professionals* (pp. 897–996). New York, NY: Academic Press.

Davis, M., Markus, K., Walters, S., Vorus, N., & Connors, B. (2005). Behavioral cues to deception vs. topic incriminating potential in criminal confessions. *Law and Human Behavior*, *29*, 683–704.

De Paulo, B., Lindsay, J., Malone, B., Muhlenbruck, L., Charlton, K., & Cooper, H. (2003). Cues to deception. *Psychological Bulletin*, *129*, 74–118.

Gudjonsson, G. (1992). *The psychology of interrogations, confessions and testimony*. Chichester: Wiley.

Gudjonsson, G. (2003). *The psychology of interrogations and confessions: A handbook*. Chichester: Wiley.

Gudjonsson, G. (2006). The psychology of interrogations and confessions. In T. Williamson (Ed.), *Investigative interviewing: Rights, research and regulation* (pp. 123–146). Cullompton, UK: Willan.

Holmberg, U., & Christianson, S. (2002). Murderers' and sexual offenders' experiences of police interviews and their inclination to admit or deny crimes. *Behavioral Sciences and the Law*, *20*, 31–45.

Horselenberg, R., Merckelbach, H., Smeets, T., Franssens, D., Peters, G., & Zeles, G. (2006). False confessions in the lab: Do plausibility and consequences matter? *Psychology, Crime & Law*, *12*, 61–75.

Horvath, F., & Jayne, B. (1994). Differentiation of truthful and deceptive suspects in behavioural analysis interviews. *Journal of Forensic Sciences*, *39*, 793–807.

Inbau, F., Reid, J., Buckley, J., & Jayne, B. (2001). *Criminal interrogation and confessions* (4th ed.). Gaithersburg, MA: Aspen.

Irving, B. (1980). *Police interrogation. A case study of current practice*. Research Study Number 2. Royal Commission on Criminal Procedure. London: HMSO.

Kalbfleisch, P.J. (1994). The language of detecting deceit. *Journal of Language and Social Psychology*, *13*, 469–496.

Kassin, S. (1997). The psychology of confession evidence. *American Psychologist*, *52*, 221–233.

Kassin, S. (2006). A critical appraisal of modern police interrogations. In T. Williamson (Ed.), *Investigative interviewing: Rights, research and regulation*. Collompton: Willan.

Kassin, S., & Fong, C. (1999). 'I'm innocent!': Effects of training on judgements of truth and deception in the interrogation room. *Law and Human Behavior*, *23*, 499–516.

Kassin, S., Goldstein, C., & Savitsky, K. (2003). Behavioral confirmation in the interrogation room: On the dangers of presuming guilt. *Law and Human Behavior*, *27*, 187–203.

Kassin, S., & Gudjonsson, G. (2004). The psychology of confessions: A review of the literature and issues. *Psychological Science in the Public Interest*, *5*, 35–67.

Kassin, S., & Kiechel, K. (1996). The social psychology of false confessions: Compliance, internalization and confabulation. *Psychological Science*, *7*, 125–128.

Kassin, S., & McNall, K. (1991). Police interrogations and confessions: Communicating promises and threats by pragmatic implication. *Law and Human Behavior*, *15*, 233–251.

Klaver, J., Rose, V., & Lee, Z. (2003). *Differential effects of minimization and maximization interrogation techniques and the role of plausibility in an experimental false confession paradigm*. Paper presented at the International Interdisciplinary Psychology and Law Conference, Edinburgh, July.

Leo, R. (1992). From coercion to deception: The changing nature of police interrogation in America. *Crime, Law and Social Change*, *18*, 33–59.

Leo, R. (1996). Inside the interrogation room. *Journal of Criminal Law and Criminology*, *86*, 266–303.

Leo, R. (2004). The 'third degree' and the origins of psychological interrogation in the United States. In G.D. Lassiter (Ed.), *Interrogations, confessions and entrapment* (pp. 37–84). New York, NY: Kluwer.

Mann, S., Vrij, A., & Bull, R. (2004). Detecting true lies: Police officers' ability to detect suspects' lies. *Journal of Applied Psychology*, *89*, 137–149.

McConville, M., & Hodgson, J. (1993). *Custodial legal advice and the right to silence*. The Royal Commission on Criminal Justice Research, Research Study No. 16. London: HMSO.

McGurk, B., Carr, J., & McGurk, D. (1993). *Investigative interviewing courses for police officers: An evaluation*. Police Research Series Paper No. 4. London: Home Office.

Meissner, C., & Russano, M. (2003). The psychology of interrogations and false confessions: Research and recommendations. *Canadian Journal of Police and Security Services*, *1*, 53–64.

Memon, A., Vrij, A., & Bull, R. (1998). *Psychology and law: Truthfulness, accuracy and credibility*. Maidenhead, UK: McGraw Hill.

Memon, A., Vrij, A., & Bull, R. (2003). *Psychology and law: Truthfulness, accuracy and credibility* (2nd ed.). Chichester: Wiley.

Milne, R., & Bull, R. (1999). *Investigative interviewing: Psychology and practice*. Chichester: Wiley.

Mortimer, A., & Shepherd, E. (1999). Frames of mind: Schemata guiding cognition and conduct in the interviewing of suspected offenders. In A. Memon, & R. Bull (Eds.), *Handbook of the psychology of interviewing* (pp. 293–315). Chichester: Wiley.

Moston, S., Stephenson, G.M., & Williamson, T. (1992). The effects of case characteristics on suspect behaviour during police questioning. *British Journal of Criminology*, *32*, 23–40.

National Crime Faculty. (2000). *A practical guide to investigative interviewing*. Bramshill, UK: National Crime Faculty and National Police Training.

Pearse, J., & Gudjonsson, G.H. (1996). Police interviewing techniques at two south London police stations. *Psychology, Crime & Law*, *3*, 63–74.

Pearse, J., & Gudjonsson, G.H. (1999). Measuring influential police interviewing tactics. *Legal and Criminological Psychology*, *4*, 221–238.

Russano, M., Meissner, C., Narchet, F., & Kassin, S. (2005). Investigating true and false confessions within a novel experimental paradigm. *Psychological Science*, *16*, 481–486.

Softley, P. (1980). *Police interrogation*. Research Study No. 61. London: Home Office.

Soukara, S., Bull, R., & Vrij, A. (2002). Police detectives' aims regarding their interviews with suspects: Any changes at the turn of the millennium? *International Journal of Police Science and Management*, *4*, 110–114.

Vrij, A. (2000). *Detecting lies and deceit*. Chichester: Wiley.

Vrij, A. (2002). 'We will protect your wife and child, but only if you confess'. In P. van Koppen, & S. Penrod (Eds.), *Adversarial versus inquisitorial justice: Psychological perspectives on criminal justice systems* (pp. 55–79). New York, NY: Kluwer.
Vrij, A. (2004). Why professionals fail to catch liars and how they can improve. *Legal and Criminological Psychology*, *9*, 159–181.
Walkley, J. (1987). *Police interrogation*. London: Police Review.
Williamson, T. (2006a). *Investigative interviewing: Rights, research and regulation*. Collompton, UK: Willan.
Williamson, T. (2006b). Towards greater professionalism: Minimising miscarriages of justice. In T. Williamson (Ed.), *Investigative interviewing: Rights, research and regulation* (pp. 147–166). Collompton, UK: Willan.

13 Examining rapport in investigative interviews with suspects: does its building and maintenance work?

Dave Walsh and Ray Bull

Introduction

Establishing rapport is felt to be critical in contributing to effective encounters between human beings (Bernieri, Davis, Rosenthal, & Knee, 1994; Hendrick, 1990; Tickle-Degnen & Rosenthal, 1990). Described by Bernieri & Gillis (2001, p. 69) as "a positive and productive affect between people that facilitates mutuality of attention and harmony", rapport development may be a more demanding task in the particular context of interviews between official investigators and those suspected of crime. In these situations, suspects may be more reluctant to talk, as doing so may lead to their incrimination in wrongdoing. Nevertheless, it has been argued that if suspects feel there is a harmonious relationship with their interviewers they will tend to talk more openly (St Yves, 2006).

Where research has been undertaken into the quality of rapport in interviews, relevant skill levels have been less than adequate. For example, Moston, Stephenson, & Williamson (1992) found in their large scale study of over 1,000 interviews that police officers spent little time establishing rapport and gathering information. Officers tended instead to directly accuse suspects from the outset that they had committed the offence. In cases where the evidence was less than strong, suspects usually denied such accusations. Thereafter, interviewers tended to repeat the original accusation which generally prompted further denials. Interviews, not unsurprisingly, came to an impasse with interviewers 'giving up' when suspects maintained their refusal to admit any wrongdoing. However, the little research that has been conducted into the nature of rapport in investigative interviewing has almost exclusively involved examination and analysis of police practice. Thus, we are largely unaware of what happens in other areas of law enforcement such as those interviews conducted by non-police officers with those suspected of tax evasion or social security benefit fraud, the latter being the focus of the present study. Those few earlier studies that have been conducted into benefit fraud interviews have found mediocrity concerning interviewing skills including those concerning rapport building (e.g. Shawyer & Milne, 2006; Walsh & Bull, 2010a; Walsh & Milne, 2008).

Background to the study

In England and Wales interviews with suspects, including those suspected of benefit fraud, are conducted under the relevant legislation (The Police and Criminal Evidence Act, 1984; henceforth referred to as PACE). The Act was introduced as a result of concerns over miscarriages of justice and aims to provide safeguards within the interviewing process. For example, PACE is intended to ensure that suspects know that (i) they can be legally represented before questioning begins, (ii) any responses they make to questions will be recorded on audio-tape and may be used as evidence, and (iii) there could be potentially detrimental implications to their subsequent defence in court if they do not answer questions put to them by investigators. In addition to its use in the criminal justice process, the mandatory audio-taping of interviews provided opportunities for researchers to examine what happens in interviews. Early studies consistently found mediocrity in interviewing skills (Baldwin, 1993; Moston et al., 1992—for a review see Milne & Bull, 1999). As a response, a new framework of interviewing called the 'PEACE' model was nationally introduced by the police. Benefit fraud investigators are also trained in the use of the model.

The PEACE model

PEACE is advocated as a more ethical and fair approach to interviewing (Milne & Bull, 1999), and is a mnemonic acronym for the five stages of interviewing—(i) **P**reparation and **P**lanning before the interview, (ii) **E**ngaging and **E**xplaining to the suspect the purpose of the interview and their rights therein, (iii) asking for an **A**ccount from the suspect (and clarifying and challenging when necessary) before (iv) bringing the interview to **C**losure and, thereafter, (v) **E**valuating the interview to ascertain where any improvements could be made). The model is not necessarily a linear one. For example, when undertaking a final summary in the Closure phase, an interviewer may identify an opportunity to resume questioning if it is identified that further clarification of the suspect's account is needed. Nevertheless, there are some tasks which solely pertain to certain interview phases. For example, interviewers would be expected to introduce themselves or inform suspects of their legal rights in the opening Engage and Explain phase.

Prior studies of interviewing in other contexts have stressed the overall importance of rapport establishment and maintenance. Thus, the present study examined benefit fraud interviews to establish whether or not opportunities to build rapport in the Engage and Explain phase are overlooked. The study also examined what impact, if any, rapport building may appear to have on overall interview quality and outcomes. Examining what attempts by interviewers were made to sustain rapport with suspects as the interview progressed on to the Account and Closure stages was also a feature of the study. Finally, the study examined whether there was any association between these efforts at maintaining rapport and the overall interview quality and outcomes.

Rapport building in interviews with suspects

In the Engage and Explain phase the PEACE model advises that interviews should commence by making a good first impression in order to begin to build rapport. For example, interviewers should demonstrate courtesy towards suspects concerning how they wish to be addressed. This type of approach can help personalise the relationship between the interviewer and the suspect (e.g., by using first name terms), which may well be crucial to the overall success of the interview (Griffiths, 2008; National Crime Faculty, 2000; Ord & Shaw, 1999).

In this initial phase of the interview it is also anticipated that a range of tasks should be conducted at this stage each of which, it is argued, can also incrementally contribute to the building of rapport. For example, certain administrative tasks are legally required to be undertaken such as all those present identifying themselves. Additionally, interviewers should state the date, time and location of the interview, as well as advising suspects that they can have a copy of the tape. Benefit fraud investigators are also required to advise suspects that they (i) are not under arrest, (ii) can leave the interview room whenever they so wish, and (iii) have the right to legal representation. Benefit fraud suspects are also asked to read a single page advisory document that informs them (i) of their rights in the interview under PACE, and (ii) the broad purpose of the interview. Suspects are also asked to confirm their understanding of this guidance. Other legally prescribed tasks involve interviewers specifically querying the reasons, whenever this occurs, as to why suspects are unaccompanied by a legal representative.

An opportunity to build rapport and establish a working relationship with suspects may occur when interviewers administer the official caution to them. The caution is designed to appraise suspects of their right to refuse to answer questions. It also advises them that any later revelations they might make (say, in court) might be looked upon adversely, questioning why defendants did not disclose this information at the earlier opportunity in the interview. Finally, the caution continues to also advise suspects that any utterances they provide are to be regarded as evidence. The caution reads;

> You do not have to say anything. But it may harm your defence if you do not mention when questioned something which you later rely on in Court. Anything you do say may be given in evidence.
>
> (Home Office, 2006, p. 78)

Several experimental studies have examined the understanding of the caution, finding that the vast majority of participants struggled to find it comprehensible (Clare, Gudjonsson, & Harari, 1998; Fenner, Gudjonsson, & Clare, 2002; Shepherd, Mortimer, & Mobasheri, 1995). Walsh & Bull (2010a), in their field study of interviews with benefit fraud suspects, found that interviewing officers rarely checked the suspects' comprehension (also Rock, 2007, in her study of professional practice conducted by the police in England and Wales). Interviewers appeared to accept on face value that an affirmative answer from suspects to the question "Do you understand?" was sufficient in itself to demonstrate to interviewers awareness of its meaning. In Walsh and Bull's study, when interviewers explored whether suspects could provide an accurate explanation of the caution, none of the suspects did. This was despite all of those suspects, whose understanding was tested in this more thorough manner, earlier answering positively that they did understand the caution. This finding suggests that any belief that any affirmative response demonstrates suspects' comprehension of their rights is an extremely precarious one.

In the context of the present study, Walsh and Bull's findings, concerning the infrequency of establishing whether suspects really do understand the caution, suggests that an opportunity to build rapport was overlooked. That is, interviewers (by not taking time to ensure such understanding) may fail to achieve (i) mutual attentiveness, (ii) positivity, and (iii) co-ordination; being the three components of Tickle-Degnen & Rosenthal's (1990) theoretical framework of rapport. Their framework will also be used to conceptualise rapport in the present study. In more detail, Tickle-Degnen and Rosenthal state that examined through a range of verbal and non-verbal behaviours *mutual attentiveness* refers to a cohesiveness of shared interest and focus. Secondly, *positivity* reflects feelings of mutual friendliness and caring. Thirdly, *co-ordination*, concerns the balance and harmony between the participants.

Rapport maintenance in interviews with suspects

In Collins, Lincoln, & Frank (2002) experimental study of forensic interviews, it was found that, of the three conditions tested (i.e., rapport, neutral, and abrupt interviewing styles), the latter two were found to be least productive in securing more co-operation (and an account) from interviewees. Indeed, some participants reported the neutral condition (displayed by indifference by the interviewer) was equally negative as the abrupt (or rude) one to building positive relationships. Similarly, Geiselman et al. (1984) found that those interviewees who felt more relaxed increased their cooperation and tried harder to recall details. However, both of these studies involved the interviewees as mock witnesses who might be argued to have a greater desire than some suspects to assist interviewers to reveal the facts.

Griffiths & Milne (2006), on the other hand, conducted a study of real life interviews with suspects. They found that those police interviewers who encouraged suspects to talk freely in the Account phase created opportunities later in that phase for increasingly probing questions to be asked, Griffiths and Milne found that this approach enabled accounts to be more closely scrutinised. Other studies (e.g. Colwell, Hiscock, & Memon, 2002; Colwell, Hiscock-Anisman, Memon, Taylor, & Prewett, 2007) have also revealed that maintaining rapport leads to an exchange of communication between interviewers and their suspects. In turn, these studies found an increased possibility of deception being later uncovered as a result of suspects providing more details. However, Oxburgh, Ost, & Cherryman (2010) have recently found that that questioning styles, rather than empathy, prompt more 'investigation related information' (IRI) from suspects. Nevertheless, Holmberg & Christianson (2002) found that many convicted offenders, who stated that their interviews had been conducted by interviewers offering an empathic and humanitarian stance, had confessed to wrongdoing. Holmberg and Christianson also found, in contrast, that those who had denied offending described their interviewers as demonstrating a dominant and judgemental approach.

Holmberg and Christianson's findings suggest that positive interviewer attitudes are also important to helping rapport flourish. However, Holmberg and Christianson's study involved (i) self-reporting by these offenders, and (ii) for some of them recollection of interviews took place several years prior to the study. Both of these factors might have affected the study's results.

As has been discussed, the literature that involves any analysis of interviewing standards by non-police agencies is sparse. Even less is known of what tasks are undertaken in interviews, which may well contribute to the mediocrity of performance and outcomes observed in the few such studies that have been conducted (see Walsh & Bull, 2010b). This present study therefore examined interviews with benefit fraud suspects conducted by non-police officers. It hypothesised that there would not be a strong association between rapport building alone and overall interview quality and the outcomes of interviews. It was also hypothesised that it would also be important for rapport to be maintained as the interview developed.

Method

Materials

The sample of interviews consisted of 115 audio-taped recorded interviews and a further 27 typed transcripts of interviews randomly sourced from five FIS teams and eight LAs throughout England, which had been conducted during the period between 2004 and 2008. Investigation teams were contacted to ask if they wished to participate and those who agreed were requested to select interviews that were no less than twenty minutes in length. (Prior research conducted by the first author had found that without this stipulation the samples sent often involved interviews that are of such short duration and simplicity that negligible research material can be satisfactorily elicited; see Walsh & Milne, 2008.) This criterion also has the potential advantage of analysing interviews of a more complex nature or those where the suspects are less compliant. Thus, it was intended that analysis of skill levels of investigators would occur in more demanding circumstances.

Specific requests could have been made for a more purposive sample that stipulated either complexity or resistance from suspects as a pre-requisite. However, it was known that this would have discouraged many of the teams from sending tapes as the extent of effort required to identify them would have been prohibitive. Examination of the size of the used tape spool in the cassette 'window' proved to be an obvious and efficient indicator of the duration of the interview, as did the length of the typed transcripts by examination of the stated interview commencement and cessation times. It was also requested that the sample of the interviews should not be those narrowly involving just one or two investigators from the team but it was preferred if they represented more widely members of each investigation team. This would increase the possibility of being provided a sample that portrayed the interviewing practices of a wide range of investigators, and not just those of a select few.

To increase the likelihood that the sample would include a range of interview outcomes, it was also requested to involve a mix of cases. This request included asking for those cases that would have been expected to go forward for some form of sanction, as well as those discontinued for reasons such as evidential shortcomings.

Procedure: the Engage and Explain phase

A first analysis involved the quality of the rapport building in the initial Engage and Explain phase using a Likert scale (previously used in earlier studies of interviewing practice; see Clarke & Milne, 2001; Shawyer, 2009; Walsh & Milne, 2008). To summarise, a rating of '1' denoted 'poor' performance where the interviewer was felt to require further training, whereas, a '2' rating denoted 'unsatisfactory' performance. A score of '3' (assessed as 'satisfactory') followed Clarke and Milne's definition of being deemed to be the minimum acceptable score under the PEACE model. Ratings of '4' and '5' referred respectively to 'skilled' and 'highly skilled' performance.

Ratings at the lower end of the scale were indicated by an absence of rapport. For example, tasks in the Engage and Explain phase undertaken in a perfunctory manner by interviewers with little or no attempt to build any working relationship. Likewise, lower assessments in the Account phase were characterised by the overuse of closed and leading questions and/or an accusatory approach. On the other hand, attempts to build rapport, epitomised by an initial approach that, whilst not too informal, was harmonious, would lead to a higher assessment. Interviewers taking time to encourage suspects to provide fuller accounts and who appeared relaxed and conversational when questioning suspects would attract higher ratings. For those scoring the highest assessment interviews would be hallmarked by a constant display of skilled behaviours.

The sample would also be examined for a quantitative analysis of the presence of several tasks expected to be conducted in the Engage and Explain phase (see Table 13.1, items 1–10). The quality of the Engage and Explain phase itself, and the overall quality of the interviewing skills, were also assessed using the same Likert scale in order to determine whether there was any association between the quality of rapport building and the quality of the Engage and Explain phase (and the subsequent overall quality of the interview). Next, the interviews were examined to identify their outcomes, divided between two classifications. The first concerned those interviews where the outcomes were either a denial or partial admission, neither of which the interviewer tested for their reliability (named 'unsatisfactory outcomes'). The second group of interview outcomes were those which resulted in the gathering of either a comprehensive account (regardless of whether any fraud was admitted) or a full and frank confession, defined as 'preferred outcomes'.

Table 13.1 Rapport related tasks/behaviours and their definitions in the interview (adapted from Clarke & Milne, 2001; Griffiths, 2008)

Task/behaviour	*Definition*
Provides introductions	Provides good initial impression and name preference in an attempt to personalise the interview
Delivers caution	Informs suspects of their legal rights in the interview
Checks understanding of caution	Thoroughly ensures that suspects understand the caution
Informs of right to tape copy	Legal requirement
Informs of right to legal advice	Legal requirement
Asks why no legal representation required	Legal requirement and ensures that suspects understand that they can have legal advice and makes explicit reason for declining this right
Explains reason for interview	Specifically informs suspects why they are being interviewed and that interview is a search for the truth
Explains interview is their opportunity to give an account	Tells suspects that will be given opportunity to tell their side of the story
Explains routines, roles, and route maps	Explains that questions will be asked in the search for the truth, that notes may be taken, outlines intended pathway of interview and potential duration. Explains roles of 'others' who are present
Provides written guidance, checking understanding	Supplies document and gives as much time as the suspect requires to read it. Asks if there any questions concerning the guidance on the document
Encourages suspect to give an account	Evidence of explicitly asking the interviewee for their first account, and allowing the interviewee to give this, without any interruptions
Development of topics	Evidence of appropriate selection of topics from the interviewee's first account (and route map).
Supplies appropriate topic structure	Interviewer moves from one topic to another in a logical structured manner
Appropriate questioning styles	Open questioning and then probing questions using closed questions for clarification only. Avoids leading, negatively loaded, multiple, overlong, forced choice questions, and statements, overtalking and interruptions
Intermittent summarising	Provides regular and accurate summarising
Explores motive	Goes beyond accepting any admission and tries to find, with understanding, why they committed offence
Explores and probes information	Goes beyond just accepting information but searches for further detail, identifying any inconsistencies
Displays active listening	Regular displays to illustrate to suspect concern and interest to encourage further information received
Maintains conversational turn taking	Ensures that conversational protocols are observed and that conversation is not one sided but a mutual encounter
Provides final summary of interview	Final summary that accurately resumes key issues discussed and captures key reposes from the suspect
Asks if suspect wishes to add or alter anything	Provides opportunity for suspect to make any amendments to their account
Informs suspects what happens next	Explains future agenda and processes
Shows equality signs	Matches suspect's style and does not belittle or talk condescendingly to or 'above' suspect. Is polite, respectful and courteous
Displays calmness	Constant and confident displays of calmness particularly when confronted by anger, hostility, aggression or resistance
Displays empathy	Exhibits a non-judgemental, open minded, understanding and concerned approach

Procedure: the Account phase

A second analysis examined the quality of the rapport in the Account phase and the number of times relevant tasks were found in the sample to have been conducted in this phase, representing further rapport opportunities (see Table 13.1, items 11–19, except 16). The exception, *exploring motive*, was not always appropriate to be conducted in every interview (e.g., in the absence of any admissions to wrongdoing). As with the tasks in the Engage and Explain phase, these tasks were assessed along the Likert scale for their skill levels. Analysis was also undertaken whether rapport skill levels in this interview phase had any association with (i) the quality of rapport building in the Engage and Explain phase, (ii) overall interview skill rating, and (iii) interview outcomes. Measures of task frequency were also conducted (except for item 16, as already explained).

Procedure: the Closure phase

A third analysis of the interviews concerned those tasks to be performed in the Closure phase (see Table 13.1, items 20–22) and this again examined (i) skill levels on the same Likert scale, (ii) frequency of occurrence, and (iii) any associations to overall skill rating and interview outcome. A final analysis was undertaken of the behaviours (items 23–25) that the existing literature suggests should be apparent throughout the interview for rapport to be continued to be present (e.g. Holmberg & Christianson 2002). The four sets of analyses examined those tasks and behaviours, as identified in Table 13.1 that make a contribution towards rapport in interviews. For example, those which encouraged suspects to talk (Collins et al., 2002; Holmberg & Christianson 2002; St Yves, 2006). These have been employed to measure PEACE interview performance in several prior studies (e.g. Bull & Cherryman, 1996; Clarke & Milne, 2001; Griffiths, 2008; McGurk, Carr, & McGurk, 1993; Walsh & Bull, 2010a; Walsh & Milne, 2008).

Inter-rater reliability

The skill levels were assessed initially by the first author of the present study, who had undergone PEACE training and had extensive professional experience of conducting fraud interviews. The second rater, who was a considerably experienced PEACE interview trainer, received guidance (as provided in Clarke & Milne, 2001) in the use of the scale by the first author. Training in the scale involved the use of two typed transcripts from the first author's investigation team (that was not part of the sample used in the present study). These two studies were chosen as they both lasted between 45–55 minutes. One of these was rated by the first author as possessing either satisfactory, skilled, or highly skilled demonstrations of rapport. The other interview involved rapport that was generally assessed to be less than the minimum standard with only rare demonstrations of satisfactory or skilled performance of certain tasks. Following the guidance, the second rater provided ratings that demonstrated comparable assessments and explanations with the first rater, suggesting that there was a mutual understanding of the scale.

Table 13.2 presents the information concerning inter-rater agreement between the two raters using 15% ($N = 22$) of the original sample of 142 interviews. Using guidelines in determining the strength of correlation (Cramer & Howitt, 2004, expressed in terms of Spearman's rho) between the two sets of raters' scores, Table 13.2 suggests that strong correlations exist regarding the overwhelming majority of

Table 13.2 Results from study concerning (a) inter-rater reliability of skill levels, (b) mean skill levels with SD, and (c) frequency of occurrence in sample

Task/behaviour	*Inter-rater reliability (Spearman's rho)*	*Skill level*	*Frequency (percentage)*
Engage and Explain tasks			
Provides introductions	0.72	3.42 (0.45)	97
Delivers caution	0.99	3.04 (0.66)	99
Checks understanding of caution	0.95	1.96 (1.21)	96
Informs suspect of right to tape copy	0.86	3.23 (0.66)	92
Informs of right to legal advice	0.95	2.77 (0.75)	95
Asks why no legal representation required	0.82	2.07 (0.41)	63
Explains reason for interview	0.91	2.35 (0.77)	74
Explains interview is their opportunity to give an account	0.77	1.58 (0.64)	51
Explains routines, roles, and route maps	0.91	1.34 (0.57)	29
Supplies written guidance, checking understanding	0.77	1.52 (0.71)	76
Account tasks			
Encourages suspect to give an account	0.65	2.57 (0.84)	90
Development of topics	0.54	2.39 (0.86)	85
Supplies appropriate topic structure	0.82	2.20 (1.06)	68
Appropriate questioning styles	0.85	2.30 (0.94)	79
Intermittent summarising	0.95	1.46 (0.73)	34
Explores motive #	0.91	1.97 (1.02)	–
Explores and probes information	0.75	2.33 (0.85)	83
Displays active listening	0.77	2.45 (0.95)	81
Maintains conversational turn taking	0.82	2.32 (0.54)	84
Closure tasks			
Provides final summary of interview	0.95	1.23 (0.70)	14
Asks if suspects wishes to add or alter anything	0.99	1.83 (0.58)	42
Informs suspects of what happens next	0.91	1.65 (0.99)	39
General behaviours			
Shows equality signs	0.85	3.06 (1.12)	88
Displays calmness	0.85	3.11 (1.01)	83
Displays empathy	0.60	2.45 (0.80)	56

Motive not assessed for presence in entire sample as only applicable in those interviews where a confession occurred.

the assessed competencies and the overall interview score, supplying confidence in the first rater's scores. (Correlations for all ratings were found to be statistically significant at the .05 level.) Interview outcomes were also subjected to the same scrutiny, finding that inter-rater reliability existed at a strong level ($rs = 0.91, p = <0.05$).

Results

The findings will be discussed by initially presenting results concerning the skills found when examining the Engage and Explain phase (before attending to the Account phase) and then proceeding to discuss the findings concerning the Account and Closure phase tasks and their relationship to rapport, before finally discussing overall interview behaviours that encourage rapport.

Rapport building in the Engage and Explain phase

Table 13.2 shows that in this initial interview phase several of the tasks were conducted in each of the interviews (e.g., *providing introductions*, *delivers caution*, and *checks understanding of caution*). However, despite this frequency the majority of tasks to be undertaken were assessed as being below PEACE standard (i.e., below a score of '3'; the exceptions being *providing introductions*, *delivers caution* and *informs suspect of right to tape copy*). It is known that many interviewing officers use a written guide that ensures that the legal requirements are not overlooked and in this regard the guide fulfils its objectives. However, this may also explain why on so many occasions this is undertaken in a rather undistinguished manner, characterised by its standard of ordinariness and expressionless indifference. For example, *delivers caution* was assessed as largely satisfactorily (but no more than that) since, whilst it was spoken at a reasonable pace, the entire caution was always delivered in a single block without interruption (as opposed to checking comprehension after each of its three parts). Further, the caution was thoroughly checked for its understanding on just sixteen per cent of occasions where suspects were asked to state their interpretation of the caution's meaning (and then on every one of these occasions only after the caution had been provided in its entirety). In most of the other instances where the checking of the caution occurred ($N = 99$) any attempts at establishing understanding was limited to the interviewer being satisfied with a 'yes' response. Other tasks believed to assist in greatly helping rapport to develop (such as *explains reason for interview*, and particularly, *explains interview is their opportunity to give an account* and *supplies written guidance, checking understanding*) were each assessed as being conducted by investigators at below PEACE standard on average. Of concern also is that in less than a third of the samples the interviewer advised the suspect of the *routines, roles and route map* of the interview. Thus, regarding rapport building in the Engage and Explain phase, sixty-five per cent ($N = 92$) were assessed as below PEACE standard ($M = 2.19$, $SD = 0.77$, $rs = 0.89, p = <0.05$).

When examining whether there was any association between the overall skill level in rapport building levels of various skills levels in the Engage and Explain phase (skill levels of entire sample; $M = 2.40$, $SD = 0.79$), $rs = 0.82$), it was found that in those sixty-six interviews where the overall rapport skill levels for the phase were at or above PEACE standard, rapport building (overall) was at a mean level of 2.64 ($SD = 0.69$). However, where the standard of the Engage and Explain phase was assessed as below PEACE standard, rapport building was rated at a mean level of 1.77 ($SD = 0.59$). This difference was significant (t (140) = 7.95, $r = 0.56$, $p = < 0.05$). Moreover, there was a significant difference in the time devoted to the Engage and Explain phase in that interviews where rapport building (overall) was at or above PEACE standard ($N = 50$) the average duration was 3.98 minutes ($SD = 0.92$), whereas for those at below PEACE standard this was 2.71 minutes ($SD = 0.88$; t (113) = 8.16, $p = < 0.01$, $r = 0.58$). This difference may well reflect the extra time taken on many of the tasks (i.e., items 1–10 in Table 13.1 above), which were themselves more frequently performed in the interviews assessed at PEACE standard or above.

In this opening interview phase there was a significant difference between those interviews rated at or above PEACE standard overall for rapport (in this phase) ($M = 2.39$, $SD = 0.78$) and those interviews where the rapport rating was below PEACE standard ($M = 2.05$, $SD = 0.73$; t (140) = 2.70, $r = 0.22$, $p = < 0.05$). However, when examining whether there was any association between rapport building in the Engage and Explain phase and the interview outcomes, there was found to be no significant effect. In those interviews with a preferred outcome, rapport was assessed on average in the Engage and Explain phase at 2.27 ($SD = 0.75$), compared to those where the interview result was an unsatisfactory outcome ($M = 2.15$, $SD = 0.78$). Also there was no difference in the duration of the Engage and Explain phase between (i) preferred outcomes ($M = 3.18$, $SD = 1.12$) and (ii) 'not-preferred' outcomes ($M = 3.17$ minutes ($SD = 1.12$).

Rapport maintenance in the Account phase

In this phase, as Table 13.2 depicts, it was found that, despite the regular presence of six of the nine key tasks that help maintain rapport, all of them were conducted at a performance level that was consistently below par (i.e., rated at less than '3'). Two of the tasks (i.e., *exploring the motive* of the suspects where confessions occurred, and *intermittent summarising)* were particularly 'poor'. Indeed, the latter only appeared in a third of the interviews, despite an average duration found in the study of nearly 30 minutes for this Account phase, suggesting that there would be much information received that may well have benefited from periodic recapitulation.

There was found a strong association between rapport quality in this phase and overall interview quality in that those interviews which contained rapport building at or above PEACE standard had a mean assessment of 3.10 ($SD = 0.67$), which is higher than those which contained rapport building at below PEACE standard ($M = 1.83$, $SD = 0.57$, t (139) = 11.98, $r = 0.71$, $p = < 0.01$). In this Account phase (in contrast to the Engage and Explain phase), there was a significant difference in that the mean rapport rating for those interviews with preferred outcomes ($M = 2.89$, $SD = 0.79$) was significantly different from those with 'no-preferred' outcomes

($M = 2.05$, $SD = 0.79$; $t(137) = 6.17$, $r = 0.47$, $p = < 0.01$). Perhaps, unsurprisingly, given these scores, rapport maintenance in the Account phase was rated at a mean score of 2.38 ($SD = 0.88$, $rs = 0.85$, $p = < 0.05$).

Rapport maintenance in the Closure phase

From examination of Table 13.2 it can be seen that the three tasks to be undertaken in this stage were each performed only in a minority of interviews, with the task of providing final summaries being notably absent. To compound this situation, the skill level, where these tasks were conducted, was consistently and considerably sub-standard. The infrequent displays of these tasks, when coupled with the few skilled examples, rendered impossible any statistical analysis relating to effects of differences in assessed rapport skills on other factors. The tendency was to rush through this stage (defined as commencing at the end of the final response from the suspect in the Account phase to the end of the interview). As such, the average duration of this phase was under two minutes, with over eighty per cent lasting less than a minute. Tasks that should be undertaken in the Closure phase might lead to a resumption of the Account phase (e.g., the conducting of final summaries may act as a catalyst for further questioning as opportunities are identified that need further clarification). However, only on one occasion in the present study did this occur.

Rapport building and rapport maintenance

Since it was found that rapport building in the initial interview phase did not necessarily (i) lead either to interviews resulting in preferred outcomes or (ii) significantly contribute to overall interview quality, this led to an analysis to see if there was any relationship between rapport quality in the Engage and Explain phase, and Account phase. Figure 13.1 shows that almost seventy per cent of those who were assessed as requiring further training in rapport building skills in the Engage and Explain phase continued to be at below PEACE standard in the Account phase. Similar findings were also revealed when examining those who were 'unsatisfactory' at rapport construction (i.e., in the Engage and Explain phase) where sixty per cent of those rated at this level when first attempting to develop rapport (i.e., in the Engage and Explain phase) also had similar failings when trying to maintain rapport in the Account phase. On the other hand, Figure 13.1 indicates that 'unsatisfactory' or 'poor' performance in the Engage and Explain phase can be remedied when the Account phase is being conducted. For example, thirty-one per cent of those rated as requiring further training (as they were assessed as 'poor') in rapport building in the Engage and Explain phase were rated as either satisfactory (13%) or skilled in rapport maintenance in the Account phase (18%). Moreover, forty-five per cent of interviewers rated as unsatisfactory in rapport development in the Engage and Explain phase were later assessed as either 'satisfactory' or 'skilled' in the Account phase.

Figure 13.1, conversely, shows that interviewers at or above PEACE standard when building rapport in the Engage and Explain phase can regress in performance standards (i.e., in the Account phase). Forty per cent of those who were rated as

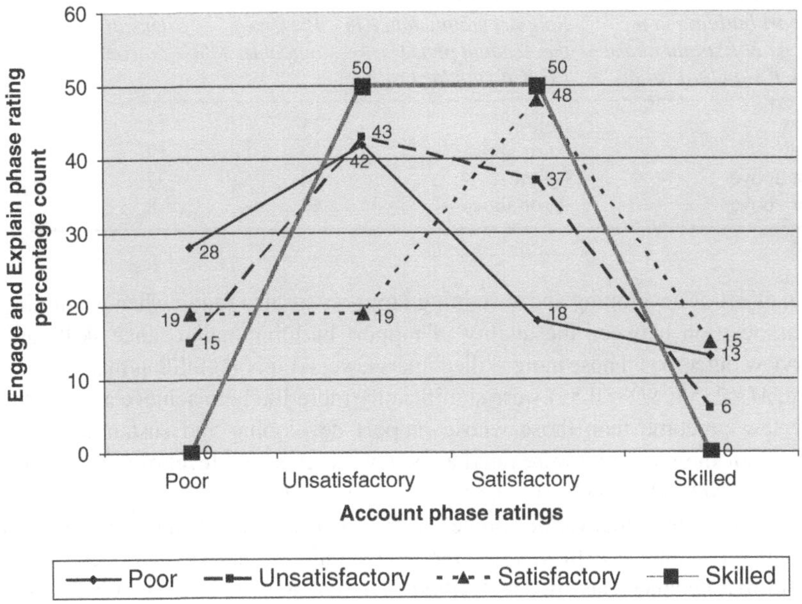

Figure 13.1 Rapport skill ratings in both the Engage and Explain, and the Account, phases.

'satisfactory' in the Engage and Explain phase fell below the minimum acceptable PEACE standard when they should be attempting to maintain rapport later in the Account phase. Moreover, all of those rated as 'skilled' at rapport building in the Engage and Explain phase did not maintain this standard of performance, with half of them being rated as no more than satisfactory and the other half being 'unsatisfactory' at sustaining rapport in the Account phase.

When examining the relationships between either rapport building and rapport maintenance and subsequent interview outcomes, Table 13.3 shows that of the assessed four levels of rapport, those who were rated as at or above PEACE standard of performance in their rapport building skills in the Account phase were, regardless of the quality of rapport building performance in the Engage and Explain phase, three times as likely to achieve either a comprehensive account from suspects or a full and frank confession (i.e., 33% vs. 11%; 42% vs. 14%) than those who were assessed as below minimum acceptable standards.

These findings appear to suggest that rapport maintenance is more strongly associated with the preferred outcomes than is rapport building. However, interviewers rated as at or above PEACE standard in both their rapport building *and* maintenance skills were over five times more likely to obtain satisfactory outcomes (42% vs. 8%). For those interviewers who achieved an 'overall interview' performance rating of at or above PEACE standard their average rapport rating (i.e., across Engage and Explain and Account phases) was found to be $M = 2.75$ (SD 0.46), which is significantly higher than those whose 'overall' performance rating was less than PEACE standard ($M = 1.94$, $SD = 0.51$; $t(137) = 9.64$, $r = 0.64$, $p = < 0.01$).

Table 13.3 Rapport building and maintenance rating & interview outcomes

Rapport building in the Engage & Explain phase PEACE standard rating	*Rapport maintenance in the Account phase PEACE standard rating*	*Preferred outcomes (%)*	*Unsatisfactory outcomes (%)*
Below	Below	11	44
Below	At or above	33	12
At or above	Below	14	37
At or above	At or above	42	8

An effect of developing and sustaining rapport was also found when examining the association between the quality of rapport building/maintenance skills and interview outcomes. Those more skilled interviewers (rapport building/maintenance score; M =2 .58, SD = 0.55) were significantly more likely to achieve a preferred interview outcome than those whose rapport developing and sustaining skills throughout the interview were rated as below the expected level of performance (M = 2.10, SD = 0.61; t (137) = 4.72, r = 0.37, p = <0.01).

Those interviews that yielded higher overall interview skill ratings *and* obtained a preferred outcome were those where rapport building was rated as 'satisfactory' and rapport maintenance classified as 'skilled'. Each of such interviews (N = 20) was also characterised by 'skilled' or 'highly skilled' displays of the general key behaviours (see Table 13.1 above, items 23–25). From Table 13.2 it can be seen that two of these general behaviours (i.e., *showing equality signs* and *displays calmness*), believed to stimulate rapport development in interviews, were on average performed at a level assessed as at least PEACE standard. The exception being *displays empathy* which occurred in only just over half of the sample. This infrequent appearance of empathy contributed to an average assessment that was below acceptable levels of quality (i.e. a score of less than '3').

Discussion

Several studies have pointed out that interviews either prefaced or characterised by good rapport development generally produce fuller accounts from suspects (Clarke & Milne, 2001; Collins et al., 2002; Griffiths & Milne, 2006; Holmberg & Christianson 2002; Walsh & Bull, 2010a). Given the importance of this task, the present study set out to examine how effectively rapport building and maintenance skills were performed, and to determine in the context of benefit fraud interviews, if there is any linkage between interview quality, interview outcome, and rapport building and rapport maintenance. In the following section, after considering the limitations of the study, the results will be discussed.

Limitations and future directions

The present study did not take into account some other factors that may have affected the results such as the (i) personality of the interviewees, (ii) time of day,

(iii) duration since offence, (iv) training background of interviewer, and (v) what might have taken place prior to the interview. In terms of the latter aspect since, in contrast to the police, benefit fraud investigators have no power of arrest or detention this probably reduces the opportunity for prior rapport to occur before the interview (say, between arrest and questioning). In which case, the confounding effects that this previous contact and communication may have on results may well be minimised in the present study.

Individual or demographic factors of interviewers or suspects were also not included, nor were any effects of case characteristics, although benefit frauds in comparison to police investigations are largely homogeneous crimes. However, it is argued that, given the scarcity of knowledge concerning benefit fraud investigative interviews this study represents an initial foray into territory that has largely been ignored. It may also be questioned whether the tasks measured contribute to rapport building and maintenance particularly those relating to the legal requirements. For example, even careful explaining of the caution by investigators may be an inhibitor to building harmonised working relations with its references to, say, 'evidence' and 'court'. However, this did not appear to be the case in the present study. Those most skilled at rapport building who took time to ensure suspects understood their legal requirements were often those who subsequently obtained most co-operation through skilled displays of rapport, particularly when excellent displays of empathy were demonstrated.

Finally, it may be argued that requesting a purposive sample may reflect a distorted view of actual practice. However, it was found that, in comparison to Walsh & Milne's (2008) study, the request for interviews of at least twenty minutes in length meant that the sample contained sufficient material to assess skills more thoroughly regardless of whether the interviews involved either more complex frauds or resistant suspects.

Finally, it is acknowledged that the study concerned one form of crime: benefit fraud. This is a largely a homogeneous type of crime, and it is recommended that further research should therefore examine other types of crime, including more serious crimes.

The Engage and Explain phase

The results of the present study suggest that there is frequently scant attention paid to the necessary skills and tasks required in the opening (i.e., Engage and Explain) interview phase, which combine to aid the construction of rapport. Whilst some interviews did contain 'skilled' rapport building, none were rated as 'highly skilled', Neither does there appear to be sufficient consideration given as to whether suspects understand their rights, with interviewers appearing to attach greater importance to the swift completion of the duties pertaining to legal requirements.

An example of this expeditious approach emerged when examining the attention given by investigators as to whether suspects understood the caution that informs them of their rights. The limited method by which comprehension was generally requested (i.e. by solely asking "Do you understand?") suggests both a hurrying of suspects through this task and an overlooking of the importance (including the legal importance) of suspects having to understand the caution. It would seem that interviewers, by adopting this approach, feel that they have completed another of the 'early' administrative tasks before, what may be seen by these professionals, as starting the interview 'proper' (i.e. the questioning of suspects).

Failing to explain the caution ignores the real possibility that suspects do not comprehend its meaning (Fenner et al., 2002; Clare et al., 1998; Shepherd et al., 1995). It is also argued that by not conducting such explanations an opportunity is missed for interviewer and suspect to work together to develop a shared understanding of its meaning, being a feature of rapport. More specifically, the rarity with which any of the essential rapport tasks in the Engage and Explain phase were performed also seems to demonstrate (i) an apparent lack of awareness of how these tasks help in rapport development, (ii) how much rapport was lacking, and (iii) a lack of awareness of the value of rapport building in encouraging the suspect to talk more freely later in the interview in the Account phase. In short, it is argued that such an approach does not meet Tickle-Degnen & Rosenthal's (1990) three essential criteria of rapport (i.e., mutual attentiveness, positivity and co-ordination).

The account phase

When examining the Account phase stage of the interview, it was often found that key 'Account' stage tasks that may well aid already established rapport to flourish tended to be neglected. For example, regular and intermittent summarising was not apparent in two-thirds of the interviews. Where this task was conducted, performance regularly fell below acceptable standards of expected professionalism. Summarising has been argued to be a key interviewing skill in as much as it provides opportunities to demonstrate a common understanding and active listening that is more likely to encourage further information (Hargie & Dickson, 2004; Milne & Bull, 1999). Rackham (2003) contends that summarising can help highlight any contradictions and gaps in the current account and therefore assist in the development of subsequent questioning strategy. It also allows the interviewer to cognitively rest, helping them to check their own understanding and organise memory for key points for later use (Milne & Bull, 1999; Shepherd, 2007).

Further, an empathic approach by investigators was found to be demonstrated in less than half the interviews. Where it was displayed, it was assessed as consistently below acceptable PEACE standards. This is a concerning finding in the light of an empathic approach being associated with interviews where suspects confess to serious criminal offending (Holmberg & Christianson 2002).

In the specific context of benefit fraud interviews, Walsh & Bull (in press) found, in their survey of the beliefs of benefit fraud investigation professionals, that there was general agreement regarding the importance of rapport, and also acknowledgement of the skills that may contribute to rapport building and (though less clearly identified) rapport maintenance. However, in contrast to these perceptions, what is suggested from the findings of the present study is that attempts to construct rapport in practice are typified by investigators apparently overlooking that the Engage and Explain phase presents opportunities to build rapport. Rather this phase seems to be viewed as an administrative exercise, only necessary to fulfil certain legal requirements before interviewers quickly turn to questioning suspects. The inattention to the necessary tasks and the briskness taken to conduct the Engage and Explain phase in the lesser skilled interviews was repeated in the Closure phase.

Concluding thoughts

Griffiths (2008) has argued that skilled interviewing should not just be assessed by the achievement of confessions but that it can equally occur in interviews where denials are robustly scrutinised by the interviewers. In recognition of this viewpoint, the present study found that skilled rapport behaviours in both the Engage and Explain, and the Account phases are more strongly associated with 'skilled' interviewing and preferred outcomes (where, if a full confession is not received, the suspect's story is examined thoroughly). However, the present study also found that it was not always the case that rapport built in the initial phase led to rapport quality in the Account phase, and in turn, to those preferred outcomes and overall good interviewing standards.

This study found that rapport can be 'lost' if tasks that sustain it are not conducted or are not attended with the required level of professionalism. This finding may well reflect that the various tasks conducted in the Account phase are more demanding (Griffiths, 2008). On the other hand, if rapport building is mediocre initially, it can be remedied in the Account phase if 'skilled' rapport is developed therein. Effective interviewing is defined in the present study as those interviews possessing a high level of skills continuously displayed throughout the interview, resulting in the preferred outcomes of a fairly elicited, but rigorously tested, comprehensive account or a full and frank confession. The present study found that effective interviewing is most likely to occur when rapport is skilfully built and then, as importantly, skilfully maintained.

References

Baldwin, J. (1993). Police interview techniques: Establishing truth or proof? *British Journal of Criminology*, *33*, 325–351.

Bernieri, F., & Gillis, J. (2001). Judging rapport: Employing Brunswik's lens model to study interpersonal insensitivity. In J. A. Hall, & F. J. Bernieri (Eds.), *Interpersonal sensitivity: theory and measurement* (pp. 67–88). Mahwah, NJ: Lawrence Erlbaum.

Bernieri, F., Davis, J., Rosenthal, R., & Knee, C. (1994). Interactional synchrony and rapport: Measuring synchrony in displays of sound and facial affect. *Personality and Social Psychology Bulletin*, *20*, 303–311.

Bull, R., & Cherryman, J. (1996). *Helping to identify skills gaps in specialist investigative interviewing*. London: Home Office Police Department.

Clarke, C., & Milne, R. (2001). *National evaluation of the PEACE investigative interviewing course*. Police Research Award Scheme Report No. PRAS/149. London: Home Office.

Clare, I. C. H., Gudjonsson, G, H., & Harari, P. M. (1998). Understanding of the current police caution (England and Wales). *Journal of Community & Applied Social Psychology*, *8*, 323–329.

Collins, R., Lincoln, R., & Frank, M. G. (2002). The effect of rapport in forensic interviewing. *Psychiatry, Psychology and Law*, *9*, 69–78.

Colwell, K., Hiscock, C.K., & Memon, A. (2002). Interviewing techniques and the assessment of statement credibility. *Applied Cognitive Psychology*, *16*, 287–300.

Colwell, K., Hiscock-Anisman, C. K., Memon, A., Taylor, L., & Prewett, J. (2007). Assessment Criteria Indicative of Deception (ACID): An integrated system of investigative interviewing and detecting deception. *Journal of Investigative Psychology and Offender Profiling*, *4*(3), 167–180.

Cramer, D., & Howitt, D. (2004). *The Sage dictionary of statistics*. London: Sage.

Fenner, S., Gudjonsson, G. H., & Clare, I. C. H. (2002). Understanding of the current police caution (England and Wales) among suspects in police detention. *Journal of Community & Applied Social Psychology*, *12*, 83–93.

Geiselman, R. E., Fisher, R. P., Firstenberg, I., Hutton, L. A., Sullivan, S. J., Avetissian, I. V., & Prosk, A. L. (1984). Enhancement of eyewitness memory: An empirical evaluation of the cognitive interview. *Journal of Police Science Administration*, *12*, 74–80.

Griffiths, A. (2008). *An examination into the efficacy of police advanced investigative interview training?* Unpublished PhD thesis. University of Portsmouth.

Griffiths, A., & Milne, R. (2006). Will it all end in tiers? Police interviews with suspects in Britain. In T. Williamson (Ed.), *Investigative interviewing: Rights, research and regulation* (pp. 167–189). Cullompton: Willan.

Hargie, O., & Dickson, D. (2004). *Skilled interpersonal communication*. London: Routledge.

Hendrick, C. (1990). The nature of rapport. *Psychological Inquiry*, *4*, 312–315.

Holmberg, U., & Christianson, S. (2002). Murderers' and sexual offenders' experiences of police interviews and their inclination to admit or deny crimes. *Behavioral Sciences & Law*, *20*, 31–45.

Home Office. (2006). *Police and criminal evidence act 1984: Codes of practice A–G*. London: Stationery Office.

McGurk, B. J., Carr, M. J., & McGurk, D. (1993). *Investigative interviewing courses for police officers: An evaluation*. Police Research Group Paper No. 4, London: Home Office.

Milne, R., & Bull, R. (1999). *Investigative interviewing: Psychology and practice*. Chichester: Wiley.

Moston, S., Stephenson, G. M., & Williamson, T. (1992). The effects of case characteristics on suspect behaviour during police questioning. *British Journal of Criminology*, *32*, 23–40.

National Crime Faculty. (2000). *A practical guide to investigative interviewing*. National Police Training College: Bramshill.

Ord, B., & Shaw, G. (1999). *Investigative interviewing explained: The operational guide to practical interviewing skills*. Woking: New Police Bookshop.

Oxburgh, G., Ost, J., & Cherryman, J. (2010). Police interviews with suspected child sex offenders: Does use of empathy and question type influence the amount of investigation relevant information obtained? *Psychology, Crime & Law*, *18*(3), 259–273.

Rackham, N. (2003). The behavior of successful negotiators. In R. Lewicki, D. Saunders, J. Minton, & B. Barry (Eds.), *Negotiation: Readings, exercises and cases* (pp. 169–181). New York, NY: McGraw-Hill.

Rock, F. (2007). *Communicating rights*. London: Palgrave Macmillan.

Shawyer, A. (2009). *Investigative interviewing: Interviewing counter fraud and deception.* Unpublished PhD thesis, University of Portsmouth.

Shawyer, A., & Milne, R. (2006). *Investigative interviewing and fraud.* Presented paper at the Second International Investigative Interviewing Conference. Portsmouth, July.

Shepherd, E. (2007). *Investigative interviewing: The conversation management approach.* Oxford: Oxford University Press.

Shepherd, E. W., Mortimer, A. K. O., & Mobasheri, R. (1995). The police caution: Comprehension and perceptions in the general population. *Expert Evidence, 4*, 60–67.

St Yves, M. (2006). The psychology of rapport: Five basic rules. In T. Williamson (Ed.), *Investigative interviewing: Rights, research and regulation* (pp. 167–189). Cullompton: Willan.

Tickle-Degnen, L., & Rosenthal, R. (1990). The nature of rapport and its nonverbal correlates. *Psychological Inquiry, 4*, 285–293.

Walsh, D. W., & Bull, R. H. (2010a). Interviewing suspects of fraud: An analysis of interviewing skills. *Journal of Psychiatry & Law, 38*, 99–135.

Walsh, D. W., & Bull, R. H. (2010b). What really is effective in interviews with suspects? A study comparing interview skills against interview outcomes. *Legal and Criminological Psychology, 15*, 305–321.

Walsh, D. W., & Bull, R. H. (in press). Evaluating investigative interviews effectively? A study of professionals' perceptions, attitudes and beliefs. *Social Psychology Review.*

Walsh, D. W., & Milne, R. (2008). Keeping the PEACE? An analysis of the taped interview performance of benefit fraud investigators within the DWP. *Legal and Criminological Psychology, 13*, 39–57.

14 Police strategies and suspect responses in real-life serious crime interviews

Samantha Leahy-Harland and Ray Bull

Introduction

Over 25 years ago, the Police and Criminal Evidence Act (1984) (PACE) introduced in England and Wales legislation governing, among other things, the interviewing of suspects. PACE had been the result of the Royal Commission on Criminal Procedure that arose in response to false confessions obtained from youths in a murder and arson case (Fisher 1977, cited in Milne & Bull, 1999). PACE Code C (Home Office, 2008, p. 38) consequently stated that 'no interviewer may try to obtain answers or elicit a statement by the use of oppression'.

A significant development arising from PACE was the introduction in the mid-1980s of a statutory requirement to provide audio recordings of all interviews with persons suspected of being involved in a criminal offence (Home Office, 2010). What really went on in the interview room was finally (possibly) open to wider scrutiny and something which a limited number of researchers were able to take advantage of. As Cherryman (1999) commented, 'an interest in the topic of investigative interviewing had been sparked' (p. 16), and research commenced relatively quickly after implementation of the new laws and procedures.

Despite the advances of PACE, oppressive interviewing and false confessions still persisted (e.g. 'the Birmingham Six') to an extent. This led to another Royal Commission in 1991 (on Criminal Justice) that was charged with examining the effectiveness of the criminal justice system in securing the convictions of the guilty and the acquittal of the innocent. A new code of practice published in the following year set out the new 'Principles of Investigative Interviewing' (Home Office, 1992), which included that:

- The role of the police is to obtain accurate information from suspects.
- Interviews should be approached with an open mind.
- Information obtained from the person who is being interviewed should always be tested against what the investigator already knows (this implying that suspects should not be told at the beginning about all of the relevant information).
- The interviewing officer need not accept the first answer given.
- Even when the suspect exercises the right to silence, the interviewer still has a right to ask questions in order to try and establish the truth (so long as the questions are relevant and not repetitive).

Williamson (1993) described this as the start of attempts to promote confidence in the concept of 'investigative interviewing', the purpose of which was 'to obtain accurate and reliable information from suspects, witness or victims to discover the truth about matters under police investigation' (p. 98). This ethos is in marked contrast to the previous overreliance on confessions.

The principles of investigative interviewing described in the Home Office circular of 1992 were developed into a standardised framework for ethical interviewing known as PEACE (Shawyer, Milne, & Bull, 2009) and endorsed by a later Home Office circular in 1993. PEACE describes the five key stages of an investigative interview: planning and preparation, engage and explain, account, closure and evaluate, and was informed by psychological principles and theories and by effective police practice (Milne & Bull, 1999). Two booklets were issued to all police officers (n = 127,000) describing the new model, followed by a national training effort where all police officers in England and Wales were subsequently trained in the model over a number of years. The essential principles of PEACE are related to fairness and openness, encouraging interviewers to avoid assumptions of guilt, to keep an open mind, and to seek the truth (Shawyer et al., 2009). The model encourages effective planning prior to the interview, and using open questions, active listening, and rapport building.

The 'tactics' or strategies encouraged by the PEACE model are in contrast to those of the 'Reid Technique' (Buckley, 2006)—a popular interviewing technique used extensively in the USA (Leo, 1996). The Reid Technique originated when Inbau and Reid published a manual that described a set of tactics to be used by interviewers (or interrogators as they called them) with suspects whose guilt interrogators believed to be certain. It comprises a two-stage process involving (i) an interview to (try to) determine if suspects were lying, and (ii) if the interviewer decided that the suspect was lying, then a nine-step interrogation was undertaken.

Although the use of many elements advocated in the Reid Technique appears to be fairly widespread in the USA (Kassin et al., 2007; Reppucci, Meyer, & Kostelnik, 2010), the model (and others like it) have been widely criticised by both academics and practitioners in the UK, as well as by those in North America (Zimbardo, 1967; Meissner, Russano, & Narchet, 2010; Yeschke, 2003). For example, Snook, Eastwood, Stinson, Tedeschini, & House (2010) summarised three key concerns with the Reid Technique: first, that police officers do not have the ability to detect deception at greater than chance levels and, in any case, tend to be more biased towards a judgement of guilt than non-police officers; second, they pointed out the lack of empirical research evidence to support claims of effectiveness; and, third, many of the techniques advocated in the model are overly coercive in nature, and risk persuading people 'both innocent and guilty, to provide information that they would not normally give freely' (p. 219).

Kassin & McNall (1991) suggested that the approaches recommended by Inbau and colleagues could be distinguished into two main types, maximisation and minimisation, both of which, they hypothesised, might well lead to innocent people confessing to crimes they did not commit. They described maximisation as where the interviewer tries to frighten the suspect into a confession by exaggerating the strength of the evidence, the magnitude of the charges, and the likely negative consequences of the case going to a full trial, and minimisation as where the interviewer lulls the suspect into a false sense of security by mitigating the crime, making excuses for the suspect, or blaming the victim. As a consequence of PACE and with the introduction of PEACE, at least in the UK, the drive for achieving a confession has been replaced with a search for the truth, and later studies post-PACE have found little evidence of such manipulative or coercive 'Reid-like' tactics (Baldwin, 1992; Moston & Engleberg, 1993), a finding reinforced by more recent studies by Bull & Soukara (2010) and Soukara, Bull, Vrij, Turner, & Cherryman (2009).

In contrast to the kind of tactics endorsed in techniques like the Reid model, PEACE focuses instead on developing officers' abilities to employ a number of specific skills including engaging a suspect in conversation by introducing all those present and explaining the purpose and format of the interview, appropriate use of questions, obtaining an initial account for subsequent exploration in a structured manner, and closing the interview (Clarke, Milne, & Bull, 2011). As explained above, since PACE, there have been a number of studies examining the usage, effectiveness, and impact of the techniques and strategies used by police interviewers, including those included within the PEACE model (e.g. Clarke & Milne, 2001; Soukara, Bull, & Vrij, 2002; and Griffiths & Milne, 2006).

For example, the importance of developing rapport (during the 'engage and explain' phase of PEACE) was emphasised in the National Crime Faculty's (1996) document on investigative interviewing. This warned police officers against using stereotypical information such as culture, clothing and speech in responding to the interviewee; it recommended instead that empathy should be used where appropriate and an interest in the individual's circumstances should be shown in order to provide an environment in which the suspect would feel free to talk. Although McGurk, Carr, & McGurk (1993) found that interviewing officers rated rapport building as the fourth most important interviewer skill, Moston & Engleberg (1993) found that it was rare to find evidence of rapport building at the beginning of interviews, a finding echoed by Clarke & Milne (2001). Milne & Bull (1999) suggest that this might be due to the fact that, since PACE, some legal advisors challenge the relevance of such 'chat' (p. 162). However, Walsh & Bull (2012) found good use of rapport to be associated with substantial information gain from suspects.

With regard to the issue of empathy, Oxburgh & Ost (2011) argued that the national guidance on using empathy was unclear and incomplete. They highlight, for example, that the Achieving Best Evidence Guidelines (Ministry of Justice, 2011) associate sympathy with empathy, but this guidance does not explain what empathy is (and how it differs from sympathy) and nor does it explain how to communicate empathy. Oxburgh, Myklebust, & Grant (2010a), Oxburgh, Ost, & Cherryman (2010b) examined the use of empathy in transcripts of 20 real-life interviews with suspected child sex offenders and found that empathy was not widely present.

A central feature of PEACE is that suspects should initially be given the opportunity to provide a full account of what happened. In a preliminary study of around

400 audio-taped suspect interviews (carried out with the Metropolitan Police), Moston & Engleberg (1993) identified that most interviewers typically began an interview by adopting an information gathering (inquisitorial) strategy and few a confession (accusatorial) strategy. In a related study, Stephenson & Moston (1994) examined over 1000 audio-recorded suspect interviews and reported that, in contrast to the 1993 study, in many cases, the suspect was confronted with the accusation against them at the very outset of questioning with no attempt to establish rapport or invite the suspect to give an alternative version of events. Similar findings were observed by Leo (1996) who sat in on 122 interviews (involving 45 detectives) in one police department in the USA and watched video recordings of a further 60 interviews conducted by two other police organisations. He found that detectives usually began by confronting the suspects with evidence suggesting their guilt, using true evidence (observed in 85 % of interviews) and also, more worryingly, false evidence (observed in 30 % of interviews).

It should be emphasised that both of these UK-based studies (Moston & Engelberg and Stephenson & Moston) analysed interviews conducted in the late 1980s, after PACE but before PEACE had been launched. A later evaluation of PEACE by Clarke & Milne (2001) found that although officers' interviewing skills seemed to have improved by that time, a number of problems still persisted. They rated 14 separate behaviours during the account phase and found that 'encouraging an account', 'keep to relevant topic', 'deals with difficulty' and 'structure and sequence' were rated at above the median level (deemed as showing adequate skill). However, a number of skills were found to be less than adequate, namely: 'exploring account', 'topic development', 'using summaries and links', and a technique called 'conversation management'. Whilst this suggests an improvement in the account phase of the interview over that observed by Moston and Engelberg, skill levels were still less than ideal.

PEACE advocates that the suspect is invited to provide a full and uninterrupted account (which might include introducing evidence) before any challenges are made. Dando & Bull (2011) tested an alternative information-gathering technique which involved revealing information (both incriminating and otherwise) at appropriate times throughout the questioning stage, as opposed to revealing all of the evidence at the beginning or end of an interview. Results revealed that the gradual release of information at opportune moments during the interview enhanced the ability to detect those suspects who were telling the truth and those who were lying (also see Dando, Bull, Ormerod, & Sandham, 2015).

The presentation of evidence as a means of challenge has intuitive appeal, but few studies have looked in any depth at the different ways in which interviewers challenge suspects. Although a study by Alison, Kebbell, & Leung (2008) found that Hong Kong officers rated 'pointing out inconsistencies' as the most important interviewing tactic in serious crime interviews, Hakkanen, Ask, Kebbell, Alison, & Granhag (2009) claim that most previous research has shown that investigators often fail to challenge suspects at all. They cited Baldwin (1993) who found that no challenge was made by the interviewers in almost 40 % of the late 1980s cases and Moston, Stephenson, & Williamson (1992) who also found an inability of officers to effectively challenge suspects. A later study by Pearse & Gudjonsson (1996) did examine use of challenges and found that challenging a lie or an inconsistency was present in around a fifth of cases but that other challenges occurred less frequently. More recently, a study by Soukara et al. (2009) examined the use of challenge in police interviews with suspects and found that 'emphasising contradictions', 'challenging the suspect's account' and 'positive confrontation' were found in at least half of the 80 suspect interviews they analysed, with 'emphasising contradictions' and 'challenging the suspect's account' being among the most common tactics used in confession interviews. Further analysis revealed, however, that these two types of challenge were actually used more in interviews where there was *less* of a shift from denial to admission. They reflected that this finding should not have been entirely unexpected as interviewers may well persist in the use of tactics with suspects who continue to deny (rather than with those who confess).

Oxburgh et al. (2010a, 2010b) state that the key principle underpinning the numerous interviewing guidance documents is 'for interviewers to gain as much detailed information as possible from the interviewee using effective, non-coercive questioning techniques' (p. 45). Oxburgh et al. (2010a, 2010b) presented a thorough review of the psychological and linguistic literature on question types, as they apply to police interviews. They found that open information-seeking questions are the most productive in terms of gaining detailed responses from the interviewee. The notion that poor questioning can lead to distorted responses and potentially false confessions is well documented (Milne & Bull, 1999; Gudjonsson, 2003; Kassin, 1997), and inappropriate or unproductive question types have been defined as including forced choice, leading and multiple questions (Milne & Bull, 1999), complex questions (Shawyer & Walsh, 2007) and opinion or statement questions (Griffiths & Milne, 2006).

Beyond the type of questions asked, a growing amount of research has focused on the potential influence of different interviewer strategies or tactics on the suspect's likelihood of confession. For example, Bull & Soukara (2010) in 2003 identified 40 interviews from their sample of 200 in which a confession occurred, although not at the start of the interview, and analysed the occurrence and timing of 17 interviewer tactics relative to the timing of the shift to admission/confession. Bull and Soukara found that seven out of the 17 interviewer tactics under observation were used in the minutes prior to a shift, and that the tactics of minimisation and maximisation were never used at any point. They suggested that confessing might be considered to be influenced by the tactics used in the preceding 15 min, and found the following tactics to be the most frequently used during this time (in order of highest to lowest frequency): disclosure of evidence, open questions, repetitive questions, followed by leading questions, handling suspect's mood, pointing out contradictions and positive contradictions. Bull and Soukara suggest that the tactics of disclosure of evidence, open questions and repetitive questions *may* to some extent influence the suspects' decision to confess; however, the authors make clear that as these tactics also occur in several different time slots during the interview (not just in the time preceding the confession), this timing may have been coincidental.

Kelly, Miller, & Redlich (2015) analysed 29 suspect interviews in which the suspect initially denied their guilt or complicity, comparing tactics used in those interviews that ended with a confession and those that did not. They found that *rapport and relationship building* was more commonly observed at the outset of the interview, decreasing towards the middle, and increasing by the end. In contrast, *emotion provocation* and *presentation of evidence* increased from the beginning of the interview to the middle and then decreased again. They also observed a slight linear increase in the use of *confrontation/competition* throughout the stages of the interview. When comparing those interviews with suspects who denied against those who offered full or partial confessions, Kelly et al. found that the levels of *rapport and relationship building* were similar across both samples. They observed low levels of *confrontation/competition* in the confession sample, in contrast to the increasing emphasis of this found in the denial sample. *Presentation of evidence* in the denial sample was observed more frequently at each stage of the interview in comparison to the equivalent stages in the confession sample. The authors suggest that the more subtle *presentation of evidence* evident in the confession sample (in contrast to the almost immediate presentation of evidence in the denial sample) may be a more effective tactic in eliciting confessions.

Walsh & Bull (2010) compared both the quality and frequency of tactics used and whether the suspect confessed or not. Their findings suggested it was not only the frequency of tactics that were related to whether a suspect confessed but also how well those tactics were used. For example, they found that disclosure of evidence and regular summarising (when used well and often) were linked with a shift from denial to admission. The authors concluded that it is insufficient just to consider what interviewers do in an interview, but that what is important is how *skilfully* and *regularly* they undertake certain tactics.

Although many studies focus on the link between tactic use and confessions, a study by Leo (1996) looked beyond whether the suspect confessed or not, to include whether the suspect provided incriminating information during the interview. He found that in around two thirds of the interviews, suspects revealed some kind of incriminating evidence (which included unintentional provision of information as well as a partial or full confession). The only factors that he found to be associated with such revelations were interview length and the number of tactics used; this led him to conclude 'that the effort and energy expended by officers is one of the most important factors in explaining successful interrogation outcomes' (p. 262). Leo also explored whether different tactics were linked to the suspect providing incriminating information and found significant associations for identifying contradictions (91 % of the interrogations in which this tactic was used), offering the suspect a moral justification or psychological excuse (90 %), praise/flattery (91 %) and appealing to the suspect's conscience (97 %).

From the overview of the literature presented above, it is clear that in the UK substantial attempts have been made to modernise the interviewing of suspects via guidance and training. However, rather few studies have yet been published on the extent to which interviewers are able to put such guidance/training into practice, especially in serious cases like murders. Equally, much of the research literature that has examined particular interviewing strategies has tended to focus solely on the association of these strategies with whether the suspect confessed or not. Specifically, the present study examines (i) the association between the strategies and questions used by police interviewers and the suspects' response and (ii) how serious crime suspects respond during a police interview.

Method

Data were obtained from recordings of real-life serious crime suspect interviews (along with associated case details). Due to the nature of the required sample and the associated difficulties with gaining access to the information, a truly randomised sample selection process (or other form of probability sampling) was not considered feasible. Instead, a mix of purposive (homogeneous) and convenience sampling methods was adopted.

The Association of Chief Police Officers (ACPO, now called the National Police Chiefs' Council) was/is an independent, professionally led strategic body which, in partnership with the government and other public bodies, leads and coordinates the direction and development of the police service in England, Wales and Northern Ireland. The ACPO Homicide Working Group and ACPO Investigative Interviewing Working Group were at the time of this research made up predominantly of senior-level police personnel along with some government and academic membership. The first author was a research representative for the Home Office (the government department responsible for policing) on both groups. Initial contact was subsequently made with both groups to request participation from police forces. Each participating force was asked for:

- audio copies of interviews with serious crime suspects from closed cases (these are considered solved by the police although this does not necessarily mean a conviction has been achieved) that had occurred in the last five years (which at the time of data collection included interviews from 2000 onwards);
- written plans or strategies prepared for the interviews;
- brief case details.

Before moving on to describe how the information was obtained, it is important to set out the definition of an *interview* used in the present study. In serious crime cases, it is very unlikely that a suspect is interviewed on only a single occasion. In part, this is dictated by the complexity of such cases: even where the suspect might admit the offence, the police still need to gather a vast amount of information to support any prosecution. Suspects also have certain rights including entitlements to breaks and rest periods. Additionally, interviewers themselves might purposefully plan to break an interview after certain topics have been covered to allow further enquiries to be made.

Most interviews of serious crime suspects therefore run over several days (and in some cases even months). Identifying though where one interview started and another ended was not straightforward. This was in a large part due to the practice of analogue audio-taping, which means that a period of questioning *has* to come to an end after 45 min (the maximum tape length). Within this 45-min period, however, a number of different scenarios can emerge:

- Questioning can be concluded early (say 20 min into the taping period) as all the relevant topics have been covered.
- Questioning could be suspended at the request of the legal advisor or suspect.
- Questioning may run to the end of the tape; new tapes are then inserted and the questioning is continued immediately.
- Questioning may continue for the full 45 min at which point it is decided to use the tape change as a natural break point, even though more questions on a similar topic may need to be asked later.

Due to the range of different potential scenarios, it was not possible to definitively say when one interview of a suspect started and another with him/her ended. For these reasons, the present study defines a single *interview* as a single audio tape, which in some instances might be only 5 min long or alternatively the full 45 min.

It is acknowledged that whilst there may be some inherent limitations in defining a single interview in this way, the practical reality of how police interviews are conducted within the UK offers some mitigation to these limitations. First, PACE dictates that a number of activities must occur at the start of each interview (e.g. introduction of persons present, date and time, caution given, right to legal advice, etc.). In the current sample of interviews, it was found that the caution, introductions and the time, date and location of the interview were provided in the vast majority of interviews, that is, at the start of each individual taped interview. Consequently, even if the interview carried on immediately after the end of the previous 45-min interview, formalities are required at the beginning of the next tape thereby arguably providing some 'distinctiveness' to each interview.

Furthermore, due to the analogue tape recording procedure used in the current sample, interviews could not last longer than around 45 min. In fact, the mean duration ($N = 407$) in the present sample was 30 min indicating that the majority of interviews were deliberately brought to a close before the end of the 45-min tape. This finding is not unexpected as PEACE and advanced interviewing techniques place great emphasis on the planning and preparation stage of the interviewing process (Soukara et al., 2002). A key feature of this planning phase is to identify discrete topics of questioning and to deploy gradual disclosure of evidence and information (Dando & Bull, 2011). Interviewing officers may therefore deliberately want to put a connected series of questions to the interviewee and then break, whilst further investigations are made and/or so the interviewing strategy can be reviewed and refreshed depending on the information provided.

Also, given the nature of the interviews in the present sample—serious crimes—the total interviewing time is considerably longer than found in other studies (Baldwin, 1993; Bull & Cherryman, 1996). So, although the mean duration of single interviews in the present study was 30 min, when the total time each suspect was interviewed was calculated, the mean duration was 3 h and

44 min. The shortest total length of interviewing for an individual suspect was 35 min and the longest was 15 h and 12 min. Inevitably, therefore, interviews in the present sample did not always occur on the same day; in fact, in some cases, the interviewing took place over several weeks. Consequently, many interviews in this sample could not be considered 'continuous' in a chronological sense.

The practical reality of the interviewing presented above, together with the mean duration of interviews in the present sample, led to the decision that each individual interview could reasonably, methodologically speaking, be treated as 'independent' of other interviews with the same suspect. Whilst the issue of independence should not affect the validity of the majority of the findings presented in this paper, it is nevertheless acknowledged that this might be more problematic when comparing strategies and question type across time segments. Readers are therefore reminded that the comparisons across time segments refer to *individual tapes* (which in the majority of cases in the present sample would be one of many interviews conducted with a single suspect but often on different topics). Consequently, readers are asked to be cautious when interpreting these results, as the findings may not be replicated if all interviews of the same suspect were analysed as a continuous 'single' interview.

Sample characteristics

A total of 407 such tape recordings were obtained from ten forces across England (representing a mix of urban and rural forces) and one force from Wales (including a mix of rural and urban areas). All interviews took place between 1999[1] and 2006, with the majority (76 %, $n = 309$) occurring between 2004 and 2006 inclusive. In these, a total of 56 different suspects were interviewed representing 45 different cases. Of these 45 cases, 41 involved a single victim (91 %), three involved two victims (7 %), and one case involved four victims (2 %).

The majority of suspects were interviewed for the offence of murder (82 %, $n = 46$), with a further three suspects for attempted murder. Three suspects were interviewed for a serious sexual offence and four for a serious assault. The majority of interviewers were male: 82 % of both primary ($n = 333$) and secondary interviewers[2] ($n = 335$). Similarly, the majority of suspects were also male (95 %, $n = 53$). The mean age of suspects was 32 years ($n = 55$), with the youngest person interviewed aged 16 and the oldest 67.

Analysing the interviews

To enable the systematic capture of the required information, it was decided that content analysis would be employed. Content analysis was used to measure a number of predefined characteristics of suspect interviews which were broken down into 5-min time segments. A coding frame was then developed in two stages. First, an initial coding frame was created that drew upon previous research involving the analysis of police interviews (Baldwin, 1992; McGurk et al., 1993; Moston & Engleberg, 1993; Cherryman, 1999; Pearse & Gudjonsson, 1999;

Table 14.1 Coding frame

Theme	*Code*
Question style	Closed Open Closed with element of open Closed-open Negative (open or closed) Multiple choice/option (open, closed, negative, repeated or statement) Statement Repetitive (open, closed, negative or statement) Ineffective
Strategy	Building rapport/showing empathy Use of silence Suspect's interest to talk Situational futility Interviewer explicitly asks suspect to tell truth/give their account of what happened Emphasising seriousness of offence Special warning (or similar) provided Showing the suspect photographs of the crime scene/victim Describing the victim's trauma and/or the family's trauma or emphasising the severity of injuries Minimisation Maximisation Describing evidence and what has happened Challenging the suspect
Conversation characteristics	Interruptions by the interviewer Interruptions by the suspect Overlapping talk
Suspect response (Only one of these codes could be selected during a single exchange)	Relevant No comment Silent Challenging Unclear/complex
Suspect behaviour (A single exchange could have any of these features)	Suspect sounds upset Suspect interrupted Suspect sounds frustrated Suspect laughed
Suspect admission (Only one of these codes could be selected during a single exchange)	Full admission Partial admission Denial

Clarke & Milne, 2001; Griffiths & Milne, 2006; Oxburgh et al., 2010a, 2010b). In addition, the relevant literature on discourse and conversation analysis was also considered (e.g. Schegloff, 2000; Schegloff & Sacks, 1973; Heydon, 2011). The coding frame used in the present study therefore drew on the coding frames used in previous research, although it did not replicate any single one in its entirety. For example, the coding frame used by Moston & Engleberg (1993), whilst lacking in detail in terms of how the interviews were assessed, some of the strategies, like direct accusations or evidence strategy, were adapted for use in the present coding frame. The study of Pearse & Gudjonsson (1999) examined real-life interview data from 18 serious criminal cases and the study identified 39 interviewing tactics, the majority of which were included in the initial stages of the development of the coding frame in the present study. In particular, following Pearse and Gudjonsson, interviews were also broken down into 5-min time segments. The rating scale used by Clarke & Milne (2001) did not include an examination of the suspect response, and since its focus was on assessing the *overall* quality of interviewer behaviour rather than on analysing the minutiae of *individual* exchanges between suspect and interviewer, the rating scale approach was not adopted in the present study. However, a large number of the criteria used in their rating scale (e.g. elements in the engage and explain section, interviewer characteristics and so on) were adopted for use.

The subsequent coding frame that was developed was then tested against a large sample of interview tapes (n = 100) and further refined. The coding frame went through a number of iterations during this stage, and the final list of codes included is shown in Table 14.1. The approach to coding was to mark the presence or absence of each code (making no judgement on quality) within each 5-min segment.

Once the coding frame was established, the second stage involved carrying out inter-rater and intra-rater reliability checks on 50 taped interviews. Both percentage agreement and Cohen's kappa were applied to the data. As might be expected, generally stronger agreement was found for intra-rater reliability than inter-rater reliability across all codes. Following Banerjee's (1999, cited in Neuendorf, 2002) guidelines, the majority of codes show acceptable levels of agreement, beyond what would have been expected by chance. The exception was the code *explains routine*, which showed poor inter-rater agreement; findings concerning this code should therefore be treated with caution. There were a number of codes (*explains grounds for arrest*, *explains purpose of interview*, *open question*, *closed question with open elements*, *statement question*, *overlapping talk* and *building rapport/ showing empathy*) which had higher but nevertheless still moderate results (under 0.75), and again, some caution is recommended when interpreting the findings associated with these codes.

Results

Suspect response

How serious crime suspects responded during these interviews was categorised as either a *relevant response*, *silence*, *no comment*, *challenging response* or *unclear/ complex response.* Analysis of all the interview tapes revealed that *relevant responses* were found to be the most frequent suspect response (a mean frequency of 76 occurrences per interview tape) with *no comment* the second most frequent, occurring on average 21 times per interview. On average, *relevant responses* were significantly more frequent ($M = 76.18$, Mdn $= 67.00$) than *no comment* ($M = 21.00$, Mdn $= 0.00$), $Z = -10.98$, $p < 0.001$. It was rare for the suspect to *challenge* the interviewer or for the suspect to answer in an *unclear or irrelevant manner. Complete silence* was also quite rare with a mean frequency of six occurrences per interview.

It was also recorded whether the suspect admitted or denied the offence ($N = 56$). It was far more common for suspects to deny the offence (64 % of suspects) than admit to it (23 % of suspects made some kind of admission, with only 7 % of these making a full admission). Only a small proportion (13 %) of suspects neither admitted nor denied, which in practice reflected either no comment or silence in response to accusations. It should be noted that a denial also included those interviews where the suspect stayed silent or made no comment but made denials via a prepared statement in interview (which either they or their legal advisor read out). It is important to highlight that *none* of the 56 suspects included in the present study changed their position from denial to admission. Nevertheless, 49 suspects were subsequently convicted (for the remaining seven, it was not possible to determine the outcome).

The pattern of strategies and question types

In terms of analysing the pattern of strategies and questions used by police interviewers, a total of 15 different strategies and 9 question types were coded for.

Strategy use This revealed that *presentation of evidence* was the most frequent strategy, by a considerable margin, occurring on average 21 times during each tape ($M = 21.41$, SD $= 16.28$). *Challenge* was the second most frequent, occurring on average around five times per tape ($M = 21.41$, SD $= 16.28$), with *explicitly asks for an account* being the third most frequently used strategy ($M = 0.83$, SD $= 1.51$).

Although evidence of rapport building was, overall, quite rare, further analysis revealed that *rapport/empathy* was significantly more frequent in the initial stages of the interview tape (the first 15 min) ($M = 0.37$) compared to the next 15 min (i.e. the middle of the interview tape) ($M = 0.26$), $Z = 2.94$, $p < 0.01$. *Minimisation* and *maximisation* were extremely rare, with only one incidence of maximisation (and none of minimisation) being observed across all interview tapes.

The mean frequency of strategy use across time segments was explored for two of the more frequent strategies: *presentation of evidence* and *challenge.* For *presentation of evidence,* there was a broadly consistent frequency across time segments, demonstrating a gradual presentation. The pattern for the strategy of *challenge* was different, with the mean frequency of challenges increasing as the interview progressed, peaking in time segments seven and eight, and then falling again in the final time segment of the interview tape. The difference in *challenges* between time segments seven ($M = 1.16$) and one ($M = 0.23$) was significant ($Z = -6.41$, $p < 0.001$).

Correlations between different strategies Bivariate (two-tailed) non-parametric correlations (Kendall's tau) were performed between the frequencies with which different strategies were used (excluding *maximisation* and *minimisation* due to the observed frequency being one or less for these codes), and the results are shown in Table 14.2. A number of significant (weak) correlations were found, including the following: *rapport/empathy* was positively correlated with *requests attention* ($T = 0.09$, $p < 0.05$) but negatively correlated with *challenge* ($T = -0.20$, $p < 0.01$); *use of silence* was positively correlated with *situational futility* ($T = 0.26$, $p < 0.01$), *explicitly asks for account* ($T = 0.20$, $p < 0.01$), *describes trauma* ($T = 0.13$, $p < 0.01$), *presentation of evidence* ($T = 0.12$, $p < 0.01$) and *challenge* ($T = 0.21$, $p < 0.01$); *suspect's interest to talk* was positively correlated with *situational futility* ($T = 0.14$, $p < 0.01$), *explicitly asks for account/truth* ($T = 0.35$, $p < 0.01$), *describes trauma* ($T = 0.11$, $p < 0.05$), *emphasises seriousness* ($T = 0.22$, $p < 0.01$), *caution reiterated* ($T = 0.20$, $p < 0.01$), *presentation of evidence* ($T = 0.13$, $p < 0.01$) and *challenge* ($T = 0.10$, $p < 0.05$).

Question types *Closed* questions were by far the most frequent type of question observed ($M = 63$, SD = 46.80). The second most frequent was *statement* questions ($M = 16.52$, SD = 16.61). *Open* questions were not particularly common: on average, only one open question was asked per interview tape ($M = 1.02$, SD = 1.88). Questions categorised as *closed with element of open* also occurred infrequently ($M = 0.27$, SD = 0.89). Consequently, the total observations of *open* and *closed with element of open* questions were combined into a single category, *open type,* for further analysis.

The non-parametric Friedman test was selected to compare the use of *open-type* questions across three categories of time: (i) the initial three time segments of an interview tape (each of 5 min), (ii) the middle three time segments and (iii) the final two time segments.[3] A significant effect was found, ($\chi^2 = 16.67$, $p < 0.001$ meaning that there was a difference identified in the frequency of *open-type* questions across the three time segments. Three paired samples Wilcoxon signed ranks tests were then used to make post hoc comparisons between conditions. A first test indicated that there was a significant difference in the scores between the initial time segments ($M = 0.81$) and the middle time segments ($M = 0.56$), $Z = -3.35$, $p = 0.001$. A second test indicated that there was a significant difference in the scores between the initial time segments ($M = 0.81$) and the final time segments ($M = 0.38$), $Z = -4.09$, $p = 0.000$. A third test indicated that there was also (although not as strong) significant difference in the scores between the middle time segments and the final time segments, $Z = -2.75$, $p = 0.006$. Essentially, this suggests that there were significantly more *open-type* questions used in the initial time segment compared to the second and third time segments.

The association between suspect response with strategies and question type

To permit further analysis of strategy use and question type with suspect response, a number of decisions were made with regard to which variables were included in the analysis: due to the small frequencies of *unclear and challenging responses,* these were excluded from further statistical analysis, and *silence* and *no comment responses* were considered sufficiently similar in function to warrant combining

Table 14.2 Significant Kendall's tau correlation coefficients between different strategies used by interviewers

Strategy		*Attention*	*Situational futility*	*Tell truth*	*Seriousness*	*Caution*	*Trauma*	*Evidence*	*Challenge*
Rapport	Correlation	0.09*	–	–	–	–	–	–	−0.20**
	Sig. (2-tailed)	0.04	–	–	–	–	–	–	0.06
Silence	Correlation	–	0.26**	0.20**	–	–	0.13**	0.12**	0.21**
	Sig. (2-tailed)	–	0.001	0.001	–	–	0.01	0.003	0.001
Interest to talk	Correlation	–	0.14**	0.35**	0.22**	0.20**	0.11*	0.13**	0.10*
	Sig. (2-tailed)	–	0.005	0.001	0.001	0.001	0.002	0.002	0.03

*$p < 0.05$; **$p < 0.01$.

into a single category, referred to as *no response*. Consequently, suspect response became a dichotomous variable: a *relevant response* versus a *no response* (combining *silence* and *no comment* responses).

Strategy use and suspect response Linear regression was employed to examine if particular strategies were associated with *suspects responding relevantly* (in comparison to *not responding*). All strategies (except *minimisation* and *maximisation* due to low frequencies) were included in the model. The overall model fit was $R^2 = 0.31$ ($p < 0.001$). Six strategies were identified as significant predictors of *suspects responding relevantly* (in comparison to *not responding*). In summary: *requests attention* ($\beta = 0.13, p < 0.01$), *rapport/empathy* ($\beta = 0.19, p < 0.001$) and *presentation of evidence* ($\beta = 0.15$, $p < 0.01$) were all significant predictors of *suspects responding relevantly.* In other words, the greater use of these strategies was associated with more *relevant responses* than if fewer of these strategies were used. In contrast, *explicitly asks for an account* ($\beta = -0.27, p < 0.001$), *emphasises seriousness of offence* ($\beta = -0.14, p < 0.01$), *special warning* ($\beta = -0.13, p < 0.01$) and *caution reiterated* ($\beta = -0.14$, $p < 0.01$) were all negatively associated with *suspects responding relevantly.* This means that less frequent use of these strategies was associated with more relevant responses (than if more of these strategies were used). No significant associations were found between *suspect response* and the following strategies: *challenge, suspect's interest to talk, use of silence, describes injuries* and *describes trauma.*

Multinomial logistic regression was also undertaken to explore the relationships between strategy use and whether the suspect *admitted, denied* or *made no response* (i.e. neither admitted nor denied). For this analysis, strategies were coded as either present or absent (rather than counts). Some strategies, due to low frequencies or lack of variation, were also excluded. The strategies subsequently included in the regression model were *requests attention, rapport/empathy, use of silence, explicitly asks for account, describes trauma* and *challenge.* The logistic regression model was statistically significant, $\chi^2 = 54.60, p < 0.001$. This analysis revealed some significant associations with *suspects either admitting or denying an offence,* in comparison to *not responding,* these being *requests attention* ($\beta = 1.63, p < 0.05$) and *rapport/empathy* ($\beta = 1.56, p < 0.01$) associated with an increased likelihood of *suspects admitting the offence* rather than *not responding*; *requests attention* ($\beta = 1.73, p < 0.05$) was also associated with an increased likelihood of *suspects denying the offence* in comparison to not responding, and use of *describing trauma* ($\beta = -1.67, p < 0.05$) was associated with a decreased likelihood of suspects *admitting an offence,* in comparison to not responding.

Strategy use and suspect interruptions On average, an *interviewer interrupted the suspect* between once and twice per tape, which was significantly fewer (M = 1.69, Mdn = 0.00) than *suspect interruptions* (M = 6.54, Mdn = 3.00), $Z = -12.98$, $p < 0.001$. A bivariate (two-tailed) Kendall's tau correlation was conducted between number of *suspect interruptions* and number of *interviewer interruptions,* and a significant correlation (across interviews) was found between the number of interviewer and suspect interruptions, $T = 0.53$, p (two-tailed) < 0.01. That is, more *suspect interruptions* occurred in the interviews that had more *interviewer interruptions*. Negative binomial regression was also undertaken to explore associations between suspect interruptions and the presence (or absence) of strategies. The key findings are that the presence of *requests attention* ($\beta = 1.05$, $p < 0.001$), *explicitly asks for account* ($\beta = 0.28$, $p < 0.05$), *presentation of evidence* ($\beta = 2.01$, $p < 0.05$) and *challenge* ($\beta = 0.39$, < 0.01) are significantly associated with increased *suspect interruptions*, and the presence of *suspect's interest to talk* ($\beta = -0.51$, $p < 0.05$), *situational futility* ($\beta = -0.49$, $p < 0.05$), *special warning* ($\beta = -1.87$, $p < 0.001$) and *reiterates caution* ($\beta = -0.74$, $p < 0.01$) are all significantly associated with fewer *suspect interruptions*. The model was significant, $\chi^2 = 126.43$ ($p < 0.001$).

Question types and suspect response Linear regression was carried out to explore the associations between question type and the suspect's likelihood to respond relevantly (or not). Greater use of *statement* ($\beta = 0.80$, $p < 0.001$) and *open-type questions* ($\beta = 0.80$, $p < 0.05$) were significantly associated with suspects responding *relevantly* (compared to *not responding*), and fewer *closed questions* ($\beta = -0.23$, $p < 0.001$) was significantly associated with *suspects responding relevantly* (compared to *not responding*). The overall model fit was $R^2 = 0.62$.

Multinomial logistic regression was also carried out to see whether question types might be associated with whether the suspect was likely to admit (either fully or in part), deny or not respond. Not all question types could be included in the analysis because of low frequencies or lack of variation (i.e. closed questions). The question types (whether present or absent) added into the model were *open*, *negative* and *repetitive* question types. The logistic regression model was statistically significant, $\chi^2 = 19.99$ ($p < 0.01$). Two significant associations were identified: the presence of *open-type* questions ($\beta = 1.12$, $p < 0.05$) was associated with an increased likelihood of *suspects admitting the offence* (in comparison to *not responding*), and the presence of *negative* questions ($\beta = 1.23$, $p < 0.01$) was associated with an increased likelihood of *suspects denying the offence* (in comparison to *not responding)*.

Discussion

The research presented here is distinctive in that it draws on a relatively large sample of real-life serious crime interviews and describes in detail the exchange between police interviewers and serious crime suspects. Few studies have examined suspect response beyond whether a confession was made or not; this study therefore makes an important contribution by exploring suspect response in greater detail and also by examining the associations between suspect response and the strategies and questions used by police interviewers. This research therefore provides a fresh insight into police interviewing of serious crime suspects (in England and Wales).

Strategies

Analysis of these real-life serious case interviews demonstrated that a range of strategies were employed by interviewers. 'Appropriate' strategies of *presentation of evidence*, *challenge* and *rapport/empathy* were among the most common strategies employed in the present sample of interviews. That *presentation of evidence* was the most frequently observed strategy is in line with other research (Bull & Soukara, 2010; Pearse & Gudjonsson, 1996; Soukara et al., 2002). Interviewers were, however, more challenging to suspects in the present study than has been observed in other earlier studies (Hakkanen et al., 2009; Baldwin, 1992) (although methodological differences between studies should be noted).

The frequency of these strategies is also in line with the ethos of investigative interviewing. For example, *explicitly asks for an account*, being the third most frequent strategy used, is a key feature of PEACE (i.e. that the suspect should be asked for a full account of what happened). The finding that the frequency of *challenges* increased as the interview tape progressed is also in line with PEACE, that challenges should occur after an initial account from the suspect is obtained. However, PEACE also recommends building rapport as an important element of an effective interview, and evidence of *rapport* in the present study was, overall, quite rare (e.g. Moston & Engleberg, 1993; Oxburgh et al., 2010a, 2010b). It is, however, worth highlighting that *rapport/empathy* was significantly more frequent in the initial stages of the interview tape (the first 15 min) compared to the next 15 min (i.e. the middle of the interview tape). So, whilst it is encouraging that the use of rapport appears to be more frequently observed in the earlier stages, the fact that overall its usage was rare aligns with the finding by Walsh & Bull (2012) that many interviewers failed to maintain rapport. The ability to develop and maintain rapport with suspects therefore might be a subject worthy of further attention during the training of serious crime interviewers.

Reassuringly, there were no observations of the controversial strategies of *minimisation* and only one instance of *maximisation,* across all interviews. This is clearly encouraging, is in line with the PEACE ethos of ethical interviewing and reinforces the findings from other UK-based studies (e.g. Soukara et al., 2009) that also found these techniques were rarely, if ever, used. With the exception of *minimisation* and *maximisation*, explicit judgements of the appropriateness (or otherwise) of the different strategies were not made in the present research. Nevertheless, the strategies that were most commonly used (*presentation of evidence*, *challenge* and *rapport/empathy*) are unlikely to generate much controversy and would on the whole be considered appropriate. Others (e.g. *situational futility*, *emphasising seriousness*) might be perceived as problematic with certain (more vulnerable) individuals. However, the authors' view is that the actual practice of these strategies in the present sample of interviews is unlikely to cause concern to many. For example, the cases under examination in this study were all extremely serious crimes—either murder or rape—and to remind suspects of that, on occasion, felt perfectly reasonable in the authors' opinion. Instead, the issue is one of degree, and infrequently used strategies, used within an appropriate context, may be cause for little concern. However, there were a handful of occasions during interviews where the *clustering* of strategies bordered on verbal aggression, tending to be towards the end of interviews where interviewers perhaps became more desperate or frustrated in their interactions with suspects. In these cases, the suspect tended to deny involvement or not respond, and their stated position never altered. In these interviews, a legal advisor was always present, and in two instances, the legal advisor raised their concerns over the questioning becoming oppressive.

A number of significant associations were observed between different strategies and how suspects responded and behaved. For example, *rapport/empathy* was associated with an increased likelihood of suspects admitting the offence. However, the fact that no suspect in this large sample changed their position from denial to admission, and that most suspects who did admit, did so early on in the questioning, possibly points to the opposite: in other words, that more *rapport/empathy* was used because the suspect was admitting. A similar point can be made with regard to the strategy of *describes trauma* which was associated with a decreased likelihood of suspects admitting an offence. *Describing the trauma of a victim* is arguably a more confrontational strategy and might only be employed because the suspect is denying the offence (if the suspect was admitting the offence, then there would be no call to use it).

Question style

In line with previous research (Read, Powell, Kebbell, Milne, & Steinberg, 2013; Snook, Luther, Quinlan, & Milne, 2012; Griffiths & Milne, 2006), *closed* questions were by far the most frequently noted type of questions used which contrasts with relevant guidance/training. Although *closed-open-type* questions were much less frequent than *closed* questions, further analysis revealed that open questions occurred more during the initial phase of each interview tape, which is in line with PEACE and aligns with Griffiths and Milne's study of serious crime interviewing in 2006.

Statement questions were the second most frequent type of question asked, which appears to be a higher frequency than that found by Snook et al. (2012) and Read et al. (2013). (It should be noted that the different methods adopted to measure question type frequency might mean the results are not wholly comparable). Whilst some studies of police interviewing identify *statement* questions as unproductive (Oxburgh et al., 2010a, 2010b), a different position was adopted in the present research. During the early stages of testing the coding frame (which initially did not include a code for statement questions), clear adjacency pairs were evident although they could not, in lexical terms, be categorised as one of the existing question types. For example:

Interviewer: John Smith said you were there that night. Were you at the Ship Inn public house that night?
Suspect: No, I wasn't there then. I was there earlier that day but left at 4 pm.
Interviewer: So, you're saying that John is incorrect in thinking that he saw you there that evening.

Using the example above ('So, you're saying that John was incorrect'), one option might be to make an inference as to the type of question it was intended to be.

However, since these types of questions were relatively frequent, it was decided that a separate code (*statement* questions) should be used to capture these. It should be emphasised therefore that in the present research, *statement* questions per se are not considered an inappropriate question type.

Statement questions, as defined in this study, might therefore benefit from further qualitative analysis of their construction and purpose. For example, *statement* questions were characterised by interviewers echoing or rephrasing something suspects had recently said, with the purpose of prompting the suspect to continue talking. As a result, some *statement* questions might be more closely aligned to how *closed-open-type* questions were categorised in this research, rather than closed. The finding that *statement* questions and *open-type* questions were significantly associated with *suspects responding relevantly* (compared to not responding) lends credence to this view. This type of issue emphasises the importance of using audio recordings as opposed to written transcripts; the intonation of a phrase (and therefore the intended function of that question) may only be noted using audio recordings as opposed to written transcripts. Although *open-type* questions are associated with suspects responding relevantly as well as an increased likelihood of suspects admitting the offence, the use of these question types might be a *consequence* of suspects responding or admitting (and not a *cause* of it).

Similarly, *negative* questions were associated with an increased likelihood of suspects denying the offence. Again, using *negative* questions with suspects that are denying offences suggests that attempts are being made to persuade the suspect of an alternative position, for example 'The evidence suggests that you were there that night, don't you agree with that?'. Whilst the use of *negative* questions is likely to receive less attention (or criticism) in cases with suspects who persist in denials (and do not change their position), there are potentially more damaging implications if suspects did change from denial to admission. However, the fact that *negative* questions are present at all may well be a cause for concern and something to be addressed in police training of interviewers.

Whilst the potentially negative consequences of certain question types are well understood, it should be emphasised that the overall frequency of *negative*, *repetitive*, *multiple* and *ineffective* questions was low in comparison to all of the other types of questions asked. This is in contrast to some studies (e.g. Soukara, 2004, found repetitive questions occurred in the vast majority of interviews) but consistent with others (e.g. Bull & Cherryman, 1996, found the use of long or overly complex questions was rare). It is also worth highlighting that analysis of simple frequencies of questions might be misleading. For example, we saw above that *repetitive* questions might well be appropriate if suspects continually interrupt or evade answering a pertinent question. Similarly, whilst *open* questions are universally considered as an appropriate question type, they might not always be effective. For example, in one case, a legal advisor specifically asked the interviewer to avoid open questions as the (young) suspect would find it easier to respond to closed, specific questions.

There were also instances when, in the authors' opinion, open questions could have been asked and were not, or where open questions were asked and very quickly suspects' replies were interrupted with a closed question (a finding consistent with that of Read et al., 2013). This suggests that there may still be some room for improvement in police use of open questions, particularly in allowing suspects the opportunity to fully respond to an open question.

One of the principles of effective questioning advocated in PEACE is to allow suspects the opportunity to provide an uninterrupted account. The pattern of interruptions and overtalking during real-life police–suspect interviews has not been well documented to date. In the present study, it was encouraging that interviewer interruptions appear therefore, at least on average, to be quite rare, and appear broadly consistent with effective practice recommendations described earlier. Also, it is worth highlighting that interviewers interrupted suspects far less than suspects interrupted interviewers.

The results showed that the presence of *negative*, *multiple*, *statement* and *repetitive* questions was associated with increased suspect interruptions. Many of these question types are considered to be unproductive, and their correlation with increased interruptions is noteworthy. Alone, this might indicate that interviewers who use unproductive questioning techniques also interrupt more, pointing to an overall lack of questioning skill. However, when one also looks at suspect interruptions, which were significantly more prevalent than interviewer interruptions, we can see that more suspect interruptions were also significantly correlated with these unproductive type questions. This might explain why more *repetitive* questions, for example, are correlated with increased suspect interruptions: questions may have to be repeated because suspects are interrupting.

Returning to the overall frequencies of these question types found in the present study, *repetitive*, *ineffective* and *negative* questions were actually quite rare. Also, *statement* questions, for reasons described above, whilst more frequent, were not, in the present study, necessarily considered unproductive. The associations identified between certain infrequently used question types, and interviewer and suspect interruptions, might therefore point to a more complex interaction of factors.

Consequently, and in line with recommendations by Oxburgh et al. (2010a, 2010b), it is advocated that the context in which questions are asked should be integral when evaluating police questioning. For example, although negative-type questions are unlikely to ever be effective or appropriate, the same may not always be true for others (i.e. *repetitive* questions). Equally, whilst *open* questions are universally considered an appropriate form of question, they might not necessarily be effective for all suspects. Similarly, *statement* questions, one of the most frequent types of questions observed in the present sample of interviews, may actually have been intended (and potentially successful) as a strategy to encourage further information from the suspect. Finally, whilst interrupting suspects might in theory always be considered ineffective practice, the suspect behaviour evident in the present sample at times arguably necessitated reasonable interruptions. For instance, interviewers might interrupt suspects who were very aggressive or who appeared to be deliberately avoiding answering the question asked.

Conclusion

This innovative research presented here progresses our understanding of how suspects respond in interviews by moving away from focusing solely on whether suspects admit or deny offences to include how suspects actually respond during interviews.

There are a number of issues with the present research that necessarily limit the findings. First, interviews were not randomly selected. Consequently, this limits the ability to generalise the findings to the wider population of serious crime suspect interviews. Nevertheless, the research did obtain interviews from a wide range of forces and so goes some way towards minimising this problem. It would therefore be useful to explore whether the findings identified here could be replicated in a larger and randomly selected sample of interviews.

Overall, the intention of this research was to enhance understanding of the actual police interviewing of serious crime suspects. As such, it focused on breadth of exploration, rather than in-depth analysis of specific issues. Consequently, further detailed (and possibly qualitative) analysis is likely to have merit. Identifying real (but anonymised) examples of good (and poor) practice might be of particular value for police training. Finally, the issue of treating each interview tape as a discrete interview has been dealt with earlier in this paper but readers are reminded that this may limit the extent to which the findings can be generalised.

Whilst questions remain over the efficacy (and appropriateness) of some strategies, the range of strategies observed here suggests that interviewing officers were not deterred from actively encouraging even the most reluctant suspects to talk or from allowing cooperative suspects full opportunity to provide a detailed account. It is important to emphasise that the finding that strategies do not appear to be particularly effective in encouraging reluctant suspects to speak does not necessarily mean that these strategies should be discounted completely. The persistence of interviewing officers in providing suspects with every opportunity and encouragement to provide their side of the story may in itself be an effective strategy for jurors to consider and in minimising the possibility of suspects devising credible but false defences later on in the criminal justice process.

This paper also provides further evidence that police questioning practice in the UK is adhering to many of the elements of skilled questioning laid down in national guidelines. However, there continues to be room for improvement. Although relatively infrequent, inappropriate question types like negative and multiple questions may leave interviewing officers open to criticism, both during and after the interview process. Although the topic of question types does feature in advanced interview training, it is possible that refresher training might be helpful especially on better use of open questions. It is also recommended that research that seeks to guide such improvements must consider the context within which a question is asked or a particular strategy is used.

In conclusion, only a handful of studies have explored the relationship between suspect response and the strategies and questions used by interviewers. In turn, only a small proportion of these have drawn on real-life data. None have specifically examined serious crime suspects. The present research is the first to address these gaps, and despite its limitations, it is hoped that the insights provided here will be of interest and use to researchers and practitioners alike.

Notes

1 Although the original request to forces was for interviews after 2000, it was decided that the interviews occurring in 1999 were close enough to the rest of the sample to permit inclusion.
2 Primary interviewers were defined as those who opened the interview and who (usually) took the predominant role in questioning. Secondary interviewers were those who (usually) took less of a role in questioning, and who initially spoke after the primary interviewer.
3 The final time segment was not included in this analysis as no open-type questions occurred in this time segment.

References

Alison, L., Kebbell, M., & Leung, J. (2008). A facet analysis of police officers' self-reported use of suspect interviewing strategies and their discomfort with ambiguity. *Applied Cognitive Psychology*, *22*, 1072–1087.

Baldwin, J. (1992). *Video taping of police interviews with suspects: An evaluation*. London: Home Office.

Baldwin, J. (1993). Police interview techniques: Establishing truth or proof. *British Journal of Criminology*, *33*(3), 325.

Buckley, J. P. (2006). The Reid technique of interviewing and interrogation. In T. Williamson (Ed.), *Investigative interviewing: Rights, research and regulation* (pp. 190–206). Cullompton: Willan.

Bull, R., & Cherryman, J. (1996). *Helping to identify skills gaps in specialist investigative interviewing: Enhancement of professional skills*. London: Home Office.

Bull, R., & Soukara, S. (2010). Four studies of what really happens in police interviews. In G. D. Lassiter, & C. A. Meissner (Eds.), *Police interrogations and false confessions: Current research, practice, and policy recommendations* (pp. 81–95). Washington, DC: American Psychological Association.

Cherryman, J. (1999). *Police investigative interviewing: Skill analysis and concordance of evaluations* (unpublished PhD thesis). University of Portsmouth, Portsmouth.

Clarke, C., & Milne, B. (2001). *National evaluation of the PEACE investigative interviewing course*. Police Research Award Scheme, Report No. PRAS/149. Home Office, London.

Clarke, C., Milne, R., & Bull, R. (2011). Interviewing suspects of crime: The impact of PEACE training, supervision and the presence of a legal advisor. *Journal of Investigative Psychology and Offender Profiling*, *8*, 149–162.

Dando, C., & Bull, R. (2011). Maximising opportunities to detect verbal deception: Training police officers to interview tactically. *Journal of Investigative Psychology and Offender Profiling*, *8*, 189–202.

Dando, C., Bull, R., Ormerod, T., & Sandham, A. (2015). Helping to sort the liars from the truth-tellers: The gradual revelation of information during investigative interviews. *Legal and Criminological Psychology*, *20*, 114–128.

Griffiths, A., & Milne, B. (2006). Will it all end in tiers? Recent developments in police interviews with suspects in Britain. In T. Williamson (Ed.), *Investigative interviewing: Rights, research, regulation* (pp. 167–189). Cullompton: Willan.

Gudjonsson, G. H. (2003), *The psychology of interrogations and confessions: A handbook*. Chichester: Wiley.

Hakkanen, H., Ask, K., Kebbell, M., Alison, L., & Granhag, P. A. (2009). Police officers' views of effective interview tactics with suspects: The effects of weight of case evidence and discomfort with ambiguity. *Applied Cognitive Psychology*, *23*, 468–481.

Heydon, G. (2011). Silence: Civil right or social privilege? A discourse analytic response to a legal problem. *Journal of Pragmatics*, *43*, 2308–2316.

Home Office. (1992). *Investigative interviewing, police circular 22/92*. London: Home Office.

Home Office. (2008). *Police and criminal evidence act 1984. Code C. Code of practice for the detention, treatment and questioning of persons by police officers*. London: Stationery Office.

Home Office. (2010). *Police and criminal evidence act 1984. Code E. Code of practice on audio recording interviews with suspects*. London: Stationery Office.

Kassin, S. M. (1997). The psychology of confession evidence. *American Psychologist*, *52*(3), 221–233.

Kassin, S. M., & McNall, K. (1991). Police interrogations and confessions: Communicating promises and threats by pragmatic implication. *Law and Human Behaviour*, *15*(3), 233–251.

Kassin, S. M., Leo, R., Meissner, C. A., Richman, K. D., Colwell, L. H., Leach, A., & La Fon, D. (2007). Police interviewing and interrogation: A self report survey of police practices and beliefs. *Law and Human Behaviour*, *31*, 381–400.

Kelly, C. E., Miller, J. C., & Redlich, A. D. (2015). The dynamic nature of interrogation. *Law and Human Behaviour*, doi:10.1037/lhb0000172

Leo, R. A. (1996). Inside the interrogation room. *Journal of Criminal Law and Criminology*, *86*, 266–303.

McGurk, B. J., Carr, M. J., & McGurk, D. (1993). *Investigative interviewing courses for police officers: An evaluation*. Police Research Group Paper No. 4. Home Office, London.

Meissner, C. A., Russano, M. B., & Narchet, F. M. (2010). The importance of a laboratory science for improving the diagnostic value of confession evidence. In G. D. Lassiter & C. A. Meissner (Eds.), *Police interrogations and false confessions: Current research, practice, and policy recommendations*. Washington, DC: American Psychological Association.

Milne, R., & Bull, R. (1999). *Investigative interviewing: Psychology and practice*. Chichester: Wiley.

Ministry of Justice. (2011). *Achieving best evidence in criminal proceedings guidance on interviewing victims and witnesses, and guidance on using special measures*. London: Ministry of Justice.

Moston, S., & Engleberg, T. (1993). Police questioning techniques in tape recorded interviews with criminal suspects. *Police Society*, *3*, 223–237.

Moston, S., Stephenson, G. M., & Williamson, T. M. (1992). The effects of case characteristics on suspect behaviour during police questioning. *British Journal of Criminology*, *32*, 23–40.

National Crime Faculty. (1996), *Investigative interviewing: A practical guide*. Bramshill: National Crime Faculty and National Police Training.

Neuendorf, K. A. (2002). *The content analysis handbook.* Thousand Oaks, CA: Sage.

Oxburgh, G., & Ost, J. (2011). The use and efficacy of empathy in police interviews with suspects of sexual offences. *Journal of Investigative Psychology and Offender Profiling, 8*, 178–188.

Oxburgh, G. E., Myklebust, T., & Grant, T. (2010a). The question of question types in police interviews: A review of the literature from a psychological and linguistic perspective. *International Journal of Speech, Language and the Law, 17*(1), 46–66.

Oxburgh, G., Ost, J., & Cherryman, J. (2010b). Police interviews with suspected child sex offenders: Does use of empathy and question type influence the amount of investigation relevant information obtained? *Psychology, Crime & Law*, doi:10.1080/1068316X.2010.481624

Pearse, J., & Gudjonsson, G. (1996). Police interviewing techniques at two south London police stations. *Psychology, Crime & Law, 3*, 63–74.

Pearse, J., & Gudjonsson, G. (1999). Measuring infuential police interviewing tactics: A factor analytical approach. *Legal and Criminology Psychology, 4*, 221–238.

Police and Criminal Evidence Act. 1984. Retrieved from: www.legislation.gov.uk/ukpga/1984/60/contents

Read, J., Powell, M. B., Kebbell, M. R., Milne, R., & Steinberg, R. (2013). Evaluating police interviewing practices with suspects in child sexual abuse cases. *Policing and Society: An International Journal of Research and Policy.* doi:10.1080/10439463.2013.784297.

Reppucci, N. D., Meyer, J., & Kostelnik, J. (2010). Custodial interrogation of juveniles: results of a national survey of police. In G. D. Lassiter & C. A. Meissner (Eds.), *Police interrogations and false confessions: Current research, practice, and policy recommendations* (pp. 67–80). Washington, DC: American Psychological Association.

Schegloff, E. A. (2000). Overlapping talk and the organisation of turn-taking for conversation. *Language in Society, 29*(1), 1–63.

Schegloff, E. A., & Sacks, H. (1973). Opening up closings. *Semiotica, 8*(4), 289–327.

Shawyer, A., & Walsh, D. (2007). Fraud and PEACE: Investigative interviewing and fraud investigation. *Crime Prevention and Community Safety, 9*, 102–117.

Shawyer, A., Milne, R., & Bull, R. (2009). Investigative interviewing in the UK. In T. Williamson, B. Milne, & S. P. Savage (Eds.), *International developments in investigative interviewing* (pp. 24–38). Cullompton: Willan.

Snook, B., Eastwood, J., Stinson, M., Tedeschini, J., & House, J. C. (2010). Reforming investigative interviewing in Canada. *Canadian Journal of Criminology and Criminal Justice, 52*(2), 215–232. doi:10.31381cjccj.52.2.215.

Snook, B., Luther, K., Quinlan, H., & Milne, R. (2012). Let 'em talk!: A field study of police questioning practices of suspects and accused. *Criminal Justice and Behavior, 39*, 1328–1338.

Soukara, S. (2004). *Investigating interviewing of suspects: Piecing together the picture.* (Unpublished doctoral dissertation). University of Portsmouth, Portsmouth.

Soukara, S., Bull, R., & Vrij, A. (2002). Police detective's aims regarding their interviews with suspects: Any change at the turn of the millennium? *International Journal of Police Science and Management, 4*(2), 100–114.

Soukara, S., Bull, R., Vrij, A., Turner, M., & Cherryman, J. (2009). What really happens in police interviews of suspects? Tactics and confessions. *Psychology, Crime & Law, 15*(6), 493–506.

Stephenson, G. M., & Moston, S. (1994). Police interrogation. *Psychology, Crime & Law, 1*, 151–157.

Walsh, D., & Bull, R. (2010). What really is effective in interviews with suspects? A study comparing interviewing skills against interviewing outcomes. *Legal and Criminological Psychology*, *15*, 305–321.

Walsh, D., & Bull, R. (2012). Examining rapport in investigative interviews with suspects: Does its building and maintenance work? *Journal of Police and Criminal Psychology*, *27*, 73–84.

Williamson, T. M. (1993). From interrogation to investigative interviewing; strategic trends in police questioning. *Journal of Community & Applied Social Psychology*, *3*, 89–99.

Yeschke, C. L. (2003). *The art of investigative interviewing*. Burlington, MA: Butterworth-Heinemann.

Zimbardo, P. G. (1967). The psychology of police confessions. *Psychology Today*, *1*, 17–27.

15 What is 'believed' or actually 'known' about characteristics that may contribute to being a good/effective interviewer?

Ray Bull

Introduction

Among the world's first publicly available research based official/government guidance documents on how best to gather information from people who may be reluctant to divulge/discuss what they knew/what they had experienced were: (i) the 1992 'Memorandum of Good Practice on Video Recorded Interviews with Children for Criminal Proceedings', drafted by a psychologist (the current author) and a lawyer (Diane Birch) (Bull, 1992, 1996), and; (ii) the 1992 booklet issued by 'The Central Planning Unit' to every police officer in England and Wales ($N = 127{,}000$) that outlined the new 'PEACE' approach to the conducting of interviews. These set out in detail (as did the subsequent 2002 government document 'Achieving Best Evidence' – mostly written by psychologists, and regularly updated since then) the ways in which information gathering interviews should be conducted, and thus the skills/abilities required of effective interviewers (it is not proposed here to review the contents of these widely available documents; see http://www.justice.gov.uk/downloads/victims-and-witnesses/vulnerable-witnesses/achieving-best-evidence-criminal-proceedings.pdf).

Ground-breaking research (Baldwin, 1993) involving real-life police interviews conducted in the late 1980s (after the electronic recording of suspect interviews became mandatory in England and Wales in 1986) found that the level of interviewing skills was poor (in the absence of appropriate training) and very few interviewees believed to be in possession of 'incriminating' information shifted during interviews from not divulging such information to doing so. Draft reports of such research studies (see Milne & Bull, 1999 for more on these 'early' studies) led the senior London police officer Tom Williamson to convene (in 1990/91) a small working party of detectives and psychologists (including Eric Shepherd, Stephen Moston and Ray Bull) that produced in 1991 a two-volume (unpublished) overview (largely written by Moston) of aspects of psychology that might be useful to the improving of such interviewing.

During the same time (i.e. in 1991), under the auspices of the national 'Association of Chief Police Officers' and the 'Home Office' (the relevant government ministry), a group of experienced detectives (drawn from several police organisations in England and Wales) worked on developing new training courses and updated interviewing principles (they were aware of the contents of our literature review mentioned above). From this evolved the 'PEACE' approach with its fundamental realisation that whether interviewees be 'suspects', 'witnesses' or 'victims', the interviewers' task should be considered to be basically the same – this being to try to obtain from them as much information as possible. Indeed one of the major principles underlying this 'new' approach was stated as being, "to obtain accurate and reliable information from suspects, witnesses or victims". Thus, information gathering is its main goal, realising that 'victims' and 'witnesses' can often be reticent to divulge relevant information. Also, 'PEACE' is used when interviewing informants, undercover officers/agents and the like (as well as terrorism suspects) about events that have not yet taken place (i.e. about the future).

In the mid-1990s, the present author was asked by the UK government to identify any skills gaps in 'PEACE'-trained, experienced police officers' interviews with suspects (in serious cases). Assisted by Julie Cherryman, we first asked many experienced detectives what they believed the most important skills were (Bull & Cherryman, 1996) – from their responses plus the relevant literature, we compiled a questionnaire. Then, a much larger sample of officers was asked to say how necessary each of the skills listed in the questionnaire was. A total of 28 skills emerged as being important, and the ones deemed most necessary were (in rank order): listening, preparation, questioning, knowledge of subject, flexibility, open mindedness, rapport, compassion/empathy.

We then obtained several dozen recordings of relevant interviews, which were independently evaluated by four 'expert' raters regarding the 28 skills plus for 'overall skill'. The eleven skills found to significantly discriminate between interviews judged overall as "skilled" and those they judged as "not skilled" were:

- communication skills; empathy/compassion;
- flexibility; keeps interviewee to relevant topics;
- responds to what interviewee says; open-mindedness;
- closed questions; interview has structure; open questions;
- appropriate use of pauses and silences; apparent use of tactics.

However, even in the more skilled interviews, some skills were not that often present (i.e. appropriate use of pauses and silences; avoidance of using closed questions; flexibility; empathy/compassion – thus these being ones training should better address). On the other hand, even in the less-skilled interviews, some skills were often present (e.g., not releasing all information at the beginning of the interview; absence of (i) inappropriate interruptions, (ii) undue pressure, (iii) long/complex questions, (iv) over-talking – skills that seem to have been absent in the earlier studies.

In their 2009 overview of what constitutes best practice when interviewing people who may possess 'incriminating' information yet may usually be unwilling to divulge this (e.g. suspected sex offenders), Read, Powell, Kebbell, & Milne noted (2009, p. 452) that "when Powell asked officers who were perceived as being particularly good at engaging threatened and marginalised" communities (e.g., Australian aboriginals), "courtesy, respect, patience, and honesty were perceived by these officers to be their most valued professional assets".

In their survey in England of experienced investigators'/interviewers' beliefs, Walsh & Bull (2011) found that participants believed good interviewers to be those who planned, built and maintained rapport, listened, remained open-minded, calm, unrushed, and well organised in terms of questioning and of evidence/information presentation. Poor interviewers were thought of as being inflexible, aggressive, unskilled planners, who missed opportunities to appropriately question and challenge what interviewees said.

In her doctoral thesis in Belgium, Smets (2012) listed 40 competencies believed to be relevant to the effective gathering of information from interviewees, which related to the five constructs of communicative, benevolent, controlled/non-reactive, careful/tenacious, and dominant/insisting (for a full list see Smets, 2012, p. 99). In their ongoing survey of interviewers (from a variety of countries) working on criminal investigations or on 'intelligence' issues, Sivasubramaniam & Goodman-Delahunty (2013) reported that being patient, showing kindness, respect and concern, and appealing to cooperation were rated highly (as were confronting with evidence of guilt, identifying contradictions in story). Various forms of 'mild' coercion were not rated at all highly.

In their recent survey of 'HUMINT' interviewers' views on 'What qualities make a good interrogator?' Russano & Narchet (2013) found 'interpersonal skills' to be most frequently mentioned, followed by 'patience', 'flexible/adaptable, 'ability to empathize', 'good communicator', and 'good listener' (these findings are similar to those of Bull & Cherryman, 1996 mentioned above). Among Russano & Narchet's (2013) participants were some with experience of interviewing 'high value targets' and these were unanimous that 'rapport-building' is the most 'effective approach'.

Beliefs about what are other important attributes of good investigators

In 2012, the experienced British police detective O'Neill was awarded a PhD for new research on the topic of 'What makes a successful volume crime investigator?'. This research (O'Neill & Milne, 2014), in part, gathered police detectives' beliefs concerning: (i) the attributes required to be successful investigators, and; (ii) how such success should be defined and measured. His first empirical study examined crime investigators' perceptions of their role, of success, and of the skills and abilities they believed to be required for it to be successful. The findings were largely consistent with prior research in that respondents ranked relatively highly topics such as communication skills, commitment, dedication, decision-making and motivation (some other 'topics', such as education, stability, empathy, training, and intelligence were ranked relatively low). The participants were also consistent with each other in believing that detections can be a main indicant of success.

His second empirical study invited investigators to identify successful investigators from amongst their peers. The respondents chose peers who were older, more experienced, and trained in investigation. They also ranked the thirty attributes on the basis of how prevalent they were in successful peers. These rankings were not entirely consistent with those found in his first study in that topics such as experience and persistence this time were ranked higher, although stability, education, training, empathy, and intelligence were still ranked lower.

Actual relationships between skills/abilities and information gain in interviews

In his 2004 doctoral thesis, the experienced Swedish detective Ulf Holmberg reported a highly innovative study in which he found (see Holmberg & Christianson, 2002) for convicted murderers and sexual offenders an association between whether they (said they) confessed/gave an account of wrong-doing and whether the police interviewing they experienced was conducted in a dominant (e.g. aggression, hostility, condemnation, impatience) or a humane (e.g. friendly, empathic) manner.

The relationship between interviewer characteristics and interview outcome/information gain was also studied in Japan by Otsuka, Wachi, Watanabe, Yokota, & Kuraishi (2011). Police officers (n = 274) who interviewed adult suspects (who denied having committed a crime when arrested but later confessed during or after being interviewed) filled in a questionnaire which included their level of 'empathic understanding'. For most types of crime studied (i.e. murder, rape, robbery) a significant positive association was found between officers' (self-reported) 'level of empathic understanding' and 'full confessions'. Zak (2012) stated his beliefs that "empathy . . . compels . . . people to share what they have with others whom they care about" (p. 19) and that "empathy requires intellectual perspective-taking" (p. 59). He noted that prior authors had identified four elements considered essential for empathy, these being shared affect, awareness of the other, mental flexibility, and emotional self-regulation which relies on executive function. In his own research (not relating directly to interviewing/interrogating) he found that "the choice of 'empathy' was directly correlated with a rise in oxytocin" (p. 54) and that "oxytocin provides further advantages by reducing . . . fear of the unknown" (p. 37). However, he noted that testosterone blocks the binding of oxytocin, inhibits people's ability to pick up social cues, and activates fear/punishment. Such findings suggest a 'biological' correlate (at least in part) for the findings of Holmberg & Christianson (2002) and of Otsuka et al. (2011).

In contrast to this Japanese finding and to Holmberg's Swedish finding, in the UK, Oxburgh, Ost, & Cherryman (2012) found no effect in real-life investigations of police interviewers' actual use of empathy on the amount of investigation-relevant information (IRI) provided by interviewees suspected of child sex offences. Oxburgh et al. (2012), not surprisingly, did find a relationship between the amount of IRI and interviewers' use of appropriate question types.

More recently Bull & Leahy-Harland (2012) found that interviewers of suspected murderers and rapists did not demonstrate a 'dominating approach' in these long-duration interviews. Instead, the strategies most frequently used were 'presentation of information', 'challenges', 'explicitly asks for account/tell truth', and 'rapport/empathy' (all of which are emphasised in 'PEACE' training). We also examined which strategies were associated with these interviewees continuing to responding relevantly and found positive associations for 'rapport/empathy', 'presentation of evidence', 'requests attention'; but negative associations for 'explicitly asks for account/tell truth', 'emphasises seriousness of offence', and 'situational futility'. Interviewer 'presentation of information/evidence' was also found by Bull & Soukara (2010) to be associated with suspects shifting from not providing relevant information to doing so.

Among the most substantial investigations concerning actual relationships between skills/abilities and information gain in real-life interviews was an analysis of interviewer skills in a large sample ($n = 142$) of recorded interviews with people suspected of 'benefit fraud'. In this Walsh & Bull (2010a) found that while investigators generally displayed ethical interviewing standards and tended to use open questioning techniques, a noticeable proportion of these interviews were not conducted skilfully. Shortcomings were particularly found in terms of rapport development, summarising, flexibility, and how investigators brought interviews to closure.

In terms of 'information gain', Walsh & Bull (2010b) examined whether interviewing in a manner that is compatible with the recommended and trained 'PEACE' approach affected outcomes. They found that good interviewing (i.e. in a manner advocated by the 'PEACE' approach) was significantly associated with the securing of fuller accounts. In particular, they assessed which of the many skills in the 'gaining of an account' phase were effective, finding these to be:

- encourages interviewee to give an account; develops topics;
- deals with difficulty; uses appropriate structure;
- uses appropriate questions; explores motive;
- challenges appropriately; explores received information;
- conversation-management; cognitive interviewing;
- self-confidence; open-mindedness; flexibility;
- communication skills; listening skills.

Walsh & Bull (2012a) also examined how the interviewers attempted to overcome suspects' initial denials of knowing about wrong-doing. They assessed 85 interviews with suspects of benefit fraud not only for interviewer tactics and skills/other attributes but also for interviewee movement/'shift' to providing relevant information. It was found that 'shifting' from (a) denying to (b) providing relevant, incriminating information indicating guilt/admissions/confessions more often occurred when certain tactics and skills/other attributes were present (many of which are recommended by 'PEACE'). Of the 22 'skills/tactics' examined, 13 were found to significantly differentiate between interviews in which suspects (i) 'shifted' versus (ii) did not 'shift'; these being:

- disclosure of evidence; emphasising contradictions;
- encouraging account; gentle prods;

- open questions; persistence;
- positive confrontation; probing questions;
- providing appropriate structure; regular summarising;
- repetitive questioning; showing concern;
- silence.

'Disclosure of evidence' was also found by Bull & Soukara (2010) to be associated with 'suspects' shifting from not providing relevant information to doing so. More recently Dando & Bull (2011) and Dando, Bull, Ormerod, & Sandham (2015) have compared the effectiveness of 'early', 'late' and 'gradual' revelation by interviewers of what they already knew that contradicted what interviews had said in interviews (also see Clemens, Granhag, & Stromwall, 2011). Found not to be effective by Walsh & Bull (2012a) were the tactics of:

- maximisation; minimisation;
- concern; interruptions;
- leading questions; intimidation;
- suggest scenario; challenging the account;
- and situational futility – some of which traditionally have been part of training in the USA (e.g., Inbau, Reid, Buckley, & Jayne, 2001).

The 'skills/other attributes' assessed were those derived from the relevant, up-to-date literature concerning what might assist a person to shift from not providing information to doing so. All eleven of these were found to significantly differentiate between those interviews in which (i) the interviewee 'shifted' from not providing relevant, incriminating information to providing a meaningful amount and (ii) the interviewee did not 'shift' from not providing. They were:

- prepared; rapport builder/keeper;
- empathic; respectful;
- active listener; calm;
- non-judgemental; communication skill;
- self-confident; open-minded;
- flexible.

Walsh & Bull (2012b) went on to study rapport in these interviews, examining its building and then its maintenance during interviews. They found that opportunities were often missed to build rapport in the initial stages. Also, where some rapport had initially been built, it was not always maintained partly because some of the tasks undertaken later in the interview (which may well have assisted rapport maintenance) were often conducted poorly. In terms of the effects of rapport they found that some of the interviewers they assessed as 'at or above PEACE standard' when building rapport in the opening 'Engage and Explain' phase regressed in the 'Gaining of an Account' phase. In fact 40% of those who were rated regarding rapport development as 'satisfactory' in the 'Engage and Explain' phase fell below the minimum acceptable PEACE standard when regarding rapport maintenance in the subsequent 'Account' phase. Moreover, all of those rated as 'skilled' at rapport building in the 'Engage and Explain' failed to maintain this standard of performance, with half of them being rated as 'no more than satisfactory' and the other half being 'unsatisfactory' at sustaining rapport in the 'Account' phase.

When examining the relationships between either rapport building/rapport maintenance and subsequent interview outcomes, those interviewers who were rated as at or above PEACE standard of performance in their rapport building skills in the 'Account' phase were, regardless of the quality of rapport building performance in the 'Engage and Explain' phase, three times as likely to achieve either a comprehensive account from the interviewees than those who were assessed as below minimum acceptable standards. These findings suggest that rapport maintenance (that will have involved rapport building) is more strongly associated with the preferred outcome than is rapport building. Interviewers rated as at or above PEACE standard in *both* their rapport building and maintenance skills were over five times more likely to obtain satisfactory outcomes. Thus, initial rapport building of itself, therefore, is not sufficient in influencing overall interview quality and outcomes, since rapport also has to be maintained throughout the interview.

Interviewees' beliefs

Only fairly recently has research been published on what 'reluctant' interviewees have to say about the skill/abilities required of effective interviewers/information gatherers. None of these published studies involve 'high value detainees'. However, it is clear from several UK court cases in recent years that people planning acts of terrorism are sometimes willing to talk comprehensively about this (and plead guilty). Of course, interviewers/investigators need to be adequately prepared for such interviews (Pearse, 2009) and be trained regarding how best to disclose incriminating information and to 'challenge' accordingly (e.g., see studies by Dando & Bull, 2011; Dando et al., 2015 – whose research was funded by a countering terrorism initiative).

In 2005, in the USA, O'Connor and Carson (two highly experienced professional interviewers) found that the predominant reason confessors (to child molestation) gave for why they confessed was the respect shown to them by the interviewers. Of the one third who did not confess/make any admissions (but who were found guilty), many said that this was because of the way they were interviewed/interrogated by the police (e.g., in a demeaning and/or coercive manner). These authors recommended on the basis of what their participants said that an investigator/interviewer needs to demonstrate to the interviewee an understanding of the latter's view of the world, developing rapport, communicating in a non-threatening and non-judgemental way while showing understanding, empathy, and respect for the interviewee as a human being. Some of the offenders commented that in their police interviews it had been made obvious to them that the interviewers felt negative towards them, which caused them not to provide information that otherwise they may well have provided.

The following year in Australia, Kebbell, Hurren, & Mazerolle (2006) arrived at similar conclusions. They made the important point that until recently most of the research concerning the obtaining of information from people who may be involved in wrong-doing had focused on false confessions rather than on how best to obtain information from actual wrong-doers. In their first study, convicted sex offenders were asked about their interviews with the police and for suggestions for the improving of such interviewing. Of great importance was their remarkable finding that prior to their police interview, only 16% said that they had planned to deny. A third had planned to give an account of wrong-doing/confess and half said that prior to being interviewed they had not yet decided whether to give an account/confess or not (somewhat similar findings were also found in a Canadian study – see Deslauriers-Varin & St-Yves, 2006, below). This finding concerning the few who had already decided not to provide relevant information flies in the face of common intuition, which was aptly summarised in 2008 by Leo, "Confessions, especially to serious crimes, are rarely made spontaneously. Rather, they are actively elicited . . . typically after sustained psychological pressure" (p. 119).

The participants' consensual suggestions for improving investigators' interviewing skills (also later reported in Kebbell, Alison, Hurren, & Mazerolle, 2010) fell into the categories of compassion, neutrality, honesty, being clear, non-aggressive. Those regarding what would make interviewees less likely to provide accounts/confess were aggressive behaviour, bias, and pressurising. When asked, "What do you think are the most important characteristics for an interviewer to have?", the consensual replies focused on an interviewer being capable, approachable, understanding, calm, non-aggressive, neutral, respectful, assertive, honest, professional, empathic, good listener, and interpersonally skilled.

In their second study, Kebbell et al. (2006) using a different sample of incarcerated male 'sex' or 'violence' participants provided information (via a 35-item questionnaire) concerning how their interviews were conducted by the police. Some of the sex offenders had confessed and some had denied. The confessors indicated that their interviews had been more ethical, humane, and less domineering than did the deniers, and to have involved the interviewer using more 'evidence presentation strategies'. Interestingly, when asked to compare the interviews that had experienced with how the police should interview, for both types of offending (i.e. sex or violence) the largest differences were for 'evidence presenting strategies' and 'ethical', followed by 'humanity' and less 'dominance'.

In this second study, the sexual offences participants each also read a number of vignettes in which the description of the police interview varied and they were asked to indicate the likelihood of each suspect confessing (also reported in Kebbell, Alison, & Hurren, 2008). This likelihood was found to be significantly greater in the 'humanity' condition than in the 'dominant' or 'cognitive distortion' conditions (and in the control condition). From these studies Kebbell et al. (2006) concluded that, "improving ethical interviewing and displays of humanity may increase the likelihood of confessions" (p. 59) and that, "dominance may reduce the likelihood of a confession" (p. 59).

In their final study, Kebbell et al. (2006) asked experienced police interviewers how those suspected of being involved in wrong-doing should be interviewed, finding a strong consensus regarding the importance of rapport and empathy: "the most common opinion amongst the participants was that a humane approach is typically preferable to a dominant or aggressive approach" (p. 82). In addition, Kebbell et al. (2006) importantly noted that, "some participants argued that catching a suspect out in a lie could be equally as effective as obtaining a confession" (p. 89) via "presenting evidence which conflicted with what the offender has said previously" (p. 91). However, they also noted that "we still do not know the best way of doing this" (p. 109). Kebbell et al. (2006) also (though rather briefly) mentioned the concept of 'reactance' (see Gudjonsson, 2003), noting that a lack of effectiveness of a domineering interrogating/interviewing style may well be due to a psychological reaction of defiance created within the interviewee. Their substantial report's concluding sentence was, "Based on these results, it seems that the most ethical approach to police interviewing may also be the most effective" (p. 110).

Vanderhallen & Vervaeke (2014) report in their study, 126 people who had just been interviewed by the police in relation to various offences and who agreed to fill in a number of questionnaires relating to: (i) their perception of the interviewers' empathy and interviewing style; (ii) their own feelings of hostility, anxiety, of being respected; (iii) their satisfaction with the interview, and; (iv) the 'working alliance' (which these researchers state consists of three subcomponents: "an *agreement* on the goal, an *agreement* on the tasks of both participants, and an emotional bond of mutual trust and acceptance . . . The working alliance is fostered and fed by an attitude of empathy, unconditional positive regard and authenticity" (p. 16)). They found that interviewees' interview satisfaction ratings were significantly related to their evaluations of the strength of the 'working alliance' and to a 'humanitarian' interviewing style.

In the same year as Kebbell et al. (2006) submitted their report, Deslauriers-Varin & St-Yves, (2006, also see St-Yves & Deslauriers-Varin, 2009) reported finding in Canada that 44% of their sample of convicted persons said they had, in fact, been ready just before their interrogation/interview commenced to confess/provide an incriminating account. However, 25% of these changed their mind during the interrogation. Similarly, of the 32% who were not already prepared to confess at the beginning of their interviews, a quarter also changed their mind.

Deslauriers-Varin, Lussier, & St-Yves (2011) describe their survey of a large number of incarcerated offenders whose official files contained information concerning whether (45%) or not (55%) they had confessed. Included in the survey was a question concerning the offenders' perceptions at the time of interrogation/interview of the strength of the police evidence against them. It was found that the confessors' perception of this was significantly stronger than the non-confessors'. Indeed, of the many factors examined in this complex study, "offenders' perception of police evidence emerged as one of the strongest predictors of confession" (p. 130). These authors concluded that "These results highlight the importance of case preparation and gathering evidence against a suspect prior to the police interrogation" (p. 142).

Actual differences between 'good' and 'not so good' investigators/interviewers

In O'Neill's (2012) third and fourth empirical studies, 'high' and 'low' performers were identified by objective means (e.g., actual rates of case clear-up/detection) and then compared, as were the high and low choice groups identified in his second study. The high detection group contained only a third of the high choice set, suggesting that respondents' ability to distinguish high performers was far from foolproof. The 'high' and 'low' performers were compared in relation to mean scores achieved on the NEO personality inventory (which assesses people in five personality domains with thirty individual facets). No significant differences were found between these two groups in relation to the domains and there was only one significant facet difference (for gregariousness that relates to a person's sociability, being part of the extraversion domain). However, 'training' significantly differentiated between the groups, with almost all those in the 'high' performing group having been trained via 'the national investigator programme', as opposed to few in the 'low' performing group.

Sear & Stephenson (1997) also found very few relationships between police interviewers' overall skill scores (as demonstrated in actual interviews of suspects) and the 'Big Five' dimensions, probably because many of these officers then exhibited "a cold, calculating and dominating approach to others" (p. 32).

In O'Neill's (2012) fifth empirical study, they compared the 'high' and 'low' groups in relation to critical thinking skills, as participants in one of his prior studies (see above) had ranked reasoning, judgement, and decision-making as relatively important to success. No significant differences were found. The sixth study compared these groups regarding intellectual capacity (as assessed using Raven's Standard Progressive Matrices) and multiple dimensions of empathy (as assessed by the 'Interpersonal Reactivity Index'). Again, no significant differences were found.

In contrast to O'Neill's substantial and ecologically valid findings of no differences, van Hemert, van den Berg, & Wijn (2012) found that people's (e.g., security personnel) appropriate reactions to role-played deviant behaviour in a museum context was positively associated with their extraversion, self-esteem, flexibility, and negatively related to their neuroticism (with intelligence having no association).

Some significant associations were also found by Ono, Sachau, Deal, Englert, & Taylor (2011) between investigators' individual differences and their performance. Their study had quite good ecological validity and involved (during training) 131 federal law enforcement agents from the Air Force Office of Special Investigations (AFOSI), with 38 of these again available one year later. Their training consisted of: (i) an eleven week long course at the US Federal Law Enforcement Training Center (FLETC); plus (ii) a further six week AFOSI course. Their FLETC training performance and their performance one year later (assessed by supervisors' evaluations) were compared to their (a) intellectual functioning/cognitive ability (assessed by tests of inductive reasoning and of vocabulary), (b) their scores on the 'Big Five' NEO PI-R personality inventory, and (c) 'emotional quotient inventory (as assessed by the short version of the EQ-i) – all these presumably assessed during training.

Their overall training performance (assessed using a seven item rating scale involving, for example, (i) 'interviews and interrogations', (ii) 'investigative mind-set', and (iii) 'interpersonal skills') was found to be related to the 'Conscientiousness' dimension of the 'Big Five' (but to no other dimensions) but not to cognitive ability nor to EQ-i scores. However, 'Conscientiousness' was only significantly (though modestly) associated with 'investigative mind-set' (as were EQ-i scores) but not with 'interviews and interrogations' nor with 'interpersonal skills'.

Their supervisory evaluations of 'job performance' one year later were significantly associated with cognitive ability, the 'Neuroticism' dimension of the 'Big Five', and EQ-i scores. When a hierarchical regression was performed, 'Neuroticism' ceased to be a significant predictor of overall job performance. EQ-i scores were found to be significantly associated with 'interviews and interrogations', as was 'Neuroticism'. Ono et al. (2011) concluded (p. 487) that the EQ-i "appears to hold significant potential for identifying applicants with effective interrogation . . . skills".

The 'Big Five' was also part of the study by Ames, Maissen, & Brockner (2012) who recently noted that "When people feel 'listened to' by would-be agents of influence their liking for, commitment to, and trust in the agents tend to increase, thereby expanding the agents' influence" (p. 345). They examined the relationships between 'listening' skill (as rated by work colleagues) and each of the 'Big Five' personality dimensions, finding associations for 'Agreeableness' and for 'Openness'. (For 'verbal expression' skill [found to be independent of 'listening' skill] there was a significant association with 'extraversion'.) These authors also noted that "Whereas personality change in adulthood may be difficult, developing listening behaviors may be more tractable" (p. 349).

Individual differences in the ability to determine if the interviewee is giving truthful/accurate information

In 2006 Aamodt and Custer presented a meta-analysis of the possible relationships between individual differences and the detection of deception, finding very few meaningful associations. Bond (2008) found within law enforcement personnel (and within students) little consistency across time in people's abilities to detect truth/deception thus implying that individual differences are unlikely to exist, as did the studies by Leach et al. (2009).

However, in his very comprehensive 2008 review of around 1,000 publications concerned with truth/lie detection Vrij commented (p. 176) that several individual difference "factors influence the ability to detect truth and lies . . . people high in self-awareness, introverts, and good actors are relatively good lie detectors, but socially anxious persons are relatively poor . . . Good lie detectors are more knowledgeable about diagnostic cues to deceit . . . listen carefully to what senders say or pay attention both to senders' speech and their behaviour, whereas poor lie detectors pay attention only to senders' behaviour".

In the years since that 2008 review a small number of newer studies have been published on this topic. For example, Peace, Porter, & Almon (2012) using the 'Big Five' personality inventory reported that students' 'openness to experience' and 'neuroticism' were positively associated with the accuracy of determining whether victims' written allegations of sexual assault were truthful/deceptive, whereas 'extraversion' was negatively associated for truthful accounts but not for false ones (though all of these significant associations were rather weak). Baker, ten Brinke, & Porter (2013) reported that students' ability to perceive and express emotion was negatively related to their ability to detect deception in TV broadcasts of individuals pleading for the safe return of a member of their family. Wright, Berry, & Bird (2012) found that people who were somewhat better at lie detection produced statements that others found more difficult to detect as truthful/deceptive. However, no effects of emotional intelligence were found.

Reinhard (2010) found that people with higher 'Need for cognition' were better truth/lie detectors and that they used content cues (i.e. plausibility) rather than non-verbal/behavioural cues. Indeed, a growing body of research is finding that relying on (and thus interviewing for) content (i.e. what interviewees say) rather than on 'visual behaviour' leads to better judgements regarding truth/lies. For example, see Mann, Vrij, & Bull's 2004 study of police officers' assessments regarding real-life interviews with suspects. Reinhard, Scharmach, & Müller (2013) also noted that in employment interviews deceivers try to exercise their impression management skills to create a positive effect by praising the interviewer or endorsing attitudes that the interviewer holds. (Investigative interviewers could seek to do the same.)

However, few if any studies have examined whether any relationships between individual differences and truth/lie detection accuracy remain stable over time. Indeed, Vrij, Mann, Robbins, & Robinson (2006) found police officers' deception detection performance not to be stable across time; as did Leach et al. (2009) who studied the detection performance of 'evaluators' (students) for adult liars/truth-tellers.

Some of the studies mentioned in the sections above could be taken to suggest that better interviewers are those who behave in a 'positive' rather than a 'negative, way. However, Forgas & East (2008) found that people in a 'negative' mood were better at detecting whether video-recorded interviewee accounts were deceptive. These authors noted that affective states can influence in interactional settings the types of information processing strategies people adopt, but that very little research had been published regarding such effects in the investigative interview/information gathering setting. They pointed out that mood could affect the ways in which available information is processed and they cited studies which found people in a negative mood process this in a more systematic and detailed way. They noted that research supports the notion that negative mood is often accompanied by a more pessimistic, cautious and avoidant interpersonal style. They also suggested that "people in a good mood . . . are less effective persuaders" (p. 1366).

Forgas & East (2008) further suggested that positive mood might "prime a more positive, trusting evaluation of a message" (p. 1363) and that people in a negative mood may well be less likely to form lenient, optimistic inferences. They cited previous studies that found negative mood to reduce tendencies to accept communications as genuine – which could especially be important where veracity judgements have to go beyond the available information. Thus, Forgas & East (2008) hypothesised that negative mood could enhance the detection of deception. In their own study they manipulated observers' mood (by film watching) and found those induced to be in negative mood to be significantly better at detecting lying than those in a positive or neutral mood, in part via a reduction in truth bias (i.e. an increase in scepticism). (No effect of mood was found for truth detection.)

In a similar vein, Reinhard & Schwarz (2012) also found negative mood to enhance deception detection (as well as truth detection). In both their first and second experiments the self-reported use of senders' verbal information was greater for those 'observers' in the negative mood group. Their third experiment enhanced knowledge by finding that such effects relate to a greater reliance on the processing of message content (e.g. consistency) rather than on non-verbal cues (the reverse being the case for positive mood). Clearly, in information gathering interviews message content is what is desired. Furthermore, as Reinhard and Schwarz noted, content cues are thought to be more diagnostic of deception/truth.

What is suggested by the above described work of Forgas & East (2008) and that of Reinhard & Schwarz (2012) is that when deciding during interviews whether the information being provided by the interviewee is likely to be valid/true, interviewers should process this information carefully. Overall, the work described in this review suggests that better information gatherers are those who can establish/maintain rapport, act 'humanely', and so on. However, while doing these 'positive' things well-trained and well-selected interviewers should not lose sight of the benefits of remaining sceptical.

Scepticism concerning an interviewee's account can arise from many sources but an important and innovative set of studies by Levine et al. (2011) looked not only at the behavioural individual differences between persons who are typically believed to be telling the truth (independently of their actual veracity) and persons who are typically thought to be lying, but also the types of cues that other people use in their attempts to differentiate between liars and truth-tellers. Other research (Bull, 2004; Vrij, 2008) has repeatedly found that it is very difficult to dissuade people from using such cues even though studies have repeatedly found such cues not actually to differentiate. Thus, an important idea is that effective interviewers might try to interview in ways that actually make such cues effective. The cues Levine et al. found most strongly to be related to people deciding if persons were sincere/truth-telling or insincere/lying included 'confident and composed', 'vocal uncertainty', 'hesitant', 'verbal uncertainty', 'pleasant and friendly', and 'plausible explanation'. Therefore, good interviewers could be those who interview in ways that cause such cues to be valid indicators (e.g. allow truth-tellers to be 'confident and composed' and 'pleasant and friendly' but cause liars to be 'hesitant', to have implausible explanations and vocal/verbal uncertainty).

Being sceptical may be easier (perhaps too much so) regarding people whose (main) language differs from that of the interviewer (or observer of an interview). For example, Da Silva & Leach (2013) found in a study of detecting deception that participants exhibited a lie-bias when assessing second-language speakers. Da Silva & Leach (2013) found similar effects for assessors who were either police officers or students. Castillo & Mallard (2012) provided an overview of how cross-cultural differences in 'social norms' might increase the likelihood of inferring deception.

Conclusion

This article has presented an overview of the published literature on what is believed or actually known about characteristics that may contribute to being a good/effective interviewer. Regarding beliefs concerning the particular abilities/skills that should be possessed by interviewers/investigators who are able to gain information from interviewees there seems to be an international consensus that the following may well be very important – preparation, planning, knowledge of topic, being well organised, flexibility, open-mindedness, communication, rapport, listening, questioning, compassion/empathy, courtesy, respect, patience, being calm, and appealing to cooperation.

Research studies on interviewees'/suspects' views, though currently rather small in number, have come internationally to a consensus that a humanitarian interviewing style is more likely to lead to comprehensive, truthful accounts. In connection with the actual relationships between skills/abilities and information gain in interviews, those which relevant research has largely found to be important include – being well prepared, use of appropriate structure, rapport, being humane/respectful, empathy, communication, requesting attention, encouraging interviewee to give an account, active listening, exploring received information, use of silences, questioning, flexibility, open-mindedness, self-confidence, remaining calm, being non-judgemental, exploring motive, regular summarising, evidence/information revelation, challenging appropriately, and emphasising contradictions.

Studies involving individual differences in interviewers' ability to determine if interviewees are giving truthful or deceptive information have found few differences that relate to 'personality'. However, the way in which interviewers conduct their interviews and the type of information they base their true/lie decisions on seems to be crucial.

References

Aamodt, M., & Custer, H. (2006). Who can best catch a liar? A meta-analysis of individual differences in detecting deception. *Forensic Examiner*, *15*, 6–11.

Ames, D., Maissen, L., & Brockner, J. (2012). The role of listening in interpersonal influence. *Journal of Research in Personality*, *46*, 345–349.

Baker, A., ten Brinke, L., & Porter, S. (2013). Will get fooled again: Emotionally intelligent people are easily duped by high-stakes deceivers. *Legal and Criminological Psychology*, *18*, 300–313.

Baldwin, J. (1993). Police interview techniques. Establishing truth or proof? *British Journal of Criminology*, *33*, 325–352.

Bond, G. (2008). Deception detection expertise. *Law and Human Behavior*, *32*, 339–351.

Bull, R. (1992). Obtaining evidence expertly: The reliability of interviews with child witnesses. *Expert Evidence*, *1*, 5–12.

Bull, R. (1996). Good practice for video recorded interviews with child witnesses for use in criminal proceedings. In G. Davies, S. Lloyd-Bostock, M. McMurran, & C. Wilson (Eds.), *Psychology, law and criminal justice*. Berlin: de Gruyter.

Bull, R. (2004). Training: General principles and problems regarding behavioural cues to deception. In P.A. Granhag & L. Stromwall (Eds.), *Detecting deception in forensic contexts*. Cambridge: Cambridge University Press.

Bull, R., & Cherryman, J. (1996). *Helping to identify skills gaps in specialist investigative interviewing: Enhancement of professional skills*. London: Home Office Police Department.

Bull, R., & Leahy-Harland, S. (2012). *Analyses of real-life police interviews with suspects: Strategies used and suspect responses*. Paper presented at the Annual Conference of the American Psychology-Law Society, Portland.

Bull, R., & Soukara, S. (2010). A set of studies of what really happens in police interviews with suspects. In G. D. Lassiter & C. Meissner (Eds.), *Interrogations and confessions*. Washington, DC: American Psychological Association.

Castillo, P., & Mallard, D. (2012). Preventing cross-cultural bias in deception judgments: The role of expectancies about nonverbal behaviour. *Journal of Cross-Cultural Psychology*, *43*, 967–978.

Clemens, F., Granhag, P., & Stromwall, L. (2011). Eliciting cues to false intent: A new application of strategic interviewing. *Law and Human Behavior*, *35*, 1–11.

Dando, C., & Bull, R. (2011). Maximising opportunities to detect verbal deception: Training police officers to interview tactically. *Journal of Investigative Psychology and Offender Profiling*, *8*, 189–202.

Dando, C., Bull, R., Ormerod, T., & Sandham, A. (2015). Helping to sort the liars from the truth-tellers: The gradual revelation of information during investigative interviews. *Legal and Criminological Psychology*, *20*, 114–128.

Da Silva, C., & Leach, A.-M. (2013). Detecting deception in second-language speakers. *Legal and Criminological Psychology*, *18*, 115–127.

Deslauriers-Varin, N., Lussier, P., & St-Yves, M. (2011). Confessing their crime: Factors influencing the offender's decision to confess to the police. *Justice Quarterly*, *28*, 113–145.

Deslauriers-Varin, N., & St-Yves, M. (2006). *An empirical investigation of offenders' decision to confess their crime during police interrogation*. Paper presented at the Second International Investigative Interviewing Conference, Portsmouth, July.

Forgas, J., & East, R. (2008). On being happy and gullible: Mood effects on scepticism and the detection of deception. *Journal of Experimental Social Psychology*, *44*, 1362–1367.

Gudjonsson, G. (2003). *The psychology of interrogations and confessions: A handbook*. Chichester: Wiley.

Holmberg, U. (2004). *Police interviews with victims and suspects of violent and sexual crimes*. Doctoral thesis, University of Stockholm.

Holmberg, U., & Christianson, S. (2002). Murderers' and sexual offenders' experiences of police interviews and their inclination to admit or deny crimes. *Behavioral Sciences and the Law*, *20*, 31–45.

Inbau, F., Reid, J., Buckley, J., & Jayne, B. (2001). *Criminal interrogations and confessions*. Gaithersburg, MD: Aspen.
Kebbell, M., Alison, L., & Hurren, E. (2008). Sex offenders' perceptions of the effectiveness and fairness of humanity, dominance, and displaying an understanding of cognitive distortions in police interviews: A vignette study. *Psychology, Crime and Law, 14*, 435–449.
Kebbell, M., Alison, L., Hurren, E., & Mazerolle, P. (2010). How do sex offenders think the police should interview to elicit confessions from sex offenders? *Psychology, Crime and Law, 16*, 567–584.
Kebbell, M., Hurren, E., & Mazerolle, P. (2006). *An investigation into the effective and ethical interviewing of suspected sex offenders*. Final report to the Australian Criminology Research Council.
Leach, A-M., Lindsay, R., Koehler, R., Beaudry, J., Bala, N., Lee, K., & Talwar, V. (2009). The reliability of lie detection performance. *Law and Human Behavior, 33*, 96–109.
Leo, R. (2008). *Police interrogation and American justice*. Boston: Harvard University Press.
Levine, T., Serota, K., Shulman, H., Clare, D., Park, H., Shaw, A., Shim, J., & Lee, J. (2011). Sender demeanour: Individual differences in sender believability have a powerful impact on deception detection judgments. *Human Communication Research, 37*, 377–403.
Mann, S., Vrij, A., & Bull, R. (2004). Detecting true lies: Police officers' ability to detect suspects' lies. *Journal of Applied Psychology, 89*, 137–149.
Milne, R., & Bull, R. (1999). Investigative interviewing: Psychology and practice. Chichester: Wiley.
O'Connor, T., & Carson, W. (2005). Understanding the psychology of child molesters: A key to getting confessions. *The Police Chief, 72*, 1–7.
O'Neill, M. (2012). *What makes a successful volume crime investigator?* Unpublished doctoral dissertation: University of Portsmouth.
O'Neill, M., & Milne, R. (2014). Success within criminal investigations: Is communication still a key component? In R. Bull (Ed.), *Investigative interviewing*. New York: Springer.
Ono, M., Sachau, D., Deal, W., Englert, D., & Taylor, M. (2011). Cognitive ability, emotional intelligence, and the 'Big Five' personality dimensions as predictors of criminal investigator performance. *Criminal Justice and Behavior, 38*, 471–491.
Otsuka, Y., Wachi, T., Watanabe, K., Yokota, K., & Kuraishi, H. (2011). *Factors that determine the level of confession in denying suspects*. Poster presented at the Annual Conference of the American Psychology-Law Society, Miami.
Oxburgh, G., Ost, J., & Cherryman, J. (2012). Police interviews with suspected child sex offenders: Does the use of empathy and question type influence the amount of investigation relevant information obtained? *Psychology, Crime & Law, 18*, 259–273.
Peace, K., Porter, S., & Almon, D. (2012). Sidetracked by emotion: Observers' ability to discriminate genuine and fabricated sexual assault allegations. *Legal and Criminological Psychology, 17*, 322–335.
Pearse, J. (2009). The investigation of terrorist offences in the United Kingdom: The context and climate for interviewing officers. In R. Bull, T. Valentine, & T. Williamson (Eds.), *Handbook of psychology of investigative interviewing*. Chichester: Wiley-Blackwell.
Read, J., Powell, M., Kebbell, M., & Milne, R. (2009). Investigative interviewing of suspected sex offenders: A review of what constitutes best practice. *International Journal of Police Science and Administration, 11*, 442–459.
Reinhard, M. (2010). Need for cognition and the process of lie detection. *Journal of Experimental Social Psychology, 46*, 961–971.

Reinhard, M.-A., Scharmach, M., & Müller, P. A. (2013). It's not what you are, it's what you know: Experience, beliefs, and the detection of deception in employment interviews. *Journal of Applied Social Psychology*, *43*(3), 467–479.

Reinhard, M., & Schwarz, N. (2012). The influence of affective states on the process of lie detection. *Journal of Experimental Psychology: Applied*, *18*, 377–389.

Russano, M., & Narchet, F. (2013). *Interrogation practices and beliefs: Does high-value target experience matter?* Paper presented at the Annual Conference of the American Psychology-Law Society, Portland.

Sear, L., & Stephenson, G. (1997). Interviewing skills and individual characteristics of police interrogators. In G. Stephenson & N. Clarke (Eds.), *Procedures in criminal justice: Contemporary psychological issues*. Leicester: British Psychological Society.

Sivasubramaniam, D., & Goodman-Delahunty, J. (2013). *An international survey of intelligence interviewing practices and beliefs*. Paper presented at the Annual Conference of the American Psychology-Law Society, Portland.

Smets, L. (2012). *Police investigative interviewing: A new training approach*. Antwerp: Maklu.

St-Yves, M., & Deslauriers-Varin, N. (2009). The psychology of suspects' decision-making during interrogation. In R. Bull, T. Valentine, & T. Williamson. (Eds.), *Handbook of psychology of investigative interviewing* (pp. 1–16). Chichester: Wiley.

Vanderhallen, M., & Vervaeke G. (2014). Between investigator and suspect: The role of the working alliance in investigative interviewing. In R. Bull (Ed.), *Investigative interviewing*. New York, NY: Springer.

van Hemert, D., van den Berg, H., & Wijn, R. (2012). *The role of competencies of security personnel in detecting deviant behaviour*. Paper presented at the conference on The Behavioural Analysis of Crime and Investigations, London, December.

Vrij, A. (2008). *Detecting lies and deceit: Pitfalls and opportunities*. Chichester: Wiley.

Vrij, A., Mann, S., Robbins, E., & Robinson, M. (2006). Police officers' ability to detect deception in high stakes situations and repeated lie detection tests. *Applied Cognitive Psychology*, *20*, 741–755.

Walsh, D., & Bull, R. (2010a). Interviewing suspects of fraud: An in-depth analysis of interviewing skills. *Journal of Psychiatry and Law*, *38*, 99–135.

Walsh, D., & Bull, R. (2010b). What really is effective in interviews with suspects? A study comparing interview skills against interview outcomes. *Legal and Criminological Psychology*, *15*, 305–321.

Walsh, D., & Bull, R. (2012a). How do interviewers attempt to overcome suspects' denials? *Psychiatry, Psychology and Law*, *19*, 151–168.

Walsh, D., & Bull, R. (2012b). Examining rapport in investigative interviews with suspects: Does its building and maintenance work? *Journal of Police and Criminal Psychology*, *27*, 73–84.

Walsh, D., & Bull, R. (2011). Benefit fraud investigative interviewing: A self-report study of investigation professionals' beliefs concerning practice. *Journal of Investigative Psychology and Offender Profiling*, *8*, 131–148.

Wright, G., Berry, J., & Bird, G. (2012). You can't kid a kidder: Association between production and detection of deception in an interactive deception task. *Frontiers in Human Neuroscience*, *6*, 1–7.

Zak, P. (2012). *The moral molecule*. New York, NY: Dutton.

Index